THE SACRED ROMANCE

DESIRE

JOHN ELDREDGE

Thomas Nelson
Since 1798

NASHVILLE   DALLAS   MEXICO CITY   RIO DE JANEIRO   BEIJING

Published in Nashville, Tennessee, by Thomas Nelson. Thomas Nelson is a registered trademark of Thomas Nelson, Inc.

Published in association with Yates & Yates, www.yates2.com.

Thomas Nelson, Inc., titles may be purchased in bulk for educational, business, fund-raising, or sales promotional use. For information, please e-mail SpecialMarkets@ThomasNelson.com.

Unless otherwise noted, Scripture quotations are taken from the HOLY BIBLE: NEW INTERNATIONAL VERSION®. © 1973, 1978, 1984 by International Bible Society. Used by permission of Zondervan Publishing House. All rights reserved.

Scripture quotations marked NLT are from *Holy Bible*, New Living Translation. © 1996. Used by permission of Tyndale House Publishers, Inc., Wheaton, Illinois 60189. All rights reserved.

Scripture quotations marked NKJV are from THE NEW KING JAMES VERSION. © 1982 by Thomas Nelson, Inc. Used by permission. All rights reserved.

Scripture quotations marked MSG are from *The Message* by Eugene H. Peterson. © 1993, 1994, 1995, 1996, 2000. Used by permission of NavPress Publishing Group. All rights reserved.

Scripture quotations marked NRSV are from NEW REVISED STANDARD VERSION of the Bible. © 1989 by the Division of Christian Education of the National Council of the Churches of Christ in the U.S.A. All rights reserved.

Scripture quotations marked NASB are from NEW AMERICAN STANDARD BIBLE®. © The Lockman Foundation 1960, 1962, 1963, 1968, 1971, 1972, 1973, 1975, 1977. Used by permission.

Scripture quotations marked KJV are from the KING JAMES VERSION.

Library of Congress Cataloguing-in-Publication Data Available

ISBN: 978-1-4002-0278-2

Printed in the United States of America
09 10 11 12 13 WC 6 5 4 3 2 1

CONTENTS

The Sacred ROMANCE

DESIRE

The Sacred

ROMANCE

Drawing Closer to the
Heart of God

1

The Lost Life of the Heart

*Thirsty hearts are those whose longings have been
wakened by the touch of God within them.*

A. W. Tozer

SOME YEARS into our spiritual journey, after the waves
of anticipation that mark the beginning of any pilgrimage have begun to ebb into life's middle years of service and busyness, a voice speaks to us in the midst of all we are
doing. *There is something missing in all of this*, it suggests. *There
is something more.*

The voice often comes in the middle of the night or the
early hours of morning, when our hearts are most unedited and
vulnerable. At first, we mistake the source of this voice and
assume it is just our imagination. We fluff up our pillow, roll
over, and go back to sleep. Days, weeks, even months go by and
the voice speaks to us again: *Aren't you thirsty? Listen to your
heart. There is something missing.*

We listen and we are aware of . . . a sigh. And under the sigh
is something dangerous, something that feels adulterous and
disloyal to the religion we are serving. We sense a passion deep
within that threatens a total disregard for the program we are
living; it feels reckless, wild. Unsettled, we turn and walk
quickly away, like a woman who feels more than she wants to
when her eyes meet those of a man not her husband.

1

We tell ourselves that this small, passionate voice is an intruder who has gained entry because we have not been diligent enough in practicing our religion. Our pastor seems to agree with this assessment and exhorts us from the pulpit to be more faithful. We try to silence the voice with outward activity, redoubling our efforts at Christian service. We join a small group and read a book on establishing a more effective prayer life. We train to be part of a church evangelism team. We tell ourselves that the malaise of spirit we feel even as we step up our religious activity is a sign of spiritual immaturity and we scold our heart for its lack of fervor.

Sometime later, the voice in our heart dares to speak to us again, more insistently this time. *Listen to me—there is something missing in all this. You long to be in a love affair, an adventure. You were made for something more. You know it.*

When the young prophet Samuel heard the voice of God calling to him in the night, he had the counsel from his priestly mentor, Eli, to tell him how to respond. Even so, it took them three times to realize it was God calling. Rather than ignoring the voice, or rebuking it, Samuel finally listened.

In our modern, pragmatic world we often have no such mentor, so we do not understand it is God speaking to us in our heart. Having so long been out of touch with our deepest longing, we fail to recognize the voice and the One who is calling to us through it. Frustrated by our heart's continuing sabotage of a dutiful Christian life, some of us silence the voice by locking our heart away in the attic, feeding it only the bread and water of duty and obligation until it is almost dead, the voice now small and weak. But sometimes in the night, when our defenses are down, we still hear it call to us, oh so faintly—a distant whisper. Come morning, the new day's activities scream for our attention, the sound of the cry is gone, and we congratulate ourselves on finally overcoming the flesh.

Others of us agree to give our heart a life on the side if it will

only leave us alone and not rock the boat. We try to lose ourselves in our work, or "get a hobby" (either of which soon
begin to feel like an addiction); we have an affair, or develop a
colorful fantasy life fed by dime-store romances or pornography.
We learn to enjoy the juicy intrigues and secrets of gossip. We
make sure to maintain enough distance between ourselves and
others, and even between ourselves and our own heart, to keep
hidden the practical agnosticism we are living now that our
inner life has been divorced from our outer life. Having thus
appeased our heart, we nonetheless are forced to give up our
spiritual journey because our heart will no longer come with us.
It is bound up in the little indulgences we feed it to keep it at
bay.

Losing Heart

The life of the heart is a place of great mystery. Yet we have
many expressions to help us express this flame of the human
soul. We describe a person without compassion as "heartless,"
and we urge him or her to "have a heart." Our deepest hurts we
call "heartaches." Jilted lovers are "brokenhearted." Courageous soldiers are "bravehearted." The truly evil are "black-
hearted" and saints have "hearts of gold." If we need to speak
at the most intimate level, we ask for a "heart-to-heart" talk.
"Lighthearted" is how we feel on vacation. And when we love
someone as truly as we may, we love "with all our heart." But
when we lose our passion for life, when a deadness sets in which
we cannot seem to shake, we confess, "My heart's just not in
it."

   In the end, it doesn't matter how well we have performed
or what we have accomplished—a life without heart is not
worth living. For out of this wellspring of our soul flows all true
caring and all meaningful work, all real worship and all sacrifice.
Our faith, hope, and love issue from this fount, as well. Because

it is in our heart that we first hear the voice of God and it is in the heart that we come to know him and learn to live in his love.

So you can see that to lose heart is to lose everything. And a "loss of heart" best describes most men and women in our day. It isn't just the addictions and affairs and depression and heartaches, though, God knows, there is enough of these to cause even the best of us to lose heart. But there is the busyness, the drivenness, the fact that most of us are living merely to survive. Beneath it we feel restless, weary, and vulnerable.

Indeed, the many forces driving modern life have not only assaulted the life of our heart, they have also dismantled the heart's habitat—that geography of mystery and transcendence we knew so well as children.

I (Brent) remember sitting in my college zoology class as my professor expounded with upraised arms—the perspiration-stained underarms of his shirt proudly exposed—that man's basic problem was that he wanted to smell (be) like a flower instead of a mammal. In physics class, the professor seemed to take satisfaction in explaining to us that the beauty of sunsets and rainbows was due only to the refraction of light through water and dust particles in the air. It was as if the miracle of light itself were somehow done away with by these explanations. I remember leaving those professors of the Age of Reason with a sense of loss, a sense of "Oh, so that's all it is." The message of my teachers was clear: Once we dispense with unhelpful mysticism and superstition, the progress of mankind will proceed unhindered.

All of us have had that experience at one time or another, whether it be as we walked away from our teachers, our parents, a church service, or sexual intimacy; the sense that something important, perhaps the only thing important, had been explained away or tarnished and lost to us forever. Sometimes little by little, sometimes in large chunks, life has appropriated the terrain meant to sustain and nourish the more wild life of the heart, forcing it to retreat as an endangered species into smaller, more secluded, and often darker geographies for its survival. As this has happened, something has been lost, something vital.

For what shall we do when we wake one day to find we have lost touch with our heart and with it the very refuge where God's presence resides?

Starting very early, life has taught all of us to ignore and distrust the deepest yearnings of our heart. Life, for the most part, teaches us to suppress our longing and live only in the external world where efficiency and performance are everything. We have learned from parents and peers, at school, at work, and even from our spiritual mentors that something else is wanted from us other than our heart, which is to say, that which is most deeply *us*. Very seldom are we ever invited to live out of our heart. If we are wanted, we are often wanted for what we can offer functionally. If rich, we are honored for our wealth; if beautiful, for our looks, if intelligent, for our brains. So we learn to offer only those parts of us that are approved, living out a carefully crafted performance to gain acceptance from those who represent life to us. We divorce ourselves from our heart and begin to live a double life. Frederick Buechner expresses this phenomenon in his biographical work, *Telling Secrets*:

> "[Our] original shimmering self gets buried so deep we hardly live out of it at all . . . rather, we learn to live out of all the other selves which we are constantly putting on and taking off like coats and hats against the world's weather."

On the outside, there is the external story of our lives. This is the life everyone sees, our life of work and play and church, of family and friends, paying bills, and growing older. Our external story is where we carve out the identity most others know. It is the place where we have learned to label each other in a way that implies we have reached our final destination. Bob is an accountant; Mary works for the government; Ted is an attorney. The Smiths are the family with the well-kept lawn and lovely children; the Joneses are that family whose children are always in trouble. Here, busyness substitutes for meaning, efficiency substitutes for creativity, and functional relationships substitute for love. In the outer life we live from *ought* (I ought to do this) rather than from *desire* (I want to do this) and management substitutes for mystery. There are three steps to a happy marriage, five ways to improve your portfolio, and seven habits for success.

There *is* a spiritual dimension to this external world in our desire to do good works, but communion with God is replaced by activity for God. There is little time in this outer world for deep questions. Given the right plan, everything in life can be managed . . . except your heart.

The inner life, the story of our heart, is the life of the deep places within us, our passions and dreams, our fears and our deepest wounds. It is the unseen life, the mystery within—what Buechner calls our "shimmering self." It cannot be managed like a corporation. The heart does not respond to principles and programs; it seeks not efficiency, but passion. Art, poetry, beauty, mystery, ecstasy: These are what rouse the heart. Indeed, they are the language that must be spoken if one wishes to communicate with the heart. It is why Jesus so often taught and related to people by telling stories and asking questions. His desire was not just to engage their intellects but to capture their hearts.

Indeed, if we will listen, a Sacred Romance calls to us through our heart every moment of our lives. It whispers to us on the wind, invites us through the laughter of good friends, reaches out to us through the touch of someone we love. We've heard it in our favorite music, sensed it at the birth of our first child, been drawn to it while watching the shimmer of a sunset on the ocean. The Romance is even present in times of great personal suffering: the illness of a child, the loss of a marriage, the death of a friend. Something calls to us through experiences like these and rouses an inconsolable longing deep within our heart, wakening in us a yearning for intimacy, beauty, and adventure.

This longing is the most powerful part of any human personality. It fuels our search for meaning, for wholeness, for a sense of being truly alive. However we may describe this deep desire, it is the most important thing about us, our heart of hearts, the passion of our life. And the voice that calls to us in this place is none other than the voice of God.

We cannot hear this voice if we have lost touch with our heart.

The true story of every person in this world is not the story you see, the external story. The true story of each person is the journey of his or her heart. Jesus himself knew that if people lived only in the outer story, eventually they would lose track of their inner life, the life of their heart he so much desired to redeem. Indeed, it was to the most religious people of his time that Jesus spoke his strongest warnings about a loss of heart.

It is tragic for any person to lose touch with the life of their heart but especially so for those of us who once heard the call in our heart and recognized it as the voice of Jesus of Nazareth. We may remember him inviting us to a life of beauty, intimacy, and adventure that we thought was lost. For others of us, when he called, it felt for the first time in our lives as if our heart had finally found a home. We responded in faith, in hope, and in love and began the journey we call the Christian life. Each day seemed a new adventure as we rediscovered the world with God by our side.

But for many of us, the waves of first love ebbed away in the whirlwind of Christian service and activity, and we began to lose the Romance. Our faith began to feel more like a series of problems that needed to be solved or principles that had to be mastered before we could finally enter into the abundant life promised us by Christ. We moved our spiritual life into the outer world of activity, and internally we drifted. We sensed that something was wrong and we perhaps tried to fix it—by tinkering with our outer life. We tried the latest spiritual fad, or a new church, or simply redoubled our commitment to make faith work. Still, we found ourselves weary, jaded, or simply bored. Others of us immersed ourselves in busyness without really asking where all the activity was headed. At one point in my own spiritual pilgrimage, I stopped to ask myself this question: "What is it that I am supposed to be *doing* to live the spiritual life in any way that is both truthful and passionately alive?"

What we want to say in these pages is simply this: *Our hearts are telling us the truth—there really is something missing!*

The Centrality of the Heart

For above all else, the Christian life is a love affair of the heart. It cannot be lived primarily as a set of principles or ethics. It cannot be managed with steps and programs. It cannot be lived exclusively as a moral code leading to righteousness. In response to a religious expert who asked him what he must do to obtain real life, Jesus asked a question in return:

> "What is written in the Law? . . . How do you read it?"
>
> He answered: "'Love the Lord your God with *all your heart* and with all your soul and with all your strength and with all your mind'; and, 'Love your neighbor as yourself.'"
>
> "You have answered correctly," Jesus replied. "Do this and you will live." *(Luke 10:26–28, italics added)*

The truth of the gospel is intended to free us to love God and others with our whole heart. When we ignore this heart aspect of our faith and try to live out our religion solely as correct doctrine or ethics, our passion is crippled, or perverted, and the divorce of our soul from the heart purposes of God toward us is deepened.

The religious technocrats of Jesus' day confronted him with what they believed were the standards of a life pleasing to God. The external life, they argued, the life of ought and duty and service, was what mattered. "You're dead wrong," Jesus said. "In fact, you're just plain dead [whitewashed tombs]. What God cares about is the inner life, the life of the heart" (Matt. 23:25–28). Throughout the Old and New Testaments, the life of the heart is clearly God's central concern. When the people of Israel fell into a totally external life of ritual and observance, God lamented, "These people . . . honor me with their lips, but their hearts are far from me" (Isa. 29:13).

Our heart is the key to the Christian life.

The apostle Paul informs us that hardness of heart is behind all the addictions and evils of the human race (Rom. 1:21–25). Oswald Chambers writes, "It is by the heart that God is perceived [known] and not by reason . . . so that is what faith is: God perceived by the heart." This is why God tells us in Proverbs 4:23, "Above all else, guard your heart, for it is the wellspring of life." He knows that to lose heart is to lose everything. Sadly, most of us watch the oil level in our car more carefully than we watch over the life of our heart.

In one of the greatest invitations ever offered to man, Christ stood up amid the crowds in Jerusalem and said, "If anyone is thirsty, let him come to me and drink. Whoever believes in me, as the Scripture has said, streams of living water will flow from within him" (John 7:37–38). If we aren't aware of our soul's deep thirst, his offer means nothing. But, if we will recall, it was from the longing of our hearts that most of us first responded to Jesus. Somehow, years later, we assume he no longer calls to us through the thirst of our heart. Like the Galatians, whom Paul rebuked for forgetting how they came to Christ, we find that something or someone has seduced us to return to our outer life and to performance as the way of salvation. This external religious self we try to maintain doesn't recognize God's voice communing with us when he comes to call us more deeply to the Romance he has set within us.

It is possible to recover the lost life of our heart and with it the intimacy, beauty, and adventure of life with God. To do so we must leave what is familiar and comfortable—perhaps even parts of the religion in which we have come to trust—and take a journey. This journey first takes us on a search for the lost life of our heart, and for the voice that once called us in those secret places; those places and times when our heart was still with us. The pilgrimage of the heart leads us to remember together what it was that first engaged us in deep ways as children: ". . . anyone who will not receive the kingdom of God like a little child will never enter it," said Jesus (Mark 10:15).

Our journey will take us to explore the hidden questions of our heart, born out of the stories of our lives. It is only by leaving home and taking a pilgrimage that we will begin to see how our own stories are interwoven with the great Romance God has been telling since before the dawn of time. It is on this pilgrimage that we begin to see that each of us has a part in the cosmic love affair that was created specifically with us in mind. Last, this pilgrimage brings us to the destination, set within all of our hearts, which in some way we have known, longed for, and been haunted by since we were children.

This book is born out of the journey that John and I have shared for several years. I have been a Christian counselor for the same length of time that John has been conducting seminars for a major Christian ministry. Both of us have at one time worked in a local church. Our lives have given us a unique look into the inner life of modern Christianity, and what we have known from our own stories has been confirmed again and again through hundreds of encounters with other believers: Most Christians have lost the life of their heart and with it, their romance with God. As we trace the steps of the journey toward God's resurrection of the heart, we hope to help you discover your soul's deepest longing and invite you to embrace it as the most important part of your life.

It is our aim to help you "guard your heart," to see more clearly the enemies of your heart and the hearts of those you love; to enable you to better enter the battle for hearts to which our Captain calls us.

Our journey begins by asking questions, putting words to the movements of the heart. "What is this restlessness and emptiness I feel, sometimes long years into my Christian journey? What does the spiritual life have to do with the rest of my life? What is it that is set so deeply in my heart, experienced as a longing for adventure and romance, that simply will not leave me alone? Does it have anything to do with God? What is it that he wants from me? Has he been speaking to me through my heart all along? When did I stop listening? When did his voice first call to me?"

2

An Unknown Romancing

We wake, if ever we wake at all, to mystery.
Annie Dillard

WHAT, OR WHO, first calls to us from the wellspring of our heart? Our external stories, the ones we live in front of the world, filled with busyness and bustle, will not give us the answer to our question. We must move to the internal story that goes on in our heart. If we are going to begin the journey toward the recovery of our heart, we must follow Frederick Buechner's advice and "listen to our lives."

> If God speaks to us at all other than through such official channels as the Bible and the church, then I think that he speaks to us largely through what happens to us . . . if we keep our hearts and minds open as well as our ears, if we listen with patience and hope, if we remember at all deeply and honestly, then I think we come to recognize, beyond all doubt, that, however faintly we may hear him, he is indeed speaking to us, and that, however little we may understand of it, his word to each of us is both recoverable and precious beyond telling. (*Now and Then*)

Our inner story is most audible early in the morning, or sometimes in the middle of the night when the inner editor that tells us how we "should" respond to the world has gone off duty. It is then that our heart speaks to us of the story that is most deeply ours. It is a story whose plot contains both mystery and magic as well as foreboding and anxiety—what philosophers call "angst." When we listen most attentively to the inner story our heart tells us about, most of us are aware that the plot revolves around two very different messages, or revelations, that have vied for our attention since we were very young. One has enchanted us while the other has dared us to rise above fear and resignation. The first has come to us in the form of a romancing that even now in my forties often fills me (Brent) with anticipation. Something wonderful woos us. The other lays siege to us in much darker hues and brings with it a foreboding that sometimes nags at the edges of our consciousness even on the most sunlit morning. Something fearful stalks us.

And yet, life's enchantment of us is, perhaps, the deeper of the two messages—the love story that first engaged our heart before the darker revelation did its work. And so it is here we will begin to "listen to our lives." If we will allow ourselves to go back to the story most of us knew as children, it is not hard to bring back the early images and sounds and aromas of life's first revelation—that of a great Romance.

Each of us has a geography where the Romance first spoke to us. It is usually the place we both long to see again and fear returning to for fear our memories will be stolen from us. My own earliest memories of the Romance come from 120 acres of New Jersey farmland, bordered by a stream to the southeast and a low and broad hillside to the northwest. As was the case with most family farms in the 1950s, the labor of both my mother and father was required by the animals and fields from early morning to dusk, leaving my sister and me to explore the mysteries of meadows and haymows.

I first remember the Romance calling to me when I was a boy of six or seven, just past dusk on a summer evening, when the hotter and dustier work of the farm had given way to another song. Something warm and alive and poignantly haunting would call to me from the mysterious borders of the farm that was my world. I would walk toward it, past the corrals where our milk cows rested, down through rows of dark green corn that towered far over my head. The corn, imperious in its height and numbers, presented its own kind of enchanted forest. Every leaf that gave way before my outstretched arms offered possible mystery. The earth was warm and brown and fragrant and seemed to invite a sort of barefooted ecstasy with no worry of stones or other debris to cause me harm.

Finally I would come to the end of the corn out into a fringe of meadow where tall grasses swayed in silvery response to the moonlight's embrace. Beyond these dancers a thin line of maple and oak trees, straight as sentinels, hid the voices calling so passionately to me from moving water where the creek formed the border of our farm. The hardwoods that guarded the creek would usher me to a sandbar below an old wooden bridge that carried the road above on into New Jersey's rich farmlands. There in the moonlight, I would squat down on my heels near the water's edge, letting my toes sink into the cool sand. Around the imprint of my foot, the sand would bleed the deep reds of rusting iron ore.

In that place I was in the middle of the singers.

The voices of crickets, katydids, and cicadas would come to me, carried above the sounds of the creek and mingled with the pungent odor of tannins. Tens of thousands of stream-side musicians sang to me the magic stories of the farms and forests. It seemed as if the songs were carried all the way from the headwaters—those mysterious beginnings of the waters that came up through the mosses and cattails in a manner no less magical than if they had been called to life by moon-dusted fairies. The creek waters would rest in the darkness under the bridge before continuing their journey. The surface stillness of the resulting pond played host to the shiny green lords of the young river, the deep-throated bullfrogs. They added their own intermittent bass notes to the melody; a call to order unheeded by the great mass of musicians.

I remember being in that place until the music of life would fill me with the knowledge of some Romance to be lived; an assurance that there was a reason to joust against dragons with wooden swords; a reason to wear not one but two pearl-handled revolvers in the cowboy stories I weaved and lived out each day; a reason to include a pretty girl who needed to be rescued, even though I was far too busy fighting the bad guys to be captured by love. The magic assured me of loves and lovers and adventures to be joined and mystery to be pursued.

The Romance of that place would surround me as I rose and returned through the cornfield in response to my mother's distant call. It comforted me with a familiarity that seemed to connect me with things that were at once very old and still becoming new. Lying on my bed, with my parents far off downstairs in another part of the house and a geography of the heart I did not then know, I would fall asleep, romanced by some unseen lover that, back then, I only knew from those singers in the summer moonlit night.

I, perhaps like you, have encountered the Romance many times since: in the golden fall of the Rockies and in the windswept sea grasses and whitecaps of bay and ocean on the Atlantic; in a quiet moment of sunlight orchestrated into parallel rays of warmth on my shoulder as I read a good book; in the eyes of certain women and the strength of certain men; in the joy of my five-year-old son turning cartwheels during a soccer game, oblivious to the demands of winning; and in rare occurrences of kindness, courage, and sacrifice by men and women I have known and reports of the same by many I have not.

In my adult years it has ebbed and flowed and usually comes as a surprise. One vivid appearance took place perhaps four years ago on a summer's evening. A couple who were longtime friends of ours before we moved to Colorado were visiting us from the East Coast. It was a difficult time for them individually and for their marriage. This particular night the four of us had gone to see *When Harry Met Sally*, a poignant comedy-drama on the subject of whether men and women could just be friends. The movie provoked much emotion in our friends and they walked down to the lake near our home to talk about their hurt and anger and their future. Our house sits on a ridge in the southern portion of our city and my wife and I sat at the table in our darkened dining room, looking out at the lights of surrounding neighborhoods.

I felt heavy and sad inside over the pain of our friends. Heavy about the unknown future of their marriage and our friendship. Sad as well at some of the distances in our own marriage that had rarely been bridged. As I put these things into words with Ginny, she reached out and took my hand. I don't remember the exact words of our conversation, but I remember her sitting there in a summer dress with her blue eyes visible even in the twilight. I know we talked about being a man and being a woman and what it was like to love and be in love. I felt as if some veil that was often suspended between us fell away for a few moments and we talked as friends. Friends who had the possibility of deeper romance.

I remember going to bed that night feeling much the same as I felt as a boy on those summer nights so long ago, stirred and enchanted by a taste of beauty and intimacy that came by surprise. The tears I shed in the moments before sleep were sad and joyous and felt not at all contradictory. When I awoke the next morning I reached for the sense of the Romance inside but I knew it was gone before I even went into the kitchen for coffee. The veil had dropped back into place and the day before me seemed to offer only the everyday responsibilities of job and family and simply going on.

Remembering these scenes from my own story, I realized that I had found part of the lost journey of my heart. As a young boy, my heart was captured by mystery: mystery that invited me to open my heart and join it in a kind of joyful exuberance; mystery that hinted of a story that existed on its own outside my own fanciful creations; a story that nonetheless invited me to be part of it as I constructed my childhood adventures; a story that offered me villains and heroes and a story line that evolved out of their conflict; a story that, along with telling me of great danger, also told me that all things would be well; a story that felt as if it began in laughter and was confident that it would bring all who were a part of it home in joyful communion.

Sadly, many of us never come to see this wooing, in whatever geography it first finds us, as having anything to do with our heart's deepest desire, our spiritual life, or our soul's destiny. This is true in part because it is a story that is very hard to capture in propositions. We have learned to tell ourselves that it is naive to trust it after we become adults, as if somehow we have outgrown it and moved on to more reasonable or "scientific" ways of thinking. We have learned to think of it as quaint, or sentimental, or the foolishness of a child. Contemporary Christianity has often taught us to mistrust it, for fear it will lead us into some New Age heresy, unwittingly giving away what most deeply belongs to Christian faith. We are certainly rarely told to listen to it, look for it, follow it to its source.

Thankfully, our heart will not totally give up on the Romance. In spite of our "maturity" or the admonitions of our teachers to avoid the "things of this world," we find ourselves with a lump in our throat at a movie when two lovers we know are meant to be together finally find each other—or don't. Another movie tells the story of a man with a noble heart. He sacrifices comfort and safety for a cause higher than mere political expediency. He is defeated, yet his spirit enthralls us with his heroism. We leave the theater with a burning in our heart; a desire to be part of such a cause.

In all of our hearts lies a longing for a Sacred Romance.

It will not go away in spite of our efforts over the years to anesthetize or ignore its song, or attach it to a single person or endeavor. It is a Romance couched in mystery and set deeply within us. It cannot be categorized into propositional truths or fully known any more than studying the anatomy of a corpse would help us know the person who once inhabited it.

Philosophers call this Romance, this heart yearning set within us, the longing for transcendence; the desire to be part of something larger than ourselves, to be part of something out of the ordinary that is good. Transcendence is what we experience in a small but powerful way when our city's football team wins the big game against tremendous odds. The deepest part of our heart longs to be bound together in some heroic purpose with others of like mind and spirit.

Indeed, if we reflect back on the journey of our heart, the Romance has most often come to us in the form of two deep desires: the longing for adventure that *requires* something of us, and the desire for intimacy—to have someone truly know us for ourselves, while at the same time inviting us to *know* them in the naked and discovering way lovers come to know each other on the marriage bed. The emphasis is perhaps more on adventure for men and slightly more on intimacy for women. Yet, both desires are strong in us as men and women. In the words of friends, these two desires come together in us all as a longing to be in a relationship of heroic proportions.

When I was a boy, I loved to jump from our haymow onto the backs of steers feeding at the hayrack directly underneath. The ensuing bareback ride was always an adventure of the highest order. I also loved to watch *The Mickey Mouse Club* on television, just to have a moment's intimacy with Annette (Funicello). I am still partly convinced our eyes met a time or two and she smiled at me. These two boyhood passions for adventure and intimacy often came together in my fantasies in a story in which I would rescue Annette from the bad guys and escape with her into the mountains where we would live happily ever after. I would be her hero. She would be my beauty. And we would always be ready to fight the bad guys again whenever the world needed us, side by side.

Whatever form each of our intimate adventures has taken in our fantasies, or in "real life," this Sacred Romance is set within all our hearts and will not go away. It is the core of our spiritual journey. Any religion that ignores it survives only as guilt-induced legalism, a set of propositions to be memorized and rules to be obeyed.

Someone or something has romanced us from the beginning with creek-side singers and pastel sunsets, with the austere majesty of snowcapped mountains and the poignant flames of autumn colors telling us of something—or someone—leaving, with a promise to return. These things can, in an unguarded moment, bring us to our knees with longing for this something or someone who is lost; someone or something only our heart recognizes. C. S. Lewis knew this longing well:

> Even in your hobbies, has there not always been some secret attraction which the others are curiously ignorant of—something, not to be identified with, but always on the verge of breaking through, the smell of cut wood in the workshop or the clap-clap of water against the boat's side? Are not all lifelong friendships born at the moment when at last you meet another human being who has some inkling (but faint and uncertain even in the best) of that something which you were born desiring, and which, beneath the flux of other desires and in all the momentary silences between the louder passions, night and day, year by year, from childhood to old age, you are looking for, watching for, listening for? You have never *had* it. All the things that have ever deeply possessed your soul have been but hints of it—tantalizing glimpses, promises never quite fulfilled, echoes that died away just as they caught your ear. But if it should really become manifest—if there ever came an echo that did

not die away but swelled into the sound itself—you would know it. Beyond all possibility of doubt you would say, "Here at last is the thing I was made for." We cannot tell each other about it. It is the secret signature of each soul, the incommunicable and unappeasable want, the thing we desired before we met our wives or made our friends or chose our work, and which we shall still desire on our deathbeds, when the mind no longer knows wife or friend or work. While we are, this is. If we lose this, we lose all.

Indeed, art, literature, and music have all portrayed and explored the Romance, or its loss, in myriad scenes, images, sounds, and characters that nonetheless speak to us out of the same story. The universality of the story is the reason Shakespeare's plays, even though they speak to us from a pastoral setting in England across four hundred years of time, speak so eloquently and faithfully that they are still performed on stages from Tokyo to New York City.

It is as if someone has left us with a haunting in our inner-heart stories that will not go away; nor will it allow itself to be captured and ordered. The Romance comes and goes as it wills. And so we are haunted by it.

What does this Romance have to do with God? Could it be that the more literal, propositional message of Christianity that we recite to each other in the Apostles' Creed is the same secret message those singers were sharing with each other and with me on those long-ago summer evenings of my boyhood? Has God left us all with the haunting of this Sacred Romance to draw us toward home?

If this poignant longing were the only deep experience of our soul, then we should not lose heart. Though we may not have tasted satisfaction yet, we would search for it all our lives. There are enough hints and clues and "tantalizing glimpses" to keep us searching, our heart ever open and alive to the quest. But there is another message that comes to all of us in varying shades and intensities, even in our early years. It often seems to come out of nowhere and for no discernible reason that we can fathom. It is dark, powerful, and full of dread. I think of it as the Message of the Arrows.

3

The Message of the Arrows

I cried when I was born and every day shows why.
George Herbert

THERE ARE ONLY TWO THINGS that pierce the human heart, wrote Simone Weil. One is beauty. The other is affliction. And while we wish there were only beauty in the world, each of us has known enough pain to raise serious doubts about the universe we live in. From very early in life we know another message, warning us that the Romance has an enemy.

The psalmist speaks of this enemy and tells us we need not fear it:

> He [God] will save you from the fowler's snare
>   and from the deadly pestilence.
> He will cover you with his feathers,
>   and under his wings you will find refuge;
>   his faithfulness will be your shield and rampart.
> You will not fear the terror of night,
>   nor the arrow that flies by day. *(Ps. 91:3–5)*

Yet we cannot deny that the Arrows have struck us all, sometimes arriving in a hail of projectiles that blocked out the sun, and other times descending in more subtle flight that only let us know we were wounded years later, when the wound festered and broke.

One of the first Arrows I (Brent) remember came on a fall morning when the green choruses of summer were no longer there to comfort me. I happened upon my mother standing by the stove one morning before school began, stirring oatmeal. She had been crying and the tears still welled up in her eyes. They were not the kind of tears shed in anger or even pain due to a momentary spat with my father. They were not due to some recently delivered message about illness or death in the family.

They were the tears of a frightened girl in her mid-twenties who could find no meeting place between the life she found herself living as wife and mother and the needs of her own wounded heart that never felt the connection with mother and father so necessary to living with courage and hope. I couldn't have put that into words back then, but I felt the fear as a palpable enemy that needed to be quickly defeated. If there was an adversary of the heart that even adults did not know how to handle, my world was much less safe than I had thought. I moved quickly to help my mother vanquish this foe in the best way I knew how.

I think I put my hand on her arm and said something like, "It will be all right." I remember feeling a separation within myself and from her even then that kept me from addressing her as Mom or Mommy. I didn't understand that the arrows were already inside both of us. She looked angry that anyone could believe anything so foolish and said something like, "It's not all right. You kids just don't know what it's like."

My stepfather was not there to show me how to fend off Arrows such as these and so they entered into me and, as I later came to know, lodged in a deep place. Still later, I came to realize he did not know how to defeat the enemy either, for himself or me.

This other Message of the Arrows that I learned on fall and winter mornings seemed as strong and often stronger than the message of those summer creek-side singers. I remember sitting in the school cafeteria alone, trying to pull the Arrows out or at least cover them over so I could enter into the banter that seemed to flow so easily from my friends. I remember being pinned down on the playground by a friend of mine who was bigger than me and feeling that I would always be in that place if I wasn't careful.

I remember standing in the kitchen of our old farmhouse in my pajamas one morning at the age of five or six when two men in felt hats and long overcoats came to ask where my parents were. They asked several questions, all of which I answered, "I don't know." Finally they turned in disgust and said in parting, "You don't know much, do you, kid?"

There were other Arrows over the years that struck in that same deep place. Arrows that carried messages about ears that were too big, and a father who never called or wrote; my stepfather, who was a cowboy, commenting to my mother that I was a town kid; another stepfather who came and went and never stayed in touch. There was a girl I loved but couldn't love (intimacy requires a heart that is released and mine was pinned down with unknown fears and grief) and so I let her go; and total confusion over what vocation I would pursue or even had any ability for. The Arrows flew and all seemed to strike close to that fearful place, a place that said that I was alone in a coldly indifferent world. And even the ones that didn't, I made sure they ended up there. I needed the message to be at least consistent that the world was clearly a fearful place.

I remember, one day in winter in my early twenties, going back to stand on the bridge over that same creek that had been so magical for me as a boy. It was two years after returning home from college. I had spent most of five years there still pursuing the Romance through parties, alcohol, and drugs, and in always making sure I was present when anything was going on. I feared that if I missed any opportunity, the magic would come while I was not there and I would miss it forever. And for a time, the Arrows seemed to be silenced by the endless possibility that "something *was* about to happen." College life hid so much disappointment behind the illusion that life hadn't really started yet. The Arrows remained silent until a disinterested office worker placed my diploma in my hand without looking up and I found myself standing on the front steps of my college administrative offices with no more reason to stay.

The Message of the Arrows

I had graduated from college without finding a love or a vocation. The adults I knew (who so often try to fill emptiness of soul with economic solutions) told me it was time to settle down and find a responsible life. I, on the other hand, felt that I had only begun to be restless. I felt there was nowhere I really belonged or even wanted to belong; that whatever story my family and friends had found to live in, my own had become a succession of meaningless chapters with no plot other than filling in the days. It was a longing for the landscape of those summer evenings of so long ago that called me again to the bridge that day. It was a hope that I would find some clarity of vision in the place I had loved so much as a boy.

I stood there that November day looking down onto a small, brown stream bordered in lifeless gray hardwoods and monochromatic fallen leaves. The waters themselves flowed listlessly over the barriers of leaves and sticks in their path, as if wearied by the constant chore of movement. In many places, the dams built by the winter debris stilled their life with little resistance. A few hundred yards off to my right stood our old farmhouse, now vacant with a large hole in the roof. The barns and sheds and corrals that had given it a reason to exist were gone. Weeds grew in a tangled confusion where the corn had once stood in ordered wildness. The weariness of it all came together in the silence of those absent August songsters from so many years ago.

I remember feeling a sharp pain in my chest that I silenced with cold anger. I thought what a fool I had been all these years to believe in the summer message of this place. Laid out before me in the light of day was obviously the reality that had always been there. It was time I stopped believing a lie. The mysterious Love and Lover that had come to me in my childhood were frauds.

I know now I placed that last Arrow in my heart that day and shoved it cleanly through. I did it to kill the tears of mourning inside that would have insisted that there was something I had lost. Yet the Haunting was still there that day on the bridge. I only understood years later that it was I myself who killed it— or tried to. If I had allowed the loss I felt to flow in the waters of my own tears, the haunting call of that long-ago summer would have remained. It was in placing a dam of hardness over the ache I felt inside that I refused to acknowledge the Haunting and even misinterpreted the message of autumn: Something Lost and Again Coming.

At some point we all face the same decision—what will we do with the Arrows we've known? Maybe a better way to say it is, what have they tempted us to do? However they come to us, whether through a loss we experience as abandonment or some deep violation we feel as abuse, their message is always the same: Kill your heart. Divorce it, neglect it, run from it, or indulge it with some anesthetic (our various addictions). Think of how you've handled the affliction that has pierced your own heart. How did the Arrows come to you? Where did they land? Are they still there? What have you done as a result?

To say we all face a decision when we're pierced by an Arrow is misleading. It makes the process sound so rational, as though we have the option of coolly assessing the situation and choosing a logical response. Life isn't like that—the heart cannot be managed in a detached sort of way (certainly not when we are young, when some of the most defining Arrows strike). It feels more like an ambush and our response is at a gut level. We may never put words to it. Our deepest convictions are formed without conscious effort, but the effect is a shift deep in our soul. Commitments form never to be in that position again, never to know that sort of pain again. The result is an approach to life that we often call our personality. If you'll listen carefully to your life, you may begin to see how it has been shaped by the unique Arrows you've known and the particular convictions you've embraced as a result. The Arrows also taint and partially direct even our spiritual life.

My own spiritual journey with Christ "began" (I've since come to know the beginning was long before I was born) when my first prayer to God since I was a boy escaped from my heart one morning at work. It was the morning after another night of searching for something or someone; searching in bars, nightclubs, and just driving the roads listening to music all with the help of enough alcohol and drugs to keep the search hopeful. I was working, installing pipe in the bottom of sewer wells. I and the men I worked with lived with a cynicism that did for us in daylight hours what the alcohol and drugs did at night. We wryly commented to each other, standing in sewage up to our chests at four in the morning, that we were as far down in life as we could get, and there was no way to go but up.

One morning, almost without my bidding, my heart cried out from its own depths, "God, help me, because I am lost." And God answered with lavish faithfulness in those "first-love" years. I began reading the Bible and it came alive in my hands and heart. A friend I knew from high school came by and told me he had "become a Christian." He invited me to attend classes with him at Philadelphia College of the Bible, where I drank in everything I was taught with hungry joy and anticipation. At night, Ralph and I would go listen to a speaker or simply hang out at a diner talking about God, life, girls, and the abundant living we were sure was ahead. That fall, I went to a retreat in the mountains of Pennsylvania and met a longhaired girl whose heart God had recently courted and won. We sat for hours, talking about our personal longings and fears. We even prayed out loud together, a totally new concept to me.

"Becoming a Christian," however, doesn't necessarily solve the dilemma of the arrows, as I was soon to realize. Mine were still lodged deep and refused to allow some angry wound inside to heal. My resulting ambivalence colored every thought, action, and relationship of those important years. One day, at my by-then fiancée's request, I sat for five hours on the shore of a lake trying to understand the doubts I had about getting married. I knew no more at the end of the day than I did at the beginning. I had no one, at that point in my life, to help me understand the ambivalence created by the Message of the Arrows. No one who could fit the contradictory messages of the two revelations (the Romance and the Arrows) into any kind of story that would allow for life's unknowns even as my heart stayed open to the intimacy of Romance. So I became my own author and killed the one to control the other. I broke my engagement. I gave up the mystery of the Romance for a story that was much more predictable—which is to say, aloneness.

I allowed the romance to revive with another girl, Ginny, who eventually became my wife, when I was twenty-eight, but the arrows refused to be silent and I lived my late twenties and early thirties in a continuing blind reaction to the two revelations that vied for my soul. An old and familiar feeling began to make itself known from somewhere in the vicinity of my heart; a loneliness, an emptiness, a kind of ache and longing for something and someone I couldn't quite define. Feeling agitated and betrayed by such adulterous feelings, I pushed them down and threw myself even more intensely into Christian involvement and service. I began teaching our church's college-and-career class, became the singles pastor, and worked with our high school kids. Ginny and I were both teachers and used our summers to go to the mission fields in Mexico and the Dominican Republic as summer assistants with Wycliffe Bible Translators and Teen Missions. I even attended those strange Christian phenomena known as "potluck suppers" in the church activity hall.

These were all good things, but there was a part of me that refused to be healed, or filled, or freed, or whatever it was that my heart refused to be silent about. And since I never bothered to ask myself many questions (at least not the right questions) about what I felt or believed, I lived those years in a tangled web of fantasy divorced from present living and reality motivated by agnosticism and resignation. I lived in reaction to a series of happenings and circumstances that I felt unable to understand or even use as a way of understanding. I lived in the place where Forrest Gump found himself as he stood at the grave of his lifelong love, Jenny. "I don't know if we each have a destiny, or if we're all just floating around accident-like, on the breeze."

Many of you reading my story can relate to an inner journey that *feels* something like my own, even though the scenes of your outer story may be very different. The sense of being part of some bigger story, a purposeful adventure that is the Christian life, begins to drain away again after those first-love years in spite of everything we can do to stop it. Instead of a love affair with God, your life begins to feel more like a series of repetitive behaviors, like reading the same chapter of a book or writing the same novel over and over. The orthodoxy we try to live out, defined as "Believe and Behave Accordingly" is not a sufficient story line to satisfy whatever turmoil and longing our heart is trying to tell us about. Somehow our head and heart are on separate journeys and neither feels like life.

Eventually this division of head and heart culminates in one of two directions. We can either deaden our heart or divide our life into two parts, where our outer story becomes the theater of the should and our inner story the theater of needs, the place where we quench the thirst of our heart with whatever water is available. I chose the second route, living what I thought of as my religious life with increasing dryness and cynicism while I found "water" where I could: in sexual fantasies, alcohol, the next dinner out, late-night violence videos, gaining more knowledge through religious seminars—whatever would slake the thirsty restlessness inside. Whichever path we choose—heart deadness or heart and head separation—the Arrows win and we lose heart.

This is the story of all our lives, in one way or another. The haunting of the Romance and the Message of the Arrows are so radically different and they seem so mutually exclusive they split our hearts in two. In every way that the Romance is full of beauty and wonder, the Arrows are equally powerful in their ugliness and devastation. The Romance seems to promise a life of wholeness through a deep connection with the great Heart behind the universe. The Arrows deny it, telling us, "You are on your own. There is no Romance, no one strong and kind who is calling you to an exotic adventure." The Romance says, "This world is a benevolent place." The Arrows mock such naïveté, warning us, "Just watch yourself—disaster is a moment away." The Romance invites us to trust. The Arrows intimidate us into self-reliance.

It is as if we have all been "set up" for a loss of heart. I think about two couples who chose to go through marriage counseling with me, not because their relationships were terrible but because both couples desired to live before God and each other with more freedom and love. Hannah and Mike (not their real names) were in their early twenties and had been married just a few months. Hannah had a difficult life before her marriage, moving from town to town with no relationship with her real father. Mike was a loner before he met Hannah, nursing the wounds from his own Arrows in solitude. Hannah and Mike both loved the outdoors and as their love for each other grew, they looked forward to a long life in the mountains with their yet-to-be-born children. One year after their marriage, I spoke at Hannah's memorial service in the Garden of the Gods. Cancer took her life almost before she had a chance to fight it.

Sam and Leslie (not their real names) came for counseling after long years of fruitful service for God on the mission field. They were still young, in their early fifties, and they knew there were some unhealed things between them that would prevent them from having the deeper intimacy they both longed for in the years ahead. They entered into looking at their marriage with courage and hope at a time in life when it would have been easy to just stay with the status quo. They looked forward to enjoying the time to come with their children and grandchildren as well as a deeper intimacy with each other. Not long ago I stood at Leslie's graveside as Sam and the children said good-bye to her, Leslie also having been struck down by cancer.

What are Mike and Sam left to conclude? Mike opened his heart only to lose everything in exactly the way he feared. Sam hoped to live out his years with Leslie, enjoying his family and the fruits of all his years of service, only to face the years ahead alone. The Arrows strike at the most vital places in our hearts, the things we care most about. The deepest questions we ever ask are directly related to our heart's greatest needs and the answers life gives us shape our images of ourselves, of life, and of God. *Who am I?* The Romance whispers that we are someone special, that our heart is good because it is made for someone good; the Arrows tell us we are a dime a dozen, worthless, even dark and twisted, dirty. *Where is life to be found?* The Romance tells us life will flourish when we give it away in love and heroic sacrifice. The Arrows tell us that we must arrange for what little life there may be, manipulating our world and all the while watching our backs. "God is good," the Romance tells us. "You can release the well-being of your heart to him." The Arrows strike back, "Don't ever let life out of your control," and they seem to impale with such authority, unlike the gentle urges of the Romance, that in the end we are driven to find some way to contain them. The only way seems to be to kill our longing for the Romance, much in the same way we harden our heart to someone who hurts us. *If I don't want so much,* we believe, *I won't be so vulnerable.* Instead of dealing with the Arrows, we silence the longing. That seems to be our only hope. And so we lose heart.

Which is the truer message? If we try to hang on to the Romance, what are we to do with our wounds and the awful tragedies of life? How can we keep our heart alive in the face of such deadly Arrows? Is it possible for Mike to risk opening his heart to love again? Can Sam ever totally trust the God he served for so long? How many losses can a heart take? If we deny the wounds or try to minimize them, we deny a part of our heart and end up living a shallow optimism that frequently becomes a demand that the world be better than it is. On the other hand, if we embrace the Arrows as the final word on life, we despair, which is another way to lose heart. To lose hope has the same effect on our heart as it would be to stop breathing. If only there were someone to help us reconcile our deepest longings with our greatest fears.

In my thirties, I didn't know that the One who answered the "religious prayer" of my mid-twenties ("God, help me, because I am lost") was the same One who wooed me so long ago in the magic of the singers and even in the harsh coldness of that November day. If I had known, the years of my religiosity would have been filled with much more joy and confusion, mourning and hope, patience and spontaneity, and conviction and uncareful love than they have been. I would have lived with a confidence that the Arrows aren't the final word. But I had lost my own story with the loss of my family as a boy, and along with it any sense of a larger story that would reconcile the two messages my heart had known.

4

A Story Big Enough to Live In

*Romance is the deepest thing in life, romance is
deeper even than reality.*

G. K. Chesterton

Is THERE a reality that corresponds to the deepest
desires of our heart? Who gets the last word—the
Romance or the Arrows? We need to know, so we are
constantly, every moment of our lives, trying to make sense out
of our experiences. We look for coherence, a flow, an assurance
that things fit together. We want, we *need* to reconcile the two
revelations Brent has been describing. Our problem is most of
us live our lives like a movie we've arrived at twenty minutes
late. The action is well under way and we haven't a clue what's
happening. Who are these people? Who are the good guys and
who are the bad guys? Why are they doing that? What's going
on? We sense that something really important, perhaps even
glorious, is taking place, and yet it all seems so *random*. Beauty
catches us by surprise and makes us wish for more, but then the
Arrows come and we are pierced. As Chesterton wrote,

> We all feel the riddle of the earth without anyone to point it out.
> The mystery of life is the plainest part of it. . . . Every stone or
> flower is a hieroglyphic of which we have lost the key; with every
> step of our lives we enter into the middle of some story which we
> are certain to misunderstand. (*Orthodoxy*)

No wonder it's so hard to live from our heart! We find ourselves in the middle of a story that is sometimes wonderful, sometimes awful, often a confusing mixture of both, and we haven't the slightest clue how to make sense of it all. Worse, we try to interpret the meaning of life with only fragments, isolated incidents, feelings, and images without reference to the story of which these scenes are merely a part. It can't be done, because, as Julia Gatta pointed out, "Experience, no matter how accurately understood, can never furnish its own interpretation." So we look for someone to interpret life for us. Our interpreters will usually be the primary people in our lives when we are young, our parents or grandparents or another key figure. They shape our understanding of the story in which we find ourselves and tell us what to do with the Romance, the Arrows, and our hearts.

Brent was often left without an interpreter as fathers came and went. I (John) was more fortunate; I had a grandfather who stepped into my life at the very moment the Arrows were about to take over, during the years my father was engulfed in the sinister battle we call alcoholism. Trained as a civil engineer, my father fell into a career in sales just when the U.S. Army glutted the market with engineers after World War II. Arthur Miller captured the tenuous nature of his life in *Death of a Salesman*: "He's a man way out there in the blue, riding on a smile and a shoeshine. And when they start not smiling back—that's an earthquake. And then you get yourself a couple of spots on your hat, and you're finished. Nobody dast blame this man." My mother went back to college and then to work to help make ends meet, and I was largely left on my own to form my understanding of the story of life and my role in it.

My grandfather, "Pop," filled an empty place in my soul at that critical moment. He was my hero, a cowboy and a gentleman in a Stetson and boots. Spending summers on his ranch was a schoolboy's dream—riding horses, chasing frogs, harassing the big old cows when I was sure no one was looking. I remember riding in his old Ford pickup, Pop with his cowboy hat and leather work gloves, waving at nearly everyone on the road. Folks seemed to wave back with a sense of respect. It gave me a settled feeling that someone was in charge, someone strong and loving.

Pop loved me as a boy and called me to be a man. He taught me to saddle and ride a horse—not merely for fun, but to take my place on a working ranch. Together we explored the open spaces of the eastern Oregon sagebrush, mending fences, tending sick cattle, fishing Huck Finn–style with willow branches and a piece of string. Early in the morning we'd go for coffee, milk, and doughnuts down at the diner where everyone knew us by name. Sunday afternoons we'd go "visiting"—calling on relatives in nearby towns and farms. Together they would sit and chat, telling family stories that gave me a sense of being part of something larger than myself. Even though my own world was shaken by the earthquake of my father's struggle, I knew there was another world where things were well and I could have a place in it.

During my teenage years visits to the ranch grew fewer and farther between. My father, fighting his own battles, was unable to teach me how to fight mine. Screaming to know someone was there for me, I tried nearly every protest available to unsupervised teens in American culture. At fifteen I was arrested for breaking and entering. I can't even remember what my parents said or did; perhaps I had already broken their hearts as only a prodigal son can. But hours later I found myself free to roam again. On the surface, I was relieved to escape punishment; far deeper, in the place in our heart where the story forms, the disappointment was more than I could bear. Why didn't they *do* something? I knew what I'd done was wrong; why wouldn't somebody show me the right way? It was a major Arrow. The message instructed me in the deep terror that there was no one strong enough to care for my soul, to pick me up and set me straight when I'd fallen. I was alone.

I was seventeen when I last saw my grandfather. The brain cancer that eventually killed him had already taken a loathsome toll. The man who had always stood larger than life was stooped and withered. His ranch, a picture of his life, was failing. I simply had no context for it, nothing larger to give it redemptive meaning. So I distanced myself from him and from the final piece of evidence that I was on my own in the world. When he died, I couldn't bring myself to attend the funeral.

Years later, in the summer of 1993, I stood by my grandfather's grave for the first time. After sixteen years I had made a pilgrimage to face the reality I had so long run from. It lay there in quiet, undeniable triumph: the Message of the Arrows.

Whether we feel it with the finality that Brent and I did, or as a lingering fear in the corner of our minds, most of us sense that we are alone in the world. No one has ever been there for us with the strength, tenderness, and consistency that we long for. Even in the best situations, people eventually let us down. Our personal drama leaves us little hope for an Author who is taking the story toward a good conclusion. Chesterton said we're certain to misunderstand the story we find ourselves in and he was right. Furthermore, those closest to us often help in the misinterpretation.

Still, we must make some sense of things. Life goes on and so must we. In order to participate or merely survive, we will find some story to live in.

Why Story?

The deepest convictions of our heart are formed by stories and reside there in the images and emotions of story. As a young boy, around the time my heart began to suspect that the world was a fearful place and I was on my own to find my way through it, I read the story of a Scottish discus thrower from the nineteenth century. He lived in the days before professional trainers and developed his skills alone, in the highlands of his native village. He even made his own iron discus from the description he read in a book. What he did not know was that the discus used in competition was made of wood with an *outer rim* of iron. His was solid metal and weighed three or four times as much as those being used by his would-be challengers. This committed Scotsman marked out in his field the distance of the current record throw and trained day and night to be able to match it. For nearly a year, he labored under the self-imposed burden of the extra weight. But he became very, very good. He reached the point at which he could throw his iron discus the record distance, maybe farther. He was ready.

My Scotsman (I had begun to closely identify with him) traveled south to England for his first competition. When he arrived at the games, he was handed the official wooden discus—which he promptly threw like a tea saucer. He set a new record, a distance so far beyond those of his competitors that no one could touch him. He thus remained the uncontested champion for many years.

Something in my heart connected with this story. *So, that's how you do it: Train under a great burden and you will be so far beyond the rest of the world you will be untouchable.* It became a defining image for my life, formed in and from a story.

Life is not a list of propositions, it is a series of dramatic scenes. As Eugene Peterson said, "We live in narrative, we live in story. Existence has a story shape to it. We have a beginning and an end, we have a plot, we have characters." Story is the language of the heart. Our souls speak not in the naked facts of mathematics or the abstract propositions of systematic theology; they speak the images and emotions of story. Contrast your enthusiasm for studying a textbook with the offer to go to a movie, read a novel, or listen to the stories of someone else's life. Elie Wiesel suggests that "God created man because he loves stories." So if we're going to find the answer to the riddle of the earth—and of our own existence—we'll find it in story.

Once upon a time the Western world had a story. Imagine you lived in the High Middle Ages. Your world was permeated with Christian imagery. You marked the days by the sound of church bells and the weeks and months according to the liturgical calendar. You lived in *anno domini*, the year of our Lord. It wasn't football season, it was Advent. Your role models were the saints, whose feast days were regular reminders of a drama greater than yourself. The architecture of the cathedral, the music, literature, and sculpture all gave you a vision of transcendence, reminding you of the central elements of that great story. Even the everyday language reflected the Christian understanding of life's story, expressions like "God be with you," "upon my soul," and "by Christ's blood." Birth and death, love and loss—all of your personal experiences would be shaped and interpreted by that larger story.

But you don't live in the Middle Ages, you live in the Postmodern Era. For hundreds of years, our culture has been losing its story. The Enlightenment dismissed the idea that there is an Author but tried to hang on to the idea that we could still have a larger story, life could still make sense, and everything was headed in a good direction. Western culture rejected the mystery and transcendence of the Middle Ages and placed its confidence in pragmatism and progress, the pillars of the Modern Era, the Age of Reason. But once we had rid ourselves of the Author, it didn't take long to lose the larger story. In the Postmodern Era, all we have left is our small stories. It's not pentecost, it's time for spring training. Our role models are movie stars, and the biggest taste of transcendence is the opening of the ski season. Our best expressions are on the level of "Have a nice day." The only reminder we have of a story beyond our own is the evening news, an arbitrary collection of scenes and images without any bigger picture into which they fit. The central belief of our times is that there is no story, nothing hangs together, all we have are bits and pieces, the random days of our lives. Tragedy still brings us to tears and heroism still lifts our hearts, but there is no context for any of it. Life is just a sequence of images and emotions without rhyme or reason.

So, what are we left to do? Create our own story line to bring some meaning to our experiences. Our heart is made to live in a larger story; having lost that we do the best we can by developing our own smaller dramas.

Look at the things people get caught up in: sports, politics, soap operas, rock bands. Desperate for something larger to give our lives transcendence, we try to lose ourselves in the smallest kinds of stories. Some of us choose the "Why does everything go wrong for me?" story. The plot of life is a tragedy, and we are playing the role of the victim of cruel circumstances. Our Arrows are our identity. This is an immensely popular story line because it relieves us of having to take any real responsibility for our lives. Victims demand to be understood, but don't you dare require anything of them.

And then there is the survivor, living in a life where the plot is a siege. The world is a dangerous and unpredictable place, so I will hunker down and survive, taking little risk, doing what I can to protect myself even if it means cutting myself off from others and from my own dreams. These stories focus on the Arrows at the expense of the Romance.

On the other hand, some of us are trying to live out a story line that preserves the Romance in some way. Though it takes a lot of energy to push the mess of life out of sight in order to maintain the belief that mystery and magic are the final word, we try. The most popular option is romantic love, the idea that somewhere out there is that special someone who will sweep you off your feet, take your breath away, with whom life would be one idyllic adventure and sex an unending ecstasy. It is the theme of popular music, the false transcendence of our day. Women especially are attracted to this story line; witness the success of novelist Danielle Steel and her imitators. The divorce rate ought to be proof enough of the failure of this story. It's not so much that lovers cannot live with each other as that they cannot live without the Haunting, which they mistook for romantic love. So they move to the next partner, trying to capture that evasive feeling again.

The leading false transcendence among men is the sports story. Men either pursue their longings for adventure through their own recreational activities or they lose themselves vicariously in their favorite players and teams, or in their children's sports. Business also fits into the story of life as a Big Game. *Sure, things are unpredictable, but some people seem to win and I'm determined to be one of them. I'll stay on top, travel light, and move fast.* We identify with a sports team or a company because we are allowed to belong to something bigger than our small worlds. Our heroes are the few winners, of course, while the losers are quickly pushed out of the camera's view.

Christians can opt for one of these, or choose a more "spiritual" version. The Religious Man or Woman is a popular story option in which we try to reduce the wildness of life by constructing a system of promises and rewards, a contract that will obligate God to grant us exemption from the Arrows. It really doesn't matter what the particular group bargain is—doctrinal adherence, moral living, or some sort of spiritual experience— the desire is the same: taming God in order to tame life. Never mind those deep yearnings of the soul; never mind the nagging awareness that God is not cooperating. If the system isn't working, it's because we're not doing it right. There's always something to work on, with the promise of abundant life just around the corner. Plenty of churches and leaders are ready to show you how to cut a deal.

All these stories comprise what James McClendon calls the "tournament of narratives" in our culture, a clash of many small dramas competing for our heart. Through baseball and politics and music and sex and even church, we are searching desperately for a larger story in which to live and find our role. All of these smaller stories offer a taste of meaning, adventure, or connectedness. But none of them offer the real thing; they aren't large enough. Our loss of confidence in a larger story is the reason we demand immediate gratification. We need a sense of being alive now, for now is all we have. Without a past that was planned for us and a future that waits for us, we are trapped in the present. There's not enough room for our souls in the present.

Our attempts to construct a story to live in eventually fail because, as Robert Jenson has said, "Human consciousness is too obscure a mystery to itself for us to script our own lives." Inevitably, we leave significant parts of our souls out of the story. If our particular version fails to take both of life's messages into account, to grant them proper weight, it will destroy us. Denying the tragedy of life requires such effort that it tears the soul apart. Believing that in the end there is only tragedy kills the most tender, "alive" parts of us. Trapped in an eternal present, we come to a sickness of heart like that of Shakespeare's Macbeth, the Scottish nobleman who sells his soul to play the role of king in his own small story. At the end of his life he laments,

> I am sick at heart. . . .
> To-morrow, and to-morrow, and to-morrow,
> Creeps in this petty pace from day to day
> To the last syllable of recorded time;
> Life's but a walking shadow, a poor player
> That struts and frets his hour upon the stage
> And then is heard no more. It is a tale
> Told by an idiot, full of sound and fury,
> Signifying nothing. (*Act V, Scene V*)

The Sacred Romance

There *is* another way, one that grants the "devil his due" in all the tragedy of life, but that also keeps hope alive that the haunting of the Romance is no illusion, either. Children aren't a bad place to look when we're trying to get beyond the cynicism of adulthood and so it shouldn't surprise us that most children have found a way of reconciling the messages. Before skepticism takes over (what we mistakenly call maturity), children intuit the true Story as a fairy tale. If you'll remember, the best fairy tales aren't romantic in the poor sense of the word. They are realistic, only more so. There are ogres and evil sorcerers and wicked stepmothers, to be sure. But they are neither the whole story nor even the heart of it. There are genuine heroes and heroines and a cause to live for that is worth dying for. There is a quest or a journey strewn with danger and the stakes could never be higher.

My boys are at the age when cowboys are among their greatest heroes. Our days are often filled with gunfights and stories of daring adventure. Several nights ago, as I was tucking seven-year-old Samuel into bed, we began talking about the future. I asked him what he wanted to do when he grows up. With a grave severity in his eye he looked at me and said, "I'm going to bring back the West." His heart knew that he was made for noble things. Our heart knows it, too, if we will let it speak to us.

Now, what is intriguing is that this metaphor is the closest one to the way in which the Scriptures present the gospel—as a Sacred Romance. If that surprises you then it is good news, for any explanation bold enough to encompass the meaning of life ought to have at least two elements: It ought to be weighty enough to sustain both messages and it ought to come as a bit of a surprise. We have lived for so long with a "propositional" approach to Christianity we have nearly lost its true meaning. As Mary Stewart Van Leeuwen says,

Much of it hinges on your view of scripture. Are you playing proof-text poker with Genesis plus the Gospels and Paul's epistles, with everything else just sort of a big mystery in between—except maybe Psalms and Proverbs, which you use devotionally? Or do you see scripture as being a cosmic drama—creation, fall, redemption, future hope—dramatic narratives that you can apply to all areas of life? (*Prism* interview)

For centuries prior to our Modern Era, the church viewed the gospel as a Romance, a cosmic drama whose themes permeated our own stories and drew together all the random scenes in a redemptive wholeness. But our rationalistic approach to life, which has dominated Western culture for hundreds of years, has stripped us of that, leaving a faith that is barely more than mere fact-telling. Modern evangelicalism reads like an IRS 1040 form: It's true, all the data is there, but it doesn't take your breath away. As British theologian Alister McGrath warns, the Bible is not primarily a doctrinal sourcebook: "To reduce revelation to principles or concepts is to suppress the element of mystery, holiness and wonder to God's self-disclosure. 'First principles' may enlighten and inform; they do not force us to our knees in reverence and awe, as with Moses at the burning bush, or the disciples in the presence of the risen Christ" (*A Passion for Truth*).

Could it be that our lives actually make sense, every part—the good and the bad? Those deep yearnings that catch us by surprise when we hear a certain song on the radio, or watch our children when they aren't aware of being watched, are telling us something that *is* truer about life than the Message of the Arrows. It seems too good to be true, which ought to raise even deeper suspicions that it is true. As Chesterton recounts in *Orthodoxy*, he "had always believed that the world involved magic: now I thought that perhaps it involved a magician. . . . I had always felt life first as a story; and if there is a story there is a storyteller."

According to the part of the story God has allowed us to see, the Haunting we sense is his calling us forth on a journey. The resurrection of our heart requires that the Sacred Romance be true and that is precisely what the Scriptures tell us. As Frederick Buechner reminds us in his wonderful book *Telling the Truth: The Gospel as Tragedy, Comedy and Fairy Tale*, the world of the gospel *is* the world of fairy tale, with one notable exception:

> It is a world of magic and mystery, of deep darkness and flickering starlight. It is a world where terrible things happen and wonderful things too. It is a world where goodness is pitted against evil, love against hate, order against chaos, in a great struggle where often it is hard to be sure who belongs to which side because appearances are endlessly deceptive. Yet for all its confusion and wildness, it is a world where the battle goes ultimately to the good, who live happily ever after, and where in the long run everybody, good and evil alike, becomes known by his true name. . . . That is the fairy tale of the Gospel with, of course, one crucial difference from all other fairy tales, which is that the claim made for it is that it is true, that it not only happened once upon a time but has kept on happening ever since and is happening still.

Let us explore together the drama that God has been weaving since before the beginning of time, which he has also placed in our heart. Who are the main players in this larger story? What is the plot? How do we fit in? As we rediscover the oldest story in the world, one that is forever young, we journey into the heart of God and toward the recovery of our own hearts. For perhaps God would be reason enough to stay open to the Romance if we knew he would keep us safe. And therein we experience a great fear and confusion.

5

The Wildness of God

*[We live our lives before] the wild, dangerous,
unfettered and free character of the living God.*
Walter Bruggeman

THE UNKNOWN Romancing or the Message of the Arrows—which captures the essence of life? Should we keep our hearts open to the Romance or concentrate on protecting ourselves from the Arrows? Should we live with hopeful abandon, trusting in a larger story whose ending is good or should we live in our small stories and glean what we can from the Romance while trying to avoid the Arrows?

Perhaps God, as the Author of the story we're all living in, would tilt the scale in a favorable direction if we knew we could trust him. And therein lies our dilemma. There seems to be no direct correlation between the way we live our lives and the resulting fate God has in store for us, at least on this earth. Abraham's grandson, Jacob, lives the life of a manipulator and is blessed. Jesus lives for the sake of others and is crucified. And we never quite know when we're going to run into the uncertainty of the part God has written for us in his play, whether our character has significant lines yet to speak or will even survive the afternoon.

I (Brent) was confronted with my own questions about him at the most elemental level when I was a fourth grader in David C. Crockett elementary school in Bryan, Texas. As a Northerner recently moved from New Jersey, I quickly discovered that there had been a Civil War and there were still amends to be made. That fall, for what seemed like weeks, the four of us from Northern states were sent to one end of the playground where we waited to be attacked by the forces of the Confederacy. And since we were considerably outnumbered, unlike those 1860s Union infantry, we were soon enough "captured" and taken to prison camp. This camp was a large mulch pile of dead leaves surrounded by chicken wire and presided over by a sixth grader named Jimmy. Jimmy's favorite form of punishment was to drag the terrified waif last captured to the middle of the pile and lower his considerable 150-pound bulk until the prisoner disappeared from view. I cannot describe the terror I felt at being taken to Jimmy. Much of any leg speed I have came from a determination to be the last one captured on a given day, in hopes that the school bell would ring before my interment.

I remember one of my friends, a boy from Ohio named Terry, being sat on so long one day that I feared he was dead. I looked around for teachers or parents or even sympathetic sixth graders who would help us. No one came. I finally yelled for Jimmy to let Terry up before he killed him. With a smile, and in best bad guy form from the movies, he rose majestically and ordered my guards to put me in Terry's place.

I remember landing in the leaves with only the thought I'd be suffocated, or worse, made to cry in front of everybody. Before Jimmy could lower himself all the way, I squirmed free, jumped the chicken wire, and raced to the far ends of the playground to outlast the recess bell. Somehow I could never find the way to express this daily terror to my parents. I felt totally alone with it.

The Question in Our Heart

Of course, all of us have lived through events such as I have described, some much, much worse and, if they took place in the setting of family, school, or work, perhaps lasting for years. The terror we enter and the seeming lack of rescue from it leave us with a deeply imprinted question about God that we hide in our heart, sometimes not allowing the light of day to touch it for years, even deep into our spiritual journey. We cover the question with rationalizations that let him off the hook and allow us to still believe, but our beliefs rest on foundations that move and quake under us. It is easy to reason that Jimmy and those sixth graders were just bad; you know, "not raised in very good homes." And of course, our rationalizations do bear a modicum of truth that keeps us from dealing with the question lodged deep in our heart, hidden from our conscious mind: "Do you care for me, God?"

What's under that question?

Blaise Pascal, in his *Pensees,* says, "The heart has its reasons that reason knows not of." What's under that question is our personal stories, often punctuated by the Message of the Arrows: parents who were emotionally absent; bedtimes without words or hugs; ears that were too big and noses that were too small; others chosen for playground games while we were not; and prayers about all these things seemingly met with silence. And embedded in our stories, deep down in our heart, in a place so well guarded that they have rarely if ever been exposed to the light of day, are other grief-laden and often angry questions: "God, why did you allow this to happen to me? Why did you make me like this? What will you allow to happen next?" In the secret places of our heart, we believe God is the One who did not protect us from these things or even the One who perpetrated them upon us. Our questions about him make us begin to live with a deep apprehension that clings anxiously to the depths of our hearts. . . . "Do you really care for me, God?"

This is the question that has shipwrecked many of our hearts, leaving them grounded on reefs of pain and doubt, no longer free to accompany us on spiritual pilgrimage. We might be able to rationalize away that question by telling ourselves that we need to be more careful, or that sometimes others are just bad. We can even breathe a sigh of relief when we realize that trouble has come from our own sin. But even the careful, legalistic, and constricted lifestyle that arises out of thinking we can avoid trouble through our own devices shipwrecks when the Arrows seem to strike us out of nowhere. What are we to make of God's wildness in allowing these things to happen?

A Part Too Large

Indeed, the things that have happened to us often suggest that the real script of the play we're all living in is "God is indifferent" rather than "God is love." Deep down in our heart, in the place where the story is formed, this experience of God as indifferent drives us to write our own scripts, as John described in Chapter 4. Job apparently lived with this anxiety about God even before his tribulations descended upon him, as evidenced by his exclamation from the ashes of his home and his life: "What I *feared* has come upon me; what I *dreaded* has happened to me" (Job 3:25).

Job was a God-fearing man and yet something in him suspected that faith in God did not necessarily translate into peace and safety. Of course, Job had no inkling of the discussion going on in heaven between God and Satan. It was a debate over whether the foundation of God's kingdom was based on genuine love or power. And astonishingly, God was placing the perception of his own integrity as well as the reputation of his whole kingdom on the genuineness of Job's heart. Eavesdrop with me on one of the most revealing conversations in the Scriptures:

> One day the angels came to present themselves before the LORD, and Satan also came with them. The LORD said to Satan, "Where have you come from?"

Satan answered the LORD, "From roaming through the earth and going back and forth in it."

Then the LORD said to Satan, "Have you considered my servant Job? There is no one on earth like him; he is blameless and upright, a man who fears God and shuns evil."

"Does Job fear God for nothing?" Satan replied. "Have you not put a hedge around him and his household and everything he has? You have blessed the work of his hands, so that his flocks and herds are spread throughout the land. But stretch out your hand and strike everything he has, and he will surely curse you to your face."

The LORD said to Satan, "Very well, then, everything he has is in your hands, but on the man himself do not lay a finger." . . .

On another day the angels came to present themselves before the LORD, and Satan also came with them to present himself before him. And the LORD said to Satan, "Where have you come from?"

Satan answered the LORD, "From roaming through the earth and going back and forth in it."

Then the LORD said to Satan, "Have you considered my servant Job? There is no one on earth like him; he is blameless and upright, a man who fears God and shuns evil. And he still maintains his integrity, though you incited me against him to ruin him without any reason."

"Skin for skin!" Satan replied. "A man will give all he has for his own life. But stretch out your hand and strike his flesh and bones, and he will surely curse you to your face."

The LORD said to Satan, "Very well, then, he is in your hands; but you must spare his life."

So Satan went out from the.presence of the LORD and afflicted Job with painful sores from the soles of his feet to the top of his head. Then Job took a piece of broken pottery and scraped himself with it as he sat among the ashes.

His wife said to him, "Are you still holding on to your integrity? Curse God and die!"

He replied, "You are talking like a foolish woman. Shall we accept good from God, and not trouble?"

In all this, Job did not sin in what he said. *(Job 1:6–12; 2:1–10)*

When Job's three friends came along and witnessed the devastation of his life, they tore their clothes, sprinkled dust on their heads, and appropriately, sat in silence with him for seven days because they saw how great his suffering was. The story doesn't tell us much about what they were feeling during those seven days, but their subsequent counsel gives us a pretty good idea of what they were thinking. Eliphaz the Temanite basically responded to Job's continued groanings by saying, "Job, you've been our man. We've watched you carefully to see how you gain God's blessings so that we can do it just like you do. You know how this religion business works. If you're innocent, you'll be okay. If you've sinned, you won't. Since you're not okay, you've obviously blown it. There can be no other explanation for what's going on here" (Job 4:1–8).

God's direct correction of Job's friends exposed the secret demand of their hearts. They, like all of us do at one time or another, had been relating to God like one of the Mesopotamian household gods that the peoples in the Middle East were so familiar with.

The cultures in the cradle of civilization lived with a pantheon of gods who themselves existed in a kind of hierarchy. There were gods of war, fertility, and harvest who were acknowledged by the culture as a whole, and under these, a litany of household gods, usually statues made of crafted wood, clay, and precious metals, that were placed on the family mantel. People related to each of these gods by means of specific rituals and ceremonies whereby their protection and favor could be gained. Each family literally "owned" their own god.

To use an illustration from our culture, these household gods were somewhat like having a mobster for a neighbor. To those outside the neighborhood, the mobster may seem fearful and somewhat sinister. But if you're his immediate neighbor and treat him with deference and respect, he may get you a good deal on aluminum siding or a new car. Or he might have a bag of dead cats deposited on the doorstep of the man down the street, who, you casually mentioned, was allowing his dog to dig in your flower beds.

When the living God of the Old Testament came along, he seemed to fit right in with this way of thinking, describing himself as the God of Abraham, Isaac, and Jacob. He gave Moses a regimen of laws, rituals, and ceremonies to be followed if the Israelites were to gain his favor. Everything should have worked out fine. The familiar household-god religion was very simple and well understood by everyone: Simply obey the prescribed rules, regulations, and rituals that the god thought were important, for whatever reason, and he would be appeased and give his blessing. The Israelites never bothered to read between the lines. They were totally unprepared and unwilling to consider the thought that they, like Job, were involved in a much bigger drama.

Indeed, when we consider how central a part Job was given in the drama God was directing, we are confronted with the reality that we, too, could be in the same position. It seems that the part God has written for us is much too big and certainly too dangerous. Paul confirms this thought in Ephesians when he tells us, "The church, you see, is not peripheral to the world; the world is peripheral to the church. The church is Christ's body, in which he speaks and acts, by which he fills everything with his presence" (1:22–23, *The Message*). Every human being is of great significance to God, but those whom God has drawn to believe in him are center stage in a drama of cosmic proportions.

When we look at Job's time on center stage, we find that God not only allows the Prince of Darkness to come before his throne, he points Job out to him and, in effect, unleashes him on the defenseless man. This is very much akin to a policeman drawing the attention of a gang of thugs to a young man walking lawfully along the street with his wife, children, and belongings. He then gives the gangsters permission to test the man's respect for the law by mugging and robbing him, and killing his children. I find myself asking, "Was this really necessary to test Job's heart? What's going on here anyway?" I want to ask, "If God is the author, producer, and director of this play, *what kind of a story is he telling?*"

I am filled with not a little outrage as well as an anxiety that wants to ask for a much smaller part in the play than Job had; or possibly even a role in a more off-Broadway production that I could help direct. You know, something like *God Helps Brent Pursue Money, Wealth, and Fame While Living a Quiet Life.* There is something frightening about being in a play in which the director may allow the plot to descend on my character from a totally unknown direction, a direction that may cause me deep emotional or even physical harm. It is something like having the stage lights dropped from high overhead during one of my scenes without telling me, leaving me no chance to change my mark before they fall.

God's artistry as Playwright of the story we find ourselves living in often seems to use up characters like trailer courts in tornado season. He assures us, notably in the Psalms, that he sees our pain and cares for us, and that our tormentors will be judged, but he still calls us firmly to our marks, regardless of disease, calamity, age, sex, or strength.

He comes to Job in the midst of his loss, pain, and indeed the nearness of death and says, referring to the ongoing discussion between Job and his friends,

> "Who is this that darkens my counsel
> with words without knowledge?
> Brace yourself like a man;
> I will question you,
> and you shall answer me" *(Job 38:2–3).*

This is followed by his lengthy interrogation of Job's understanding of even the physical creation, much less any more profound issues. I must admit there is something in me as a man that feels strangely respected by this approach while another part of me thinks, *How unfeeling and cold.*

When God comes to call Jeremiah to be his prophet of hard sayings to Judah, Jeremiah protests, saying, "'Ah, Sovereign LORD . . . I do not know how to speak; I am only a child.' But the LORD said to me, 'Do not say, "I am only a child." You must go to everyone I send you to and say whatever I command you. Do not be afraid of them, for I am with you and will rescue you,' declares the LORD" (Jer. 1:6–8).

God is saying that these things will be done through Jeremiah's dependence on his strength and provision, and that he will rescue him. Yet there is something about God's rescues that make them a little less timely than dialing 911. He leaves Abraham with his knife raised and ready to plunge into Isaac's heart, and Isaac waiting for the knife to descend; he leaves Joseph languishing for years in an Egyptian prison; he allows the Israelites to suffer four hundred years of bondage under the Egyptians and leaves those same Israelites backed against the Red Sea with Pharaoh's chariots thundering down on them. He abandons Jesus to the cross and does not rescue him at all. And then there are those of us who, along with the saints under heaven's very altar, are groaning under the weight of things gone wrong, waiting for that same Jesus to return and sweep us up with him in power and glory. "How long, O Lord?" we whisper in our weariness and pain.

Indeed, God calls us to battles where the deck appears stacked in favor of those who are his enemies and ours, just to increase the drama of the play. And there is the clear picture, even from God himself, that he does so to enhance his own glory.

In C. S. Lewis's novel *The Lion, the Witch, and the Wardrobe,* of The Chronicles of Narnia series, four children, Peter, Susan, Edmund, and Lucy, pass through the wardrobe's portal to find the kingdom of Narnia imprisoned under the spell of the White Witch. Aslan the lion, who is the king of Narnia, is nowhere to be found. Although rumor has it "He is on the move," he appears to have abandoned his kingdom to the White Witch, who spends her leisure time turning the inhabitants into lawn statuary.

The four children set out to explore this strange and somewhat frightening new country that is locked under evil's spell. They come upon Mr. and Mrs. Beaver, a husband and wife still faithful to Aslan. The Beavers assure the children that Aslan is about to return to set things right and that prophecy suggests that they have a very important, even central part to play in the drama about to unfold. Indeed, they learn they are to actually rule with Aslan from Cair Paravel itself, Aslan's royal city.

Faced with all this fearful yet exciting news, Lucy and Susan's thoughts go to what Aslan is actually like. If he is a king who is safe, they reason, that will certainly be of great comfort in light of the battle being all but lost.

"Is—is he a man?" asked Lucy.

"Aslan a man!" said Mr. Beaver sternly. "Certainly not. I tell you he is the King of the wood and the son of the great Emperor-Beyond-the-Sea. Don't you know who is the King of Beasts? Aslan is a lion—*the* lion, the great Lion."

"Ooh!" said Susan, "I'd thought he was a man. Is he—quite safe? I shall feel rather nervous about meeting a lion."

"That you will, dearie, and no mistake," said Mrs. Beaver; "if there's anyone who can appear before Aslan without their knees knocking, they're either braver than most or else just silly."

"Then he isn't safe?" said Lucy.

"Safe?" said Mr. Beaver; "don't you hear what Mrs. Beaver tells you? Who said anything about safe? 'Course he isn't safe. But he's good. He's the King, I tell you."

When we were young, most of us loved adventure. There is something about the unknown that draws us, which is why we like stories so much. But I like to leave the theater at the end of the play, knowing that the dilemma of evil has been resolved by the characters on the stage or screen. Like Peter, Susan, Lucy, and Edmund, to find ourselves not as spectators but as central characters in the play itself is somewhat daunting. The stakes are truly high, sometimes literally life or death, and God rarely if ever yells "Cut!" just as the dangerous or painful scene descends upon us. No stunt doubles come onto the set to take our places. Many of us feel that we have been playing these kinds of scenes ever since we were children. We wonder if the hero will ever show up to rescue us.

We would like to picture goodness as being synonymous with safety. When we think of God being good, we perhaps picture someone like Al on the popular TV program, *Home Improvement*. He is someone who carefully plans out each task ahead of time and has all the proper tools and safety equipment in place; someone who has thought out every possible danger ahead of time and made allowances to ensure our safety as his workmate; someone who goes to bed early, gets plenty of rest, and wears flannel shirts as a mark of his reliability.

Being in partnership with God, though, often feels much more like being Mel Gibson's sidekick in the movie *Lethal Weapon*. In his determination to deal with the bad guy, he leaps from seventh-story balconies into swimming pools, surprised that we would have any hesitation in following after him. Like Indiana Jones's love interests in the movies, we find ourselves caught up in an adventure of heroic proportions with a God who both seduces us with his boldness and energy and repels us with his willingness to place us in mortal danger, suspended over pits of snakes.

One strain of the modernist school of art is famous for creating "masterpieces" by standing back twenty feet and hurling paint onto the canvas. In answer to those who would criticize such a careless approach, they argue that chance is the real artist at work in this life and they do not want to interfere with its creative process. Our experience of what God is doing is sometimes felt from the perspective of one of those paint molecules. We come crashing onto the canvas who knows where, intermingled with whatever the fates bring along next.

Indeed, one of Satan's most powerful whisperings to us is that we are expendable. He may admit that we are part of God's plan for his own glory but only in the same way Napoleon used his soldiers to establish his empire. When the going got rough in the Russian winter campaign, Napoleon hightailed it back to Paris in his carriage, leaving Marshall Ney and the remnants of the once Grand Army to make it back the best way they could.

At one point in the long, arduous campaign of delivering to Judah the bad news of coming judgment and futile calls for repentance, Jeremiah explodes with thoughts that have apparently been building in him for a while with regard to God's use of him:

> O LORD, you deceived me, and I was deceived;
> you overpowered me and prevailed.
> I am ridiculed all day long;
> everyone mocks me.
> Whenever I speak, I cry out
> proclaiming violence and destruction.
> So the word of the LORD has brought me
> insult and reproach all day long.
> But if I say, "I will not mention him
> or speak any more in his name,"
> his word is in my heart like a fire,
> a fire shut up in my bones.
> I am weary of holding it in;
> indeed, I cannot. *(Jer. 20:7–9 NIV)*

Jeremiah complains that not only has God written a play that casts him in a devastating role, but that he has also placed a fire in his heart that will not let him leave the play even if he wants to. And there is this fire in all of us, felt as a desire for intimacy and a hunger for meaning, that we must literally kill if we want to escape the play.

To all of these charges, God is unrepentant, even as he was with Job. His response to these things is basically along the lines of, "I AM WHO I AM, I do what I do. I am good. What are you going to do with me?" Ironically, at the end of his interrogation by God, Job picks himself up and repents. He goes away with a sense of "Oh, now I get it. I was foolish to have lost perspective." God turns to Job's friends, who have been expounding the standard household-god formula to Job, "If you don't sin, things will go well [i.e., you can control your destiny]"—and tells them quite plainly they know nothing about him. He tells them he will have his *friend* Job pray for them.

Faced with the Message of the Arrows and a part too big that God the Cosmic Playwright insists is ours, with little clarity on the meaning and relationship of our scenes and character to the larger play, it appears more than sensible to opt out and go off-Broadway. Even though the smaller plays we write are often just pieces of stories, becoming our own directors and playwrights at least promises a level of control over the script. We hope we can eliminate most of the relational unknowns along with the villain and live in our smaller stories with some modicum of peace and quiet.

What is this drama God has dropped us into the middle of? What act of the play are we in and what do our scenes have to do with the larger story being told? Is our well-being even a consideration in the story line?

There is a stirring scene in Shakespeare's play *Henry V* that perhaps gives us a glimpse of what God is up to, both in the larger story he is telling as well as his purpose in our own lives, as he makes us a part of all this. Henry, the Christian king of England, has invaded France. After several battles, his army is worn down to six or seven thousand weary, hungry, and sick soldiers, dogged by rain and cold and thoughts of perhaps never seeing home again. The French army, fresh and thirty thousand strong, sends a courier to offer Henry the opportunity to avoid certain and ignominious defeat by surrendering. The hearts of Henry's army are divided as to the wisdom of battle. The king knows that hearts divided are hearts already defeated and he delivers a stirring speech on St. Crispin's day, capturing his soldiers' hearts up into something much larger:

> We would not die in that man's company
> That fears his fellowship to die with us.
> This day is call'd the feast of Crispian:
> He that outlives this day, and comes safe home,
> Will stand a tip-toe when this day is nam'd,
> And rouse him at the name of Crispian.
> He that shall live this day, and see old age,
> Will yearly on the vigil feast his neighbors,
> And say, tomorrow is Saint Crispian.
> Then will he strip his sleeve and show his scars,
> And say, These wounds I had on Crispin's day.
> Old men forget; yet all shall be forgot,
> But he'll remember with advantages
> What feats he did that day: then shall our names,
> Familiar in their mouths as household words . . .
> Be in their flowing cups freshly remember'd.
> This story shall the good man teach his son;
> And Crispin Crispian shall ne'er go by,
> From this day to the ending of the world,
> But we in it shall be remembered. (*Act IV, Scene III*)

Stirred to the core by the power of these words, Henry's men throw themselves into the battle with abandon and defeat the French in a total rout. King Henry calls his men to something that transcends safety and common sense. He calls them to battle and suffering that will bring them all a glorious remembering in the hearts of men. His words rouse something that burns within their hearts; something set there for the purposes of a king.

The battles God calls us to, the woundings and cripplings of soul and body we all receive, cannot simply be ascribed to our sin and foolishness, or even to the sin and foolishness of others. When Jesus and the disciples were on the road one day, they came upon a man who had been blind since birth. "Rabbi, who sinned, this man or his parents?" they asked him. "Neither this man nor his parents sinned," said Jesus, "but this happened so that the work of God might be displayed in his life." And with that, Jesus spat on the ground, made some mud to place on the man's eyes, and healed him (John 9:1–7).

Many of us who are reading these words have not yet received God's healing. The display of God's works through our wounds, losses, and sufferings is yet to be revealed. And so, we groan and we wonder.

A Strange Redemption

Yet there is something else God knows about us that causes him, like Henry V, to exhort us on into battle, or sometimes, even enter into battle against us. Most of us are convinced at some level in our heart that our main difficulty is the capriciousness of life. If we could ever overcome the damage of others' sins against us and just be loved better by those around us, and perhaps love a little better ourselves, we reason, we would be free to live well. For the most part, we don't see ourselves as people who are deeply committed to following the path to death. The way we want to live feels so right—so much like life—the only problem seems to be the way others treat us and God's indifference to our pleas for help. Some core part of all of our hearts is convinced that life would flow along smoothly if God were only a little more like those Mesopotamian household gods. The truth is, we all come into this world with a predilection to live life under our own terms and according to our own understanding.

We tell ourselves that we were not this way until the Arrows came and the Arrows certainly do deepen and justify our proclivity to reject God. Yet Jesus tells us through Paul in the third chapter of Romans that "There is no one righteous, not even one; there is no one who understands, no one who seeks God. All have turned away. . . ." (vv. 10–12). "There is a way that seems right to a man," says Proverbs 14:12, "but in the end it leads to death."

Genesis gives us an in-depth account of God using both crippling and blessing over the years of the patriarch Jacob's life to show him that his salvation and hope were in a more redemptive story than his own cleverness and manipulation could create; one that God was authoring. This is not the way we often see it, though. In our experience, it feels more as if God just allows bad things to happen to us out of indifference or malice. There is a fascinating illustration of a modern-day Jacob, a man trying to find redemption in a smaller story, along with God's fierce determination to disrupt and entice him back into the larger play, in the popular movie *Forrest Gump*. Forrest is a likable man of borderline intelligence who grew up struggling with leg braces due to polio and all of the cruel tauntings that those who are different often suffer. He is thrown into seemingly random scenes in American history much like the white feather that drifts with the wind throughout the movie. He finds himself in Vietnam under the leadership of Lieutenant Dan, a rough but capable man, whose family has produced a long line of military heroes killed in combat. Lieutenant Dan is confident that dying with honor on the field of battle is his redemption. When he is rescued by Forrest from a firefight, his wounds require both legs to be amputated above the knee. He and Forrest, also wounded, are consigned to the same hospital ward where one night the rageful Lieutenant Dan drags Forrest from his bed. He proceeds to choke and curse him for destroy-ing his life by saving him.

"I was supposed to die on the battlefield, Gump!" rages Lieutenant Dan. "I used to be Lieutenant Dan. Now look at me. I'm just a . . . cripple."

In response, Forrest observes with poignant simplicity, "You *still* Lieutenant Dan," leaving him to collapse in grief and despair.

Lieutenant Dan, like all of us to one extent or another, is convinced that who he is, is inextricably tied to a self-redemp-tive story that alone will bring him recognition, honor, self-respect—indeed, salvation. When that is taken from him, he is engulfed by shame, anger, and despair. He goes to New York City and enters into a purgatorial story of his own making, killing all desire for redemption. He lives off of his veteran's benefits in a haze of alcohol, drugs, and sex with prostitutes. When Forrest comes to see him, Lieutenant Dan relates to him that some of the other veterans at the V.A. Hospital have been telling him he should trust in Jesus. "Can you believe it, Gump?" he remarks bitterly. "They tell me that Jesus will *walk* with me on the streets of heaven." But Lieutenant Dan can see no larger story than the one that has been stolen from him. He continues to pursue the destruction of his soul with the same zeal with which he once pursued glory on the battlefield.

On New Year's Eve, God the Wild One disrupts him again. Lieutenant Dan has corralled Forrest into going back to his apartment with two prostitutes to ring in the New Year with hedonistic disdain. The prostitutes play the game, each of them pretending great attraction to Lieutenant Dan and Forrest. When Forrest is uncomfortable with his "date's" advances, he clumsily resists. With the play she is acting out ruined, she spits out, "What's wrong with this retard?" and begins to berate For-rest.

And here, Lieutenant Dan finds out he has not been able to

totally kill his heart. He is filled with rage at this treatment of Forrest and orders both of the women to leave, prompting a barrage of derogatory epithets from them as they exit. With his heart again exposed, he is brought to the realization that he still cares. And with this realization, he is plunged into something beyond despair. The scene ends with a close-up of the death mask of his face stretched over a heart "filled" with inconsolable emptiness.

But God is not through with Lieutenant Dan.

Forrest travels to the Gulf of Mexico to try his hand at captaining a shrimp boat, a plan inherited from his army buddy, Benjamin Blue, who was killed in the same firefight that took Lieutenant Dan's legs. Forrest is bringing his boat back to the dock one afternoon after another fruitless day casting for shrimp. On the dock, cigar clenched in his teeth, his wheelchair adorned with an "America—My Kind of Place" sticker is Lieutenant Dan, ready to try his hand as Forrest's first mate.

The strangeness of hope has once again provoked him to another try at self-redemption from his self-imposed hell. But once again, the Divine Disrupter thwarts his efforts. Lieutenant Dan confidently directs Forrest to where he is sure the shrimp are hiding, only to have their nets repeatedly regurgitate onto the deck a collage of old tires, license plates, leather shoes, and a clam or two. By this time, Lieutenant Dan is convinced that God is working against him somehow. He passively assents to Forrest's petitioning the Almighty for his favor as a member of the congregation of an otherwise all-black church. As Forrest sways disharmoniously with the other choir members and handles the praying, Lieutenant Dan sits in the rear of the church, violently downing whiskey and waiting for Forrest to appease this uncooperative household god that has attached himself to his life.

The ensuing days' shrimping brings no more harvest than before. With storm clouds gathering in the background, a completely frustrated and furious Lieutenant Dan rages, "Where . . . is this God of yours, Gump? I wish your Jesus were here right now!" And Forrest comments to his listeners with rare irony, "It's funny Lieutenant Dan said that 'cause right then, God showed up." God sends a storm that puts the boat in mortal danger of being destroyed. Unbowed, Lieutenant Dan lashes himself to the mast, filled with joy at this opportunity to finally have it out with his tormenter. He curses God and dares him to sink the boat. But God has another purpose for Lieutenant Dan. He allows the storm to rage until his anger is spent but does not kill him. Later, we learn that Forrest and Lieutenant Dan's boat has been the only survivor in the entire shrimping fleet. As they once again ply the shrimping grounds, now without competition, their hoists and nets strain to release one cascading swarm of shrimp after another onto the deck of their boat.

As Forrest recounts the story of their becoming millionaires to a credulous but kind lady at a bus stop, he asks if she would like to know what happened to Lieutenant Dan. As he describes the scene to her, we see Lieutenant Dan sitting on the rail of their shrimping boat. The anger and fear so long entrenched there are gone. In their place is a kind of reflective surprise, like that of a man who has been redeemed in a most unexpected way. "Forrest," says Lieutenant Dan in a quiet, almost shy voice, "I never thanked you for saving my life." And with that, he hoists his legless body over the side. As Forrest hurries to the rail with some concern over his intentions, we see Lieutenant Dan backstroking peacefully through the water with a gentle smile on his face. As the camera moves away, we leave him swimming up the reflected gold highway of the sunset on the water, even as Forrest remarks, "I think Lieutenant Dan finally made his peace with God."

And again, we wonder. What is it that Lieutenant Dan has discovered? What healing has he received even though his legs are unrestored?

So often, like Lieutenant Dan before his healing, we feel that God is not only unconcerned with our plight, but that he is actually working against us. And sometimes, we are right. The story of Lieutenant Dan is a poignant and revealing portrayal of God's fierce intentions to use both crippling and blessing to redeem us from our self-redemptive and purgatorial stories. Indeed, in the seventeenth chapter of Acts, Paul gives the Athenians the stunning news that every single thing in the lives of both nations and individuals is orchestrated with this sole objective that they might seek God (vv. 26–28). This revelation requires some reflection. We are used to thinking of the great movements of history, even the movements in our immediate relationships, as being impersonal, if not arbitrary. But with God, who notes the fall of every sparrow, the events of our lives are thoughtfully and thoroughly orchestrated to bring about our redemption. The days of our lives were ordered and numbered before there was one of them, says the psalmist (139:16). And yet, the ways of his redemption often leave us trembling and fearful.

Frederick Buechner, in his novel *Son of Laughter*, nonetheless invites us to relationship with this Wild Deity through the words of Jacob. Jacob's journey has come full circle, the smaller story he was attempting to live through deception and manipulation has been rewritten by the purposes of the Wild Romancer who is God. He is once again in need of redemption, his sons, Simeon and Levi, having just murdered Hamor and Shechem along with all their people for the rape of their sister, Dinah. Jacob is ready to let Simeon and Levi die in turn to cleanse (redeem) his family from the curse of the household gods Rachel (his wife) stole from her father's house, having brought them with her on this journey home.

Instead, the Fear (the only name by which Jacob knows God) commands him to sacrifice a red heifer and use the ashes to purify his sons and himself. Noting that they are cleansed on the outside, Jacob laments that the household gods still control them internally with their promises of earthbound blessing. He exhorts his family to give the Fear their hearts' trust even as he buries all the household gods under the oak tree where Abraham so long ago built his altar in memory of the three angels come to pledge him God's covenant. Here are Jacob's words to us through Buechner:

> The unclean blood no longer clung to our hands, but the small gods clung still to our hearts. They clung with silver fingers, with fingerless hands of wood and baked clay. Like rats, the gods gibbered in our hearts about the rich gifts they have for giving to us. The gods give rain. The swelling udder they give and the sweet fig, the plump ear of grain, the ooze of oil. They give sons. To Laban they gave cunning. They give their names as the Fear, at the Jabbok, refused me his when I asked it, and a god named is a god summoned. The Fear comes when he comes. It is the Fear who summons. The gods give in return for your gifts to them: the strangled dove, the burnt ox, the first fruit. There are those who give them their firstborn even, the child bound to the altar for knifing as Abraham bound Isaac till the Fear of his mercy bade the urine-soaked old man unbind him. The Fear gives to the empty-handed, the empty-hearted, as to me from the stone stair he gave promise and blessing, and gave them also to Isaac before me, to Abraham before Isaac, all of us wanderers only, herdsmen and planters moving with the seasons as gales of dry sand move with the wind. In return it is only the heart's trust that the Fear asks. Trust him though you cannot see him and he has no silver hand to hold. Trust him though you have no name to call him by, though out of the black night he leaps like a stranger to cripple and bless.

"Do you really care for me, God?"

Can we trust this stranger who leaps out upon us? Could it be that his glory and our well-being really are part of the same script?

If only we understood his heart more clearly. . . .

6

God the Ageless Romancer

*So long as we imagine it is we who have to look for
God, we must often lose heart. But it is the other way
about—He is looking for us.*

Simon Tugwell

CAN IT POSSIBLY get any more uncertain than this? We so long for life to be better than it is. We wish the beauty and love and adventure would stay and that someone strong and kind would show us how to make the Arrows go away. We hope that God will be our hero. Of all the people in the universe, he could stop the Arrows and arrange for just a little more blessing in our lives. He can spin the earth, change the weather, topple governments, obliterate armies, and resurrect the dead. Is it too much to ask that he intervene in our story? But he often seems aloof, almost indifferent to our plight, so entirely out of our control. Would it be any worse if there were no God? If he didn't exist, at least we wouldn't get our hopes up. We could settle once and for all that we really are alone in the universe and get on with surviving as best we may.

This is, in fact, how many professing Christians end up living: as practical agnostics. *Perhaps God will come through, perhaps he won't, so I'll be hanged if I'll live as though he had to come through. I'll hedge my bets and if he does show up, so much the better*. The simple word for this is *godlessness*. Like a lover who's been wronged, we guard our heart against future disappointment.

In my sophomore year in high school I (John) fell in love with a beautiful junior named Joy. Our first dates were romantic, exciting, and full of adventure. I gave her my heart. One day several months into the relationship, I was trying in vain to thumb a ride home when I saw her car approaching. My heart leaped with anticipation, but Joy whizzed past in her convertible with another guy at the wheel. Adding insult to injury, she waved gaily as they rushed by. I felt the fool, which is what we often do when we feel betrayed. And I never gave her my heart again.

Everyone has been betrayed by someone, some more profoundly than others. Betrayal is a violation that strikes at the core of our being; to make ourselves vulnerable and entrust our well-being to another, only to be harmed by those on whom our hopes were set, is among the worst pain of human experience.

Sometimes the way God treats us feels like betrayal. We find ourselves in a dangerous world, unable to arrange for the water our thirsty souls so desperately need. Our rope won't take the bucket to the bottom of the well. We know God has the ability to draw water for us, but oftentimes he won't. We feel wronged. After all, doesn't Scripture say that if we have the power to do someone good, we should do it (Prov. 3:27)? So why doesn't God?

As I spoke with a friend about her painful life, how reckless and unpredictable God seems, she turned and with pleading eyes asked the question we are all asking somewhere deep within: "How can I trust a lover who is so wild?" Indeed, how do we not only trust him, but love him in return? There's only one possible answer: You could love him if you *knew* his heart was good. In the movie *The Last of the Mohicans*, brave Nathaniel has captured the heart of the beautiful Cora. With tremendous courage and cunning, he rescues her from an ambush set by the black-hearted Magua, leader of a warring tribe. Nathaniel leads Cora, her sister, and a few other survivors to a hidden cave behind a waterfall. Just when it appears they will escape and live happily ever after, Magua and his savages discover their hideout. Once captured, the women may be spared but the men will surely be executed. With no powder for their rifles, Nathaniel's only chance is to leap from the falls; by saving himself, he will live to rescue Cora another day. One of the other men calls him a coward, accusing him of foul and selfish motives. How is Cora feeling? What looks like abandonment may not be. Her only hope in the face of such wildness lies in the goodness of Nathaniel's heart. At this point, it's all she has to go on. It's all we often have to go on too.

Does God have a good heart? In the last chapter Brent spoke of God as the Author of the story, which is how most people see him if they see him at all. And, as Hamlet said, there's the rub. When we think of God as Author, the Grand Chess Player, the Mind Behind It All, we doubt his heart. As Melville said, "The reason the mass of men fear God and at bottom dislike him is because they rather distrust his heart, and fancy him all brain, like a watch." Do you relate to the author when reading a novel or watching a film? Caught up in the action, do you even think about the author? We identify with the characters in the story precisely because they are *in* the story. They face life as we do, on the ground, and their struggles win our sympathy because they are our struggles also. We love the hero because he is one of us, and yet somehow rises above the fray to be better and wiser and more loving as we hope one day we might prove to be.

The Author lies behind, beyond. His omniscience and omnipotence may be what create the drama, but they are also what separate us from him. Power and knowledge don't qualify for heart. Indeed, the worst sort of villain is the kind who executes his plans with cold and calculated precision. He is detached; he has no heart. If we picture God as the mastermind behind the story—calling the shots while we, like Job, endure the calamities—we can't help but feel at times what C. S. Lewis was bold enough to put words to: "We're the rats in the cosmic laboratory." Sure, he may have our good in mind, but that still makes him the "vivisectionist"—the experimenter.

We root for the hero and heroine, even come to love them, because they are living *in* the drama. They feel the heartache, they suffer loss and summon courage and shed their own blood in their struggles against evil. What if? Just what if we saw God not as Author, the cosmic mastermind behind all human experience, but as the central character *in* the larger story? What could we learn about his heart?

I worked as an actor in Los Angeles for a number of years. In the theater, when you're preparing to act a part, you want to "get into the skin" of your character, to discover his motives. What makes him tick? Why does he do the things he does? Every human action has a motive behind it. Nathaniel jumps from the waterfall, leaving Cora behind. Why? He lives to fight another day. Why does he live to fight again? Beneath simple motives lie deeper purposes. What is it that drives this hero throughout the course of his life? His love for Cora. Here might be the key to our dilemma: The Scriptures are written from the perspective that God is the hero of the story. Let's revisit the drama with the view of God as lead actor. What is his motive? How does life affect him?

The Larger Story

Act I: His Eternal Heart

All good fairy tales begin with "Once upon a time," and so it is with the truest fairy tale of all. *In the beginning*, which is to say, once upon a time, is used twice in the Scriptures. There is the first verse of Genesis, of course, but we cannot start there because when the curtain goes up on Genesis chapter 1, it is actually going up on later events, the human story. We're after God's story, the drama from his perspective, so we would do better to start with the opening lines from the gospel of John, which take us back even farther to the once upon a time before time: "In the beginning was the Word, and the Word was with God, and the Word was God. He was with God in the beginning."

The story that is the Sacred Romance begins not with God alone, the Author at his desk, but God in relationship, intimacy beyond our wildest imagination, heroic intimacy. The Trinity is at the center of the universe; perfect relationship is the heart of all reality. Think of your best moments of love or friendship or creative partnership, the best times with family or friends around the dinner table, your richest conversations, the acts of simple kindness that sometimes seem like the only things that make life worth living. Like the shimmer of sunlight on a lake, these are reflections of the love that flows among the Trinity. We long for intimacy because we are made in the image of perfect intimacy. Still, what we don't have and may never have known is often a more powerful reminder of what *ought* to be.

Our story begins with the hero in love. As Buechner reminds us, "God does not need the Creation in order to have something to love because within himself love happens."

And yet, what kind of love? There are selfish forms of love, relationships that create closed systems, impenetrable to outsiders. Real love creates a generous openness. Have you ever been so caught up in something that you just had to share it? When you are walking alone in the woods, something takes your breath away—a sunset, a waterfall, the simple song of a bird—and you think, *If only my beloved were here.* The best things in life were meant to be shared. That is why married lovers want to increase their joy by having children. And so it is with God.

"Father," Jesus says, "I want those you gave me to be with me, right where I am. I want them to be one heart and mind with us" (John 17). Overflowing with the generosity that comes from the abundance of real love, he creates us to share in the joy of this heroic intimacy. One early mystic says we were created out of the laughter of the Trinity.

Sunday afternoons were my favorite days during summers on my grandfather's ranch. That's when we'd go "visiting," calling on second cousins, great aunts, adopted friends, and other relatives at their farms. I remember having a warm, settled feeling as I sat on the porch and listened to the older folks remembering the shared stories of their lives. My sense of security grew from an awareness that all this had been going on before me, that though I was part of it, I wasn't responsible for it. It didn't depend on me. You've heard that children care more that their parents love each other than that they love them and this is the reason why. It's the assurance that there is something grand and good going on that doesn't rest on your shoulders, something that doesn't even culminate in you, but rather invites you up into it.

And so it is with God's story. Before any of our complex and sometimes overwhelming smaller stories began, there was something wonderful already going on: Once upon a time, were Father, Son, and Holy Spirit—the kind of home we've been looking for all our life. From the beginning, we know that God is a lover at heart, from all eternity.

Act II: His Heart Betrayed

There was another scene before ours. In Act II, there came angels. We're not given a great deal of insight into the life of angels, but we do know that God opened his heart and home to a heavenly host before us. And for the most part, they seem thrilled to be a part of things. Scripture never shows us a bored angel. Quite the contrary. We also know there was a cosmic divorce, a betrayal in the heart of the universe. Satan, then named Lucifer, turned on his Maker. He rose up against his sovereign Lord, and with him legions upon legions of angels. There was war in heaven. In *Paradise Lost*, John Milton wrestled with the heights of poetic imagery to capture the drama of this scene:

> How shall I relate
> To human sense th' invisible exploits
> Of warring spirits? how, without remorse,
> The ruin of so many, glorious once
> And perfect while they stood.

He tells the story of a majestic heavenly banquet thrown by the Father in honor of the Son. The first member of the Trinity, generous of heart, freely gives center stage to the second member of the Trinity. Satan is unable to endure the glory bestowed on Jesus. Satan is jealous for himself and this kind always ends in murder. Believing that he should have center stage, Satan draws a multitude of angels into battle against the throne of God:

> Arms on armor clashing brayed
> Horrible discord; dire was the noise
> Of conflict; overhead the dismal hiss
> Of fiery darts in flaming volleys flew
> So under fiery cope together rushed
> Both battles main with ruinous assault
> And inextinguishable rage. All heaven
> Resounded; and, had earth been then, all earth
> Had to her centre shook.
> Deeds of eternal fame were done,
> But infinite; for wide was spread
> That war, and various; sometimes on firm ground
> A standing fight; then, soaring on main wing
> Tormented all the air; and all air seemed then
> Conflicting fire. Long time in even scale
> The battle hung, till Satan
> No equal, ranging through the dire attack

Of fighting seraphim confused, at length
Saw where the sword of Michael smote, and felled
Squadrons at once; with huge two-handed sway.

At the approach of Satan, the great archangel Michael "from his warlike toil surceased," turning to confront the betrayer of their heaven:

Author of evil, unknown till thy revolt . . .
How hast thou disturbed
Heaven's blessed peace, and unto Nature brought
Misery, uncreated till the crime
Of thy rebellion. How hast thou instilled
Thy malice into thousands, once upright
And faithful, now proved false . . .
Heaven casts thee out.

Satan mounted his rebellion through the power of one idea: God doesn't have a good heart. Though it seems almost incomprehensible, he deceived a multitude of the heavenly host by sowing the seed of doubt in their minds that God was somehow holding out on them. After the insurrection is squelched, that question lingers in the universe like smoke from a forest fire. Sure, God won, but it took force to do it. Power isn't the same thing as goodness. As the lead actor in the story, God *seems* generous and self-giving, but perhaps he's just big. Maybe his motive is simply to be in charge. At the end of Act II, our hero's heart has been called into question.

Act III: His Heart on Trial

When the curtain goes up on the story of humanity, we see God in a flurry of breathtaking dramatic actions that we rather blandly call "creation." Remember, we're looking for the motives of his heart. Why is he doing all this? We know he already had the perfect relationship and that he has suffered a betrayal in the heart of heaven simply for the offense of sharing it. Now we see him preparing to woo our hearts with a world that is beautiful and funny and full of adventure. Don't rush ahead to the Fall. Stay here a moment and feel God's happiness with it all. Yosemite and Yellowstone and Maui and the Alps; mangoes and blackberries and cabernet grapes; horses and hummingbirds and rainbow trout. "The morning stars sang together and all the angels shouted for joy" (Job 38:7 NIV).

God creates man and woman and sets them in Paradise. How long had he been planning this? Are we merely the replacement for the angels he lost, the first date he can find on the rebound? The first chapter of Ephesians gives a look into God's motives here:

> Long before he laid down earth's foundations, he had us in mind, had settled on us as the focus of his love, to be made whole and holy by his love. Long, long ago he decided to adopt us into his family through Jesus Christ. (What pleasure he took in planning this!) He wanted us to enter into the celebration of his lavish gift-giving by the hand of his beloved Son. . . . Long before we first heard of Christ and got our hopes up, he had his eye on us, had designs on us for glorious living. (*The Message*)

God begins our courtship with a surprise. Taking the blindfold off, he turns us around and reveals his handmade wedding present. "Here," he says. "It's yours. Enjoy yourselves. Do you like it? Take it for a spin." A lavish gift indeed. What's he up to? Flowers, chocolates, exotic vacations, dinners at the finest restaurants—any person would feel pursued. But what are his intentions? Surprisingly, we see in the first glimpse of God's wildness the goodness of his heart—he gives us our freedom. In order for a true romance to occur, we had to be free to reject him. In *Disappointment with God*, Philip Yancey reminds us that the powers of the Author aren't sufficient to win our hearts.

> Power can do everything but the most important thing: it cannot control love. . . . In a concentration camp, the guards possess almost unlimited power. By applying force, they can make you renounce your God, curse your family, work without pay, eat

human excrement, kill and then bury your closest friend or even your own mother. All this is within their power. Only one thing is not: they cannot force you to love them. This fact may help explain why God sometimes seems shy to use his power. He created us to love him, but his most impressive displays of miracle—the kind we may secretly long for—do nothing to foster that love. As Douglas John Hall has put it, "God's problem is not that God is not able to do certain things. God's problem is that God loves. Love complicates the life of God as it complicates every life."

The wildness of giving us freedom is even more staggering when we remember that God has already paid dearly for giving freedom to the angels. But because of his grand heart he goes ahead and takes the risk, an enormous, colossal risk. The reason he didn't make puppets is because he wanted lovers. Remember, he's inviting us up into a romance. Freedom is part of the explanation for the problem of evil. God is the author of some storms directly; but he is the author of the possibility of all storms in giving us freedom. And *we* opened Pandora's box.

Can you imagine if on your honeymoon one of you sneaked off for a rendezvous with a perfect stranger? Adam and Eve kicked off the honeymoon by sleeping with the enemy. Then comes one of the most poignant verses in all Scripture. "What is this you have done?" (Gen. 3:13). You can almost hear the shock, the pain of betrayal in God's voice. The fall of Adam and Eve mustn't be pictured as a crime like theft, but as a betrayal of love. In love God creates us for love and we give him the back of our hand. Why? Satan gets us to side with him by sowing the seed of doubt in our first parents' minds: "God's heart really isn't good. He's holding out on you. You've got to take things into your own hands." And Paradise was lost.

Yet there was something about the heart of God that the angels and our first parents had not yet seen. Here, at the lowest point in our relationship, God announces his intention never to abandon us but to seek us out and win us back. "I will come for you." *Grace* introduces a new element of God's heart. Up till this point we knew he was rich, famous, influential, even generous. Behind all that can still can hide a heart that is less than good. Grace removes all doubt.

And then the long story of God's pursuit of humanity begins. Satan wanted center stage: He wanted to be the main character, he wanted to be the point. His plan now is to ruin the Sacred Romance, to get us all caught up in our own little socio-dramas by telling us that we are the point. You can see how humanity goes along with this. Cain murders Abel; Lamech threatens to murder everyone else. Humanity grows worse and worse until God says in pain, "I'm sorry I ever made them." But he doesn't give up. First with Noah, then Abraham, then Israel, we see God pursuing a people whose hearts will be for him, with whom he can share the joy of the larger story. But their faithfulness lasts about as long as the morning dew.

How is God feeling by this point? As a person *in the story*, what is his heart experience? When we reach the prophets, we get a glimpse at what it feels like to be God. Reading the prophets, says Yancey, is like hearing a lovers' quarrel through the apartment wall. Eavesdrop on the argument and catch a glimpse of his heart:

> I long to be gracious to you. You are precious and honored in my sight, because I love you. But you—come here, you . . . you . . . offspring of adulterers. You have made your bed on a high and lofty hill, forsaking me, you uncovered your bed, you climbed into it and opened it wide. You have been false to me. Yet . . . I will take delight in you, as a bridegroom rejoices over his bride, so will I rejoice over you. *(From Isaiah)*

> I remember the devotion of your youth, how as a bride you loved me. . . . What fault did you find in me that you strayed so far from me? You are a swift she-camel running here and there, sniffing the wind in her craving—in her heat who can restrain her? Should I not punish them for this? Should I not avenge myself? I have loved you with an everlasting love; I have drawn you with lovingkindness. What have I done to make you hate me so much? *(From Jeremiah)*

I will answer you according to your idols [your false lovers] in order to recapture your heart. *(From Ezekiel)*

Return to me and I will return to you. Yet you have said harsh things about me. You have said, "There's no pay-off in this relationship. It's not worth loving God." *(From Malachi)*

After this, four hundred years of silence. God doesn't call and when we do he won't answer the phone. You can almost imagine him nursing his wounds, wondering where it all went wrong. And then an idea comes to him. Here is Kierkegaard's version of the story:

Suppose there was a king who loved a humble maiden. The king was like no other king. Every statesman trembled before his power. No one dared breathe a word against him, for he had the strength to crush all opponents. And yet this mighty king was melted by love for a humble maiden. How could he declare his love for her? In an odd sort of way, his kingliness tied his hands. If he brought her to the palace and crowned her head with jewels and clothed her body in royal robes, she would surely not resist—no one dared resist him. But would she love him?

She would say she loved him, of course, but would she truly? Or would she live with him in fear, nursing a private grief for the life she had left behind? Would she be happy at his side? How could he know? If he rode to her forest cottage in his royal carriage, with an armed escort waving bright banners, that too would overwhelm her. He did not want a cringing subject. He wanted a lover, an equal. He wanted her to forget that he was a king and she a humble maiden and to let shared love cross the gulf between them. For it is only in love that the unequal can be made equal. (as quoted in *Disappointment with God*)

The king clothes himself as a beggar and renounces his throne in order to win her hand. The Incarnation, the life and the death of Jesus, answers once and for all the question, "What is God's heart toward me?" This is why Paul says in Romans 5, "Look here, at the Cross. Here is the demonstration of God's heart. At the point of our deepest betrayal, when we had run our farthest from him and gotten so lost in the woods we could never find our way home, God came and died to rescue us." We don't have to wait for the Incarnation to see God as a character in the story and learn something of his motives. But after the Incarnation there can be no doubt.

There is so much more to say. Jesus left to prepare our place in heaven; the Spirit has come to empower us to continue the invasion of the kingdom, which is primarily about freeing the hearts of others to live in the love of God. There is so much in our own heart that remains to be released. Our enemy has not given up yet and his target is also our heart. And what of Act IV, the coming adventures of heaven? All that is for the chapters ahead. Let's stop here and try to bring this into focus.

What is God like? Is his heart good? We know he is the initiator from first to last. As Simon Tugwell reminds, God is the one pursuing us:

> So long as we imagine that it is we who have to look for God, we must often lose heart. But it is the other way about; He is looking for us. And so we can afford to recognize that very often we are not looking for God; far from it, we are in full flight from him, in high rebellion against him. And He knows that and has taken it into account. He has followed us into our own darkness; there where we thought finally to escape him, we run straight into his arms. So we do not have to erect a false piety for ourselves, to give us the hope of salvation. Our hope is in his determination to save us, and he will not give in. (*Prayer*)

When we feel that life is finally up to us it becomes suffocating. When we are the main character, the world is so small there's barely room to move. It frees our souls to have something going on before us that involves us, had us in mind, yet doesn't depend on us or culminate in us, but invites us up into something larger. And what about the Romance and the Arrows? It wasn't supposed to be like this. Once upon a time we lived in a garden; we lived in the place for which we were made. There were no Arrows, only beauty. Our relationships weren't tainted with fear, guardedness, manipulation, quid pro quo. Our work was rewarding; we received more than we gave. There is beauty, and we so long for it to last; we were made for the Garden. But now there is affliction also, and that is because we live East of Eden. The Arrows seem like the truest part of life, but they are not. The heart of the universe is still perfect love.

Finally, if we try to relate to God primarily as Author, we will go mad or despair—pretty much the same thing. I just can't imagine the characters of a novel affecting the author that much. He may like them, hate them, be intrigued with mapping out their development, but they don't impact him the way the people in his real life do. He doesn't live with them as flesh-and-blood lovers. But when we see God as the Hero of the story and consider what he wants for us, we know one thing for certain: We affect him. We impact the members of the Trinity as truly as they do each other.

It is only when we see God as the Hero of the larger story that we come to know his heart is good.

Where does that leave us? What is our role in the cosmic drama? Are we bit players, added for dramatic tension, color, comic relief? Neil Anderson has written that while "The most important belief we possess is true knowledge of who God is. . . . The second most important belief is who we are as children of God." In the next chapter, we'll explore our role in the story.

7

The Beloved

I am my beloved's and his desire is for me.
Song of Songs

HELEN OF TROY must have really been something. Two kingdoms went to war over her; thousands of men gave up their lives so that one might have her. Hers was "the face that launched a thousand ships." Helen was the wife of Menelaus, King of Greece, in the ninth Century, B.C. Their home was a peaceful mediterranean kingdom until the arrival of Paris, Prince of Troy. Paris fell in love with Helen and, depending on the version of the story you've heard, she with him. Under the cover of night, Paris stole away with Helen and took her back to Troy. It was the beginning of the Trojan War. Menelaus and his brother Agamemnon amassed a mighty Greek army and set off in one thousand ships to lay siege on Troy, all to win Helen back.

Few have ever felt so pursued. Sometimes we wonder if we've even been *noticed*. Father was too busy to come to our games, or perhaps he jumped ship altogether. Mother was lost in a never-ending pile of laundry or, more recently, in her own career. We come into the world longing to be special to someone and from the start we are disappointed. It is a rare soul indeed who has been sought after for who she is—not because of what she can do, or what others can gain from her, but simply for herself. Can you recall a time when a significant someone in your life sat you down with the sole purpose of wanting to know your heart more deeply, fully expecting to enjoy what he found there? More people have climbed Mt. Everest than have experienced real pursuit, and so what are we left to conclude? There is nothing in our hearts worth knowing. Whoever and whatever this mystery called *I* must be, it cannot be much.

"In fact," we continue, "if I am not pursued, it must be because there is something wrong with me, something dark and twisted inside.' We long to be known and we fear it like nothing else. Most people live with a subtle dread that one day they will be discovered for who they really are and the world will be appalled.

The wife of a close friend was seeing a counselor to sort through some of her own Arrows. After several private sessions she asked her husband, who is a pastor, to come along. As the day of the event drew near, his quiet dread swelled to full-fledged panic. The night before their joint session the pastor had a dream in which the counselor uncovered his true self, then leaped up from her chair and ran out of the office and down the street, screaming, "My God—he's a pastor!"

We come into the world with a longing to be known and a deep-seated fear that we aren't what we should be. We are set up for a crisis of identity. And then, says Frederick Buechner, the world goes to work:

> Starting with the rather too pretty young woman and the charming but rather unstable young man, who together know no more about being parents than they do the far side of the moon, the world sets in to making us what the world would like us to be, and because we have to survive after all, we try to make ourselves into something that we hope the world will like better than it apparently did the selves we originally were. That is the story of all our lives, needless to say, and in the process of living out that story, the original, shimmering self gets buried so deep that most of us hardly

end up living out of it at all. Instead, we live out all the other selves which we are constantly putting on and taking off like coats and hats against the world's weather. (*Telling Secrets*)

Think about the part you find yourself playing, the self you put on like a costume. Who cast you in this role? Most of us are living out a script that someone else has written for us. We've not been invited to live from our heart, to be who we truly are, so we put on these false selves hoping to offer something more acceptable to the world, something functional. We learn our roles starting very young and we learn them well: Joey's the smart kid and his role is to be smart. He'll help you with your homework and grow up to be a computer programmer. Karen is the victim of abuse, struggling against overwhelming odds. She's been given the role of being used. The pretty girls get to be the cheerleaders, the others are sent to the library. The athletic boys are picked for the team, the others are simply picked on. Either we're chosen for the wrong reasons or not chosen at all.

What does any of this have to do with our heart? God created each of us with a unique identity, a role in the larger story, but early on we've been handed a revision by the other players in our life.

"Well, then," the realist might say, "don't let people affect you so much. Be your own person. Believe in yourself." Those who've tried realize that this advice just isn't enough for the healing of your soul and the recovery of your true identity. The deepest Arrows we've known are lodged in the places of our self-identity and no amount of positive thinking or self-affirmation will remove them. There are words that have been spoken, repeated a thousand times, and they play like a recording in our inner thoughts: "stupid," "incompetent," "ugly," "unlovable"—the list goes on and on.

There are images, too, scenes from our lives that speak more deeply even than words. In the second grade I (John) wet my pants in school one day. We were watching a film and I was too embarrassed to interrupt class to ask permission to leave. I tried to hold it as long as I could, but the film was longer. A puddle formed beneath my desk. Mortified, fearing the Arrows of playground taunts, I tried a cover-up and claimed my thermos had broken. The teacher sent me to the office for the nurse to call my parents to bring a pair of dry pants. No one was home. In a moment of real need, when I so desperately wanted someone to be there for me, I was alone. Something clicked within me; an image settled in that place, which captured the message that I had better never blow it again because there wouldn't be anyone to pick me up when I fell. So much of my perfectionism as an adult is energized by that image: Never be in a place of need.

Deep within the Arrows stay, poisoning our self-perceptions, until someone comes along with the power to take them away, free us from all the false selves we use to weather the world's weather, and restore to us our true identity. Without such a person, we are lost in the smaller stories, anxiously looking about, hoping for a clue as to who we really are. We read the opinions that others hold of us like a report card on how we're doing. Parents of teenagers warn them against the riptides of peer pressure, but who of us does not to some degree succumb? Fashion is an enduring testimony to the fact that we live quite consciously before the eyes of others. And for such we were made. We were created to live in community, not a hall of mirrors. Philosopher and author Gabriel Marcel uses an experience from daily life to reveal the way in which we establish a sense of self:

> Take, for instance, the child who brings his mother flowers he has just been gathering in the meadow. "Look," he cries, "I picked these." Mark the triumph in his voice and above all the gesture . . . which accompanies his announcement. The child points himself out for admiration and gratitude: "It was I, I who am with you

here, who picked these lovely flowers, don't go thinking it was Nanny or my sister; it was I and *no one else*." (*Homo Viator*)

Luke, my two-year-old, found me one Saturday morning puttering in the garage. "'Mere," he said, in a tone and with an expression that allowed no room for debate. He turned and I followed him into the family room. "Sit." I sat down, my curiosity fully engaged. "Watch!" He climbed onto his WonderColt and began to ride with great passion, a cowboy on some dangerous mission in which he would be the hero. Something outside the window drew my attention and I looked away, a very big mistake. "Watch *me*!" he demanded. Luke wanted what we all want—to play our part, to live our lives before the eyes of another. Actually, he wanted more than simple recognition. He wanted praise, admiration, applause—in short, he wanted glory.

How could it be otherwise? We are created in the image of God, or more precisely, *as a reflection of the Trinity*. If we really understood this wonderful truth deep in our hearts, it would probably bring revival in our day. Consider just two essential realities that flow from this fact. First, as we observed in the previous chapter, the Trinity is a community and so to be made in its image means we are relational at our core. "Our creation is by love, in love and for love," writes psychologist Gerald May. But there is more. The Trinity is a society whose members draw their identities from the others. The Father wouldn't be a father if it weren't for his relationship to the Son and to us. He might be "God," "Jehovah," even "Almighty," but never "Abba, Father." Of course the Son would never have been one if not for the presence of the Father. But because of his relationship to the other members of the Trinity, Jesus has been and forever will be the Son of God. And just like my son, Luke, and all children, what he craves most, his greatest prize, is the applause of the Father. "Father, I want those you have given me to be with me where I am, and to see my glory, the glory you have given me because you loved me before the creation of the world" (John 17:24).

Identity is not something that falls on us out of the sky. For better or for worse, identity is *bestowed*. We are who we are in relation to others. But far more important, we draw our identity from our impact on those others—*if* and *how* we affect them. We long to know that we make a difference in the lives of others, to know that we matter, that our presence cannot be replaced by a pet, a possession, or even another person. The awful burden of the false self is that it must be constantly maintained. What happened to Helen of Troy when her hips began to bulge and her face sag? Did she leap from bed each morning to the mirror, fearing that the effects of the passing years would make her less and less lovable? Our dilemma is hers: We think we have to keep doing something in order to be desirable. Once we find something that will bring us some attention, we have to keep it going or risk the loss of the attention.

And so we live with the fear of not being chosen and the burden of maintaining whatever it is about us that might get us noticed and the commitment never to be seen for who we really are. We develop a *functional* self-image, even if it is a negative one. The little boy paints his red wagon a speckled gray with whatever Father left in the can after putting a new coat on the backyard fence. "Look what I did!" he says, hoping for affirmation of the wonderful impact his presence has on the world. The angry father shames him: "What do you think you're doing? You've ruined it." The boy forms an identity: *My impact is awful; I foul good things up. I am a fouler.* And he forms a commitment never to be in a place where he can foul things up again. Years later, his colleagues wonder why he turned down an attractive promotion. The answer lies in his identity, an identity he received from the impact he had on the most important person in his world and his fear of ever being in such a place again.

A little girl draws her father's attention only when he wants to use her for his sexual perversions. *I am sexually dangerous,* she concludes. *I am a dirty little girl.* She lives with the tremendous rift in her soul caused by the ambivalence of abuse. On the one hand, the attention felt good. She was made for intimacy. Yet the only intimacy she's ever known was violating. Years later, she becomes the efficient, competent head of women's ministry at church. She's known as a tireless worker and a real servant— but there isn't a man who is drawn to her in any intimate way. She carefully avoids all compliments and keeps any potential relationships at a purely "ministry" level. She can't take the risk of being attractive sexually. Long ago she learned that intimacy leads to violation, that the sensual parts of her are dirty and so she hides them well beneath a false self of Christian service.

For the past thirty years, I have found my identity and earned my living by being up front, first as an actor, then as a public speaker. That script began in the second grade when I fell in love with my teacher, Mrs. McGrath. She was young and pretty and she *noticed* me, noticed that I could speak well in front of the class and so she picked me to narrate the school play. Something deep within me was stirred, touched. I gave a brilliant reading and all the mothers cried. *Ahha!* my little foolish heart concluded, *this is my part—this is how I will find glory!* And for thirty years I have lived out that part, rarely offering the truest parts of me and so rarely feeling alive and connected with anyone. You cannot have intimacy out of a false self.

There is no escaping your identity. You will not live beyond how you see yourself; not for long. If "Failure" is the part you're playing, you will fail. The Performers will perform, the Seductive will seduce, the Victims will be victimized, the Nobodies will fade away, and the Somebodies will do whatever it is that made them feel like somebody, donning coat and hat according to the weather. Again, what we are doing in this costume ball of life is looking to avoid exposure while at the same time trying to offer something that will bring us glory.

As a young girl my friend Susan was lost in a busy household full of brothers and sisters and seldom seen by distracted parents. One day she made a necklace from pumpkin seeds, a simple craft to pass the time. For some odd reason the necklace captured her father's attention. "Hey, everybody, look at this, will ya? Look at what Susan made!" Years later, as she reflected back on what seemed a trivial moment, she remembered the power she seemed to suddenly possess: "People came alive at something I did!" Does it come as a surprise to learn that she is now makes her living as a creative designer?

It's not that her father's attention and affirmation were wrong; it's just that they were the exception, not the rule. When we live with so little love, we will grasp onto what we do receive in a way that becomes defining. Those moments may not reveal our true identity and calling, but they're all we've got.

We will draw our identity from outside ourselves; the question is, from whom? In the end, it will be from those moments and those people on whom we've had the biggest impact. Think again about Helen of Troy. Why "of Troy"? Wasn't she really Helen of Greece, Menelaus's wife? In calling her "Helen of Troy" we are forever reminded of the impact she had on the mediterranean world of the tenth century B.C. She is not Helen the Beauty or Helen Like No Other Woman. Those are qualities she could possess alone. No, she is Helen of Troy, which really means something like Helen the Fought Over, Helen the Captive and Rescued, Helen the Pursued. Her identity is inseparable from her relationships; it has been bestowed upon her. Maybe she enjoyed the attention, maybe not. Perhaps in the end she merely played the part of the rare art object, stolen from Menelaus's palace to be put on display in Troy. I hope that someone in all those thousands was pursuing her for her heart. But whatever else she felt, as the center of an international crisis Helen must have known beyond a shadow of a doubt that *she mattered.*

The gospel says that we, who are God's beloved, created a cosmic crisis. It says we, too, were stolen from our True Love and that he launched the greatest campaign in the history of the world to get us back. God created us for intimacy with him. When we turned our back on him he promised to come for us. He sent personal messengers; he used beauty and affliction to recapture our hearts. After all else failed, he conceived the most daring of plans. Under the cover of night he stole into the enemy's camp *incognito*, the Ancient of Days disguised as a newborn. The Incarnation, as Phil Yancey reminds us, was a daring raid into enemy territory. The whole world lay under the power of the evil one and we were held in the dungeons of darkness. God risked it all to rescue us. Why? What is it that he sees in us that causes him to act the jealous lover, to lay siege both on the kingdom of darkness and on our own idolatries as if on Troy—not to annihilate, but to win us once again for himself? This fierce intention, this reckless ambition that shoves all conventions aside, willing literally to move heaven and earth— what does he want from us?

We've been offered many explanations. From one religious camp we're told that what God wants is obedience, or sacrifice, or adherence to the right doctrines, or morality. Those are the answers offered by conservative churches. The more therapeutic churches suggest that no, God is after our contentment, or happiness, or self-actualization, or something else along those lines. He is concerned about all these things, of course, but they are not his primary concern. What he is after is *us*—our laughter, our tears, our dreams, our fears, our heart of hearts. Remember his lament in Isaiah, that though his people were performing all their duties, "their *hearts* are far from me" (29:13 *italics added*). How few of us truly believe this. We've never been wanted for our heart, our truest self, not really, not for long. The thought that God wants our heart seems too good to be true.

Craig, my closest friend, whom I've known for almost

twenty years, is a man I deeply respect. His life is full with many of the qualities I so want to reflect: insight, love, courage, a wonderful sense of odd humor, a man of sad gravity as the occasion requires. We live in separate states and our visits are rare and precious. As we were walking in the fields near my home one day, he was speaking about the future in a way that assumed we would be friends for life. Something stirred within me, and I heard my heart wonder, *Why would he want to be friends with me? What could he possibly see in me?* I was surprised by the honesty of my heart in response to being pursued, enjoyed. We just don't think there is anything desirable in us. And yet, we want to be desired. We were made for glory, for the attention that the Trinity gives to each other, and we can't live without it.

Things Are Not What They Seem

The reason we enjoy fairy tales—more than enjoy them—the reason we *identify with them* in some deep part of us is because they rest on two great truths: The hero really has a heart of gold and the beloved really possesses hidden beauty. In the last chapter, I hope you got a glimpse of God's good heart. But what about the second great truth—could we possess hidden greatness? It seems too good to be true.

Remember, the theme of veiled identity runs through all great stories. As Buechner reminds us, "Not only does evil come disguised in the world of the fairy tale but often good does too." The heroines and heroes capture our heart because we see long before they ever do their hidden beauty, courage, greatness. Cinderella, Sleeping Beauty, Snow White—they're not simple wenches after all. The beast and the frog—they're actually princes. Aladdin is "the diamond in the rough." If the narrative of the Scriptures teaches us anything, from the serpent in the Garden to the carpenter from Nazareth, it teaches us that things are rarely what they seem, that we shouldn't be fooled by appearances.

Your evaluation of your soul, which is drawn from a world filled with people still terribly confused about the nature of *their* souls, is probably wrong. As C. S. Lewis wrote in *The Weight of Glory,*

> It is a serious thing to live in a society of possible gods and goddesses, to remember that the dullest and most uninteresting person you talk to may one day be a creature which, if you saw it now, you would be strongly tempted to worship, or else a horror and a corruption such as you now meet, if at all, only in a nightmare. . . . There are no *ordinary* people. You have never talked to a mere mortal.

Imagine if Cinderella's story ended this way: "And the Prince married Grimheld, one of the brutish, wicked stepsisters, who complained about everything and picked her nose during the wedding." It's not far from our understanding of the gospel. The familiar refrain goes something like this: "You are a sinner, a traitor, a depraved wretch—pond scum, really. But God, in order to show the world what a great guy he is, will let you in anyway." We can't start with the Fall in our understanding of who we are and our role in the story. That's like coming into the movie twenty minutes late. But most Christian efforts to explain the story begin there. The whole idea of a fall assumes a starting place from which to plummet and given what a big deal the Bible makes of the Fall, it must have been from a pretty high place. "Boy trips, stubs toe" doesn't make the evening news. "Skydiver jumps, chute fails" does. The higher the original position, the bigger the story. Nobody's surprised when the neighborhood mutt runs off, plays the mongrel, sows a few wild oats, and kicks off a great night by rummaging through the trash. But what's the response if the Queen of England is found rolling around in the alley?

Yes, we are not what we were meant to be, and we know it.

If, when passing a stranger on the street, we happen to meet eyes, we quickly avert our glance. Cramped into the awkward community of an elevator, we search for something, anything to look at instead of each other. We sense that our real self is ruined, and we fear to be seen. But think for a moment about the millions of tourists who visit ancient sites like the Parthenon, the Colosseum, and the Pyramids. Though ravaged by time, the elements, and vandals through the ages, mere shadows of their former glory, these ruins still awe and inspire. Though fallen, their glory cannot be fully extinguished. There is something at once sad and grand about them. And such we are. Abused, neglected, vandalized, fallen—we are still fearful and wonderful. We are, as one theologian put it, "glorious ruins." But unlike those grand monuments, we who are Christ's have been redeemed and are being renewed as Paul said, "day by day," restored in the love of God.

Why is it that thousands of years later, Helen's story still has the power to haunt us? Isn't it that we long to believe beauty really could do that—there really might be someone worth launching a thousand ships to regain and someone willing, out of passionate love, to launch those ships? God has launched his ships for us. Could it be that we, all of us, the homecoming queens and quarterbacks and the passed over and picked on, really possess hidden greatness? Is there something in us worth fighting over? The fact that we don't see our own glory is part of the tragedy of the Fall; a sort of spiritual amnesia has taken all of us. Our souls were made to live in the Larger Story, but as Chesterton discovered, we have forgotten our part:

> We have all read in scientific books, and indeed, in all romances, the story of the man who has forgotten his name. This man walks about the streets and can see and appreciate everything; only he cannot remember who he is. Well, every man is that man in the story. Every man has forgotten who he is. . . . We are all under the

same mental calamity; we have all forgotten our names. We have all forgotten what we really are. (*Orthodoxy*)

Every woman is in some way searching for or running from her beauty and every man is looking for or avoiding his strength. Why? In some deep place within, we remember what we were made to be, we carry with us the memory of gods, image-bearers walking in the Garden. So why do we flee our essence? As hard as it may be for us to see our sin, it is far harder still for us to remember our glory. The pain of the memory of our former glory is so excruciating, we would rather stay in the pigsty than return to our true home. We are like Gomer, wife of the prophet Hosea, who preferred to live in an adulterous affair rather than be restored to her true love. Like Helen, we participated in our capture, though we were duped into it. And like Helen, our king has come for us, in spite of our unfaithfulness. If it is true that our identity comes from the impact we have on others, then our deepest and truest identity comes from the impact we've had on our most significant Other. Listen to the names he has given us: "No longer will they call you Deserted. . . . They will be called the Holy People, the Redeemed of the LORD; and you will be called Sought After" (Isa. 62:4, 12).

In other words, *we* are the ones to be called Fought Over, Captured and Rescued, Pursued. It seems remarkable, incredible, too good to be true. There really is something desirable within me, something the King of the universe has moved heaven and earth to get. George Herbert reached for words to express his wonder:

"My God, what is a heart
That thou shouldst it so eye and woo
Powering upon it with all thy art
As if thou hadst nothing else to do?" (*Mattens*)

King David used a similar refrain:

"What is man that you are mindful of him,
the son of man that you care for him?
You made him a little lower than the heavenly beings
and crowned him with glory and honor" *(Ps. 8:4–5).*

The Scriptures employ a wide scale of metaphors to capture the many facets of our relationship with God. If you consider them in a sort of ascending order, there is a noticeable and breathtaking progression. Down near the bottom of the totem pole we are the clay and he the Potter. Moving up a notch, we are the sheep and he the Shepherd, which is a little better position on the food chain but hardly flattering; sheep don't have a reputation as the most graceful and intelligent creatures in the world. Moving upward, we are the servants of the Master, which at least lets us into the house, even if we have to wipe our feet, watch our manners, and not talk too much. Most Christians never get past this point, but the ladder of metaphors is about to make a swift ascent. God also calls us his children and himself our heavenly Father, which brings us into the possibility of real intimacy—love is not one of the things a vase and its craftsman share together, nor does a sheep truly know the heart of the shepherd, though it may enjoy the fruits of his kindness. Still, there is something missing even in the best parent-child relationship. Friendship levels the playing field in a way family never can, at least not until the kids have grown and left the house. Friendship opens a level of communion that a five-year-old doesn't know with his mother and father. And "friends" are what he calls us.

But there is still a higher and deeper level of intimacy and partnership awaiting us at the top of this metaphorical ascent. We are lovers. The courtship that began with a honeymoon in the Garden culminates in the wedding feast of the Lamb. "I will take delight in you," he says to us, "as a bridegroom rejoices over his bride, so will I rejoice over you," so that we might say in return, "I am my beloved's and his desire is for me."

Lady Julian of Norwich was given a series of revelations into the sufferings of Christ and the glory of the gospel. She was taken into the heart of God and upon her return she concluded quite simply, "We are his lovers." The bridal imagery often fails to capture a man's heart, but consider: God is neither male nor female. Both genders together are needed to reflect his image and he transcends them both. The question every woman is asking goes something like, "Am I lovely? Do you want me?" The question every man is asking is, "Do I have what it takes? Am I adequate?" As men and women, we want to be chosen for different reasons, but we both want to be chosen, to be welcomed into the heart of things, invited into the Drama to live from our heart. We both want love, the adventure of intimacy, and this is what God's pursuit means for men and for women.

> O Living Flame of Love . . .
> How Gently and how lovingly
> Thou wakest in my bosom,
> Where alone thou secretly dwellest;
> And in Thy sweet breathing
> Full of grace and glory,
> How tenderly Thou fillest me with Thy love.

These words, penned by St. John of the Cross in his book *Living Flame of Love*, capture the heart-cry of every soul for intimacy with God. For this we were created and for this we were rescued from sin and death. In Ephesians, Paul lets us in on a little secret: We've been more than noticed. God has pursued us from farther than space and longer ago than time. Our romance is far more ancient than the story of Helen of Troy. God has had us in mind since before the Foundations of the World. He loved us before the beginning of time, has come for us, and now calls us to journey toward him, with him, for the consummation of our love.

Who am I, really? The answer to that question is found in the answer to another: What is God's heart toward me, or, how do I affect him? If God is the Pursuer, the Ageless Romancer, the Lover, then there has to be a Beloved, one who is the Pursued. This is our role in the story.

In the end, all we've ever really wanted is to be loved. "Love comes from God," writes St. John. We don't have to get God to love us by doing something right—even loving him. "This is love: not that we loved God but that he loved us and sent his Son as an atoning sacrifice for our sins." Someone has noticed, someone has taken the initiative. There is nothing we need to do to keep it up, because his love for us is not based on what we've done, but who we are: His beloved. "I belong to my lover, and his desire is for me" (Song 7:10).

8

The Adversary: Legends of the Fall

*The great snake lies ever half awake, at the bottom of
the pit of the world, until he awakens in hunger.*

T.S. Eliot

WE ARE THE SONS AND DAUGHTERS of God, even more,
the Beloved, pursued by God himself. The images
John has given us in the last two chapters do indeed,
"take our breath away." We might think that, having our heart
and mind bolstered by these images of beauty and truth, we
would live our lives with courage and energy that arise out of
the exuberant hope we have in the future. But there is another
voice that whispers in our ear a very different message: a message in a minor and condemning key; a key that dilutes or even
erases the truths John has portrayed so well. Some of this music
in minor key we can ascribe to the pathos of living on this side
of the Fall. Along with the creation itself, we will experience an
inner groaning until Christ returns to wipe away every tear and
establish his kingdom with us in joy and laughter.

But what is the source of the persistent accusations in our
head and heart? It is a voice that speaks to us in tones and words
vaguely familiar. The words and accusations that slide almost
unnoticed into our consciousness are words we have heard
before, sometimes from parents, peers, or the enemies of our
youth. The voice (sometimes voices) that accuses us is so familiar

we have learned to think of it as our own. Many of us have learned to use the voice to help us control life's unknowns—or so we think. It is a voice that constantly questions the wisdom of hope and the life of faith and love that flows from it.

It is the voice of our adversary.

Ezekiel gives us a portrait of this mortal enemy, before his revolt, in his prophecy against the king of Tyre, which is also a description of the angel that energized this king's heart:

> You were the model of perfection,
> full of wisdom and perfect in beauty.
> You were in Eden,
> the garden of God;
> every precious stone adorned you:
> ruby, topaz, and emerald,
> chrysolite, onyx and jasper,
> sapphire, turquoise and beryl.
> Your settings and mountings were made of gold;
> on the day you were created they were prepared.
> You were anointed as a guardian cherub,
> for so I ordained you.
> You were on the holy mount of God;
> you walked among the fiery stones.
> You were blameless in your ways
> from the day you were created
> till wickedness was found in you.
> Through your widespread trade
> you were filled with violence,
> and you sinned.
> *So I drove you in disgrace from the mount of God,*
> and I expelled you, O guardian cherub,
> from among the fiery stones.
> Your heart became proud
> on account of your beauty,
> and you corrupted your wisdom
> because of your splendor.
> So I threw you to the earth;

I made a spectacle of you before kings.
(Ezke. 28:12–17, italics mine)

The apostle John gives us, in more detail, the result of Lucifer's presumption:

And there was war in heaven. Michael and his angels fought against the dragon, and the dragon and his angels fought back. But he was not strong enough, and they lost their place in heaven. The great dragon was hurled down—that ancient serpent called the devil or Satan, *who leads the whole world astray. He was hurled to the earth, and his angels with him. (Rev. 12:7–9, italics mine)*

Our enemy is the angel Lucifer, son of the morning, one of the first and highest angels God created. He is the antagonist in the sacred romance—the great villain. All other villains are only a shadow of him. He is the one God gave a place of honor and trust "among the fiery stones" of the courts of heaven and who sees God face-to-face even to this day. He is one who spurned God's love and lost everything good through the sin of presumption. His desire was, and still is, to possess everything that belongs to God, including the worship of all those whom God loves. And God, as the Author of the great Story in which we are all living, has mysteriously allowed him a certain freedom to harass and oppress the other characters in the play, sometimes in a severe manner.

In some ways, due to his great age and dark wisdom, Satan knows us better than we know ourselves. The one purpose of his heart is the destruction of all that God loves, particularly his beloved. He stalks us day and night, as the Lord tells us through Peter: "Your enemy the devil prowls around like a roaring lion looking for someone to devour" (1 Peter 5:8). Peter makes it clear he is talking especially to believers, saying in verse 9, "Resist him, standing firm in the faith, because you know that *your brothers* throughout the world are undergoing the same kind of sufferings" (emphasis mine).

As I (Brent) read these words, several questions come immediately to mind, among them these: "Wait a minute, God. How did I get in the middle of this fight? Why do you give your enemy the freedom to attack me? And where am I to expect his attacks? A roaring lion should be fairly easy to identify. Where is this enemy of yours who is now also mine? What is his strategy to separate me from you and how does he carry it out?"

A Heart for Revenge

What is clear is that Satan has lost the battle. Twice. The first time he was hurled in disgrace from the walls of heaven by Christ and his angels. The second time, he was unable to hold the crucified Christ within the gates of hell and was forced to hand over to him the keys to death and Hades. But for a time he is placed on what feels like a very long leash to do what he can among us with his roaring.

As we pick up the drama of Satan's defeat in heaven at the end of Act II, which John described to us in Chapter 6 through Paradise Lost, we find Satan lying facedown in the lake of fire after having been hurled from the walls of heaven on the third day of his great battle with God and his angels. In shock that such a great force as his could have actually been defeated, he drags himself to a nearby island. He raises his head to see his angelic army strewn across the lake of fire like "autumn leaves"—the glow of heaven still upon them. Beelzebub, his chief lieutenant, convinces him to speak, that the sound of his voice might yet instill courage and hope in his legions.

Having lost everything with no chance for redemption, Lucifer, now Satan, tries to quiet the tears of his own heart and assure his legions that this place will never be able to hold such celestial spirits as they. He uses the despair, impotent rage, and hatred for God that they all feel to stir them to consider what "mature counsel" will once again give them hope and direction. Lucifer and his war chiefs have lost their heavenly names but Milton refers to them by the names their notoriety on the earth will earn them. Moloch urges all-out assault on heaven and if they die in the process, so be it. At least the streets of heaven will run red with blood. Belial, the consummate politician, advises a policy of laying low so that perhaps God will eventually forget about them and they can then do what they want. Mammon basically says, "Guys, we can own this joint without God here to bug us. We'll run a numbers racket never before seen under heaven." It is at this point that Beelzebub breaks in to the dialogue with exasperation:

> What sit we then projecting peace and war?
> War hath determin'd us and foil'd us with loss
> Irreparable; terms of peace, yet none
> Vouchsaf't or sought; for what peace will be giv'n
> To us enslav'd, but custody severe,
> And stripes, and arbitrary punishment . . .
> Nor will occasion want, nor shall we need
> With dangerous expedition to invade
> Heav'n, whose high walls fear no assault or Siege
> Or ambush from the Deep. What if we find
> some easier enterprise? . . .

Having expressed how futile it would be to place any hope in invading heaven or somehow pulling one over on God and establishing their own kingdom, Beelzebub advocates a different approach to gaining revenge against God by destroying or seducing God's new and favored race called man.

> There is a place
> (If ancient and prophetic fame in Heav'n
> Err not) another place, the happy seat
> Of some new Race call'd Man, about this time

To be created, like to us, though less
In power and excellence, but favour'd more
Of him who rules above; so was his will
Pronounc'd among the Gods, and by an Oath,
That shook Heav'n's whole circumference, confirm'd.
Thither let us bend all our thoughts, to learn
What creatures there inhabit, of what mould,
Or substance, how endu'd, and what their Power,
And whence their weakness, how attempted best,
By force or subtlety: Though Heav'n be shut,
And Heav'n's high Arbitrator sit secure
In his own strength, this place may lie expos'd
The utmost border of his Kingdom, left
To their defense who hold it: here perhaps
Some advantageous act may be achiev'd
By sudden onset, either with Hell fire
To waste his whole Creation, or possess
All as our own, and drive as we were driven,
The puny habitants, or if not drive,
Seduce them to our Party, that their God
May prove their foe, and with repenting hand
Abolish his own works. This would surpass
Common revenge, and interrupt his Joy
In our Confusion, and our Joy upraise
In his disturbance; when his darling Sons
Hurl'd headlong to partake with us, shall curse
Their frail Originals, and faded bliss,
Faded so soon. *(italics mine)*

Being unable to defeat God through raw power, Satan's legions decide to wound God as deeply as possible by stealing the love of his beloved through seduction. And having "seduced them to his party," to ravish them body and soul; and having ravished them, to mock them even as they are hurled to the depths of hell with God himself unable to save them because of their rejection of him. This is Satan's motivation and goal for every man, woman, and child into whom God ever breathed the breath of life. Like a roaring lion, he "hungers" for us.

God could have given up on the love affair with mankind. He could have resorted to power and demanded our loyalty, or given us a kind of spiritual lobotomy that would take away our choice to love him. Even now, he could easily obliterate our enemy and demand the allegiance of our hearts, but the love affair that began in the laughter of the Trinity would be over, at least for us. And Satan's accusation that the kingdom of God is established only through raw power would be vindicated.

Once we understand God's desire to possess our heart through love rather than power, we can fathom even more deeply the depths of God's anguish as he pleads with Israel through the prophets to give up their spiritual adultery and return to his love. We can also comprehend the fierceness of his jealousy for the heart and spiritual well-being of his chosen ones as he raises up nations and armies to obliterate the society and culture that have become a breeding ground for the enemy's seduction of their heart. "I do this so you will know that it is I Who am the Lord your God" is the heart message he brings to Israel in Ezekiel and Jeremiah. "And when you have been stripped naked and ravished, your hearts will again call out to me for rescue and I will come and destroy your enemies."

All of us have had poignant ecstasies of heart over a love affair that subsequently turned to immobilizing pain and shock as we realized that our lover could actually know us and yet leave us for another. But have you ever dated someone and you just knew, from the first time you met her, that she was the one you wanted to spend your life with? As you laughed and talked and marveled together, you felt your love deepen to a heart bond that you knew you never wanted to free yourself from. And have you ever been shocked to find one day that the one you loved so deeply and who you thought loved you just as passionately, had been dating other guys and, moreover, was spending more and more of her time with your worst enemy?

Have you ever had to literally turn a lover over to a mortal enemy to allow her to find out for herself what his intentions toward her really were? Have you ever had to lie in bed knowing she was believing his lies and was having sex with him every night? Have you ever sat helplessly by in a parking lot, while your enemy and his friends took turns raping your lover even as you sat nearby, unable to win her heart enough so she would trust you to rescue her? Have you ever called this one you had loved for so long, even the day after her rape, and asked her if she was ready to come back to you only to have her say her heart was still captured by your enemy? Have you ever watched your lover's beauty slowly diminish and fade in a haze of alcohol, drugs, occult practices, and infant sacrifice until she is no longer recognizable in body or soul? Have you ever loved one so much that you even send your only son to talk with her about your love for her, knowing that he will be killed by her? (And in spite of knowing all of this, he was willing to do it because he loved her, too, and believed you were meant for each other.)

All this and more God has endured because of his refusal to stop loving us. Indeed, the very depth and faithfulness of his love for us, along with his desire for our freely given love in return, are what give Satan the ammunition to wound God so deeply as he carries out his unceasing campaign to make us into God's enemy.

The journey of our individual hearts, as well as the heart of an entire nation or culture, really distills into this warfare for our heart's devotion. It is the central plot of the Sacred Romance, Act III, life here on earth. Indeed, all of the subplots of our lives come out of it. Satan has camouflaged this simplicity with a thousand other religions, psychologies, philosophies, knowledges, and mysticisms over the centuries, but the embers of the love affair, sustained by God's faithfulness, have refused to die and grow completely cold.

Satan's Grand Strategy

God and Satan each have a design, a battle plan, to capture our heart's devotion. The intimacy, beauty, and adventure of the Sacred Romance are placed and nurtured in the deepest longings of our heart by God himself. God's grand strategy, birthed in his grace toward us in Christ, and nurtured through the obedience of disciplined faith, is to release us into the redeemed life of our heart, knowing it will lead us back to him even as the North Star guides a ship across the vast unknown surface of the ocean.

If we were to find ourselves living with total freedom, Jesus informs us through his summary of the law in Luke 10:26–28, we would find ourselves loving God with all of our heart and our neighbors as ourselves. Jesus said further, "You will know the truth [me], and the truth will set you free."

The enemy knows this as well and his strategy to capture us is simply the opposite: to disconnect us from our heart and the heart of God toward us by any means possible. It is what he no doubt had to do to his own heart to bear the loss of heaven. Milton captures this terrible picture in earlier lines from *Paradise Lost* as Lucifer tries to speak to his fallen legions: "Thrice he assay'd [tried to speak], and thrice in spite of scorn, Tears such as angels weep burst forth. . . ."

Before Lucifer could become a true citizen of hell, he had to kill the desires of his own heart. He did it with scorn and much scorn was required. And this is his strategy with each of us: to kill the desire that would eventually lead us back to the One who loves us, using all the forms of shame, contempt, apathy, anesthesia, and perversion at his disposal.

The core of Satan's plan for each of us is not found in

tempting us with obvious sins like shoplifting or illicit sex. These things he uses more as maintenance strategies. His grand tactic in separating us from our heart is to sneak in as the Story-teller through our fears and the wounds we have received from life's Arrows. He weaves a story that becomes our particular "Message of the Arrows." Counting on our vanity and blind-ness, he seduces us to try to control life by living in the smaller stories we all construct to one degree or another. He accuses God to us and us to God. He accuses us through the words of parents and friends and God himself. He calls good evil and evil good and always helps us question whether God has anything good in mind in his plans for us. He steals our innocence as chil-dren and replaces it with a blind naïveté or cynicism as adults.

At the same time Satan is at work reinterpreting our own individual stories in order to make God our enemy, he is also at work dismantling the Sacred Romance—the Larger Story God is telling—so that there is nothing visible, as John wrote earlier, "to take our breath away." He separates beauty from truth and thus our thirst from our religious practice and the obedience of faith. He dismantles our church liturgical seasons that tell the story of a great love affair—of Paradise lost—and just when we believed everything to be hopeless—Paradise regained. He replaces the love affair with a religious system of do's and don'ts that parch our hearts and replaces our worship and communion services with entertainment. Our experience of life deteriorates from the passion of a grand love affair, in the midst of a life-and-death battle, to an endless series of chores and errands, a busy-ness that separates us from God, each other, and even from our own thirstiness.

"But can you really trust the thirst of your heart?" the enemy whispers in my ear. "Doesn't Jeremiah, God's own prophet, even say 'The heart is deceitful beyond all things and beyond cure'?" And the answer to that is, "Yes. Once my heart is sepa-rated from the life of the Sacred Romance, offered to me through the atonement of Christ, and left to seek out life on its own terms, there is no perversity it will not sink to." Part of Satan's grand strategy of separating us from our heart, once Jesus has drawn us to an awareness of being his sons and daughters through believing faith, is to convince us that our heart's desires are *at core* illegitimate. He comes in as the Storyteller and whispers to us: "Do you really think you are somebody special? Can you ever satisfy God's law without killing your heart and earning your keep? Do you think God really loves you beyond your usefulness? Hasn't your own experience taught you this is true?"

"Cinderella," the beloved fairy tale of our youth, captures wonderfully Satan's tactics as the Storyteller. As you remember, Cinderella lived with her stepsisters, a shrewish pair who made her sleep with the coal in the furnace room and had her convinced she would never be anything more than a maid. I remember thinking as I looked at the pictures of Cinderella in my child's storybook, "Doesn't she know how beautiful she is? Can't she see she is so different from her stepsisters both inside and out? Why doesn't she just look in the mirror?"

But the voices of the stepsisters were loud and Cinderella could only see in her mirror darkly. She continued to take their abuse and serve them right up until the invitation to the Prince's Ball came. When Cinderella shyly suggested that she might like to go, the stepsisters mock her to scorn for thinking she would fit in with people of such grace and beauty. As she helps stuff them into their costumes and does her best to hide their ludicrous ugliness, they continue to mock her foolishness in thinking that the prince would ever want anything to do with her. When God's grace comes in the form of Cinderella's fairy godmother and dresses her in a beautiful gown, she does finally look in the mirror and sees clearly her great beauty, but she believes it is all due to magic.

Of course, the prince recognizes her as the one he has been looking for all of his life. He spends the evening dancing with her, totally enraptured in her presence. As the clock strikes twelve, Cinderella fears being exposed for the homely house-maid she believes she is and runs from the room, losing a glass slipper in the process. Even though she still has the other glass slipper in her possession, she does not come forward when she hears the prince is searching the city for the one who can wear the dainty shoe.

Once again, the stepsisters' voices have convinced her that she is contemptible in soul and body, good only for the home-liest of tasks. Fortunately for Cinderella, the prince is a roman-tic who will not give up searching the city until he has found her, and they live happily ever after. And so it will be with us who are the beloved of the great Prince who is Jesus. It is this destiny that so enrages our enemy and makes him determined to destroy the love affair that he can never have a part in.

A Disguised Roar

Earlier in the chapter, I quoted Peter's warning that Satan is like a roaring lion, seeking whom he may devour, and asked where we are to look for the lion's roar. Satan lost his place in heaven because God and his angels were simply more powerful. As John explained earlier, it is the issue of whether God is really good that is not resolved, and this argument is still going on, at least in our sector of the cosmos. As Beelzebub said, "Drive them as we were driven, / The puny Habitants, or if not drive, / *Seduce them to our Party*, that their God may prove their foe."

Having lost the battle of power, both in being driven from heaven and in failing to hold Christ captive to death and hell, Satan's tactic in separating us from our heart until that day when he regains enough power to embody the Antichrist is to seduce us to his party by making us believe that it is God who is our enemy. It is as the Storyteller that he enters Act III of the play (the Creation and Fall) in the Garden of Eden, employing his strategy of deception until he can return to the raw power he would like to use. He comes to the man and the woman in the Garden with his roar disguised. He comes as one who is concerned with whether God really has their best interests at heart. He begins to test how well the man and the woman really know the story line God has revealed to them by asking a question: "He said to the woman, 'Did God really say, "You must not eat from any tree in the garden"?' The woman said to the serpent, 'We may eat fruit from the trees in the garden, but God did say, "You must not eat fruit from the tree that is in the middle of the garden, and you must not touch it, or you will die"'" (Gen. 3:1–3).

Contrary to the popular idea that Adam was not present at this point, possibly made so by Milton himself in *Paradise Lost*, Adam *was* present for this whole conversation, as is made clear in verse 6. God's original words to Adam were, "You are free to eat from any tree in the garden; but you must not eat from the tree of the knowledge of good and evil, for when you eat of it you will surely die" (Gen. 2:16–17). Eve adds the line, "[We] must not touch it, or [we] will die." She doesn't quite have the story straight, either because Adam had not made it clear to her or because she just didn't hear it with total accuracy. Either thought is somewhat incredible since this was before the Fall, but sin and evil always have a time of ripening before they bear their fruit.

Satan hears this flaw in Eve's lines and is emboldened to go further in his deception by directly contradicting the story line God gave to Adam. "'You will not surely die,' the serpent said to the woman. 'For God knows that when you eat of it your eyes will be opened, and you will be like God, knowing good and evil'" (Gen. 3:4–5). Satan's seduction of our heart *always* comes in the form of a story that offers us greater control through knowing good and evil rather than the unknowns of relationship.

The Cosmic Argument

And so it has gone ever since Adam lost his title as prince of the earth to the evil one. God, through the beauty of his creation, through the prophets, the Scriptures, and his Spirit who is in the world, and in those who believe through Christ, has continued to tell the story of his love for us, of what great beauty and significance we have in his eyes, along with his plans to bring us to intimacy with himself and all that is good. He exhorts us to trust in good in the midst of great evil. David Wilcox captures the poignant drama of this paradox God asks us to embrace in the lyrics to his song, "Show the Way":

> Look, if someone wrote a play just to glorify
> What's stronger than hate, would they not arrange the stage
> To look as if the hero came too late he's almost in defeat
> It's looking like the Evil side will win, so on the Edge
> Of every seat, from the moment that the whole thing begins
> It is . . .
> Love who makes the mortar
> And it's love who stacked these stones
> And it's love who made the stage here
> Although it looks like we're alone
> In this scene set in shadows
> Like the night is here to stay
> There is evil cast around us
> But it's love that wrote the play
> For in this darkness love can show the way.
> ("Show the Way," David Wilcox, © 1994 Irving Music, Inc., and Midnight Ocean Bonfire Music (BMI), All rights reserved. Used by permission. Warner Brothers Publications U.S., Inc., Miami, FL 33014)

Satan continues to use the evil that he himself creates to tell us a very different story. In his version, good is gained through our own understanding, not through a relationship with God. Life is gained by appropriating what we can see with our own eyes and by controlling any unknown Arrows that may strike us rather than living in the bigger Story God is telling. Jesus invites us to thirst. Satan invites us to control through performance of one kind or another.

His first goal, of course, is to make sure we never meet the Prince who is Jesus of Nazareth or experience a taste of the Great Ball. But once we have, Satan's second and lifelong purpose with each of us is to make sure we never know who we really are; indeed, to keep us living the life of a cellar maid rather than a princess. Even though we who are believers *have* tasted the Ball and the love of the Prince in beginning ways, the voices of the stepsisters continue to speak to us in tones varying from whispers to shouts; and like Cinderella, each of us has our own years as a "cellar maid" that the enemy can whisper to us about, causing us to wonder if this isn't who we really are after all.

The point is: We do not experience the story of our lives on rationally or emotionally neutral ground.

When I was young, I read a little book called *The Devil and Don Camillo*. It was the story of a Catholic priest whose heart was set to follow God. On one of his shoulders sat a small devil and on the other an angel, both of whom traveled with him wherever he went. As he encountered the events of each day, each spirit whispered intently in his ear its interpretation of the event and how it should be handled. This is perhaps as good an illustration of our situation as any I have come across. Satan's ministers constantly whisper to us their interpretation of the story of our lives in soul-specific ways. They use the events of our particular journey and bits and pieces of the lines spoken to us by parents, ministers, sweethearts, spouses, and perfect strangers. They weave these lines together into our particular Message of the Arrows that says there is no Sacred Romance, no larger Story that God is directing that is very good. They seduce us to the smaller stories of control and indulgence that so many of us find ourselves living, afraid to venture out any farther on the Christian journey. Satan is constantly at work deconstructing the Sacred Romance in our heart so that he may more easily seduce us to the smaller stories he is telling.

Given all this, it becomes crucial that we become a generation of storytellers who are both recapturing the glory and joy of the Sacred Romance even as we tell each other our particular stories, so that we can help each other, through God's Spirit, see his plan of redemption at work in us. In evangelical circles so often we try to apply formulas to each other with total disregard for where we are in our own story. For instance, there is a place on each of our journeys where we need to spend some time pursuing our emotions to see what heart-room they lead us to that may need tending. At other times, we need to acknowledge that a particular emotion is there but simply continue to live by faith. "You can't really study people," said C. S. Lewis, "you can only get to know them." We come to know God by coming to know the Sacred Romance he is telling. We come to understand who we are by telling each other our stories in light of the Sacred Romance.

Let me give an example of what I mean by "telling our story" from my own life. One of the deepest Arrows from my story has been the departure of three fathers, none of whom made any great effort to stay in contact or let me know that I was a significant loss. I mention this not to gain sympathy. Each of you who is reading these words has your own Arrows, some much worse than mine, others seemingly not as dramatic but perhaps even more poisonous due to their "invisibility." For instance, there is the daughter whose parents provide her every opportunity and meet every physical need, yet totally ignore her heart. I have talked about these things with my own father before he died as well as each of my stepfathers and we have reached a kind of peace that has allowed my Father in heaven to do much beginning healing. For some of us, that healing will come without the reconciliation with those who have harmed us. Nothing is impossible with God.

Having made these disclaimers, let me describe briefly how Satan, through his ministers, has woven these Arrows into a message in my life that has a very recognizable purpose for me as it does for you; it is to continue my life separated emotionally and spiritually from myself, my friends, and my family, as well as God my Father—*simply filling in time*. It is partly how my father ended his life, wandering from coffee shop to coffee shop and vacation to vacation, and to some extent, how my stepfathers struggled with theirs as well. They had no story powerful enough to sustain their waning years.

For my stepfathers, it was an end that did not appear totally unglamorous. They were both cowboys and cowboys wear aloneness with a certain heroism. It is their scripts that I have partially adopted. For other men, the script may be anesthesia or order or making money (for women, the script revolves around the heart issue of beauty or the avoidance of it)—whatever is sufficient to occupy the thirst of our heart enough that we don't need God.

My fathers' leavings gave the enemy a pernicious story line to work with; a stepsisters' message that his ministers have whispered in my ear constantly over the years. "You are on your own. There is no one to fall back on. You'd better figure out how to handle this. There's something wrong with you. Other fathers don't leave. It's all going to end badly. You're going to end up invisible and alone. Why don't you just give up this foolish idea that God cares and at least enjoy life in the ways you know you can."

Many of these thoughts have been with me from early on. They have been the energy that drove me to implement my own life script, making it up as I went along. They have been part of the energy that drove me to get a doctorate. They are even part of the energy driving me to write this book, though

I can confess that part of myself more easily than I used to. Those sentences are woven through and have partly energized the whole journey of my life. Thankfully, there are other sentences God has spoken into my life that are growing stronger even as the stepsisters' message dims.

Some of the sentences the enemy accuses each of us with have been there since we were young; others were added in the ensuing years as Satan saw opportunity to strengthen our fear and cynicism through "interpreting" those events in our lives that seem to verify our particular Message of the Arrows. His purpose is to convince us that we need to create a story to live in that is not as dangerous as the Sacred Romance. As long as we do not admit that the deep things of our heart are there— the rejection and hurt, the shame and sorrow, the anger and rage—these rooms of our heart become darkened and the enemy sets up shop there to accuse us.

I am not just speaking metaphorically or poetically when I refer to the enemy accusing us. Each of us, Christians included, is oppressed directly and specifically by the enemy in the way I am describing. This attack happens in the spiritual realm, using the sentences and voices we are familiar with from the past. We feel as if we are simply speaking to ourselves in our heads. And this is the enemy's first deception: "I am not here. It's just you struggling with all these things." Cinderella's stepsisters convinced her that it was her ugliness that brought her to her fate as a cellar maid rather than their harsh and condemning treatment of her. Many of us live our whole lives being defeated by this accusation. And indeed, deep in our hearts, the anxiety, shame, and self-contempt we often feel *are* like the attack of a roaring lion no matter what calmness or other personality device we learn to cover it with on the outside. We hide the lion's roar because he has convinced us that it is just us and we would be roundly scorned if we were to admit these things to others.

When the adversary is involved, the intensity of feelings

provoked by the everyday occurrences of life can be compared to gasoline poured on a fire. The fire would burn (i.e., we would hurt) even without the gasoline, but its additional fuel totally consumes the kindling of our souls in an inferno of shame and contempt. We feel ashamed for and contemptuous of ourselves as well as scornful of the people who have "caused" us such pain. They literally become our enemies that must be appeased or defeated. Meanwhile, the real enemy who caused this conflagration sits unnoticed in the background, full of glee. The whole experience is somewhat like being slapped in the back of the head in the school hallway. You turn around to find a boy next to you and slap him back, while the real culprit is already yards away enjoying the conflict he has instigated.

C. S. Lewis captures the destiny of the soul that Satan has in mind for each of us in his novel *The Great Divorce*. In the opening scene, we find ourselves at a bus stop in hell, from which we can see tiny pinpoints of light, each of which represents a dwelling. The bus stop is for those who might wish to travel to the outskirts of heaven and consider one last time if they would wish to be citizens there. Each dwelling visible to us is isolated from the others by darkness and great distance. From the different directions a few individuals move toward the bus stop, filled with great fear and ambivalence about leaving their familiar soul dwellings.

Lewis takes us to the window of one of these lone houses and invites us to look in. As we do so, we find Napoleon Bonaparte pacing back and forth muttering something to himself. As we listen more intently, we find him remembering his lost empire with great agitation: "It was Ney's fault. It was Josephine's fault. It was the Russians' fault." With horror, we realize that he is caught for all eternity in the failure of his particular small story, that of victorious and beloved emperor. Any of us who have spent any time rehashing how we were perceived at a party can relate to the torment of such a fate.

Satan uses the Arrows that strike all of us this side of the Fall and weaves them into a story line to convince us that we cannot live without the disguise of our false self, the role we are playing out in what John and I have been calling our "smaller story." Our smaller stories are constructed along the plotlines of control and gratification. Once we begin to live by this false self, Satan and his minions sabotage the story to make sure we are exposed. Then he mocks us for our foolishness and hypocrisy for hiding behind such a facade in the first place. Other times, he simply leaves us to die in costume.

It has only been within the last five years that I have known that his script for me existed, and only in the last two that it has become increasingly clear how the enemy uses it tactically on a day-to-day basis. The seeds of the strategy are also visible in the other members of my family, seeds planted long ago to swell and bear bitter fruit in the right time. Each of our ancestral families also has a story that the enemy is busily reinterpreting according to that family's particular Arrows. (In this day and age, we have come to understand these things through the story line of psychology and genetics; e.g., the Joneses have always suffered with dependent personality disorder.) One theme in my own family line, for instance, is that of emotionally unprotected or neglected individuals marrying for safety rather than emotional intimacy.

It is not an issue of *whether* we are being assaulted by our particular Message of the Arrows, it is a matter of whether we recognize *how* our particular script reads. All of us are partly living out the story line the enemy offers us. This idea may seem too dramatic. Most of us, perhaps, live in not a terribly evil place in the moralistic sense of the word. We simply live where busyness, or apathy, or struggle with circumstances that won't change occupies most of our energy. And the enemy is perfectly happy to leave us in such a place practicing our religion. We are already defeated. The lion, if he roars at us at all, only does so internally about certain things we need to get under control or keep hidden with regard to the smaller stories we are counting on for life.

Spiritual Warfare and Deeper Communion with God

On the other hand, once we begin thinking of all the deceptions the enemy is about with regard to our lives, we have a tendency to become obsessed with him, fearful of what he is going to do next. Once we take him seriously, he switches from his tactic of "I'm not here" to one of having us worry about him day and night, which is almost a form of worship. God graciously showed me this several years ago while I was in the midst of an intense, three-year spiritual battle on behalf of a client who had spent years in the control of a satanic cult.

One night, David (not his real name) called me on the phone at three in the morning, in the midst of painful spiritual torment. We talked and prayed and I began to read from the Psalms. Finally, I could hear by his deep breathing that he had fallen asleep. As I lay on my dining room floor, pondering whether to leave the phone off the hook and build up a huge phone bill or hang up and risk having the beeping of the phone-off-the-hook signal wake David, something wonderful and strange took place.

In my heart, I heard a voice say, "Brent, forget about the battle. You're here with me now. Rest." I looked up, actually expecting to see God in some way, or perhaps an angel. What I did see was the light in the room *change*. I find myself wanting to say it grew more distinct, almost more personal. I only know I discovered that my hand was raised in the air in worship. I didn't decide to raise it. I am not, by any means, an expressive person in the charismatic sense of the word. It was simply as if there was no other appropriate response and my hand acted accordingly. For several minutes I basked in what I can only describe now as God's warmth and love toward me. The epiphany ended with me reading the Twenty-third Psalm and others it seemed the Lord had chosen to assure me that I was not alone in the battle.

From that night on, I had a whole new understanding of what both God our Father and the enemy of our souls are about once we leave behind the deception that Satan is not there and enter into the spiritual warfare that is part of the Sacred Romance, Act III. Again, Satan's desire is to keep us away from communion with God. He doesn't care how he does it.

God's intention, on the other hand, is to use spiritual warfare to draw us into deeper communion with himself. Satan's device is to isolate us and wear us out obsessing about what he has done and what he will do next. And he is very effective in using our particular Message of the Arrows to do it. God desires to use the enemy's attacks to remove the obstacles between ourselves and him, to reestablish our dependency on him as his sons and daughters in a much deeper way. Once we understand that, the warfare we are in begins to feel totally different. It is not really even about Satan anymore, but about communion with God and abiding in Jesus as the source of life. The whole experience begins to feel more like a devotional.

Through my own experience, I begin to see more clearly that God is so confident in the good that he is willing to allow our adversary latitude in carrying out his evil intentions for the purpose of deepening our communion with himself.

I do not mean to say this lightly. Sometimes there is a great cost to be paid in the establishing of the kingdom of God in our heart and in the heavenlies. The suffering and death of Jesus were required to bring about the life of the Resurrection. And Christ tells us through Paul that we are fellow sufferers with him. But the issue becomes more about our resolve to trust God's goodness than obsessing about the enemy's cloak-and-dagger warfare. The only reason to focus on what the adversary is doing at all is so that we can recognize the sentences of the stepsisters when we hear them and rebuke them with the truths of who we really are in the great Story God is telling. As we do so, we glorify God by trusting that his Story is the truth.

Indeed, part of God's victory over the enemy of our souls, which we will be invited to take part in, will be an open mocking of Satan and his forces in view of all the peoples of the earth along with the angelic hosts. We are given a picture of the enemy's defeat, which is the culmination of Act III of the Sacred Romance, by Isaiah:

> "Those who see you stare at you [Satan], they ponder your fate:
> 'Is this the man who shook the earth
> and made kingdoms tremble,
> the man who made the world a desert,
> who overthrew its cities and would not let his captives go home?'"
> (14:16).

"You're the one we've been scared of all this time? You're the one we've been believing?" we will ask incredulously. And we will turn and walk away in the embrace of the Prince, never to speak Satan's name again. But in the meantime, our adversary will continue to use our Message of the Arrows, along with doubts about the goodness of the Prince, to lure us to spend our lives with less-wild lovers than God.

9

Less-Wild Lovers

It is the nature of desire not to be satisfied, and most human beings live only for the gratification of it.

Aristotle

IN THE TIME of our innocence, we trusted in good because we had not yet known evil. On this side of Eden and our own experience of the Fall—whatever our own Arrows have been and however the adversary has woven them together into our particular Message of the Arrows—it appears that we are left to find our way to trust in good, having stared evil in the face.

Most of us remember the time of our innocence as a Haunting. I (Brent) mean innocence not as being sinless but as that time before our experience with the Arrows crystallized into a way of handling life which is the false self. The Haunting calls to us unexpectedly in the melody and words of certain songs that have become our "life music": the crooked smile of a friend; the laughter of our children (or their tears); the calling to mind of a mischievous face that still believed in joy; the smell of a perfume; the reading of a poem; or the hearing of a story. However the Haunting comes, it often brings with it a bitter-sweet poignancy of ache, the sense that we stood at a crossroads somewhere in the past and chose a turning that left some shining part of ourselves—perhaps the best part—behind, left it behind with the passion of youthful love, or the calling of a heart vocation, or simply in the sigh of coming to terms with the mundane requirements of life.

Whenever I hear the old Frankie Avalon song "Venus," I see the blue eyes and dark hair of my first adolescent love, Kathleen. And I can feel the familiar Haunting seize my heart with palpable waves of longing and regret. We stood under the mistletoe together and I was afraid to kiss her. Even though our family moved to another state not long after, I thought for a long time it was that lost kiss that brought about the loss of the Sacred Romance; Romance that at sixteen is so embodied in first love. I felt there was something I could have done to hold on to the Sacred Romance by holding on to Kathleen.

And each of us has points of contact where the transcendence of the Romance has seared our heart in the fragrance of lovers, geographies, and times. They are captured there and return to haunt us with their loss whenever we return, or are returned, to their heart locale. At the end of the movie *A River Runs Through It*, the author, Norman MacLean, stands as an old man in the Montana river that defined the life of his family, now all gone. He casts for rising trout and something else. He tells us,

> Now nearly all those I loved and did not understand in my youth are dead, even Jesse [his wife]. But I still reach out to them . . . when I am alone in the half-light of the canyon, all existence seems to fade to a being with my soul and memories and the sounds of the Big Blackfoot River and a four count rhythm and the hope that a trout will rise. . . . I am haunted by waters.

My best friend experiences the Haunting whenever he reads the words of Robert Frost's poem "Nothing Gold Can Stay":

> Nature's first green is gold,
> Her hardest hue to hold.
> Her early leaf's a flower;

But only so an hour.
Then leaf subsides to leaf.
So Eden sank to grief,
So dawn goes down to day.
Nothing gold can stay.

The poem hangs on his office wall as a reminder of something lost.

Yet the people and times and places through which the Romance has seared us will betray us if we think that the Romance is *in* them, C. S. Lewis tells us:

> . . . it (is) not *in* them, it only comes through them and what (comes) through them (is) longing. . . . They are not the thing itself; they are only the scent of a flower we have not found, the echo of a tune we have not heard, news from a country we have never visited.

It is Lewis's way of telling us that the Romance is both set within us, and still out on the road ahead of us—a Haunting that calls us to pilgrimage.

At one time or another, though, most of us forget the Haunting, or try to; for it often threatens to cripple us, leaving us bent over and unable to deal with the everyday things that life requires to be done. We all, to some extent, take that shining something in us that felt magical and passionate as children, that something that later swirled amid the confusion of sexual passion and our longing for heart intimacy—we take it and push it through the loneliness, ache, and turmoil of life—through various stages of disconnection and hardness to another abiding place: a kind of resignation. There is something inside of us that says, "This is the way it is. I had better learn to deal with it." Thinking Act III, Scene 2 (the Fall) will go on forever, we lose heart.

In C. S. Lewis's science fiction novel, *Perelandra*, the story's protagonist, Ransom, is sent to the planet Venus to hinder Satan's attempts to seduce that planet's first woman, Tinidril.

He encounters her still in her innocence on the floating islands Lewis tells us cover the planet.

> Beautiful, naked, shameless, young—she was obviously a goddess: but then the face, the face so calm that it escaped insipidity by the very concentration of its mildness. . . . Never had Ransom seen a face so calm, and so unearthly, despite the full humanity of every feature. He decided afterwards that the unearthly quality was due to the complete absence of resignation, which mixes, in however slight a degree, with all terrestrial faces. This was a calm no storm had ever preceded.

Resignation is not just the sigh that groans with something gone wrong. Such a sigh can be redemptive if it does not let go of the Haunting we have all experienced of something presently lost. Resignation is the acceptance of the loss as final, even as I chose to interpret it on the bridge that long-ago November day. It is the condition in which we choose to see good as no longer startling in its beauty and boldness, but simply as "nice." Evil is no longer surprising; it is normal.

It is from this place of heart resignation where many of us, perhaps all of us at one time or another, having suffered under the storm of life's Arrows, give up on the Sacred Romance. But our heart will not totally forsake the intimacy and adventure we were made for and so we compromise. We both become, and take to ourselves, lovers that are less dangerous in their passion for life and the possible pain that comes with it—in short, lovers that are less wild.

Those of us who have been drawn to understand that God is our Father through conversion in Christ recapture the Romance again—for a while. We find ourselves again in the throes of first love. The Romance we thought we had left behind once more appears out on the road ahead of us as a possible destination. God is in his heaven and all seems right in the universe.

But this side of Eden, even relationship with God brings us

to a place where a deeper work in our heart is called for if we are to be able to continue our spiritual journey. It is in this desert experience of the heart, where we are stripped of the protective clothing of the roles we have played in our smaller stories, that the Message of the Arrows reasserts itself. Healing, repentance, and faith are called for in ways we have not known previously. At this place on our journey, we face a wide and deep chasm that refuses us passage through self-effort. And it is God's intention to use this place to eradicate the final heart walls and obstacles that separate us from him.

> I will go before you
> and will level the mountains;
> I will break down gates of bronze
> and cut through bars of iron.
> I will give you the treasures of darkness,
> riches stored in secret places,
> so that you may know that I am the LORD,
> the God of Israel, who summons you by name. *(Isa. 45:2–3 NIV)*

The Road Not Taken

God's imagery of going before us lets us know that he desires us to go on a journey. This is not so frightening. Most of us are aware that the Christian life requires a pilgrimage of some sort. We know we are sojourners. What we have sometimes not given much thought to is what kind of a journey we are to be taking.

"The line separating good and evil passes not through states, nor between political parties either—but right through every human heart," said Aleksandr Solzhenitsyn in the *Gulag Archipelago*. Not realizing it is a journey of the heart that is called for, we make a crucial mistake. We come to a place in our spiritual life where we hear God calling us. We know he is calling us to give up the less-wild lovers that have become so much a part of our identity, embrace our nakedness, and trust in his goodness.

As we stand at this intersection of God's calling, we look down two highways that appear to travel in very different directions. The first highway quickly takes a turn and disappears from our view. We cannot see clearly where it leads but there are ominous clouds in the near distance. It is hard to say if they hold rain, snow, or hail, or are still in the process of fermenting whatever soul weather they intend to unleash upon us. Standing still long enough to look down this road makes us aware of an anxiety inside, an anxiety that threatens to crystallize into unhealed pain and forgotten disappointment. We check our valise and find no up-to-date road map but only the torn and smudged parchment containing the scribbled anecdotes and travelers' warnings by a few who have traveled the way of the heart before us. They encourage us to follow them but their rambling journals give no real answers to our queries on how to navigate the highway.

"Each heart has its own turns and necessary overnights," they say. "Only God knows where your road leads. But come ahead. The journey is purifying and the destination is good." Faced with such mystery and irritating vagueness, we cast our glance down the other highway. It runs straight as far as we can see, with the first night's lodging visible in the appropriate distance. Each mile is carefully marked with signs that promise success on the leg of the journey immediately ahead if their directions are carefully followed. The crisp map we take from our valise assures us that heart baggage is not needed on this journey and would only be in the way.

As we turn to look at the old parchment one more time, our eyes find the sentences left by one former traveler, "Don't be afraid of embracing the disappointment you feel, old or new. Don't be scared of the unreasonable joy either. *They're* the highway markers home. I've gone on ahead. Yours Truly."

We snort with disdain at such quaint sentiments, and our choice made, we stuff the parchment into our valise and strike off down the straight highway of discipline and duty. All goes well for a while, sometimes for years, until we begin to realize that we're really not feeling much anymore. We find ourselves struggling to weep with those who weep or even rejoice with those who rejoice. Mostly we don't bother looking people in the eye. They may want to engage us and nothing much inside feels very engaged. Our passions begin to show up in inappropriate fantasies and longings interspersed with depression, anxieties, and anger we thought we had left behind. With a start, we realize our heart has stolen away in the baggage. It is taking the journey with us but under protest.

We redouble our efforts at discipline to get it to knuckle under but it refuses. Some of us finally kill it well enough that it no longer speaks as long as we're occupied. Any quasiredemptive busyness will do. We look as if we're still believing. Others of us decide the deadness is too high a price to pay and agree to let our heart have a secret life on the side. We even try to be passionate about our faith but the fiery embers that once sustained it have turned to cool gray ash, the evidence that life was indeed once present.

"Two roads diverged in a yellow wood," wrote Robert Frost in perhaps his most well-known poem, "The Road Not Taken":

> "And sorry I could not travel both
> And be one traveler, long I stood
> And looked down one as long as I could
> To where it bent in the undergrowth. . . ."

Ironically, having ignored the road that "bent in the undergrowth" and taken the more traveled highway of discipline and duty, we find ourselves at the same place of heart resignation we left so many years ago before we were Christians. We arrive at the Vanity Fair that John Bunyan describes in *The Pilgrim's Progress*. It is a familiar city populated with many of the companions we had hoped to leave behind: deadness of spirit, lack of loving-kindness, lust, pride, anger, and others. Nonetheless, having been out on the Christian journey for a number of years by now, we assume that this is as close to the Celestial City as we're ever going to get. We set up housekeeping and entertain ourselves as well as possible at the booths in the Fair that sell a variety of soul curiosities, games, and anesthetics.

The curiosities sold at the fair are endless in their diversity, many of them good in and of themselves: Bible study, community service, religious seminars, hobbies we try to convince ourselves are eternally transcendent (e.g., "Wow, I can't wait to ski deep powder!"), service to our church, going out to dinner. But we find ourselves doing them more and more to quiet the heart voice that tells us we have given up what is most important to us.

Life in Vanity Fair

Not even the most concrete of us live in a totally black-and-white world. Even so, we tend to fall into two groups when it comes to taking up housekeeping with these less-wild lovers—lovers who promise to deliver us from the Haunting of the Sacred Romance God has placed in our heart. Those of us in the first group choose anesthesia of the heart through some form of *competence* or *order*. These may be expressed in countless arenas: a clean desk, perfect housekeeping, Scripture memory and Bible study, a manicured lawn, a spotless garage, preparing and hostessing dinner parties that would make Martha Stewart proud, sending your boys to the best sports camps to ensure they (we) never experience disappointment that might provoke thirst, formulaic religion that has three-step solutions to every problem—the list is endless.

We don't stop to consider that the curse God announced to Adam and Eve dictates that we will never be under control, either in our vocations (we will not defeat the thorns and thistles of life), nor our relationships (Eve would desire to control Adam, but would fail). God's intentions here strike us as strange if not sadistic until we remember that Satan's offer to Eve was that she could bring about her own redemption through knowing good and evil.

If we were to try to picture the one who anesthetizes her heart to control life's Arrows as a wife, we would see a soul occupied by a seemingly redemptive busyness—involvement with her household and community that is productive and worthwhile. When her husband comes home from work, she is satisfied with a peck on the cheek and a few pleasant words about the day. She doesn't mind lovemaking if it's not too spontaneous but she rarely if ever pursues it. An evening of television or a good book would do just as well. Like Cinderella, she often settles into the lesser role of maid and housekeeper rather than risk rejection by wanting romance. Her husband will feel guilty—even accused—for wanting anything more with her. If he expresses his sadness over something lost in their love affair, she chides him for his melancholy spirit.

Sadness on this order, sadness about something they once had together but had lost, is what God was so often expressing to Israel (and to us) through the prophets. He was continually trying to invite her into a lovers' quarrel while she kept hearing his words on the level of an attack on how well she was performing her duties. One with an anesthetized heart hears God with Israel's ears.

The heart sentences of one who has taken on some form of anesthesia to tame her own heart as well as the heart of anyone who would want a romance with her, sound something like this: "My heart is not available for any love affair that requires engagement. I live only to avoid the surprises that the wildness of your desire, or mine, might bring. And if you were smart, you would do the same."

And underneath those brusque sentences is a person's story.

For some of us who have chosen anesthesia to tame our heart and the hearts of those who would love us, there is a hail of fierce and identifiable Arrows whose damage we try to contain by simply closing the door to the damaged heart places. For others of us, it was perhaps living in an atmosphere too fragile to bear the weight of our unedited souls. We grew up with a certain civility under which was an unadmitted demand that things be good. We learned that nothing considered "not nice" could be entered into without our world being in danger of shattering. Those around us let us know in no uncertain terms they needed us to be less-wild lovers. Sometimes whole cultures put this demand on us. Rosemary Daniell, in her book, *Fatal Flowers*, describes how the Southern culture she grew up in demanded that she literally divide her soul in two to be acceptable: a helpless Southern belle who was nonthreatening to men and Southern society, and a competent, independent career woman who could make up any family deficiency.

Our adversary also seduces us to abide in certain emotions that act as less-wild lovers, particularly shame, fear, lust, anger, and false guilt. They are emotions that "protect" us from the more dangerous feelings of grief, abandonment, disappointment, loneliness, and even joy and longing, that threaten to roam free in the wilder environs of the heart. These are feelings that frighten us, sometimes even long years into our Christian journey.

As I (Brent) write this chapter, Ginny and I are walking through a time in our marriage where we are trying to allow some of the sadness we both feel, due to years of misconnection and detachment in a certain area of our relationship, to be felt and expressed. Over the years, we have kept the feelings at bay with a bantering anger out of fear of where they might lead us (divorce?) if we admitted them. Having allowed ourselves to mourn, we both feel that there is a greater possibility of deeper romance in the years ahead.

If those of us in the first cadre of less-wild lovers choose to control our desire through various kinds of "stay-at-home" anesthesia, we who hang out in the emotional nightclubs of Vanity Fair choose a different kind of control: *indulgence.* We put our hope in meeting a lover who will give us some form of immediate gratification, some taste of transcendence that will place a drop of water on our parched tongue. This taste of transcendence, coming as it does from a nontranscendent source, whether that be an affair, a drug, an obsession with sports, pornography, or living off of our giftedness, has the same effect on our souls as crack cocaine. Because the gratification touches us in that heart-place made for transcendent communion, without itself being transcendent, it attaches itself to our desire with chains that render us captive.

A few years ago, I was counseling with a Christian man just ending a yearlong affair. He was married to an attractive and energetic woman who was also a believer, and he knew that he really loved her. He also began to understand that whatever it was that attracted him to the affair, it was not the woman herself, but something she represented. As we talked of making his break with her final, he wept with grief, immersed in the fear that some shining, more innocent part of himself would be left behind with the affair—left behind and, perhaps, lost forever.

And this is the power of addiction. Whatever the object of our addiction is, it attaches itself to our intense desire for eternal and intimate communion with God and each other in the midst of Paradise—the desire that Jesus himself placed in us before the beginning of the world. Nothing less than this kind of unfallen communion will ever satisfy our desire or allow it to drink freely without imprisoning it and us. Once we allow our heart to drink water from these less-than-eternal wells with the goal of finding the life we were made for, it overpowers our will, and becomes, as Jonathan Edwards said, "like a viper, hissing and spitting at God" and us if we try to restrain it.

"Nothing is less in power than the heart and far from commanding, we are forced to obey it," said Jean Rousseau. Our heart will carry us either to God or to addiction.

"Addiction is the most powerful psychic enemy of humanity's desire for God," says Gerald May in *Addiction and Grace*, which is no doubt why it is one of our adversary's favorite ways to imprison us. Once taken captive, trying to free ourselves through willpower is futile. Only God's Spirit himself can free us or even bring us to our senses.

If God's experience of being "married" to us, who are his Beloved, is sometimes that of being tied to a legalistic controller in the ways I've described in the paragraphs on anesthetizing our heart, at other times it is more like that of being married to a harlot whose heart is seduced from him by every scent on the evening breeze. In our psychological age, we have come to call our affairs "addictions," but God calls them "adultery." Listen again to his words to the Israelites through Jeremiah:

> "You are a swift she-camel
> running here and there, a wild donkey accustomed to the desert,
> sniffing the wind in her craving—
> in [your] heat [how can I] restrain [you]?
> Any males that pursue [you] need not tire themselves;
> at mating time they will find [you]
> Do not run until your feet are bare
> and your throat is dry" *(Jer. 2:23–25)*.

God is saying, "I love you and yet you betray me at the drop of a hat. I feel so much pain. Can't you see we're made for each other? I want you to come back to me." And Israel's answer, like that of any addict or adulterer, is: "It's no use! / I love foreign gods, / and I must go after them" (Jer. 2:25).

Perhaps we can empathize with the ache God experienced as Israel's "husband" (and ours when we are living indulgently). Having raised Israel from childhood to a woman of grace and beauty, he astonishingly cannot win her heart from her adulterous lovers. The living God of the universe cannot win the only one he loves, not due to any lack on his part, but because her heart is captured by her addictions, which is to say, her adulterous lovers.

Many of us have had the experience of not being able to bridge the distance between ourselves and others, whether they be parents, friends, or lovers. Whether the distance is caused by unhealed wounds or willful sin in our lover's heart—or our own—we experience their rejection as our not "being enough" to win them. Unlike God, we begin to think of ourselves as having a problem with self-esteem.

Whereas God became even more wild in his love for us by sending Jesus to die for our freedom, most of us choose to both become and take on lovers that are less wild. We give up desiring to be in a relationship of heroic proportions, where we risk rejection, and settle for being heroes and heroines in the smaller stories where we have learned we *can* "turn someone on" through our usefulness, cleverness, or beauty (or at least turn ourselves on with a momentary taste of transcendence).

The list of our adulterous indulgences is endless: There is the exotic dancer, the religious fanatic, the alcoholic, the adrenaline freak, the prostitute with a man, the man with a prostitute, the eloquent pastor who seduces with his words, and the woman who seduces with her body. There is the indulgent lover who never really indulges physically, but spends his life in a kind of whimsy about what is lost, like Ashley in *Gone with the Wind*. What these indulgent lovers have in common is the pursuit of transcendence through some gratification that is under their control.

In the religions of the Fertile Crescent, access to God (transcendence) was attempted through sexual intercourse with temple prostitutes. Perhaps, as we indulge our addictions, we are doing no less than prostituting ourselves and others in this very same way. "Every man who knocks on the door of a brothel is looking for God," said G. K. Chesterton.

At first glance, those of us who live by indulgence—illicit affairs of the heart—appear to have a certain passion that is superior to those who live by anesthesia. But it is a passion that must be fed by the worship or use of the other and so it is a passion that does not leave us free to love. Indulgence leaves us empty and primed for the next round of thirst quenching in an endless cycle that Solomon described as "vanity of vanities." Jimi Hendrix, one of our modern-day poets, just before his death of a drug overdose, said it this way: "There ain't no livin' left nowhere."

Life on that first road where the signs promised us life would work if we just applied the right formula—the road that seemed so straight and safe when we first set out on it—gives us no wisdom as to what we're to do with the depth of desire God has placed within us. It is desire that is meant to lead us to nothing less than communion with him. If we try to anesthetize it, we become relational islands, unavailable to those who need us; like the father who lowers his newspaper with annoyance at the family chaos going on around him, but makes no move to speak his life into it.

If we try to gain transcendence through indulgence, soon enough familiarity breeds contempt and we are driven to search for mystery elsewhere. So the man having an affair must have another and the man who is an alcoholic must drink more and more to find the window of feeling good. "There is only One Being who can satisfy the last aching abyss of the human heart, and that is the Lord Jesus Christ," said Oswald Chambers.

At the Edge of the Abyss

What, then, is the way of that less-traveled second road—the road that is the way of the heart?

We usually think of the middle years of the Christian life as a time of acquiring better habits and their accompanying virtues. But inviting Jesus into the "aching abyss" of our heart, perhaps has more to do with holding our heart hopefully in partial emptiness in a way that allows desire to be rekindled. "Discipline imposed from the outside eventually defeats when it is not matched by desire from within," said Dawson Trotman. There comes a place on our spiritual journey where renewed religious activity is of no use whatsoever. It is the place where God holds out his hand and asks us to give up our lovers and come and live with him in a much more personal way. It is the place of relational intimacy that Satan lured Adam and Eve away from so long ago in the Garden of Eden. We are both drawn to it and fear it. Part of us would rather return to Scripture memorization, or Bible study, or service—anything that would save us from the unknowns of walking with God. We are partly convinced our life is elsewhere. We are deceived.

"We are half-hearted creatures," says Lewis in *The Weight of Glory*, "fooling about with drink and sex and ambition [and religious effort] when infinite joy is offered us, like an ignorant child who wants to go on making mud pies in a slum because he cannot imagine what is meant by the offer of a holiday at the sea. We are far too easily pleased."

The desire God has placed within us is wild in its longing to pursue the One who is unknown. Its capacity and drive is so powerful that it can only be captured momentarily in moments of deep soul communion or sexual ecstasy. And when the moment has passed, we can only hold it as an ache, a haunting of quicksilver that flashes a remembrance of innocence known and lost and, if we have begun to pass into the life of the Beloved, a hope of ecstasies yet to come.

At some point on our Christian journey, we all stand at the edge of those geographies where our heart has been satisfied by less-wild lovers, whether they be those of competence and order or those of indulgence. If we listen to our heart again, perhaps for the first time in a while, it tells us how weary it is of the familiar and the indulgent.

We find ourselves once again at the intersection with the road that is the way of the heart. We look down it once more and see what appears to be a looming abyss between the lovers we have known and the mysterious call of Christ, which we now realize is coming from the other side. Jesus appears to be holding out his hand to us even as he calls us. He tells us he will provide a bridge over the chasm if we will abide in him. We hear his words, but such language is strange to us, sounding like the dialects of many who have used us or consumed us and then left us along the highway, exposed and alone. We pull back. Many of us return to Vanity Fair and mortgage our heart to purchase more of what is religiously or materially familiar.

A few of us arouse our spirit and take a step toward the chasm. We dig into our valise and pull out the old and torn parchment of road map and journal entries left by those who have traveled the way of the heart before us; the ones we had treated with such disdain. This time the words intrigue us. We realize they are telling us something about our heart that is true. One of them writes:

> Tis hard for us to rouse our spirits up—
> It is the human creative agony
> Though but to hold the heart an empty cup
> Or tighten on the team the rigid reign.
> Many will rather lie among the slain
> Than creep through narrow ways the light to gain—
> Than wake the will, and be born bitterly.
> (George MacDonald, *Diary of an Old Soul*)

Yet, "holding our heart an empty cup" and "tightening on the team the rigid reign" is language we are not familiar with. Our lovers have so intertwined themselves with our identity that to give them up feels like personal death. Indeed, they have kept us from knowing the emptiness of our heart's cup. We wonder if it is possible to survive without them. We look once more at the journal to see if this sojourner ahead of us can offer any encouragement. He writes:

> But we who would be born again indeed,
> Must wake our souls unnumbered times a day
> And urge ourselves to life with holy greed.
> Now open our bosoms to the wind's free play,
> And now, with patience forceful, hard, lie still
> Submit and ready to the making will,
> Athirst and empty, for God's breath to fill.

We are surprised and somewhat anxious at his words. We had expected him to give us religious instruction. Instead, he commands us to be greedy in our thirst, to open the windows of our heart to the "wind's free play." "What does this look like?" we ask.

"The answer is somewhat surprising," answers one who is standing at the chasm with us. "It is surprising because it happens in the context of everyday relationships and vocation." She tells us a story of how her own less-wild lover held her prisoner one day. She is a counselor, she says. Not long ago, two of her clients expressed their thankfulness for her help, saying she had done more for them in two sessions than previous counselors had done in months. Strangely, she found herself angry with them, admonishing them not to expect her to do "what they must do for themselves." As she reflected on her surprising anger, it became clear to her that she did not yet totally trust that she could live in freedom as a woman who was truly enjoyable. When her clients complimented her, her old less-wild lover of living by competence shouted at her that she had better keep coming across with counseling insights or her clients would no longer value her. It was how she had survived as a child and for a moment, she forgot the hope that God has placed something in her that is truly enjoyable, separate from her competence.

As she finishes her story, we puzzle over the truth that setting her heart free depends so deeply on trusting in her own beauty; on hoping in what is wildly good. We remember that the last line of the inscription on the gates of hell in Dante's *Inferno* reads, "Abandon all hope, ye who enter here." We pull out another of the old journals and read the apostle Peter's warning that our adversary is constantly at work (the lion seeking to devour us) to convince us that there is nothing wildly good, either in us, in God, or in his plans for the future of our love affair. "There is no such thing as true goodness," our adversary roars, "and if there is, it's deadly dull."

We wonder if it is our enemy who has convinced us that "good" is synonymous with "nice": the way we would be required to behave in Aunt Suzy's parlor on a warm summer afternoon when we would rather be swinging from a rope over the swimming hole.

It strikes us that to hope in the kind of goodness that would set our heart free, we must be willing to allow our desire to remain haunted. This side of the Fall, true goodness comes by surprise, the old writings tell us, enthralling us for a moment in heaven's time. They warn us it cannot be held. Something inside knows they are right, that if we could do so, we would set up temples to worship it and the Sacred Romance would become prostitution. We understand that we must allow our desire to haunt us like Indian summer, where the last lavish banquet of golds and yellows and reds stirs our deepest joy and sadness, even as they promise us they will return in the fragrance of spring.

Intrigued by these things and feeling the wind's free play on our face in a way we have almost forgotten, we seriously consider stepping out down the road we have so long feared and avoided. Just then our old lovers reach out for us with a vengeance. They promise us they will fill our heart to overflowing again if we will just give them one more chance. They even promise to become more religious if that will help.

Drawn by the familiar sound of their voices, and still somewhat anxious about the unknown journey ahead of us, we reach
into our briefcase one last time to see if there is any solution to
such double-mindedness. We find these words written by
another traveler who also faced the chasm that has tortured and
perplexed us so deeply. He assures us that even our deep ambivalence is part of the journey of the heart and that only severe mea-
sures by God himself can free us. He exhorts us to pray like this:

> Batter my heart, three personed God; for you
> As yet but knock, breathe, shine and seek to mend.
> That I may rise and stand, o'erthrow me and bend
> Your force, to break, blow, burn and make me new,
> I, like an usurped town, to another due,
> Labor to admit you, but, oh, to no end;
> Reason, your viceroy in me, me should defend;
> But is captive and proves weak or untrue.
>
> Yet dearly I love you and would be loved fain;
> But am betrothed unto your enemy;
> Divorce me, untie or break that knot again,
> Take me to you, imprison me, for I,
> Except you enthrall me, never shall be free,
> Nor ever chaste, except you ravish me.
>   (John Donne, "Batter My Heart")

Partly afraid to pray for such bold movement from the wild
God who loves us, we sit down to reflect on our plight. But this
time, we are honest with ourselves. We admit that Vanity Fair
really never *has* felt like home. We confess that we are truly captured by the less-wild lovers we have taken on, hoping that they
would protect us from the Arrows even as they quenched our
thirst. And we cannot deny, like it or not, that our lives have
always been entwined with the characters in the Sacred
Romance. We have lived under the hail of life's Arrows, some
dragonlike in their ferocity, others—the everyday nits—small
but continually troublesome. The Sacred Romance has touched

us for a moment, but then has gone. It strikes us that we have nothing to lose. We get up and grip our valise for the unknown journey ahead of us. Something makes us search in it for an old scrap of paper. The words scrawled on it always bothered us when we came across them back in Vanity Fair. Now we read them for assurance:

Two roads diverged in a wood, and I-
I took the one less traveled by,
And that has made all the difference.

We strike off down the road feeling much more alive than we have in a while. We are clueless as to how we will cross the abyss, but we feel a gladness to be on our way. Nonetheless, many questions nag at our consciousness as we walk. How are we to understand this journey which so few dare to travel? How are we to bring all of the characters and plots of the Sacred Romance together in our hearts and minds in a way that allows us to be transformed by the Story God is telling? Do we have all we need for the journey? Did we pack carefully enough to travel this more unknown road that is the way of the heart? Perhaps we should return home and get a few more things and a good night's rest before we undertake such a pilgrimage. All these things are on our heart as we begin.

10

On the Road

*But we who would be born again indeed, must wake
our souls unnumbered times a day.*
George MacDonald

EVERY GREAT STORY involves a quest. In J. R. R. Tolkien's *The Hobbit*, Bilbo Baggins ran from the door at a quarter till eleven without even so much as a pocket handkerchief and launched on an adventure that would change his life forever. Alice stepped through the looking glass into Wonderland; Lucy, Edmund, Susan, and Peter stumbled through the wardrobe into Narnia. Abraham left "his country, his people and his father's household" to follow the most outlandish sort of promise from a God he'd only just met, and he never came back. Jacob and his sons went to Egypt for some groceries and four hundred years later the Israel nation pulled up stakes and headed for home. Peter, Andrew, James, and John all turned on a dime one day to follow the Master, their fishing nets heaped in wet piles behind them. The Sacred Romance involves for every soul a journey of heroic proportions. And while it may require for some a change of geography, for every soul it means a journey of the heart.

In *Pilgrim's Progress*, John Bunyan's seventeenth-century allegory of the Sacred Romance, there is a man who comes to see his own story as he has never seen it before, and he is appalled by what he sees. He longs for life, real life, which is to say, eternal life, and he knows that to stay where he is means death. He has no more sense of direction than that he must go and find the path that leads to the Celestial City, his heart's true home. Against the protestations of family and friends, in rejection of all the comforts of his smaller story, he launches on a remarkable adventure: "So I saw in my dream" Bunyan wrote, "that the man began to run." A good place to start. But as Bunyan tells it, "he had not run far from his own door" before the characters in his small story ran to fetch him back, crying out all the threats and excuses they could think of. "But the man put his fingers in his ears, and ran on, crying, 'Life! life! eternal life!'"

This man becomes Pilgrim and the story of his journey is the story of our own. Entering into the Sacred Romance begins with a decision to become a pilgrim of the heart. As Gabriel Marcel reminds us, the soul is a traveler: "It is of the soul and of the soul alone that we can say with supreme truth that 'being' necessarily means 'being on the way' (*en route*)." We are, he says, "*homo viator*," which means "itinerant man," man or woman on pilgrimage. The choice before us now is to journey or to homestead, to live like Abraham the friend of God, or like Robinson Crusoe, the lost soul cobbling together some sort of existence with whatever he can salvage from the wreckage of the world. Crusoe was no pilgrim; he was a survivor, hunkered down for the duration. He lived in a very, very small world where he was the lead character and all else found its focus in him. Of course, to be fair, Crusoe was stranded on an island with little hope of rescue. We *have* been rescued, but still the choice is ours to stay in our small stories, clutching our household gods and false lovers, or to run in search of life.

Eyes for the Romance

We've gone from a creek side in New Jersey to the Cosmic Drama begun before the foundations of the world. We've met the main players in the Sacred Romance and gotten to know something of their true identities, their motives, and their roles in the story. Let's come back now to the daily grind of our own experience to answer the question, "What does all this look like in real life?" How is God wooing us through flat tires, bounced checks, and rained-out picnics? What is he after as we face cancer, sexual struggles, and abandonment? Does knowing that we are his Beloved make any difference at all? Would recognizing Satan's temptations and our less-wild lovers help us to live as freer men and women? What difference does all this make, anyhow?

The short answer is, it gives us *a way of seeing that reveals life for the romantic journey it truly is.*

Entering into the Sacred Romance begins with eyes to see and ears to hear. Where would we be today if Eve had looked at the serpent with different eyes, if she had seen at once that the beautiful creature with the charming voice and the reasonable proposition was in fact a fallen angel bent on the annihilation of the human race? Failure to see things as they truly are resulted in unspeakable tragedy. From that point on, the theme of blindness runs throughout Scripture. It's not merely a matter of failing to recognize temptation when we meet it; like Elisha's servant, we often fail to see the drama of redemption as well. As prophet to Israel, Elisha proved to be a major military liability for the Aramaeans. Every time these enemies of Israel planned an ambush, the man of God spoiled their fun by betraying their position to the otherwise unsuspecting people of God. Furious, the king of Aram decided to take out Israel's "radar" by killing Elisha. He learned where the prophet was holed up and sent an army to surround the city. The drama unfolds through the eyes of Elisha's servant:

> When the servant of the man of God got up and went out early the next morning, an army with horses and chariots had

surrounded the city. "Oh, my lord, what shall we do?" the servant asked.

"Don't be afraid," the prophet answered. "Those who are with us are more than those who are with them."

And Elisha prayed, "O LORD, open his eyes so he may see." Then the LORD opened the servant's eyes, and he looked and saw the hills full of horses and chariots of fire all around Elisha. *(2 Kings 6:15–17)*

Needless tó say, Elisha's servant suddenly saw from a whole different perspective. I (John) think it's safe to assume he also experienced a bit of emotional relief—a recovery of heart. What for him had undoubtedly been a harrowing encounter became an exciting adventure.

The apostle Paul experienced an even greater surprise on the road to Damascus. Thinking he was doing God a favor, he was hell-bent on crushing a tiny religious movement called the Way. But he had the plot and the characters completely confused. Paul, known at that time as Saul, was playing the role of Defender of the Faith, when in fact he was Persecutor of Christ. It took a bout of blindness to bring things into focus, and when the scales fell from his eyes he never saw things the same way again. Paul later explained to the Romans that human sin and suffering are the result of foolish and darkened hearts, brought on by a refusal to see the Sacred Romance. It should come as no surprise that his most fervent prayer for the saints was that the scales would fall from the eyes of our heart so that we might not miss the Sacred Romance (Eph. 1:18–19).

Several years ago I went through one of the most painful trials of my proféssional life. The story involves a colleague whom I will call Dave, a man I hired and with whom I had labored several years in ministry. We spent many hours on the road together, speaking to churches about the Christian life. A point came when I needed to confront Dave about some issues in his life that were hurting his own ministry and the larger purposes of our team. In all fairness, I think I handled it poorly, but I was totally unprepared for what happened next. Dave turned on me with the ferocity of a cornered animal. He fabricated lies and spread rumors in an attempt to destroy my career. His actions were so out of proportion it was hard to believe we were reacting to the same events. He went to the head pastor in an attempt to have me dismissed. The attempt failed, but our friendship was lost and several others were hurt in the process.

In the midst of the crisis, I spoke with Brent one afternoon about the turn of events and the awful pain of betrayal. He said "I wonder what God is up to in all this?"

"God?" I said. "What's *he* got to do with it?" My practical agnosticism was revealed. I was caught up in the sociodrama, the smaller story, completely blind to the true story at that point in my life. Brent's question arrested my attention and brought it to a higher level. In fact, the process of our sanctification, our journey, rests entirely on our ability to see life from the basis of that question. As the poet William Blake warned long ago, "Life's dim window of the soul distorts the heavens from pole to pole, and leads you to believe a lie, when you see with, not through, the eye."

Allow me, then, to review what we have encountered. First, our lives are not a random series of events; they tell a Story that has meaning. We aren't in a movie we've arrived at twenty minutes late; we are in a Sacred Romance. There really is something wonderful that draws our heart; we are being wooed. But there is also something fearful. We face an enemy with vile intentions. Is anyone in charge? Someone strong and kind who notices us? At some point we have all answered that question "no" and gone on to live in a smaller story. But the answer is *"yes"*—there is someone strong and kind who notices us. Our Story is written by God who is more than author, he is the romantic lead in our personal dramas. He created us for himself and now he is moving heaven and earth to restore us to his side. His wooing seems wild because he seeks to free our heart from the attachments and addictions we've chosen, thanks to the Arrows we've known.

And we—who are we, really? We are not pond scum, nor are we the lead in the story. We are the Beloved; our hearts are the most important thing about us and our desire is wild because it is made for a wild God. We are the Beloved, and we are addicted. We've either given our heart to other lovers and can't get out of the relationships, or we've tried our best to kill desire (often with the help of others) and live lives of safe, orderly control. Either way, we play into the hands of the one who hates us. Satan is the mortal enemy of God and therefore ours as well, who comes with offers of less-wild lovers, hoping to deceive us in order to destroy our heart and thus prevent our salvation or cripple our sanctification. These are the stage, the characters, and the plot in the broadest possible terms. Where do we go from here?

Setting Out

We are faced with a decision that grows with urgency each passing day: Will we leave our small stories behind and venture forth to follow our Beloved into the Sacred Romance? The choice to become a pilgrim of the heart can happen any day and we can begin our journey from any place. We are here, the time is now, and the Romance is always unfolding. The choice before us is not to make it happen. As Chesterton said, "An adventure is, by its nature, a thing that comes to us. It is a thing that chooses us, not a thing that we choose." Lucy wasn't looking for Narnia when she found it on the other side of the wardrobe; in a way, it found her. Abraham wasn't wandering about looking for the one true God; he showed up with an extraordinary invitation. But having had their encounters, both could have chosen otherwise. Lucy could have shut the wardrobe door and never mentioned what had happened there. Abraham could have opted for life in Haran. The choice before us is a choice to *enter in*.

So much of the journey forward involves a letting go of all that once brought us life. We turn away from the familiar abiding places of the heart, the false selves we have lived out, the strengths we have used to make a place for ourselves and all our false loves, and we venture forth in our hearts to trace the steps of the One who said, "Follow me." In a way, it means that we stop *pretending*: that life is better than it is, that we are happier than we are, that the false selves we present to the world are really us. We respond to the Haunting, the wooing, the longing for another life. Pilgrim begins his adventure toward redemption with a twofold turning: a turning *away* from attachment and a turning *toward* desire. He wanted life and so he stuck his fingers in his ears and ran like a madman ("a fool," to use Paul's term) in search of it. The freedom of heart needed to journey comes in the form of detachment. As Gerald May writes in *Addiction and Grace*,

> *Detachment* is the word used in spiritual traditions to describe freedom of desire. Not freedom *from* desire, but freedom *of* desire. . . . An authentic spiritual understanding of detachment devalues neither desire nor the objects of desire. Instead, it "aims at correcting one's own anxious grasping in order to free oneself for committed relationship to God." According to Meister Eckhart, detachment "enkindles the heart, awakens the spirit, stimulates our longings, and shows us where God is."

With an awakened heart, we turn and face the road ahead, knowing that no one can take the trip for us, nor can anyone plan our way. When he sets out, Bunyan's Pilgrim has no map, no itinerary, no step-by-step travelogue with each day's adventure carefully planned out. All he has is his desire and a general idea that the way of life lies somewhere along the road ahead. As the poet Wallace Stevens wrote, "The way through the world is more difficult to find than the way beyond it." So many of the programs of modern Christianity with three steps to this and seven steps to that and a principle for everything are in fact an effort not to journey at all. More often than not, they are pursued with a desire to hunker down and make life work, here, now. The Sacred Romance is not something to be managed, but to be lived. We cannot remove the element of mystery from the road before us nor can we eliminate the dangers. But we can learn from pilgrims who have gone before something of the road conditions, the weather, the hazards, and the places of rest and refreshment.

On the Road: Dragons and Nits

Life, said Woody Allen, is divided between the horrible and the miserable. A cynical assessment, perhaps, but if we're honest we'll have to admit our journey is hardly along the primrose path. Pretending that life is easier and more blessed than it really is hinders our ability to walk with God and share him with others. Faith is not the same thing as denial. Blessings come, to be sure. But they tend to be infrequent, unpredictable, and transient. In the day-to-day pattern of things, our journey is shaped more often by *dragons* and *nits*—crises that shake us to the core and persistent troubles that threaten to nag us to death. Dragons and nits: Are they tragic events and random inconveniences, or are they part of the plot through which God redeems our heart in very personal ways?

Mary is a good friend of mine who lost her permanent front teeth through an accident in early adolescence. Years later, she struggled to finally resolve the issue with dental caps. What should have been a simple procedure took weeks, then months. Appointment after appointment, the caps were either the wrong color, the wrong shape, or the wrong size. When she finally did get a pair that she could live with, the glue didn't hold. Where was the Sacred Romance in such a mundane and yet withering struggle? Why didn't God ride in as hero and provide a beautiful set of caps? Wouldn't that have been the loving thing to do? As the ordeal continued, a major issue of her heart surfaced. Mary's teeth had long been for her a symbol of her struggle with the question of her inner beauty. Her teeth were a source of shameful arrows lodged deep. A seemingly irrelevant nit that God refused to take away became an opportunity to face a fundamental question the heart of every woman asks: Am I lovely? Without the nit, the deeper issue of her heart would never have come up. Once it did, the real battle began.

The Accuser stepped in with a subtle, deadly stream of thoughts: "Look, just settle for the wrong caps and get on with your life. Your desire for beauty is nothing more than vanity. Things will never change. God doesn't care for your heart or he would have taken care of your teeth." And finally, "This is who you really are: unlovely and unlovable."

Each time Mary looked in the mirror, these sentences urged her to lose heart. Some days, the crisis felt as if it would crush her spirit; on other days, she just felt dumb. Meanwhile, Mary's false lovers took their cue and began offering to help her deal with the pain. Food promised to take away her heartache; busyness lured her to bury it beneath a deluge of Christian service. Even the faith practiced by the charismatic church she attends offered to lift her beyond the struggle if she would only focus on the Lord and worship more frequently.

Thankfully, her True Love was persistent in his pursuit of her heart, refusing to let her take the easy way out. The question of her inner beauty broke to the surface one day, and, fortunately, a friend with eyes for the Romance was there to help her see what was at stake. Once Mary finally turned and faced the core issue, God was able to speak words of loving reassurance: "You are lovely, Mary, and I want you to offer your inner beauty, your womanly heart to the world." Through a seemingly insignificant and unspiritual issue like dental caps, God spoke healing to Mary's heart and invited her up into the Sacred Romance.

If we'll take time to reflect, the nits of our lives and the way we typically respond to them both have a *theme*, a pattern that reveals something important about our heart, something God is after. Mary's theme was the suppression of her beauty under "more spiritual distractions." Satan tempts us toward cynicism, resignation, and an offer of a safer or even a more exciting life if we will simply renounce our True Love and follow him.

The dragons are far more dramatic. The doctor announces he's found a lump; your spouse announces she is no longer in love with you. They are dragons because they strike at the core of our deepest fears. This is the dark night of the soul, when we face the implications of Job's question: *God could stop this. Why doesn't he?* Satan leaps in with a reaffirmation of the first temptation: "God isn't really your kind advocate after all." We're faced with a choice to fall back, clutch up, seize control, or enter more deeply into our lives and our beliefs and release more thoroughly to the love of God.

The Sentences We Live By

I'll never have the love I want. The sentence rose up from some deep place within me as I lay in bed one morning, looking for a reason to get up. My wife, Stasi, and I had been going through one of the hardest times we'd ever encountered in our marriage. Some days we both wondered if we would even make it; other days we wondered if we even wanted to. The wounds were too deep, the barriers too high; it just didn't seem worth the effort. Divorce seemed like a perfectly reasonable way out.

Beneath the anger and the disappointment lurked a far more defining issue of my heart. Years ago, when my father checked out of my life into alcoholism, an Arrow lodged deep within: *You are on your own.* In order to control that Arrow I made a resolution in my heart: *I won't need anyone, not deeply. I can make it without love.* But as the years rolled by, my heart refused to live in my self-created isolation. I looked for someone to fill the void in my life left by my father. I chose Stasi as the lucky girl. Beneath the stated marriage vows of "for better or for worse," what I was really saying was, "Stasi, I'm going to give you the opportunity of a lifetime. No one has ever really loved me the way I so desperately want to be loved, but I'm going to give you that chance. It lies in your power to validate my soul."

The pressure is more than any human being can bear. Even if she were a perfect woman, Stasi could never come through. But like all of us, she came into marriage with a set of demons all her own. Though she didn't face something as awful as alcoholism, her struggles seemed to me a terrible repeat of my father's because I felt the effect to be the same: I felt alone. Smelling blood, Satan closed in like a shark with suggestions like, "You don't have to put up with this, you know. There are options, other women. Besides, things will never change with Stasi." I turned to my false loves, losing myself in my career and spending my free time escaping through fly-fishing. I prayed that God would simply take away the trials in our marriage, but he didn't. I tried to live beyond my longing to be loved, but I couldn't. The stakes were incredibly high: a loss of heart, of our marriage, and the perpetuation of the family curse onto our boys.

There, in the wee hours of the morning, when our heart has the chance to catch us with its most honest thoughts, the sentence rose from the depths of my soul: *I'll never have the love I want.* The aching wound from years before was present to me again. And there God was able to begin to waken me to the Romance. Browsing through Scripture I read 1 John 4:7, a simple sentence, one I had probably read a thousand times before: "Love comes from God." It brought more hope than I had ever known. It spoke to the wound because the wound was awakened and I was ready to hear. As the weeks progressed, I embraced my longing to be loved and turned the validation of my soul over to my Father in heaven. Sometime later, while on a business flight to the West Coast, I was thinking about love and those words from 1 John. A new sentence arose in my heart: *I have the love I wanted all my life.*

Both dragons and nits take us into the deep places of the soul, uncovering the sentences we have long lived by. It was in the depths of his personal tragedies that Job uttered the ruling sentence of his heart: "What I feared has come upon me" (3:25). In other words, "I knew it! I knew I couldn't really trust God—not with the things that matter most." Job's idol was control and God was determined to save him from it. When the nits and dragons come, we ask God to remove them and when he doesn't, we take charge of our own well-being since it appears no one else will. The dragons and nits reveal to us (and to our community) where our attachments and addictions lie. In other words, they reveal where our heart is, other than captured by the love of God.

But there is more. Life on the road takes us into our heart, for *only when we are present in the deep sentences can God speak to them.* That's why the story is a journey; it has to be lived, it cannot simply be talked about. When we face trials, our most common reaction is to ask God, "Why won't you relieve us?" And when he doesn't, we resignedly ask, "What do you want me to do?" Now we have a new question: "Where is the Romance headed?"

There is another great "revealing" in our life on the road. We run our race, we travel our journey, in the words of Hebrews, before "a great cloud of witnesses" (12:1). When we face a decision to fall back or press on, the whole universe holds its breath—angels, demons, our friends and foes, and the Trinity itself—watching with bated breath to see what we will do. We are still in the drama of Act III and the heart of God is still on trial. The question that lingers from the fall of Satan and the fall of man remains: Will anyone trust the great heart of the Father, or will we shrink back in faithless fear?

As we grow into the love of God and the freedom of our own hearts, we grow in our ability to cast our vote on behalf of God. Our acts of love and sacrifice, the little decisions to leave our false loves behind and the great struggles of our heart reveal to the world our true identity: We really are the sons and daughters of God.

What to Bring Along

In her essay *An Expedition to the Pole*, Annie Dillard describes the provision carried along by nineteenth-century explorers in their search for the North Pole:

> Each sailing vessel carried an auxiliary steam engine and a twelve-day supply of coal for the entire projected two or three years' voyage. Instead of additional coal . . . each ship made room for a 1,200-volume library, "a hand-organ playing fifty tunes," china place settings for officers and men, cut-glass wine goblets, and sterling silver flatware. . . . The expedition carried no special clothing for the Arctic, only the uniforms of Her Majesty's Navy.

Years later, Inuit eskimos came across frozen remains of the expedition, men dressed in their finery and pulling a lifeboat laden with place settings of sterling silver and some chocolate. Their naïveté is almost beyond comprehension, but perhaps it will motivate us to be better outfitted for our own journey. What does one take on an expedition of the heart? What do we need to be prepared for?

Our journey begins with desire, "not for a raise," says poet David Whyte, "but for another life." Desire sets us on our way, yet what will keep desire alive? Enemies of desire lurk all along the way—fear, self-contempt, disappointment—these and a hundred other demons of the road are enough to extinguish the flame of the heart. Hamlet, that famous Prince of Denmark, gave poetic expression to the dilemma we all face: Why press on when there is little to look forward to?

> Who would fardels [burdens] bear,
> To grunt and sweat under a weary life,
> But that the dread of something after death,
> The undiscovered country, from whose bourn
> No traveller returns, puzzles the will,
> And makes us rather bear those ills we have
> Than fly to others that we know not of?
> (*Act III, Scene I*)

In other words, it's better to stay in the safety of the camp than venture forth on a wing and a prayer. Who knows what dangers lie ahead? This was the counsel of the ten faithless spies sent in to have a look at the Promised Land when the Jews came out of Egypt. Only two of the twelve, Joshua and Caleb, saw things differently. Their hearts were captured by a vision of what might be and they urged the people to press on. But their voices were drowned by the fears of the other ten spies and Israel wandered for another forty years. Without the anticipation of better things ahead, we will have no heart for the journey.

One of the most poisonous of all Satan's whispers is simply, "Things will never change." That lie kills expectation, trapping our heart forever in the present. To keep desire alive and flourishing, we must renew our vision for what lies ahead. Things will not always be like this. Jesus has promised to "make all things new." Eye has not seen, ear has not heard all that God has in store for his lovers, which does not mean "we have no clue so don't even try to imagine," but rather, *you cannot outdream God*. Desire is kept alive by imagination, the antidote to resignation. We will need imagination, which is to say, we will need *hope*. I will say more about this in Chapter 12.

Well into his journey toward the Celestial City, Pilgrim

grows impatient with his progress. He leaves the narrow path for what he believes will be a shortcut, but is captured by the Giant Despair and held in the dungeon of Doubting Castle. Under the harsh treatment of Despair, Christian loses heart nearly to the point of taking his own life.

Julia Gatta describes impatience, discouragement, and despair as the "noonday demons" most apt to beset the seasoned traveler. As the road grows long we grow weary; impatience and discouragement tempt us to forsake the way for some easier path. These shortcuts never work, and the guilt we feel for having chosen them only compounds our feelings of despair. What is a pilgrim to do? Listen in on the whispers of Pilgrim and his companion, Hopeful, in their dungeon:

> Pilgrim: Brother, what shall we do? The life we now live is miserable. For my part I know not whether it is best to live, or to die.

> Hopeful: My brother, remember how valiant thou hast been heretofore? Apollyon could not crush thee, nor could all that thou didst hear, or see, or feel, in the Valley of the Shadow of Death. What hardship, terror and amazement hast thou already gone through. . . . remember how thou playedst the man at Vanity Fair, and was neither afraid of the chain, nor cage, nor yet of bloody death? . . .

> Now a little before it was day, good Christian, as one half amazed, broke out in this passionate speech: What a fool am I, to lie in a stinking dungeon when I may as well walk with liberty. I have a key in my bosom called Promise, that will open any lock in Doubting Castle.

Pilgrim lay in despair because he had forgotten. Hopeful urges him to *remember*, both all he had been through as well as the assurances he has from the One who called him on the journey. Life on the road requires recollection of our Love's past deeds on our behalf and his promise of continued faithfulness to us. We will need courage and patience and those are strengthened by remembering. We will need memory, which is to say, we will need *faith*.

Faith looks back and draws courage; hope looks ahead and keeps desire alive. And meantime? In the meantime we need one more item for our journey. To appreciate what it may be, we have to step back and ask, what is all this for? The resurrection of our heart, the discovery of our role in the Larger Story, entering into the Sacred Romance—why do we pursue these things? If we say we seek all of this for our own sake, we're right back where we started: lost in our own story. Jesus said that when a person lives merely to preserve his life, he eventually loses it altogether. Rather, he said, give your life away and discover life as it was always meant to be. "Self-help is no help at all. Self-sacrifice is the way, my way, to finding yourself, your true self" (Matt. 16:25, *The Message*). Self-preservation, the theme of every small story, is so deeply wrong because it violates the Trinity, whose members live to bring glory *to the others*. The road we travel will take us into the battle to restore beauty in all things, chief among them the hearts of those we know. We grow in glory so that we might assist others in doing so; we give our glory to increase theirs. In order to fulfill the purpose of our journey, we will need a passion to increase glory; we will need *love*.

Memory, imagination, and a passion for glory—these we must keep close at hand if we are to see the journey to its end. Dragons and nits and the noonday demons lie in wait. But the road is not entirely rough. There are oases along the way. It would be a dreadful mistake to assume that our Beloved is only waiting for us at the end of the road. Our communion with him sustains us along our path.

11

Desert Communion: Learning to Live on Heaven's Shores

Our nature makes us wish for rest, that is to say, an increase in being.

St. Augustine

WE'VE BEEN FOLLOWING the story line of the Sacred Romance for ten chapters since I (Brent) first posed the question in Chapter 1, "What is it that I am supposed to *do* as a Christian for the rest of my life?" Hopefully that question begins to dim for you as it does for me as the story line of the Sacred Romance begins to grip us. It is awesome to think that we are truly God's Beloved, the Bride he is preparing to reveal in all her beauty before the courts of heaven. It is joyous to consider that in his exotic goodness, he is even using the dragons and nits to free us into our true identities as sons and daughters of God, and collectively as the bride of Christ. We are indeed his Betrothed and have already received the first seal of his love in his Spirit that dwells in us.

Every courtship, at least every healthy one, is moving toward a deeper heart intimacy that is the ground for the consummation of the relationship spiritually, emotionally, and physically. The first question in the orthodox confessions of faith tests our awareness of this wonderful truth when it asks, "What is the chief end and purpose of man?" And the answer: "To know God and enjoy knowing him forever."

If we hear that answer as creatures of the Enlightenment, that is to say, the Age of Reason, the answer does not take our breath away. The word *know* has been captured in service of the intellect and so when we think of knowing God, images of learning more about him immediately come to mind. With a sigh, we consider what book we might buy or what Bible study we might attend to understand more clearly God's attributes. But what if we were sitting in a sidewalk café overhearing the following exchange between a fiancée and her betrothed?

She: "I'm so looking forward to our wedding day. I do love you so much. I really wish I could see more of you. There's so much about you I want to know better."

He: "Yes, dear, I know. I'm going to send you a book that describes more about my life. I'm sure you'll get a lot out of it."

She: "I'll be glad to read it. But I just want to hold your hand. [She continues somewhat mischievously.] I just want to kiss you."

He: "I'm sure you do, beloved. Let me send you a tape describing the role of physical affection at different stages of courtship. You'll find it worthwhile, I'm sure."

She: (Somewhat disappointed) "That's wonderful, darling. It's just that I so look forward to our wedding day. I want to be with you so badly. I think of us being, you know, 'together,' day and night."

He: "Yes, intimacy is important. I'd like to send you to a weekend seminar that really should be quite helpful."

About this time, most of us would say, "What a stiff. This guy doesn't have a clue how to love this woman. Why doesn't she dump him for somebody who's still breathing?" Yet, this is very much the way we often carry on our love affair with God. We picture him as being much like the man in the café, and so we sigh, try to push down our disappointment, and go on being good Christians. But listen with me to excerpts from another conversation between two lovers:

Lover: "How beautiful you are, my darling! Oh, how beautiful! Your eyes are doves."

Beloved: "How handsome you are, my lover! Oh, how charming! And our bed is verdant."

Lover: "Show me your face, let me hear your voice; for your voice is sweet, and your face is lovely. . . . Your mouth is like the best wine."

Beloved: "May the wine go straight to my lover, flowing gently over lips and teeth. I belong to my lover, and [your] desire is for me. Come, my lover, let us go to the countryside, let us spend the night in the villages. . . ."

Is this not a conversation that truly does begin to take our breath away? Do we not find ourselves wanting to follow these lovers to the country just to be close to such passion? This is not a conversation from the latest dime-store romance but from the Song of Solomon. God does not give us this look through the bedroom window at the love affair between Solomon and the Queen of Sheba just to be voyeuristic. As we turn from the window and look into his eyes, we realize that this is the kind of passion he feels for us and desires from us in return—an intimacy much more sensuous, much more exotic than sex itself.

Many of us would run to meet God in such a way if we only knew where to find him. But where . . . how is he to be found with this kind of intimacy? And, too, we don't go from being strangers to lovers in an instant. There are the conversations between a father and son or daughter to be held first, and the platonic intimacy of good friends. Some of us have had our hearts seared by the tainted desire of those who should have loved us platonically but rather used our desire for love to violate us emotionally and sexually. Our hearts shrink back from such imagery, as they will until we have received healing. Yet, the intimacy represented by married love is what God desires with each of us and so the imagery of courtship is what we must consider.

When we first think of being in a relationship with God, we probably picture him as somewhat flashy, even as many of us tried to be (at least us guys) when we were dating. He gave Jacob visions of angels descending and ascending to heaven; he parted the Red Sea for Moses and made the sun stand still for a day so the Israelites could win a battle. He definitely makes an impression. But you kind of wonder what he's like when you're alone with him. Would he just stay the life of the party, still playing to the crowd?

Two images from the Scriptures show us a very different side of God. In Revelation 2:17, John tells us that when we get to heaven, God will give us a white stone with a name on it that only he knows; the kind of name one lover calls another in private because it reveals something very personal about their relationship. A second picture of the way God desires to commune with us is found in 1 Kings 19 where we find the prophet Elijah worn out and afraid, fleeing from Jezebel. She has been trying to kill him ever since he did the same to her prophets. God tenderly ministers to Elijah, twice bringing him food and water. Elijah, strengthened, travels forty days and forty nights until he reaches Mt. Horeb, where he goes to sleep in a cave. The Lord wakes him and listens to his lament about what it is like to be God's prophet. Elijah is worn out from "doing" and badly in need of restoration of spirit. A great wind strikes the mountain, followed by an earthquake and a fire. And God is in none of these. Finally, Elijah hears a "gentle whisper." And it is in the gentle whisper that he finds God.

And so it is with us. God is not "out there somewhere" in some dramatic way, waiting to commune with us by earthquake or fire or signs in the sky. Instead, he desires to talk with us in the quietness of our own heart through his Spirit, who is in us.

It is his voice that has whispered to us about a Sacred Romance. What do you hear when you listen for that gentle, quiet voice?

What I so often hear, or feel, is a restlessness, a distractedness where it seems that dozens if not hundreds of disconnected or scattered thoughts vie for my attention. Bits and pieces of my smaller story, and sometimes major edifices, flash onto the screen: what other people think of me and what I need to do to win them. Anger, ego, lust, and simply blankness of spirit all take turns occupying my heart.

Indeed, when I first listen to my heart, what I often hear is the language and clatter of my old "lovers" and not much else. There seems to be no stillness or rest. If I try to hold still, my soul reacts like a feather in the afternoon breeze, flitting from place to place without purpose or direction. I almost seem invisible in the noise or blankness. Theologians refer to this condition as "ontological lightness," the reality that when I stop "doing" and simply listen to my heart, I am not anchored to anything substantive. I become aware that my very identity is synonymous with activity.

Many of us sense that this is true in our vocation, our religion, and even our recreation. When we are trying to get to know who people are, we typically ask what they do. I am a counselor. You are a businessman. It is how we tend to think of ourselves. In the religious arena, the question may take the form of what we believe. Ann Jones believes in consubstantiation, so she is a Lutheran. You believe in five-point Calvinism, so you are a Presbyterian. John Smith believes in fellowship suppers and informal worship services, so he is an evangelical.

Our whole American culture is infected with ontological lightness, celebrities and pro athletes being the most dramatic examples of this victimization of our souls that ruins us for any substantive love relationship. They are anchored only to their performances and out of their performances come their identities—and ours who worship them. As soon as they stop performing, their identities—and ours—disappear.

As men, if we have not anesthetized ourselves and become invisible by choice, we try to anchor ourselves to some form of competence. David Letterman, in a recent interview, basically said that his sense of himself was only grounded in the twenty-four-hour period between shows. If the last show was good, he felt good about himself. If the audience didn't respond, he felt horrible. Women in our culture, feminism notwithstanding, often try to ground themselves in being valued for their external beauty. Marilyn Monroe went to nightclubs disguised in a black wig long after she was famous to see if she could still attract a man as Norma Jean. She felt the emptiness as soon as she was no longer being flirted with, even after clearly establishing her identity as the world's most beautiful woman. And the emptiness consumed her in the end.

As Christians, we often feel the ungrounded restlessness of our ontological lightness even in our prayers. We find ourselves praying for God to "do" this, or for him to help us "do" that. Our prayers seem to originate from somewhere near the surface of our skin rather than any deep place inside. We go away feeling that we have not communed, that we have not put down our burdens, and indeed, we haven't.

Sinning is also a way of anchoring ourselves in a small romance that will give us a moment's satisfaction without losing control of the Arrows. Often when we are talking about a person who has lived a sinful life, we say what a "shell" she has become, ruefully pointing out that she has lost what once made her substantively human. C. S. Lewis, once again, captures the final condition of those who have never found themselves in his novel *The Great Divorce.* When the busload of citizens from hell go to the outskirts of heaven and step out of the bus, heaven's grass is so substantive that it hurts their feet to walk on it. They have become shadowy wraiths who are forced to expend tremendous amounts of energy just to take a step across heaven's meadows. Most of them return to the bus, preferring the "comfort" of hell.

We, too, experience the spiritual life not as a love affair, but as burdensome, heavy, exhausting and alien in our condition of ontological lightness. Jesus calls to us as his loved ones and says: "Come to me, all you who are weary and burdened, and I will give you rest. Take my yoke upon you and learn from me, for I am gentle and humble in heart, and you will find rest for your souls. For my yoke is easy and my burden is light" (Matt. 11:28–30).

And I find myself answering, "I don't know how to rest in you, Jesus. When I try to reach out for you, all I see are the outstretched arms of my old lovers waving, demanding, and enticing me back to them. All I can hear is the clatter of their voices. Where are you in all of this confusion?"

Two years ago, worn out by three years of spiritual battle, I found myself asking the question this way: "Jesus, if your Spirit abides in me in the person of the Holy Spirit, who is my Comforter, why do I so often feel alone and you seem so far away?" What came to me in response were Jesus' words in John 15:5, "I am the vine; you are the branches. If a man remains in me and I in him, he will bear much fruit; apart from me you can do nothing." Jesus was saying, "Living spiritually requires something more than just not sinning or doing good works. In order to live in the kingdom of heaven, you must abide in me. Your identity is in me."

If I'm not abiding in Jesus, then where is it that I abide? I asked myself.

I began to notice that when I was tired or anxious, there were certain sentences I would say in my head that led me to a very familiar place. The journey to this place would often start with me walking around disturbed, feeling as if there was something deep inside that I needed to put into words but couldn't quite capture. I felt the "something" as an anxiety, a loneliness, and a need for connection with someone. If no connection came, I would start to say things like "Life really stinks. Why is it always so hard? It's never going to change." If no one noticed that I was struggling and asked me what was wrong, I found my sentences shifting again to a more cynical level: "Who cares? Life is really a joke." Surprisingly, I noticed by the time I was saying those last sentences, I was feeling better. The anxiety was greatly diminished.

My "comforter," my abiding place, was cynicism and rebellion. From this abiding place, I would feel free to use some soul cocaine—a violence video with maybe a little sexual titillation thrown in, perhaps having a little more alcohol with a meal than I might normally drink—things that would allow me to feel better for just a little while. I had always thought of these things as just bad habits. I began to see that they were much more; they were spiritual abiding places that were my comforters and friends in a very spiritual way; literally, other lovers.

The final light went on one evening when I read John 15 in *The Message*. Peterson translates Jesus' words on abiding this way: "If you make yourselves at home with me and my words are at home in you, you can be sure that whatever you ask will be listened to and acted upon." Jesus was saying in answer to my question, "I have made my home in you, Brent. But you still have other comforters you go to. You must learn to make your home in me." I realized that my identity had something to do with simply "staying at home."

It also dawned on me that holiness, surprisingly, also comes not out of doing but out of staying at home, with who and where we are and with who and where God is in us. Indeed, we will only have the courage to leave home and continue to live as pilgrims out on the road if we have some sense that our true home abides within us in the Spirit of Christ and that we can do the same with him. And in the meantime, out of this abiding,

Jesus transforms us. Our identity begins to coalesce, not out of doing, but out of living with a good friend for a number of years and simply finding we have become more like him.

I began to see that there was a different heart journey that I had to take to learn to abide in Christ. It is the journey George MacDonald describes in his poem that I quoted in Chapter 9:

> Tis hard for (us) to rouse (our) spirits up—
> It is the human creative agony
> Though but to hold the heart an empty cup
> Or tighten on the team the rigid rein
> Many will rather lie among the slain
> Than creep through narrow ways the light to gain—
> Than wake the will, and be born bitterly.
> (*Diary of an Old Soul*)

By going to my abiding place of cynicism and rebellion, I was filling my heart cup with something that made the emptiness go away for a moment. I was "lying among the slain" rather than creeping out onto the unknown narrow path that leads to abiding in the comfort of Jesus. I began to reject the cynical thoughts when they came to comfort me and replace them with words of faith: "Jesus, I don't know how to heal myself of this anxiety. I don't even clearly understand it. But I will not anesthetize it with other lovers. I cling to you and trust in your healing."

At times, I experienced a different kind of peace. At other times, Jesus would bring certain of his words to mind: "I know the plans I have for you," he says in Jeremiah 29:11, "plans to prosper you and not to harm you, plans to give you hope and a future." Rather than indulge in my less-wild lovers, I began at times to tighten on the team the rigid rein and simply stand (rest) in faith. Spiritual warfare began to intensify as the adversary saw me not agreeing with him that life was hopeless and thus threatening to take away his footholds (perhaps strongholds) in my heart.

Besides these false comforters that we abide in, there are also the less-wild lovers I spoke of in Chapter 9 that are intertwined with our heart because they give us an identity. Whether it be accumulating great wealth, being seen as profound due to our knowledge and cleverness of speech, being physically attractive, or any of the hundreds of other small stories we have learned to abide in, we live in fear that we will sooner or later be exposed and our identities will be stripped from us. We redouble our efforts at "doing" to prevent this calamity, and again, in our ontological lightness, our lack of being anchored in anything substantive, we experience the spiritual life as burdensome and exhausting. We are unable to walk the meadows of the spiritual life.

We all want to be someone's hero or someone's beauty, to be in a relationship of heroic proportions. Contrary to legalistic forms of self-denial, we need to feel free to admit this without embarrassment. It is a core longing God himself placed within us and a deep part of our identity as men and women. It is in how we go about being heroes and beauties that is the issue. For each of us, the enemy has convinced us that we need our less-wild lovers and smaller stories to have an identity, indeed to even survive. Once we start depending on them for life, he sabotages our smaller stories so that we are exposed in our ontological lightness. Then he mocks us for our foolishness. He literally runs us into the ground with envy, anxiety, shame, discouragement, renewed efforts to rewrite our small stories so they work, and finally, depression and despair. Many of us are spiritually and emotionally ill from the process I've just described. What theo-logians have called "ontological lightness," Freud referred to as "hysteria." We are more familiar with it being called "neurosis." Jesus simply calls it the symptoms of our adultery.

"Come to me, all you who are weary and burdened, and *I* will give you rest," says Jesus. Most of us think of spiritual progress as requiring us to do more, even as our heart cries out to us to lay our burdens down. We renew our efforts at Bible study, Scripture memory, and Christian service, fearing that we will be discovered in our weakness and need. We try to use whatever small story we have been living in—competence, gifted speaking, service to others, and so on—to cross the chasm between living in the flesh and living spiritually, when only Christ can carry us to rest. The kinds of "doing" we have learned are not weighty enough to allow us to walk in the spiritual fields of the kingdom of God.

God speaks to Israel through the prophet Isaiah when she is surrounded by enemies and making every effort to appease them through diplomacy, gifts, treaties, and bribes, and says this to her:

> "You went to Molech with olive oil
> and increased your perfumes.
> You sent your ambassadors far away;
> you descended to the grave itself!
> You were wearied by all your ways,
> but you would not say, 'It is hopeless.'
> You found renewal of your strength,
> and so you did not faint" *(Isa. 57:9–10).*

God calls Israel to repent by admitting her weariness and fainting. Instead, she looks for ways to use her personal assets to redeem herself. Jesus spoke to the people about rest and thirst. The Pharisees demanded that they obey a constantly growing weight of religious laws and traditions, and chastised them for staggering under the load. They led people in the exact opposite direction from where their salvation lay—in admitting their weariness and fainting. As long as they hoped in their self-sufficiency, they would not call out to God and receive forgiveness, healing, and restoration.

So many of our contemporary churches operate on this same system of guilt. When our people are crying out for communion and rest, we ask them to teach another Sunday school class. When they falter under the load, we admonish them with Scriptures on serving others. One wonders what would happen if all activity motivated by this type of guilt were to cease for six months. Much of organized Christianity would collapse even as the Pharisees saw happen to their own religious system. As Jesus talked about thirst and rest, he brought people to the reality of their own heart.

It is impossible to live the spiritual life in the ontological lightness of doing because our hearts and minds become enemies rather than allies. Neither are we free to love or serve. The problem is not that people are not important enough to us. It is that they are *too* important—we need their approval too much in our ontologically light condition of living in our smaller stories.

God desires to use even the dragons and nits to reveal our true identities in all of our ontological density. God comes to the Israelites in Exodus 23:29–30 and tells them that he will not drive their enemies from the land in a day because they are not substantive enough to hold the land and it would become desolate and overrun with wild animals. He tells them that he will drive out their enemies as they become able to hold it. They must learn to rest in him. It is from the place of abiding in him that they will be able to hold on to what is theirs. James tells us in the introductory thoughts to his letter that we should count it all joy when we fall into various trials because God will use them to make us substantive. He tells us that this will happen as we learn to trust totally in God rather than halfway counting on our own devices with God as a fallback (being double-minded).

When we hear the phrase "trust totally in God," most of us probably sigh, hearing it as one more requirement that we have never been able to live up to. But what if we were to listen to our hearts, and hear it as a need to faint, a need to lay down our "doings" and simply make our needs known to Christ, and rest in him?

The Desert Tradition

How do we go about actually "doing" rest?

When Jesus was preparing for his public ministry, as well as his battle with Satan, he went to the desert—away from the synagogue, away from people, away from family and friends. Matthew tells us that God's Spirit led Jesus into the desert to be tempted by the devil. He prepared for spiritual battle by separating himself from all dependency on the provisions of this world, starting with the most basic: food. He fasted for forty days. He abided in prayer, in communion with his Father in heaven. When Satan came to test him with the things of this world, he answered him not with intellectual argument, but rested in the truth of Scripture. And when he had resisted the devil by abiding in the Spirit, angels came and ministered to him.

There is a place on each of our spiritual journeys where the Spirit also desires to lead us into the desert. We hear him calling to us in the restlessness and weariness of our own heart. The first time the Spirit speaks to us, we don't know it is him. We assume we are just not doing enough to be spiritual, and so we renew our religious efforts instead of fainting. Sometimes, like Samuel when God spoke to him in the night, we go through this process two or three times before we realize it is God speaking to us in our heart and follow him into the desert.

The desert tradition begun by Jesus was continued in the third and fourth centuries by a group of men and women known as "the Desert Fathers." They lived in caves and simple dwellings in the deserts south of Israel and committed themselves to prayer, solitude, and silence along with a separation from the provisions of this world. "Society," says Thomas Merton in *The Wisdom of the Desert*, "was regarded [by the Desert Fathers] as a shipwreck from which each single individual had to swim for his life. . . . These were men who believed that to let oneself drift along, passively accepting the tenets and values of what they knew as society, was purely and simply a disaster." Adds Henri Nouwen, in *The Way of the Heart*, "Without solitude, we remain acolytes of our society and continue to be entangled in the illusions of the false self."

In order to learn who we really are, we must have a place in our lives where we are removed from the materialism, entertainment, diversion, and busyness that the Vanity Fair of our society and culture immerse us in. The things sold at the booths in the Fair are tranquilizers that separate us, and protect us, from the emptiness and need of our heart. As we leave these less-wild lovers behind and enter into solitude and silence in our own desert place, the first thing we encounter is not rest, but fear, and a compulsion to return to activity. In *The Ascent to Truth*, Thomas Merton says,

> We look for rest and if we find it, it becomes intolerable. Incapable of the divine activity which alone can satisfy [rest] . . . fallen man flings himself upon exterior things, not so much for their own sake as for the sake of agitation which keeps his spirit pleasantly numb . . . [The distraction] diverts us aside from the one thing that can help us to begin our ascent to truth . . . the sense of our own emptiness.

"In the middle of the road of my life," says Dante, "I awoke in a dark wood." Our emptiness is often the first thing we find when we face honestly the story going on in our heart. It is the desert's gift to us. George MacDonald encourages us to embrace it as a friend by "leaving the heart an empty cup," and proceeding. But what do we do with our emptiness if we stay with our heart? If we try to pray, our minds fill with busy, disconnected petitions that start with the words, "God, help me to do this or that better, have more faith, read the Bible more." The busy petitions of our minds seem to leave something inside our chest cavity unexpressed, something that is trying to tell us about the way things are.

"Our mind is busy with oughts," says Nouwen in *The Way*

of the Heart, while "the heart instructs us on what is. The renewing of our mind takes place through our hearts." He quotes Theophan, the recluse, who says, "To pray is to descend with the mind into the heart, and there to stand before the face of the Lord, ever present, all-seeing, within you." If we allow our mind simply to listen, we perhaps begin to hear our heart speak—faintly, beneath the clatter. It says, "I am so weary, so lost. I have no energy to redeem myself. How I long for rest."

Our mind hears these words and realizes it is of no use to ask God to give us energy to make our way back up the cliff over which we have fallen. We need the Good Shepherd to come and get us. If we allow our heart to give our mind the words to pray, we say, "Jesus, help me. All my lovers have failed me. Forgive me. I cannot quench my thirst. Give me the water of life."

Not long ago, I was preparing one of my lectures for the Sacred Romance series that John and I were presenting in Colorado Springs. John's talk the week before had deeply touched people with the understanding of God's grace and love for them. A friend came by the table where I was sitting in our neighborhood bagel shop and kiddingly remarked, "My husband says his life was changed after last week's talk, so you better come up with something good."

Part of my smaller story has been to use my gifts as a teacher and thinker to win people's admiration—to be someone's hero. At the thought that perhaps I might be the second-best speaker in this series, I was overcome with waves of shame, a feeling of being exposed. The adversary was quickly there with reminders of past failures and the resulting pain. For a minute, I considered redoubling my efforts to come up with a good talk that week—to look up new quotes, find a really good movie clip to illustrate my points.

But this particular time, I simply listened to what my heart was telling me. It spoke to me about weariness and the fear of being found lacking; of having nothing that would make me anyone's hero. I left the bagel shop and drove to the open space that surrounds our neighborhood. I got out and began walking, feeling deeply agitated and dejected over being trapped in such a foolish place. Anyone who has ever had the thing you depended on for life threatened will know what I am describing. I had no energy to think up prayers or even any sense of what to pray for. I began to repeat a simple sentence in my head, "Jesus, you are faithful to cleanse me from all my sins." I did not try to exegete it or convince myself to believe it. I simply let it linger and resonate between my head and heart for whatever Jesus chose to do with it. After not many minutes, I felt something begin to break up deep down inside, a feeling of loneliness and longing acknowledged. There was a release that brought tears. I sensed that Jesus was ministering to me in a quiet and tender way, in a place years distant and much deeper in my spirit than just feelings provoked by the events of that particular morning. A sensation of freedom and well-being rose up from the very place inside that moments ago had felt such agitation.

Bringing what was happening back up into my head in order to put words to it, I can only say it was as if Jesus were telling me, "I understand your ache, Brent. I know how you've wanted to be someone's hero. It's okay. Rest in my love." There were no words of admonishment or exhortations to try harder. I understood, in some ways for the first time, that my sin really *has* been cleansed by Jesus and is no longer an issue between us. I knew in my heart, in a way I perhaps hadn't before, the depth of Jesus' love for me on the cross. I felt like I was home.

Resting in Jesus is not applying a spiritual formula to ourselves as a kind of fix-it. It is the essence of repentance. It is letting our heart tell us where we are in our own story so that Jesus can minister to us out of the Story of his love for us. When, in a given moment, we lay down our false self and the smaller story of whatever performance has sustained us, when we give up everything else but him, we experience the freedom of knowing that he simply loves us where we are. We begin just to *be*, having our identity anchored in him. We begin to experience our spiritual life as the "easy yoke and light burden" Jesus tells us is his experience. We become ontologically substantive.

In Matthew 24, Jesus tells us that in the last days, people will have lost the Sacred Romance altogether. Having no anchor, their faith will grow cold and they will be literally swept away in panic, as all but what cannot be shaken, is shaken. Only those of us who are securely anchored in him in our heart will be left standing to share the Sacred Romance with those who are lost.

We have come to the shores of heaven together, to the border of the region where our Christianity begins to move from a focus on doing to one of communion with Christ, our Lover and Lord. The spiritual disciplines of silence, solitude, meditation (heart prayer), fasting, and simplicity practiced by Christ and passed on to us by the traditions of the Desert Fathers bring us through our emptiness and thirst into the presence of God. Many fine books have been written on the practice of the spiritual disciplines, among them, *Celebration of the Disciplines and Prayer*, by Richard Foster; *The Way of the Heart*, by Henri Nouwen; and *The Spirit of the Disciplines*, by Dallas Willard. I recommend these as resources to help the reader journey more deeply into God's heart, which is our true home.

When we begin to abide in God's heart, the blades of grass on heaven's outskirts no longer puncture our feet. Here and there, a fresh and exotic scent reaches us from heaven's very borders. From my own experience of it, I liken it to a trip my family and I took to the Grand Canyon five years ago. Finally, after hours on end of traveling through the dry, featureless terrain of Arizona's deserts, we began climbing through the pine forests of the Kaibab Plateau, heading toward the Grand Canyon. The higher we drove, the clearer the air seemed to become, and the sweeter the scent of pine. We wondered aloud that we had been so uncomfortable hours before. The canyon itself came on us in a lavender and pink and yellow hugeness that swept my breath away. Even though I knew it was coming and that we would soon see it, I was not prepared for its exotic, spiritual beauty. I wept in joy without really understanding why. And I knew there were many days of beauty and exploration ahead.

Such will be the coming kingdom of heaven.

12

Coming Home

The door on which we have been knocking all our lives will open at last.

C. S. Lewis

My wife, Stasi, reads the end of novels first. Until recently, I (John) never understood why. "I want to know how the story ends, to see if it's worth reading," she explained. "A story is only as good as its ending. Even the best stories leave you empty if the last chapter is disappointing.

"But the opposite is also true," she added. "A really tragic story can be saved by a happy ending."

"But doesn't knowing the end take away the drama?" I asked.

"It only takes away the fear and frees you to enjoy the drama. Besides, some things are too important to be left to chance," she said, and turned back to her book.

A story is only as good as its ending. Without a happy ending that draws us on in eager anticipation, our journey becomes a nightmare of endless struggle. Is this all there is? Is this as good as it gets? On a recent flight I was chatting with one of the attendants about her spiritual beliefs. A follower of a New Age guru, she said with all earnestness, "I don't believe in heaven. I believe life is a never-ending cycle of birth and death." *What a horror*, I thought to myself. *This Story had better have a happy ending.* St. Paul felt the same. If this is as good as it gets, he said, you may as well stop at a bar on the way home and tie one on; go to Nordstrom's and max out all your credit cards; bake a cake and eat the whole thing. "Let us eat and drink, for tomorrow we die" (1 Cor. 15:32).

Our hearts cannot live without hope. Gabriel Marcel says that "hope is for the soul what breathing is for the living organism." In the trinity of Christian graces—faith, hope, and love—love may be the greatest but hope plays the deciding role. The apostle Paul tells us that faith and love depend on hope, our anticipation of what lies ahead: "Faith and love . . . spring from the hope that is stored up for you in heaven" (Col. 1:5). Our courage for the journey so often falters because we've lost our hope of heaven—the consummation of our Love Story. No wonder we live like Robinson Crusoe, trying to cobble together the best life we can from the wreckage of the world; we think we're stuck here forever. Of course, our less-wild lovers seem irresistible—we see them as our only shot at some relief. The reason most men, to quote Thoreau, "live lives of quiet desperation" is that they live without hope.

Several years ago I joined some friends for a weekend of fly-fishing on the Snake River in Jackson Hole, Wyoming. It was a last fling of fall, before the long winter set in with my heavy responsibilities at home, work, and in grad school. I had looked forward to the adventure for months, but the weekend hadn't lived up to my expectations. The weather was lousy, the fishing dreadful. As the weekend drew to a close, I found myself tense and irritable, trying desperately to squeeze joy out of diminishing hopes. *This is it?* I thought to myself. *This is as good as it's going to be?* Standing together in the river Saturday evening, empty-handed, my friend announced almost as an afterthought that he had arranged a float down a wild section of the river with a famous guide for our last day together. The weather was predicted to be clear and the fishing was practically guaranteed to be fabulous.

In a moment, everything changed. The evening light took on a rich, golden quality; the fall colors became vivid; I noticed the musical rushing of the waters for the first time and my fishing buddies suddenly seemed to me a truly decent bunch of guys. The pressure I had placed on the vacation was lifted as my heart recovered hope. I was released by the promise of better things to come.

The story may seem silly (particularly for those who do not fly-fish), but it reveals one of the most important truths of the human heart: If for all practical purposes we believe that this life is our best shot at happiness, if this is as good as it gets, we will live as desperate, demanding, and eventually despairing men and women. We will place on this world a burden it was never intended to bear. We will try to find a way to sneak back into the Garden and when that fails, as it always does, our heart fails as well. If truth be told, most of us live as though this life *is* our only hope, and then we feel guilty for wanting to do exactly what Paul said he would do if that were true.

In his wonderful book *The Eclipse of Heaven*, A. J. Conyers put it quite simply: "We live in a world no longer under heaven." All the crises of the human soul flow from there. All our addictions and depressions, the rage that simmers just beneath the surface of our Christian facade, and the deadness that characterizes so much of our lives has a common root: We think this is as good as it gets. Take away the hope of arrival and our journey becomes the Battan death march. The best human life is unspeakably sad. Even if we manage to escape some of the bigger tragedies (and few of us do), life rarely matches our expectations. When we do get a taste of what we really long for, it never lasts. Every vacation eventually comes to an end. Friends move away. Our careers don't quite pan out. Sadly, we feel guilty about our disappointment, as though we ought to be more grateful.

Of course we're disappointed—we're made for so much more. "He has also set eternity in the hearts," (Eccl. 3:11). Our longing for heaven whispers to us in our disappointments and screams through our agony. "If I find in myself desires which nothing in this world can satisfy," C. S. Lewis wrote, "the only logical explanation is that I was made for another world."

If faith and love hang on hope, if a life without hope is as Paul says "to be pitied" (1 Cor. 15:19), then shouldn't we devote ourselves to recovering a vision for the end of our story in as vivid colors as our imagination can conceive?

I knew a man who as a young boy hated the idea of heaven. He would puzzle and embarrass his Sunday school teachers by stating quite boldly, whenever the subject of heaven was brought up, that he didn't want to go there. Finally, one of them had the sense to ask him why. His answer? "I don't like peas." He had heard the familiar Christmas carol "Silent Night," with the lovely refrain "Sleep in heavenly peace" and thought it referred to the vegetable. Like any red-blooded boy he figured there had to be better things to do.

Our images aren't much better. We speak so seldom of heaven and when we do, the images are sickly: fat babies fluttering around with tiny wings, bored saints lazing on shapeless clouds, strumming harps and wondering what's happening back on earth where the real action is.

The crisis of hope that afflicts the church today is a crisis of *imagination*. Catholic philosopher Peter Kreeft writes:

> Medieval imagery (which is almost totally biblical imagery) of light, jewels, stars, candles, trumpets, and angels no longer fits our ranch-style, supermarket world. Pathetic modern substitutes of fluffy clouds, sexless cherubs, harps and metal halos (not halos of *light*) presided over by a stuffy divine Chairman of the Bored are a joke, not a glory. Even more modern, more up-to-date substitutes—

Heaven as a comfortable feeling of peace and kindness, sweetness and light, and God as a vague grandfatherly benevolence, a senile philanthropist—are even more insipid. Our pictures of Heaven simply do not move us; they are not moving pictures. It is this aesthetic failure rather than intellectual or moral failures in our pictures of Heaven and of God that threatens faith most potently today. Our pictures of Heaven are dull, platitudinous and syrupy; therefore, so is our faith, our hope, and our love of Heaven. . . . It doesn't matter whether it's a dull lie or a dull truth. Dullness, not doubt, is the strongest enemy of faith, just as indifference, not hate, is the strongest enemy of love. (*Everything You Wanted to Know About Heaven*)

If our pictures of heaven are to move us, they must be moving pictures. So go ahead—dream a little. Use your imagination. Picture the best possible ending to your story you can. If that isn't heaven, something better is. When Paul says, "No eye has seen, no ear has heard, no mind has conceived what God has prepared for those who love him" (1 Cor. 2:9), he simply means we cannot outdream God. What is at the end of our personal journeys? Something beyond our wildest imagination. But if we explore the secrets of our heart in the light of the promises of Scripture, we can discover clues. As we have said from Chapter 1, there is in the heart of every man, woman, and child an inconsolable longing for intimacy, for beauty, and for adventure. What will heaven offer to our heart of hearts?

Intimacy

Our longing for intimacy gives us the greatest scent of the joys that lie ahead. Being left out is one of life's most painful experiences. I remember the daily fourth-grade torture of waiting in line while the captains chose their teams for the kickball games. As each captain took turns choosing a player, descending from best to worst, our rank in fourth-grade society was reinforced. Though others fared worse than I—"Don't make us take

Smitty, we had him last time"—I was never the first to be chosen. No one ever said, "Wait—we get Eldredge this time!" I didn't feel wanted; at best, I felt tolerated. And then there was junior high cafeteria. After buying lunch, you carried your tray out into the dining room, looking for a place to eat. There was an unspoken hierarchy that determined where you could sit. One day, I dared to test that caste system. With modest courage I walked over to the table filled with the "cool" kids, but before I could sit down, one of them sneered, "Not here, Eldredge, we're saving this for someone else."

These are some of the ways I learned the lesson that I was on the outside. Throughout our lives, each one of us lives with a constant nagging that we never quite fit in, we never truly belong. We've all had enough experiences to teach us that we will never be allowed into the "sacred circle," the place of intimacy. Even those who are chosen to be part of the "in" crowd are never chosen for who they truly are. So we hide parts of ourselves to try and fit in, or kill our desire to be an insider, rather than let our longing lead us toward the true intimacy for which we were designed.

On the other hand, there is the joy of having someone save a place for us. We walk into a crowded room at church or at a dinner party and someone across the way waves us over, pointing to a chair he's held on to especially for us. For a moment we feel a sense of relief, a taste of being on the inside. Now consider Jesus' words in John 14:2—"I am going . . . to prepare a place for you." Christ promises that he is saving a place in heaven especially for each of us. When we walk into the crowded excitement of the wedding feast of the Lamb, with the sound of a thousand conversations, laughter and music, the clinking of glasses, and one more time our heart leaps with the hope that we might be let into the sacred circle, we will not be disappointed. We'll be welcomed to the table by our Lover himself. No one will have to scramble to find another chair, to make room for us at the end of the table, or rustle up a place setting. There will be a seat with our name on it, held open at Jesus' command for us and no other.

Heaven is the beginning of an adventure in intimacy, "a world of love," as Jonathan Edwards wrote, "where God is the fountain." The Holy Spirit, through the human authors of Scripture, chose the imagery of a wedding feast for a reason. It's not just any kind of party; it is a *wedding* feast. What sets this special feast apart from all others is the unique intimacy of the wedding night. The Spirit uses the most secret and tender experience on earth—the union of husband and wife—to convey the depth of intimacy that we will partake with our Lord in heaven. He is the Bridegroom and the church is his bride. In the consummation of love, we shall know him and be known. There we shall receive our new name, known only to our Lover, which he shall give to us on a white stone (Rev. 2:17).

George MacDonald, a theologian with a poet's heart, has explored the promises of heaven more richly than perhaps any other man. He explains what the stone implies:

> It is the man's own symbol—his soul's picture, in a word—the sign which belongs to him and to no one else. Who can give a man this, his own name? God alone. For no one but God sees what the man is. . . . It is only when the man has become his name that God gives him the stone with the name upon it, for then first can he understand what his name signifies. . . . Such a name cannot be given until the man *is* the name . . . that being whom He had in His thought when He began to make the child, and whom He kept in His thought through the long process of creation that went to realize the idea. To tell the name is to seal the success—to say "In thee also I am well pleased." (*Unspoken Sermons*)

The stone will free us to enjoy the riches of heaven, for in order to share in this heavenly intimacy, we must have the freedom of heart enjoyed by Adam and Eve before the Fall, who were naked and *felt no shame*. This is the freedom from sin, or as Kreeft has said, "from what makes us not ourselves. We will be free to be the true selves God designed us to be." Shame kills intimacy. The soul that still is in some way hiding cannot enjoy the fullness of knowing what characterizes the love between God and the saints in heaven. But then we shall be perfect; our loved ones will be perfect as well. All that has ever stood between us will be swept away and our heart will be released to real loving. The intimacy that begins between God and his people will be enriched and echoed by our communion with each other. The deepest longing of our heart—our longing to be part of the sacred circle, to be inside—reveals to us the greatest of the treasures heaven has in store. For we were made in and for the most sacred circle of all. Lewis says,

> The sense that in this universe we are treated as strangers, the longing to be acknowledged, to meet with some response, to bridge some chasm that yawns between us and reality, is part of our inconsolable secret. And surely, from this point of view, the promise of glory, in the sense described, becomes highly relevant to our deep desire. For glory meant good report with God, acceptance by God, response, acknowledgment, and welcome into the heart of things. The door on which we have been knocking all our lives will open at last. (*The Weight of Glory*)

Beauty

"And they all lived happily ever after." Where? Doing what? As wonderful as it will be to have our longing for relationship filled to overflowing, it is not enough. Our heart has other longings that heaven draws forth. There is so much more to the human soul and so much more to the riches God has prepared for those who love him. In the same way that life sharpens our yearning to be welcomed into the sacred circle of intimacy, so it awakens another ache from deep within—our longing for beauty.

The Ritz Carlton Laguna Beach is one of the most luxurious hotels in southern California. Nestled on a bluff above its private cove with white sandy beach, the hotel exudes romance. Its mediterranean architecture lifts the Ritz out of space and time, creating a fairy-tale ambiance. Arches and tile walkways lead to fountained courtyards and terraces with breathtaking views of the Pacific. The tropical climate nourishes a lush canopy of purple and red bougainvillea, whimsical flower gardens, rich green lawns, and swaying palms. Staying at the Ritz, one can almost forget, if for a moment, that the Fall ever happened. Stasi and I enjoyed a weekend of escape there thanks to a business conference I was asked to attend.

Late one evening I slipped away from the meeting to wander the grounds alone. I felt restless inside and thought a walk might be calming. Something drew me through the terraces toward the ocean. As I wandered over the beautifully manicured lawns, more luxuriant than any carpet, the sounds of music and laughter from parties inside mingled with the scent of the flower beds in the warm ocean breeze. My restlessness grew. Standing on the edge of the cliff with the crashing of the waves below and the shining of the stars above, I felt the restlessness swell into an ache. As Simone Weil said, there are only two things that pierce the human heart: beauty and affliction. I was run clean-through by the beauty of it all, overcome by an ache for a home I have never seen.

I have had this experience many times, whether walking along the Napali Coast in Hawaii, flying over the glaciers of Alaska, or noticing the simple rays of sunshine falling on the kitchen table. Yet it always takes me by surprise. We grow so used to living in a world soiled by the Fall that our soul's desire for beauty lies dormant deep within, waiting for something to awaken it. During a visit to Westminster Cathedral in England, a friend of mine got lost and by accident came into that glorious sanctuary by a rather commonplace side door. Stepping around the corner he was totally unprepared for the majesty he suddenly found himself engulfed by: the sweeping architecture, the glory in stone and spire and glass. At that very moment a choir broke into song, their angelic harmonies filling the massive cathedral. "I don't know what happened," he later told me, "but I broke down and began to weep."

"Each and every instance of beauty," writes Mark Helprin, "is a promise and example, in miniature, of life that can end in balance, with symmetry, purpose and hope." We long for beauty and the promise that it speaks. Our revulsion to the ugly is the counterpart to our desire for beauty. I used to hate the part of my daily commute that took me through the worst sections of Washington, D.C.: abandoned buildings, burned-out cars, desolate neighborhoods. It was a symbol of the triumph of evil, chaos, and death. My heart grieved to see such devastation and I breathed a sigh of relief as I passed through the wreckage and drove into the farmlands of Maryland. But we must be careful here; as Lewis said, one of the mistakes we so often make when captured by an object of beauty, whether it's a place, a person, or a work of art, is to assume the longing in our heart is for the thing before us. The Ritz and Westminster and farm meadows—these are shadows of the realities to come. The beauty of the tabernacle carried by Israel through the desert was a type of the real item in heaven. So it goes with all things on earth: The beauty that so captures our heart and is so fleeting draws us toward the eternal reality.

We long for beauty, and when the biblical writers speak of heaven, they use the most beautiful imagery they can. You can almost hear the agony of the writer trying to get it right while knowing he falls far short of what he sees. In the book of Revelation, St. John uses the word *like* again and again. "And He who was sitting was like a jasper stone and a sardius in appearance; and there was a rainbow around the throne, like an emerald in appearance. . . . Before the throne there was . . . a sea of glass like crystal" (4:3, 6 NASB). The beauty cannot be captured, only alluded to by the most beautiful things on earth.

I believe the beauty of heaven is why the Bible says we shall be "feasted." It's not merely that there will be no suffering, though that will be tremendous joy in itself; to have every Arrow we've ever known pulled out and every wound dressed with the leaves from the tree of life (Rev. 22:2). But there is more. We will have glorified bodies with which to partake of all the beauty of heaven. As Edwards wrote, "Every faculty will be an inlet of delight." We will eat freely the fruit of the tree of life and drink deeply from the river of life that flows through the city. And the food will satisfy not just our body but our soul. As Lewis said,

> We do not want merely to *see* beauty, though, God knows, even that is bounty enough. We want something else which can hardly be put into words—to be united with the beauty we see, to pass into it, to receive it into ourselves, to bathe in it, to become part of it. (*The Weight of Glory*)

And so we shall.

Adventure

What will we do in heaven? The Sunday comics picture saints lying about on clouds, strumming harps. It hardly takes your breath away. The fact that most Christians have a gut sense that earth is more exciting than heaven points to the deceptive powers of the enemy and our own failure of imagination. What do we do with the idea of "eternal rest"? That sounds like the slogan of a middle-class cemetery. We know heaven begins with a party, but then what? A long nap after the feast? The typical evangelical response—"We will worship God"—doesn't help either. The answer is certainly biblical, and perhaps my reaction is merely a reflection on me, but it sounds so one-dimensional. Something in my heart says, *That's all? How many hymns and choruses can we sing?*

We will worship God in heaven, meaning all of life will

finally be worship, not round after round of "Amazing Grace." The parable of the minas in Luke 19 and the talents in Matthew 25 foreshadow a day when we shall exercise our real place in God's economy, the role we have been preparing for on earth. He who has been faithful in the small things will be given even greater adventures in heaven. We long for adventure, to be caught up in something larger than ourselves, a drama of heroic proportions. This isn't just a need for continual excitement, it's part of our design. Few of us ever sense that our talents are being used to their fullest; our creative abilities are rarely given wings in this life. When Revelation 3 speaks of us being "pillars in the temple of our God," it doesn't mean architecture. Rather, Christ promises that we shall be actively fulfilling our total design in the adventures of the new kingdom.

Act IV—heaven—is the continuation of the Story that was interrupted by the Fall. God made the earth and entrusted it to us, to bring order and increase beauty. We were to be his regents, reigning with his blessing and authority. That arrangement was corrupted by the Fall so that the earth no longer responds to our leadership as it once did. When Christ accomplished our redemption, he didn't do it to place us on the bench for eternity. He restored us to put us back in the game. He even subjected the earth to a time of futility until the day it will be "liberated from its bondage to decay and brought into the glorious freedom of the children of God" (Rom. 8:21). We will then co-reign with Christ. "St. Peter for a few seconds walked on the water," Lewis reminds us, "and the day will come when there will be a re-made universe, infinitely obedient to the will of glorified and obedient men, when we can do all things, when we shall be those gods that we are described as being in Scripture."

Part of the adventure will be to explore the wonders of the new heaven and new earth, the most breathtaking of which will be God himself. We will have all eternity to explore the mysteries of God, and not just explore, but celebrate and share with one another. Here is a remarkable thing to consider: Your soul has a unique shape that fits God. We are not all the same, but unique creations each of us. Therefore, as MacDonald says,

> Every one of us is something that the other is not, and therefore knows something—it may be without knowing that he knows it— which no one else knows: and . . . it is everyone's business, as one of the kingdom of light and inheritor in it all, to give his portion to the rest. (*Unspoken Sermons*)

This may be why the angels Isaiah sees flying around the throne room of God are crying "holy, holy, holy," not to God, but *"to one another"* (6:3, italics mine). They are calling each other to see what they see of the majesty and beauty of God, so that their joy might be increased as they celebrate Him together. Every experience of delight takes on a fuller dimension when we share it. This is why we so often feel in the midst of some wonderful moment, "how I wish my beloved were here."

The exploration of heaven shall also include our knowing of each other. How could it not? How can love be complete without the freedom to be naked and unashamed? More than unashamed, we shall be *celebrated*. It is one of the sorrows of our present life: the separation we feel even from those closest to us. Married people can be the loneliest on earth, not for some failure of the marriage, but because they have tasted the best there is of human relationships and know it is not all it was meant to be. In *A Tale of Two Cities*, Charles Dickens captures that sense of mystery each human soul is to another.

> A wonderful fact to reflect upon, that every human creature is constituted to be that profound secret and mystery to every other. A solemn consideration, when I enter a great city by night, that every one of those darkly clustered houses encloses its own secret; that every room in every one of them encloses its own secret; that every beating heart in the hundreds of thousands of breasts there, is, in some of its imaginings, a secret to the heart nearest it!

But in heaven that veil shall be removed as well, not to our shame and embarrassment, but to our utter delight. Remember, we will be perfect, meaning we will be the soul that God had in mind all along. And then, as MacDonald says,

> We shall have the universe for our own, and be good merry children in the great house of our father. I think then we shall be able to pass into and through each other's very souls as we please, knowing each other's thought and being, along with our own, and so being *like* God. When we are all just as loving and unselfish as Jesus; when, like him, our one thought of delight is that God is, and is what he is; when the fact that a being is just another person from ourselves is enough to make that being precious. (*The Heart of George MacDonald*)

And there is, of course, the exploration of our own lives. We know a time will come for us to look back with our Lord over the story of our lives. Every hidden thing shall be made known, every word spoken in secret shall be uttered. My soul shrinks back; how will this not be an utter horror? The whole idea of judgment has been terribly twisted by our enemy. One evangelistic tract conveys the popular idea that at some point shortly upon our arrival in heaven the lights will dim and God will give the signal for the videotape of our entire life to be played before the watching universe: every shameful act, every wicked thought. How can this be so? If there is "*now* no condemnation for those who are in Christ Jesus" (Rom. 8:1, *italics mine*), how is it possible there will be shame later? God himself shall clothe us in white garments (Rev. 3:5). Will our Lover then strip his beloved so that the universe may gawk at her? Never.

However God may choose to evaluate our lives, whatever memory of our past we shall have in heaven, we know this: It will only contribute to our joy. We will read our story by the light of redemption and see how God has used both the good and the bad, the sorrow and the gladness for our welfare and his glory. With the assurance of total forgiveness we will be free to know ourselves fully, walking again through the seasons of life to linger over the cherished moments and stand in awe at God's grace for the moments we have tried so hard to forget. Our gratitude and awe will swell into worship of a Lover so strong and kind as to make us fully his own.

Arrival

Brent and I have tried to put words to many of the questions we believe every heart is asking. Well into the Christian journey, two new questions began to haunt us: Will I make it to the end? and, Will it be good when I get there?

Several years into our marriage Stasi and I reached one of the lowest moments of our lives. Sitting over the breakfast table one morning, the subject of divorce was raised in a rather casual way, as if it were a question about the raspberry jam. We had drifted apart, I knew that, but until that moment I didn't realize just how far. Over the next few days I made an emergency plan. We would go to the mountains for a holiday in hopes of recovering some of the ground we had lost. We had honeymooned in Yosemite and I thought that might be the place to look again for a lost romance.

We set out the day after Christmas on a warm and sunny morning. But as the hours wore on, a snowstorm was building in the mountains ahead. Evening fell and with it came the snow, softly at first, then heavier and harder. Our car began to slip and spin on the icy road. It was dark when we reached the entrance to the park. Up ahead, I could see the cars before us turning around and heading back down the mountain. *Oh Lord,* I prayed, *please—not now, not when so much is riding on this.* The ranger told us that the roads had become treacherous and a blizzard was raging higher in the mountains. Several cars had already slid off the highway. He recommended we turn back but left the choice to us.

"We're going on," I said. As the hours dragged on, the snow blanketed the road and dark woods all around. We were alone. *Will we make it?* I wondered to myself. *Can it possibly be good even if we do?* My knuckles were white from clutching the steering wheel. The tension in the car was thick, a palpable reminder of the reason we had come.

Just when I was about to abandon hope, twinkling lights appeared through the trees ahead. As we rounded the bend, the Wawona Hotel came into view—a gorgeous, white Victorian inn with garlands hanging from the balcony and a massive Christmas tree in the window. The snowfall eased and the flakes were now falling softly, gently. We could see a fire roaring in the large stone fireplace, casting a romantic glow over the couples who lingered over dinner. Currier and Ives never printed a more beautiful scene. As I pulled our car into safety, a deer ambled from the woods and across the white meadow before us. The sense of arrival was almost too much to bear. We had made it! The beauty of it all seemed to speak the promise of a life restored. As we walked into our room, we discovered a bottle of champagne on ice—a gift some friends had sent ahead. That weekend we turned a corner in our marriage and began the healing we now enjoy.

For now, our life is a journey of high stakes and frequent danger. But we have turned the corner; the long years in exile are winding down and we are approaching home. There is no longer any question as to whether we will make it and if it will be good when we get there. "I am going there to prepare a place for you," Jesus promised. "And if I go and prepare a place for you, I will come back and take you to be with me" (John 14:2–3).

One day soon we will round a bend in the road and our dreams will come true. We really will live happily ever after. The long years in exile will be swept away in the joyful tears of our arrival home. Every day when we rise, we can tell ourselves, *My journey today will bring me closer to home; it may be just around the bend.* All we long for we shall have; all we long to be, we will be. All that has hurt us so deeply—the dragons and nits, the Arrows and our false lovers, and Satan himself—they will all be swept away.

And then real life begins.

EPILOGUE

Remembering Toward Heaven

The Road goes ever on and on
Down from the door where it began.
Now far ahead the Road has gone,
And I must follow, if I can,
Pursuing it with eager feet,
Until it joins some larger way.

J. R. R. Tolkien

THE SACRED ROMANCE calls to us every moment of our lives. It whispers to us on the wind, invites us through the laughter of good friends, reaches out to us through the touch of someone we love. We've heard it in our favorite music, sensed it at the birth of our first child, been drawn to it while watching the shimmer of a sunset on the ocean. It is even present in times of great personal suffering—the illness of a child, the loss of a marriage, the death of a friend. Something calls to us through experiences like these and rouses an inconsolable longing deep within our heart, wakening in us a yearning for intimacy, beauty, and adventure. This longing is the most powerful part of any human personality. It fuels our search for meaning, for wholeness, for a sense of being truly alive. However we may describe this deep desire, it is the most important thing about us, our heart of hearts, the passion of our life. And the voice that calls to us in this place is none other than the voice of God.

We set out to discover if there is in the wide world out there a reality that corresponds to the world within our heart. Hopefully, we have helped you see in new ways that Chesterton was right: Romance *is* the deepest thing in life; it is deeper even than reality. Our heart is made for a great drama, because it is a reflection of the Author of that story, the grand Heart behind all things. We've seen how we lose heart when we lose the eternal Romance, which reminds us that God sought to bring us into his sacred circle from all eternity, and that despite our rejection of him, he pursues us still. The Arrows and the Haunting both find their place in Act III of that drama, in which we now live. But this act is drawing to a close. Our Lover has come to rescue us in the person of Jesus; he has set our heart free to follow him up and into the celebration that begins the adventures of Act IV.

Where do we go from here? "This life," wrote Jonathan Edwards, "ought to be spent by us only as a journey towards heaven." That's the only story worth living in now. The road goes out before us and our destination awaits. In the imagery of Hebrews, a race is set before us and we must run for all we're worth. Our prayers will have been answered if we've helped to lift some of the deadweight so that your heart may rise to the call, hear it more clearly, respond with "eager feet." Our final thoughts echo the advice found in Hebrews 12:2–3:

> Let us fix our eyes on Jesus, the author and perfecter of our faith, who for the joy set before him endured the cross, scorning its shame, and sat down at the right hand of the throne of God. Consider him who endured such opposition from sinful men, so that you will not grow weary and lose heart.

This marvelous passage is familiar to many of us, so lest we should become dull to its power due to its familiarity, consider Eugene Peterson's translation from *The Message*:

> Keep your eyes on *Jesus*, who both began and finished this race we're in. Study how he did it. Because he never lost sight of where he was headed—that exhilarating finish in and with God—he could

put up with anything along the way: cross, shame, whatever. And now he's *there*, in the place of honor, right alongside God. When you find yourselves flagging in your faith, go over that story again, item by item, that long litany of hostility he plowed through. *That* will shoot adrenaline into your souls!

Jesus remembered where he was headed and he wanted to get there with all his heart. These two themes, memory and desire, will make all the difference in our journey ahead. Without them, we will not run well, if we run at all. We have tried to do honor to the riches of memory and desire in the preceding chapters of this book. Let me (John) explore them more deeply now, as a man goes through his essential belongings one last time before setting out on a long and dangerous quest.

Living from Desire

Jesus ran because he wanted to, not simply because he had to or because the Father told him to. He ran "for the joy set before him," which means he ran out of *desire*. To use the familiar phrase, his heart was fully in it. We call the final week of our Savior's life his Passion Week. Look at the depth of his desire, the fire in his soul. Consumed with passion, he clears the temple of the charlatans who have turned his Father's house into a swap meet (Matt. 21:12). Later, he stands looking over the city that was to be his bride but now lies in the bondage of her adulteries and the oppression of her taskmasters. "O Jerusalem, Jerusalem," he cries, ". . . how often I have *longed* to gather your children together, as a hen gathers her chicks under her wings, but you were not willing" (Matt. 23:37, *italics mine*). As the final hours of his greatest struggle approach, his passion intensifies. He gathers with his closest friends like a condemned criminal sitting down to his last meal. He alone knows what is about to unfold. "I have *eagerly desired* to eat this Passover with you," he says, "before I suffer" (Luke 22:15, italics mine). Then on he presses, through the intensity of Gethsemane and the passion of the cross. Is it possible he went through any of it halfheartedly?

When the going gets rough, we're going nowhere without desire. And the going will get rough. The world, the minions of darkness, and your own double-mindedness are all set against you. Just try coming alive, try living from your heart for the Sacred Romance and watch how the world responds. They will hate you for it and will do everything in their power to get you to fall back into the comfort of the way things were. Your passion will disrupt them, because it sides with their own heart which they've tried so hard to put away. If they can't convince you to live from the safer places they have chosen, they will try intimidation. If that fails, they'll try to kill you—if not literally, then at the level of your soul.

Jeremiah lived the struggle of desire. He knew the deep ambivalence of living for the Sacred Romance. His decision to trust in the love of God and join the battle for the hearts of his people made him an outcast, a pariah. Like the Master he served, he was "despised and rejected by men." After years of opposition, getting tossed naked into the bottom of wells, plots against his life, the shame of false accusations and the loneliness of isolation, Jeremiah has had it. He is ready to throw in the towel. He lets the passion of his soul forth, directly at God:

> O LORD, you deceived me, and I was deceived;
> you overpowered me and prevailed.
> I am ridiculed all day long;
> everyone mocks me. . . .
> So the word of the LORD has brought me
> insult and reproach all day long.
> But if I say, "I will not mention him
> or speak any more in his name,"
> his word is in my heart like a fire,
> a fire shut up in my bones.
> I am weary of holding it in;
> indeed, I cannot. *(20:7–9)*

This aching prophet gives words to the dilemma of desire. He says, in effect, "You put this Romance in my heart, you drew me out on this wild adventure—how could I keep from following? But now that I have, it has only brought me the fury of my community. And what's worse, I cannot walk away. I'm trapped by my desire for you." Jeremiah may have become a prophet initially out of a sense of duty, but now he is caught up in the Sacred Romance because he can't help it. Paul voiced the same dilemma: "Woe to me if I do not preach the gospel!" (1 Cor. 9:16). When the going gets rough, *ought* is not enough to keep you going.

You may recall the movie *Chariots of Fire*, which tells the story of two Olympic runners: Eric Liddell and Charles Abrams. Both are passionate about running, but in very different ways. Abrams runs because he is driven; he runs in order to prove something. He is a cheerless man whose whole life is motivated by ought, by duty, by the law. Liddell runs because he can't help it. "When I run," he says, "I feel God's pleasure." He knows a freedom of heart that Abrams can only watch from a distance. Abrams uses discipline to subdue and kill his heart. Liddell is so freed by grace that when he runs, Abrams says, "He runs like a wild animal—he unnerves me." "Where," Liddell asks, "does the power come from to see the race to its end? It comes from *within*." It comes from desire.

"The whole life of the good Christian," said Augustine, "is a holy longing." Sadly, many of us have been led to feel that somehow we ought to want less, not more. We have this sense that we should atone for our longings, apologize that we feel such deep desire. Shouldn't we be more content? Perhaps, but contentment is never wanting *less;* that's the easy way out. Anybody can look holy if she's killed her heart; the real test is to have your heart burning within you and have the patience to enjoy what there is now to enjoy, while waiting with eager antic-ipation for the feast to come. In Paul's words, we "groan inwardly as we wait eagerly" (Rom. 8:23). Contentment can only happen as we increase desire, let it run itself out toward its fulfillment, and carry us along with it. And so George Herbert prayed,

> Immortal Heat, O let thy greater flame
> Attract the lesser to it: let those fires,
> Which shall consume the world, first make it tame;
> And kindle in our hearts such true desires,
> As may consume our lusts, and make thee way.
> Then shall our hearts pant thee. (*Love*)

There may be times when all we have to go on is a sense of duty. But in the end, if that is all we have, we will never make it. Our Hero is the example. He's run on before us and he's made it, he's there now. His life assures us it can be done, but only through passionate desire *for the joy set before us*. Or, as Peterson has it, "that exhilarating finish in and with God." The road ahead will take us into a deepening and a focusing of our desire. As author James Houston has experienced, "The desire that really gives life is to know God. This desire is never satisfied, for it is one that grows with its fulfillment; and our relationship with God changes and leads to a constant deepening of our desires" (*The Heart's Desire*).

As our soul grows in the love of God and journeys forth toward him, our heart's capacities also grow and expand: "Thou shalt enlarge my heart" (Ps. 119:32 KJV). A friend of mine is a missionary to Muslims in Senegal. He tells me that after conversion, Muslims will often notice flowers for the first time. Prior to salvation, Muslims in that arid country live a very utilitarian existence. Things are valued only for what they can do. Their houses are dull and drab; trees are only appreciated if they are fruit trees; if they have a function. It is as if the Muslims have lived without beauty for their whole lives and now, having their souls released from bondage, they are freed into the pleasures of God's creative heart. I'm struck by the parallels to modern fundamentalism. Their hatred of pleasure is not a sign of their godliness; quite the opposite. The redeemed heart hungers for beauty.

But the sword cuts both ways. While our heart grows in its capacity for pleasure, it grows in its capacity to know pain. The two go hand in hand. What, then, shall we do with disappointment? We can be our own enemy, depending on how we handle the heartache that comes with desire. To want is to suffer; the word *passion* means to suffer. This is why many Christians are reluctant to listen to their hearts: They know that their dullness is keeping them from feeling the pain of life. Many of us have chosen simply not to want so much; it's safer that way. It's also godless. That's stoicism, not Christianity. Sanctification is an awakening, the rousing of our souls from the dead sleep of sin into the fullness of their capacity for life.

Desire often feels like an enemy, because it wakes longings that cannot be fulfilled in the moment. In the words of T. S. Eliot,

"April is the cruelest month, breeding
Lilacs out of the dead land, mixing
Memory and desire" (*The Waste Land*).

Spring awakens a desire for the summer that is not yet. Awakened souls are often disappointed, but our disappointment can lead us onward, actually increasing our desire and lifting it toward its true passion.

I am a lucky man. I have a family and friends who love me well. But they also let me down. When I feel the pain of their failure, I have several options. I can retreat into cynicism ("Isn't that the way life really is?") and deaden the pain by killing my desire. Or I can become more demanding ("You will never do that again"), manipulating them and in a way increasing my addiction to relationship. Or I can let it be a reminder that a day is coming when we will all live in perfect love. I can let the ache lead me deeper into my heart and higher toward heaven. And this is where memory comes in. Desire keeps us moving forward; memory keeps us moving in the right direction.

Rehearsing the Story

If we choose the way of desire, our greatest enemy on the road ahead is not the Arrows, nor Satan, nor our false lovers. The most crippling thing that besets the pilgrim heart is simply forgetfulness, or more accurately, the failure to remember. You *will* forget; this isn't the first book you've read in search of God. What do you remember from the others? If God has been so gracious as to touch you through our words, it will not have been the first time he has touched you. What have you done with all the other times? I have had enough encounters with God to provide a lifetime of conviction—why don't I live more faithfully? Because I forget.

I am humbled by the story of the golden calf. These people, the Jews God has just delivered from Egypt, have seen an eyeful. First came the plagues; then the Passover; then the escape from Pharaoh's armies and last-minute rescue straight through the Red Sea. After that came the manna: breakfast in bed, so to speak, every morning for months. They drank water from a rock. They heard and saw the fireworks at Mt. Sinai and shook in their sandals at the presence of God. I think it's safe to say that this band of ransomed slaves had reasons to believe. Then their leader, Moses, disappears for forty days into the "consuming fire" that enveloped the top of the mountain, which they could see with their own eyes. While he's up there, they blow the whole thing off for a wild bacchanalian party in honor of an idol made from their earrings. My first reaction is arrogant: How could they possibly be so stupid? How could they forget everything they've received straight from the hand of God? My second is a bit more honest: That's me; I could do that; I forget all the time.

Spiritual amnesia is so likely that from Genesis to Revelation, the Scriptures are full of the call to remember. "Only be careful," says our Lover, "and watch yourselves closely so that you do not forget the things your eyes have seen or let them slip from your heart as long as you live" (Deut. 4:9). How then can we keep these things in our hearts? How can we, in the words of Dan Allender, "reclaim the treasures of memory for our life's journey"? The author of Hebrews answers, "Rehearse the story. Go over it item by item—particularly the central scene."

The cross of Christ is, as T. S. Eliot said, "the stillpoint in a turning world." Everything before leads up to it; everything that follows flows from it. It is the climax of the story, the centerpiece of the whole drama. As Paul says, "For what I received I passed on to you as of first importance: that Christ died for our sins according to the Scriptures, that he was buried, that he was raised on the third day according to the Scriptures, and that he appeared to Peter, and then to the Twelve" (1 Cor. 15:3–5).

We must be careful here or these will only be religious words. We interpret them, they carry meanings and associations for us. And the true meaning gets lost if we forget either the Story of which this scene is the climax or its meaning for our own story. *How* we remember is as important as *what* we remember. It seems impossible that the truths about the death and resurrection of Jesus could become lost or rote, but it happens all the time. Witness the number of dead, lifeless churches in your own city. This is inevitable when we fail to remember, or when we remember only with a purely propositional approach to Scripture. We can possess volumes of doctrinal knowledge and it can all be true, but if it is separated from reality—especially the life of the heart—it becomes of no consequence to us. Robert Jenson uses this example:

> At various places in the New Testament, Jesus' death is called a "sacrifice," in order to make its meaning instantly clear. In the ancient world, sacrifices were offered on every street corner, and every infant

understood what they were supposed to accomplish. When Christian preachers said, "Jesus' death has done what sacrifices attempt to do," the light was turned on, and hearers could respond, "So that is what is supposed to be so great about him. . . ." Preachers still talk about Jesus as the "great sacrifice," but then have to spend twenty minutes explaining what that means. If the gospel thereby gets said at all—which is unlikely—it is the subsequent explanation that does it and not the propositions with "sacrifice." (*Story and Promise*)

This is why we must remember the death and resurrection of Jesus of Nazareth in the larger context of the Sacred Romance. That Story gives the propositions their significance.

On the other hand, the truth of the gospel becomes meaningless when all we have is "story." Was this Jesus divine, or merely a great man? The question fostered a major controversy for the church in the fourth century. Leaders on both sides of the debate started with the same narrative (the Gospels) but came to very different conclusions. The Council of Nicea was called, from which we get the Nicene Creed, one of the central articles of the church and a defining propositional statement on the divinity of Christ. Brent and I have taken a great risk in our use of the story motif, because in the twentieth century liberal theologians have used "narrative" as a way of dismantling any objective interpretation of Scripture. However, we cannot escape the fact that the Scriptures are given to us in the shape of a story.

Our acts of remembering must therefore involve both essential truths and dramatic narrative. I believe we need to hold the creeds in one hand and our favorite forms of art in the other. There are films, books, poems, songs, and paintings I return to again and again for some deep reason in my heart. Taking a closer look, I see that they all tell me about some part of the Sacred Romance. They help wake me to a deeper remembrance. As Don Hudson has said, "Art is, in the final analysis, a window on heaven."

Now that we are on our way, Satan will do everything he can

to steal the Romance. One way he does this is to leave us only propositions, or worse, "principles," like "the management techniques of Jesus" or "the marketing methods of Jesus." The heart cannot live on facts and principles alone; it speaks the language of story and we must rehearse the truths of our faith in a way that captures the heart and not just the mind.

Let us return again to that central scene and see what it is the author of Hebrews wants us to see in order to follow our Hero in the race ahead. How did Jesus sustain his passionate heart in the face of brutal opposition? *He never lost sight of where he was headed.* He had a vision for the future that was grounded in the past. In the story of the Last Supper, we are told that Jesus knew "he had come from God and was returning to God," and lived his life of selfless love to the end. He remembered both where he had come from and where he was going (John 13:3). And so must we.

Where We Have Come From

We rehearse the Sacred Romance because it interprets the rest of our experience. As Jenson says, "The story about Jesus is gospel because it is the key to our stories." Part of our journey forward is a journey backward into our stories, to bring all the events of our lives—the Arrows and the Haunting—into the light of the Sacred Romance for their proper interpretation. Answers mean nothing without real questions. We lost heart initially because we had no one to tell us how to reconcile the Haunting and the Arrows, or if we did, our interpreters often got the story wrong. Redemptive remembering is where we develop a life script by interpreting the past, with both the Arrows and the Haunting, in a way that gives energy to the present and direction to the future.

If we refuse to go and get them, the Arrows will remain lodged within us, poisoning the waters of our heart, coloring our real convictions about life and draining away our vitality for the journey. Several years ago a friend at work took me aside to say, "I don't know if you're aware of this, but you are intimidating your colleagues." I wanted to laugh, because I didn't feel intimidating at work; much of the time I felt small and scared. But his words provoked a search that led me first to the realization that I was in fact a very driven person (the reason my colleagues experienced me as intimidating). As I began to wonder why, I journeyed back to the day I was arrested as a teenager and the Arrow that lodged with the message "You are on your own." Though I had been a Christian for many years and knew all the promises about God always being with me, they had no power in my soul. The Arrow remained defining and I lived from its perspective.

As I entered into that heart-room where this particular Arrow had struck, the wound felt tender and new. With Brent's help, I was able to bring it into the light of the Sacred Romance for God to touch, heal, and reinterpret. Standing again in that place, I had ears to hear Jesus tell me I am not on my own, that he will never leave or forsake me. Faced with a real question, the real answer meant something. The healing process is still under way and there are days when I can be a driven man, but much less so than before. That Arrow has lost its power. But it would still be there if all I had done was tell myself, "Be nicer to the people at work."

Where We Are Headed

Redemptive remembering also reclaims the Haunting we've known. I want to own a ranch; it is one of my most frequent daydreams. Does that come as a surprise? My most romantic moments in life came as a boy on my grandfather's ranch and there is a part of me that so wants to return to those golden summer days. The pull is especially powerful when life is pressing in and really requiring me to be a man. Somewhere in my heart, I want to be a boy again, riding in Pop's pickup. The longing is good, but it can remain trapped in time, attached to a particular place. I just received a letter from my grandmother telling me she sold the ranch. What am I to do with that part of my heart? Is it sold off with the ranch; does it die with the passing of that era?

Sometimes, we need to lose the very things that have brought us a taste of the Romance in order for our heart to move toward the real thing. Otherwise they become a false transcendence. The most unredemptive kind of remembering is what many people call "nostalgia." How sad to visit elderly friends and relatives to find them sitting around listlessly, pining for "the good old days." They have no life in the present and little vision for the future, because they are locked in the past. So even our best memories can prevent our running the race set before us until we see them in the light of the real Romance. My last visit to the ranch was such a time. As I walked into the back porch, the sound of the screen door brought a flood of memories. I felt again in that moment how "called out" I felt by my grandfather in those days. And then it struck me that it was *God* calling me out through my grandfather, and he calls me still. The Sacred Romance honors those memories by revealing them for what they are: hints of a deeper reality. I yearn for the day when I shall be forever young, free to ride the fields of heaven with my grandfather, my father, and my sons.

Finally, we were meant to remember together, in community. We need to tell our stories to others and to hear their stories told. We need to help each other with the interpretation of the Larger Story and our own. Our regular times of coming together to worship are intended to be times of corporate remembrance. "This, God has done," we say; "this, He will do." How different Sunday mornings would be if they were marked by a rich retelling of the Sacred Romance in the context

of real lives. This is a far cry from the fact-telling, principle list-
ing, list keeping that characterizes much of modern worship.

One of the reasons modern evangelicalism feels so thin is
because it is merely modern; there is no connection with the
thousands of years of saints who have gone before. Our community of memory must include not only saints from down the
street, but also those from down the ages. Let us hear the stories of John and Teresa from last week, but also those of St.
John of the Cross and Teresa of Avila, to name only two. Let us
draw from that "great cloud of witnesses" and learn from their
journeys, so that our memory may span the story of God's relationship with his people.

Remembering is not mere nostalgia; it is an act of survival,
our way of "watching over our hearts with all diligence." In *The
Brothers Karamazov*, the gentle Alyosha says, "And even if only
one good memory remains with us in our hearts, that alone may
serve some day for our salvation." Jesus seems to capture this
moment in the parable of the prodigal son. It's a classic story of
how one man tries to capture the Romance through the false
transcendence of wine, women, and song. His small story col-
lapses in on him and it appears all is lost. There, in the pigsty,
he is on the verge of destruction. Would it not have been easy
enough for him to kill his heart with sentences like, "This is
where it all ends. This is what life is truly about. Whatever it was
my heart was searching for, it is all a lie. There is no real
Romance and I am nothing but a fool." The drama of this parable is so true to life. He raises that last arrow, ready to drive it
through his heart, when suddenly, he *remembers*. And he hits
the road for home.

When I consider all that is at stake in this journey I am on,
how vulnerable are my heart and the hearts of those I love, how
quickly I forget, I am moved to fall on my face and cry out to
God for the grace to remember. George MacDonald says it better in poetry.

> Were there but some deep, holy spell, whereby
> Always I should remember thee. . . .
> Lord, see thou to it, take thou remembrance's load:
> Only when I bethink me can I cry;
> Remember thou, and prick me with love's goad.
> When I can no more stir my soul to move,
> And life is but the ashes of a fire;
> When I can but remember that my heart
> Once used to live and love, long and aspire—
> Oh, be thou then the first, the one thou art;
> Be thou the calling, before all answering love,
> And in me wake hope, fear, boundless desire.
> (*Diary of an Old Soul*)

The final burden of remembrance does not rest on us; if it did, we should all despair. Returning to the passage from Hebrews that I quoted earlier, Jesus is called the "author and perfecter of our faith" (12:2). He is the One who put the romance in our hearts and the One who first opened our eyes to see that our deepest desire is fulfilled in him. He started us on the journey and he has bound himself to see us through. Even though we may for long seasons forget him, he does not forget us.

> "I am always with you;
> you hold me by my right hand
> You guide me with your counsel,
> and afterward you will take me into glory. . . .
> My flesh and my heart may fail,
> but God is the strength of my heart
> and my portion forever" (*Ps. 73:23, 26*).

Nor will he leave us without reminders along the way. "The world is fairly studded and strewn," writes Annie Dillard, "with unwrapped gifts and free surprises . . . cast broadside from a generous hand." Our heart can be restored to life and the smallest things become heavy with transcendence when we ask one simple question: What is this telling me about the Sacred Romance?

This summer, I found it in the crickets. After tucking my boys in bed, with the requisite several glasses of water, trips to the potty, and prayers, the house finally grew quiet. I stood at the upstairs window looking out on our backyard and in the darkness, with the warm breeze caressing my face, I listened. Perhaps it was the long winter then behind us, perhaps it was the long winter of the soul that went along with it, but there was in the song of the crickets something that released my heart. Memories of all the summers past rose and mingled with the promise of the summer that would now come again. Beneath that, something deeper spoke, something at once young and yet very old. It whispered the promise of the summer that was soon coming, which would never pass into fall.

Bibliography

Buechner, Frederick. *Son of Laughter*. San Francisco: Harper San Francisco, 1993.

———. *Telling Secrets*. San Francisco: Harper San Francisco, 1991.

———. *Telling the Truth: The Gospel as Tragedy, Comedy and Fairy Tale*. San Francisco: Harper and Row, 1977.

Dickens, Charles. *A Tale of Two Cities*. New York: Portland, 1988.

Dillard, Annie. *Teaching a Stone to Talk*. New York: Harper and Row, 1982.

Donne, John. *Donne*. New York: Knopf, 1995.

Dooley, David, ed. *The Collected Works of G. K. Chesterton*. Vol. I. San Francisco: Ignatius, 1986.

Frost, Robert. *Robert Frost's Poems*. New York: Washington Square Press, 1946.

Groom, Winston. *Forrest Gump*. Produced by Steve Tisch and Wendy Fineman; directed by Robert Zemekis. Paramount Pictures, 1994.

Hein, Rolland, ed. *The Heart of George MacDonald*. Wheaton: Harold Shaw, 1994.

Hutchinson, F. E., ed. *The Works of George Herbert*. Oxford: Oxford University Press, 1972.

Houston, James. *The Heart's Desire*. Oxford: Lion, 1992.

Jenson, Robert. *Story and Promise*. Ramsey: Siglar, 1989.

Kierkegaard, Sooren. *Philosophical Fragments.*, trans. David Swenson. Princeton, NJ: Princeton University Press, 1962. As quoted in Yancey, Philip. *Disappointment with God.* New York: Harper Paperbacks, 1988.

Kreeft, Peter. *Everything You Ever Wanted to Know About Heaven But Never Dreamed of Asking.* San Francisco: Ignatius, 1990.

Lewis, C. S. *The Great Divorce.* New York: Simon and Schuster, 1946; Touchstone, 1996.

———. *The Lion, the Witch, and the Wardrobe.* New York: Macmillan, 1950; Collier Books, 1970.

———. *Perelandra.* New York: Macmillan, 1944.

———. *The Weight of Glory.* Grand Rapids: Eerdmans, 1949.

MacDonald, George. *Diary of an Old Soul.* Minneapolis: Augsburg, 1994.

———. *Unspoken Sermons.* As Quoted in Lewis, C. S., ed. *George MacDonald: 365 Readings.* New York: Macmillan, 1947.

Maclean, Norman. *A River Runs Through It.* Chicago: Univ. of Chicago Press, 1976.

May, Gerald. *Addiction and Grace.* San Francisco: Harper San Francisco, 1988.

McGrath, Alister. *A Passion for Truth.* Downers Grove, IL: InterVarsity, 1996.

Merton, Thomas. *The Ascent To Truth.* San Diego: Harcourt and Brace, 1951.

———. *The Wisdom of the Desert.* New York: New Directions, 1960, 1963. Quoted in Henri J. M. Nouwen, *The Way of the Heart.* New York: Ballantine Books, 1981.

Nouwen, Henri J. M. *The Way of the Heart.* New York: Ballantine Books, 1981.

Ricks, Christopher, ed. *Milton: Paradise Lost and Paradise Regained.* New York: Signet, 1968.

St. John of the Cross. *The Living Flame of Love.*, trans David Lewis. London: Thomas Baker, 1934.

Tugwell, Simon. *Prayer*. Ireland: Veritas.

Van Leeuwen, Mary Stewart. *Prism*, February 1995.

Wiersbe, Warren, ed. *The Annotated Pilgrim's Progress*. Chicago: Moody, 1980.

Wilcox, David. "Show the Way"; © 1994 Irving Music, Inc., and Midnight Ocean Bonfire Music (BMI). Used by permission of Warner Brothers Publications U.S., Inc., Miami, FL 33014.

Wright, William Aldis. *The Complete Works of William Shakespeare*. Garden City, NY: Garden City, 1936.

Yancey, Philip. *Disappointment with God*. New York: Harper Paperbacks, 1988.

Acknowledgments

BRENT CURTIS: Any creative work is in some sense indebted to every person who has had an impact on one's life, for good or for bad. At this moment, I would like to thank some of those whose lives and hearts have contributed in special ways to what is written here.

I want to give much thanks to Jan and Sharon, my partner and my secretary, respectively, for their heartfelt suggestions and encouragement; my partner Laura for facing with me the loneliness of spiritual warfare; Randy Raysbrook, for sharing with me the fruit of his own exploration of the place of the heart in the spiritual life; and Bruce Nygren, for trusting John and me and for editing our work with a light hand.

To Ralph and Isaac, who have walked with me in different times and on different legs of the journey as brothers of the heart—you have impacted my life in eternal ways; and to John, whose heart and courage in pursuing God flow through the pages of this book intermingled with my own—I thank God for each of you.

To my sisters, Candy, Angelita, and Brenda, and my brother, Donnie: The years of growing up have mingled your joys, sorrows, and struggles with my own in ways that are with me always. To you, Mom, for always wanting our best; and to Paul, Don, and my own father, Frederick—from each of you I learned something about being a man.

To you, Drew and Ben, for all the times of "block from the

hallway," prison tag, wrestling, and laughing at silly things. I love you both with all my heart and pray this book will be a window on the deepest thing that has guided my own life's journey. As well, may it be a light and a compass, part of guiding your own way home to the Lord Jesus Christ, who gave you to Mom and me out of his love.

Last, to you, Ginny, for loaning me your eyes and heart in reading the manuscript and for your patience over the years with my rough edges. Remember the black sand beach in New En-gland and the wedding ring captured on the last pull of the rake? In anticipation and hope, I dedicate this book to you.

JOHN ELDREDGE: Thanks to you, Dad, for teaching me to fish, introducing me to the West, and for our years together on the water and in the woods. And to you, Mom, for introducing me to the theater, to Shakespeare, and literature; and to both of you, for your love to me.

Thanks to you, Brent, for the idea of this book and for the immense courage and grace it took to collaborate.

Thanks to my wife, Stasi, whose great heart has been to mine an inspiration beyond words, love too deep for telling. I dedicate this book to you.

And from both of us, our gratitude and heartfelt love to Jesus of Nazareth, Author and Finisher of the Sacred Romance.

About the Authors

The late BRENT CURTIS was a counselor in private practice and the author of *Guilt*, published in 1992 by NavPress. He was killed in a climbing accident in 1998.

JOHN ELDREDGE is the author of numerous books including *Fathered by God, Walking with God, Epic, Waking the Dead, Wild at Heart* and coauthor of *Captivating* and *The Sacred Romance*. John, his wife, Stasi, and their three sons live in Colorado where they pursue adventure in the mountains, the woods, and on the rivers. He is also founder of Ransomed Heart, a ministry helping men and women discover the heart of God.

DESIRE

THE JOURNEY WE MUST TAKE TO FIND THE LIFE GOD OFFERS

FOR BRENT

INTRODUCTION

There's an old proverb I've come to love and appreciate very much. "Above all else, guard your heart, for it is the wellspring of life" (Proverbs 4:23). The wisdom of the passage is simply this—to lose heart is to lose everything. Because everything that makes a life worth living flows from the heart. Intimacy, romance, love. Adventure and meaning and purpose. Courage and sacrifice and joy. The list could go on and on. We need this wellspring of life within us if we would live and not merely "get by."

So then, how do we guard our heart? How do we even know what our heart is up to, or how it's doing, or where it's headed? In some sense, you have to read the whole of Scripture to get a good answer. But I can give you one secret to your heart—desire. What you do with desire is what you do with your heart. How you handle your deep desires is how you handle your heart. It's that straightforward.

Desire is powerful. One of the most powerful forces in our lives. At least, it was meant to be.

But we're not quite sure how we feel about desire, really. Or what to do with it. Desire feels . . . messy. You see those books out there promising you, "The life you dream of is yours to have! Follow your desire!" It sounds good. But we've all seen people try it and fail. They leap to a new career, or open themselves up to intimacy, or start up a project they've always dreamed about. And it comes crashing down, they come limping home. Seems like the only guy who can pull it off is the author of the book making all the promises. And we wonder, "Is it worth risking, opening myself up to my desires?"

Then you've got the other camp, often coming from well-intended church folk who warn, "Don't even think about it. Desire is only going to get you into trouble." And, there's reason to believe them. We've seen the affairs, the addictions, the financial ruin and all the other heartache brought on by someone "following their desire." It looks utterly reasonable to simply kill desire. And call it sanctification. The path of maturity.

Both camps are right, in a way. And they're both wrong. Desire *can* lead us to the life we were meant to live. And, desire can get us into a heap of trouble, too. Or just profound disappointment. Desire is a lot like love in that way. When it's good, it's really good. And when it's bad, it's really bad. Many people fear love for that very reason. Just as they fear desire. But a life without love can hardly be called living. The same holds true when we abandon our heart's deep desires. Instead of guarding the wellspring of life within us, we cap it with a cement plug and try to get on with life.

It doesn't really work. You end up losing heart. And that is an awful place to find yourself.

I believe desire is a gift from God. After all, the Psalms say things like, "May he give you the desire of your heart," (20:4) and, "Praise the Lord, O my soul . . . who satisfies your desires with good things so that your youth is renewed like the eagle's" (103:5), and "You open your hand and satisfy the **desires** of every living thing" (145:16). Clearly, God is not opposed to desire. Far from it. He gave us a heart that desires deeply, and he uses those desires to draw us to himself, and to the life he created us to live.

What we need to learn is how to listen to desire, how to *interpret* it. Desire is speaking to us, all the time. It is one of the deepest voices of the heart. A voice many of us have never been taught to understand. Desire can lead us to the life we were meant to live. It can shape our hopes and dreams, fill them with passion and determination. It can sustain us in times of distress and suffering, too. It can lead us to God. If we will listen closely.

That is why we *must* take the journey of desire, the path of learning to listen to desire, and sort it through, and find in it the treasure God has for us. In fact, when I first published this book, it was called *The Journey of Desire*. But I don't think anyone understood the title. And the book came at an unfortunate time, right before the release of another book called *Wild at Heart*, which ended up eclipsing it. This little gem sort of fell between the cracks. But it has so much to offer, so much hope and guidance for this dangerous journey of the heart we call living.

To live life fully—that is to say, to live life as God meant for us to live—demands a full recovery of our heart. You need that wellspring flowing swift and clear and true. And that, my friends, waits upon how you handle your heart's desire. So, we are re-releasing this book in hopes that it will be a great gift and a blessing to you. Yes, it is risky entering into the realm of desire. "It's a dangerous business," Bilbo admitted, "going out of your door. You step into the Road, and if you don't keep your feet, there is no knowing where you might be swept off to." But it's a far, far greater risk not to. Would you spend your whole life shut up inside, gathering cobwebs and dust?

The adventure calls. The future awaits. How you handle your heart's desire will in great measure determine what becomes of your life. So let us take the journey together.

ONCE UPON A time there lived a sea lion who had lost the sea.

He lived in a country known as the barren lands. High on a plateau, far from any coast, it was a place so dry and dusty that it could only be called a desert. A kind of coarse grass grew in patches here and there, and a few trees were scattered across the horizon. But mostly, it was dust. And sometimes wind, which together make one very thirsty. Of course, it must seem strange to you that such a beautiful creature should wind up in a desert at all. He was, mind you, a sea lion. But things like this do happen.

How the sea lion came to the barren lands, no one could remember. It all seemed so very long ago. So long, in fact, it appeared as though he had always been there. Not that he belonged in such an arid place. How could that be? He was, after all, a sea lion. But as you know, once you have lived so long in a certain spot, no matter how odd, you come to think of it as home.

CHAPTER ONE

OUR HEART'S
DEEPEST SECRET

We are never living, but hoping to live.

—PASCAL

It seems to me we can never give up longing and wishing while we are alive. There are certain things we feel to be beautiful and good, and we must hunger for them.

—GEORGE ELIOT

And I still haven't found what I'm looking for.

—U2

There is a secret set within each of our hearts. It often goes unnoticed, we rarely can put words to it, and yet it guides us throughout the days of our lives. This secret remains hidden for the most part in our deepest selves. It is the desire for life as it was meant to be. Isn't there a life you have been searching for all your days? You may not always be aware of your search, and there are times when you seem to have abandoned looking altogether. But again and again it returns to us, this yearning that cries out for the life we prize. It is elusive, to be sure. It seems to come and go at will. Seasons may pass until it surfaces again. And though it seems to taunt us, and may at times cause us great pain, we know when it returns that it is priceless. For if we could recover this desire, unearth it from beneath all other distractions, and embrace it as our deepest treasure, we would discover the secret of our existence.

You see, life comes to all of us as a mystery. We all share the same dilemma—we long for life and we're not sure where to find it. We wonder if we ever do find it, can we make it last? The longing for life within us seems incongruent with the life we find around us. What is available seems at times close to what we want, but never quite a fit. Our days come to us as a riddle, and the answers aren't handed out with our birth certificates. We must journey to find the life we prize. And the guide we have been given is the desire set deep within, the desire we often overlook or mistake for something else or even choose to ignore.

The greatest human tragedy is to give up the search. Nothing is of greater importance than the life of our deep heart. To lose heart is to lose everything. And if we are to bring our hearts along in our life's journey, we simply must not, we cannot, abandon this desire. Gerald May writes in *The Awakened Heart*,

> There is a desire within each of us, in the deep center of ourselves that we call our heart. We were born with it, it is never completely satisfied, and it never dies. We are often unaware of it, but it is always awake . . . Our true identity, our reason for being, is to be found in this desire.

The clue as to who we really are and why we are here comes to us through our heart's desire. But it comes in surprising ways, and often goes unnoticed or is misunderstood. Once in a while life comes together for us in a way that feels good and right and what we've been waiting for. These are the moments in our lives that we wish could go on forever. They aren't necessarily the

"Kodak moments," weddings and births and great achievements. More often than not they come in subtler, unexpected ways, as if to sneak up on us.

Think of times in your life that made you wish for all the world that you had the power to make time stand still. Are they not moments of love, moments of joy? Simple moments of rest and quiet when all seems to be well. Something in your heart says, *Finally—it has come. This is what I was made for!*

WHISPERS OF JOY

It was the final evening of our summer vacation. We had spent nine wonderful days in the Tetons hiking and swimming, laughing and playing, enjoying rare and wonderful time together as a family in a stunningly beautiful place. During our explorations, we had discovered a quiet pond in the woods, about a half hour's walk from camp, where wildlife would often come in the evening. This night, we planned to arrive at dusk and stay until night fell to see what nature might reveal. The sun was setting behind us as we arrived, and far off in the east massive thunderheads were building above the Absarokas, cloud upon cloud, giant castles in the sky. The fading day was slowly turning them peach, then pink, then gray.

A pair of trumpeter swans were swimming across our little pond, looking for all the world like something from a fairy tale. My wife and I sat together with our three boys on a spot of grass near the water's edge, our backs against a fallen log. Across the pond lay a meadow, the stage for the evening's drama. As light began to fade, a bull moose with a massive rack emerged from the willows directly across the meadow from where we sat. He spotted us and stopped; we held our breath. Silently, he disappeared into the trees as mysteriously as he had come. Before we could be disappointed, a cow moose and her calf appeared from another part of the meadow, wandering along grazing. We watched them as night continued to fall.

A cool breeze stirred the pines above us. Crickets began their twilight chorus. The cow lay down in the tall grass, but we could still see her calf. Sandhill cranes were calling and answering one another around the marsh with their haunting, primeval cries. The boys huddled closer to us. A beaver swam by our feet, making a V through the surface of the pond, faded with the light to a gunmetal gray. Far off in the distance, lightning was beginning within those cloud fortresses, flashes of glory. A small herd of elk came out to graze at the far end of the meadow, just as darkness was settling in. Finally, as if not to be left out, a lone coyote began to howl. It was one of the most breathtaking nights I have ever experienced in the wilderness, a living work of art. As the Scottish poet George MacDonald knew so well, something is calling to us in moments like these.

> Yet hints come to me from the realm unknown;
> Airs drift across the twilight border land,
> Odored with life;
> . . . whispers to my heart are blown
> That fill me with a joy I cannot speak,
> Yea, from whose shadow words drop faint and weak.
>
> (*Diary of an Old Soul*)

I know these years are passing quickly, and the time will come when our boys will no longer want to vacation with us. They will find other loves and form other ties, and our lives will never be the same again. Sitting there with them in the woods, clutching their flashlights, whispering to each other about each passing mystery, I would have given anything to stop the clock, turn it back if only for a few days, let us live it all again. But the seasons pass with or without our permission, and I knew in my heart we could not stay. For a moment, we were all caught up in something bigger and more beautiful than we had ever known, "suspended above the earth," as Norman MacLean says, "free from all its laws, like a work of art. And I knew just as surely and just as clearly, that life is not a work of art, and that the moment could not last."

ECHOES FROM THE PAST

Sometimes these moments go unrecognized as they unfold, but their secret comes to us years later in our longing to relive them. Aren't there times in your life that if you could, you would love to return to? I grew up in Los Angeles but spent my boyhood summers in Oregon where both my mother's and my father's parents lived. There was a beauty and innocence and excitement to those days. Woods to explore, rivers to fish, grandparents to fuss over me. My parents were young and in love, and the days were full of adventures I did not have to create or pay for, but only live in and enjoy. Rafting and swimming in the Rogue River. Playing in the park. Huckleberry pie at Becky's along the road to Crater Lake. We all have places in our past when life, if only for a moment, seemed to be coming together in the way we knew in our hearts it was always meant to be.

> There was a time when meadow, grove, and stream,
> The earth, and every common sight,
> To me did seem
> Appareled in celestial light,
> The glory and the freshness of a dream . . .
> Heaven lies about us in our infancy;

Shades of the prison-house begin to close
Upon the growing boy,
But he beholds the light, and whence it flows.
He sees it in his joy; . . .
At length the man perceives it die away,
And fade into the light of common day.
(*Ode, Intimations of Immortality from Recollection of Childhood*)

Wordsworth caught a glimpse of the secret in his childhood, saw in it hints from the realm unknown. We must learn the lesson of these moments, or we will not be able to bring our hearts along in our life's journey. For if these moments pass, never to be recovered again, then the life we prize is always fading from view, and our hearts with it. It isn't until the kids are out of the house that you realize how precious were those years. The inflatable pool in the backyard. The stockings hung up at Christmastime. First steps and first home runs and first dates. We fill photo albums with all these moments, trying to hang on to them somehow. We hate to see them slip away. Our losses seem to say that the life we prize will never be ours, never come to stay. But the secret is coming to us even in our greatest losses.

SHOUTS OF LAMENT

I did not know how much Brent meant to me until I lost him. He was killed last year at this time, in a climbing accident. We had taken a group of men to the mountains on a retreat, believing that to help a man recover his heart, you must take him out of the office, away from the television, and into the wild. We planned three days at a ranch in Colorado where we would bring rock climbing, fly-fishing, and horseback riding together with talks on the journey of a man's heart. Brent was leading the climbing on day two when he fell. The loss was unspeakable for many, many people. Ginny lost her husband. Ben and Drew lost their daddy. Many people lost the only man who had ever fought for their hearts.

I lost the truest friend I have ever known. Brent was more than my partner; he was for me the rarest of gifts—his heart saw what mine saw. Our friendship was a shared journey, a mutual quest, for the secret of our souls. It took us into the mountains, into literature and music, into the desperate battle raging all around for the hearts of others as well. We laughed and grieved and scorned and yearned all along the way. When he lost his son in a mountaineering accident, Nicholas Wolterstorff wrote,

> There's a hole in the world now . . . A center, like no other, of memory and hope and knowledge and affection which once inhabited this earth is gone. Only a gap remains. A perspective in this world unique in this world which once moved about in this world has been rubbed out . . . There's nobody who saw just what he saw, knows what he knew, remembers what he remembered, loves what he loved . . . Questions I have can never now get answers. The world is emptier. (*Lament for a Son*)

This is silly, really, and a little embarrassing, but I find myself turning suddenly when I see a silver gray Jeep pass by. I look to see if it is his, if he is there. Brent is gone; I know that. How I know that. But still, I find myself doing a double take when I see a Jeep like his. Something rises in me, something beyond reason. A hope that perhaps it is his, that he is driving past me again. The other day I was in a parking lot and saw a beat-up old Cherokee with a rack on top. I stopped, went over, and looked. I know in my head that this is ridiculous. Brent is gone. But my heart refuses at some level to accept it. Or rather, my yearning for things to be right is so strong that it overrides my logic and turns my head, in hope against hope, every time.

"The heart," Blaise Pascal said, "has its reasons which reason knows not of." Something in us longs, hopes, maybe even at times believes that this is not the way things were supposed to be. Our desire fights the assault of death upon life. And so people with terminal illnesses get married. Prisoners in a concentration camp plant flowers. Lovers long divorced still reach out in the night to embrace one who is no longer there. It's like the phantom pain experienced by those who have lost a limb. Feelings still emanate from that region where once was a crucial part of them, and they will sometimes find themselves being careful not to bang the corner of a table or slam the car door on a leg or an arm long since removed. Our hearts know a similar reality. At some deep level, we refuse to accept the fact that this is the way things are, or must be, or always will be.

Simone Weil was right; there are only two things that pierce the human heart: beauty and affliction. Moments we wish would last forever and moments we wish had never begun. What are we to make of these messengers? How are we to interpret what they are saying? The playwright Christopher Fry writes,

> The inescapable dramatic situation for us all is that we have no idea what our situation is. We may be mortal. What then? We may be immortal. What then? We are plunged into an existence fantastic to the point of nightmare, and however hard we rationalize, or however firm our religious faith, however closely we dog the heels of science or wheel among the starts of mysticism, we cannot really make head or tail of it. ("A Playwright Speaks: How Lost, How Amazed, How Miraculous We Are")

And what does Fry say we do with our dilemma? The worst of all possible reactions:

We get used to it. We get broken into it so gradually we scarcely notice it.

THE SAME OLD THING

Something awful has happened; something terrible. Something worse, even, than the fall of man. For in that greatest of all tragedies, we merely lost Paradise—and with it, everything that made life worth living. What has happened since is unthinkable: we've gotten used to it. We're broken in to the idea that this is just the way things are. The people who walk in great darkness have adjusted their eyes. Regardless of our religious or philosophical beliefs, most of us live as though this life is pretty much the way things are supposed to be. We dismiss the whispers of joy with a cynical "Been there, done that, bought the T-shirt." That way we won't have to deal with the haunting.

I was just talking with some friends about summer vacations, and I recommended that they visit the Tetons. "Oh, yeah, we've been there. Nice place." Dismissal. And we deaden our sorrows with cynicism as well, sporting a bumper sticker that says, "Life sucks. Then you die." Then we try to get on with life. We feed the cat, pay the bills, watch the news, and head off to bed, so we can do it all again tomorrow.

Standing before the open fridge, I'm struck by what I've just watched. Famine in Africa. Genocide . . . where? Someplace I can't even pronounce. I think it used to be part of the Soviet bloc. Corruption in Washington. Life as usual. It always ends with the anchor folding his notes and offering a pleasant "Good night." Good night? That's it? You have nothing else to say? You've just regaled us with the horrors of the world we live in, and all you can say is "Good night"? To be fair, he did promise more details—with film—at eleven. Just once I wish he would pause at the close of his report, take a long, deep breath, and then say, "How far we are from home," or "If only we had listened," or "Thank God, our sojourn here is drawing to an end." It never happens. I doubt it ever will. And not one of us gives it a second thought. It's just the way things are. Anytime I ask my neighbor how life is going, he always replies, "Same old thing."

Think with me for a moment. How has life turned out differently from the way you thought it would? If you are single, did you want to be? If you are married, is this the marriage you hoped for? Do you long to have children, or in having them, are you delighted with the course they've chosen for their lives? Your friendships—are they as rich and deep and lasting as you want? When the holidays roll around, do you look forward with eager anticipation to the time you'll spend with the people in your life? And afterward, as you pack away the decorations and clean up the mess, did the reality match your expectations?

How about your work, your place in the world—do you go to bed each night with a deep sense of having made a lasting contribution? Do you enjoy ongoing recognition for your unique successes? Are you even working in a field that fits you? Are you working at all? Now, what if I told you that this is how it will always be, that this life as you now experience it will go on forever just as it is, without improvement of any kind? Your health will stay as it is; your finances will remain as they are, your relationships, your work, all of it.

It is hell.

IN DEFENSE OF DISCONTENT

By the grace of God, we cannot quite pull it off. In the quiet moments of the day we sense a nagging within, a discontent, a hunger for something else. But because we have not solved the riddle of our existence, we assume that something is wrong—not with life, but with us. *Everyone else seems to be getting on with things. What's wrong with me?* We feel guilty about our chronic disappointment. *Why can't I just learn to be happier in my job, in my marriage, in my church, in my group of friends?* You see, even while we are doing other things, "getting on with life," we still have an eye out for the life we secretly want. When someone seems to have gotten it together, we wonder, *How did he do it?* Maybe if we read the same book, spent time with him, went to his church, things would come together for us as well. We can never entirely give up our quest. May reminds us,

> When the desire is too much to bear, we often bury it beneath frenzied thoughts and activities or escape it by dulling our immediate consciousness of living. It is possible to run away from the desire for years, even decades, at a time, but we cannot eradicate it entirely. It keeps touching us in little glimpses and hints in our dreams, our hopes, our unguarded moments. (*The Awakened Heart*)

He says that even though we sleep, our desire does not. "It is who we are." We *are* desire. It is the essence of the human soul, the secret of our existence. Absolutely nothing of human greatness is ever accomplished without it. Not a symphony has been written, a mountain climbed, an injustice fought, or a love sustained apart from desire. Desire fuels our search for the life we prize. Our desire, if we will listen to it, will save us from committing soul-suicide, the sacrifice of our hearts on the altar of "getting by." The same old thing is not enough. It never will be.

The secret that begins to solve the riddle of our lives is simply this: we are the sea lion who lost the sea. Life as usual is not the life we truly want. It is not the life we truly need. It is not the life we were made for. If we would only listen to our hearts, to what G. K. Chesterton called our "divine discontent," we would learn the secret of our existence. As he wrote in *Orthodoxy*, "We have come to the wrong star . . . That is what makes life at once so splendid and so strange. The true happiness is that we *don't* fit. We come from somewhere else. We have lost our way."

The meaning of our lives is revealed through experiences that at first seem at odds with each other—moments we wish would never end and moments we wish had never begun. Those time-less experiences we want to last forever whisper to us that *they were meant to*. We were made to live in a world of beauty and won-der, intimacy and adventure all our days. Nathaniel Hawthorne insisted, "Our Creator would never have made such lovely days, and given us the deep hearts to enjoy them, above and beyond all thought, unless we were meant to be immortal."

There is more to these days than pictures tucked away in photo albums, fading as the memory fades from view. We use a statement to try to console ourselves with what we think is the irrecoverable loss: "All good things come to an end." I hate that phrase. It's a lie. Even our troubles and our heartbreaks tell us something about our true destiny. The tragedies that strike us to the core and elicit the cry, "This isn't the way it was sup-posed to be!" are also telling the truth—it *isn't* the way it was supposed to be. Pascal writes,

> Man is so great that his greatness appears even in knowing him-self to be miserable. A tree has no sense of its misery. It is true that to know we are miserable is to be miserable; but to know we are miserable is also to be great. Thus all the miseries of man prove his grandeur; they are the miseries of a dignified person-age, the miseries of a dethroned monarch . . . What can this incessant craving, and this impotence of attainment mean,

unless there was once a happiness belonging to man, of which only the faintest traces remain, in that void which he attempts to fill with everything within his reach? *(Pensées)*

Should the king in exile pretend he is happy there? Should he not seek his own country? His miseries are his ally; they urge him on. Let them grow, if need be. But do not forsake the secret of life; do not despise those kingly desires. We abandon the most important journey of our lives when we abandon desire. We leave our hearts by the side of the road and head off in the direction of fitting in, getting by, being productive, what have you. Whatever we might gain—money, position, the approval of others, or just absence of the discontent itself—it's not worth it. "What good will it be for a man if he gains the whole world, yet forfeits his soul?" (Matt. 16:26 NIV).

TAKING UP THE QUEST

We must return to the journey. Wherever we are, whatever we are doing, we must pick up the trail and follow the map that we have at hand. Desire, both the whispers and the shouts, is the map we have been given to find the only life worth living. You may think you are following the map of desire when all you are doing is serving it slavishly, unthinkingly. It is not the same. We must *listen* to desire, look at it carefully, let it guide us through the false routes and dead ends. C. S. Lewis advises us,

I knew only too well how easily the longing accepts false objects and through what dark ways the pursuit of them leads us. But I also saw that the Desire itself contains the corrective of all these errors. The only fatal error was to pretend you had passed from desire to fruition, when, in reality, you had found either nothing, or desire itself, or the satisfaction of some different desire. The dialectic of Desire, faithfully followed, would retrieve all mistakes, head you off from all false paths, and force you to live through . . . a sort of [experiential] proof. (*The Pilgrim's Regress*)

The only fatal error is to pretend that we have found the life we prize. To mistake the water hole for the sea. To settle for the same old thing. Fry called such a life "the sleep of prisoners." You might remember the movie *The Shawshank Redemption*, the story of prison life in the Northeast in the 1940s. The film focuses on the journey of two men's hearts through the trials and temptations of incarceration. Red, the ringleader and most seasoned of the prisoners, explains what happens when you live within those walls too long: "At first, these walls, you hate them. They make you crazy. After a while you get used to 'em, don't notice 'em anymore. Then comes the day you realize you need them." That is the most tragic day of all—to prefer slavery to freedom, to prefer death to life. We must not stay in this sleep. The time has come for us to wake, to arise from our slumber. As the Scriptures say, "Wake up, O sleeper, rise from the dead" (Eph. 5:14 NIV). And so MacDonald prayed,

When I can no more stir my soul to move,
And life is but the ashes of a fire;
When I can but remember that my heart
Once used to live and love, long and aspire—
Oh, be thou then the first, the one thou art;
Be thou the calling, before all answering love,
And in me wake hope, fear, boundless desire.
(*Diary of an Old Soul*)

Bringing our heart along in our life's journey is the most important mission of our lives—and the hardest. It all turns on what we do with our desire. If you will look around, you will see that most people have abandoned the journey. They have lost heart. They are camped in places of resignation or indulgence, or trapped in prisons of despair. I understand; I have frequented all those places before and return to them even still. Life provides any number of reasons and occasions to abandon desire. Certainly, one of the primary reasons is that it creates for us our deepest dilemmas. To desire something and not to have it—is this not the source of nearly all our pain and sorrow?

THERE WAS A time, many years back, when the sea lion knew he was lost. In those days, he would stop every traveler he met to see if he might help him find his way back to the sea.

But no one seemed to know the way.

On he searched, but never finding. After years without success, the sea lion took refuge beneath a solitary tree beside a very small water hole. The tree provided refuge from the burning rays of the sun, which was very fierce in that place. And the water hole, though small and muddy, was wet, in its own way. Here he settled down and got on as best he could.

CHAPTER TWO

THE DILEMMA OF DESIRE

I never knew the dusk could break my heart
So much longing folding in
I'd give years away to have you here
To know I can't lose you again.

—FERNANDO ORTEGA

Who needs a heart when a heart can be broken?

—TINA TURNER

I am almost committing an indecency. I am trying to rip open the
inconsolable secret in each one of you—the secret which hurts so
much that you take your revenge on it by calling it names like
Nostalgia and Romanticism and Adolescence.

—C. S. LEWIS

High on the slopes of the world's tallest mountain, slightly less than twenty-nine thousand feet above the level of the sea, the climber has halted in his tracks. He can go no farther. His whole life has come down to this. After years of planning and preparation, he has trekked halfway across the globe to a strange country high in the Himalayas. He has drained his bank account and damaged his relationships. His career has suffered. He has sacrificed everything in his life for this moment. But none of that matters now. He is exhausted. His breathing is labored. He is forced to pause after each step for three heaving breaths, followed by another step, then a pause. As he creeps along a razor's edge of snow, each move requires an agonizing amount of concentration. Oxygen deprivation reduces his mental faculties to those of a small child. Ahead of him rises the Hillary Step, a forty-foot wall of nearly vertical ice. It is all that stands between him and the goal of his life. But he is not sure he can go on.

I am haunted by the stories of people who make the summit of Everest. Such incredible devotion is required, such total focus of body, soul, and spirit. Reaching the top of the world's tallest mountain becomes for those who try the central driving force of their lives. The goal is remarkable and the journey uncertain. Many climbers have been lost on the mountain. Those who reach the summit and return safely are among a rare and elite group of mountaineers in the world. Why do they do it? *How* do they do it?

Jon Krakauer recounted the desperate tale of the ill-fated '96 expedition in his book *Into Thin Air*: "There were many, many fine reasons not to go, but attempting to climb Everest is an intrinsically irrational act—a triumph of desire over sensibility." It is a feat begun in desire that can be accomplished only through desire. Krakauer explained how one of his climbing partners attained the summit: "Yasuko had been propelled up the mountain by the unwavering intensity of her desire."

Desire—it's the only way you will ever make it. Take marriage, for instance. Or singleness. Either makes for a far more difficult and arduous ascent than Everest, in large part because it does not seem so. The struggles are not heightened and focused into one month of do or die; rather, they stretch on across a lifetime. So it is with any act of faith or of hope—anything, in other words, that makes a life worth living. How can we possibly sustain such an intrinsically irrational act as love if we've killed our desire? May honestly admits,

> Choosing love will open spaces of immense beauty and joy for you, but you will be hurt. You already know this. You have retreated from love countless times in your life because of it. We all have. We have been and will be hurt by the loss of loved ones, by what they have done to us and we to them. Even in the bliss of love there is a certain exquisite pain: the pain of too much beauty, of overwhelming magnificence. Further, no matter how perfect a love may be, it is never really satisfied . . . In both joy and pain, love is boundless. (*The Awakened Heart*)

Desire is the source of our most noble aspirations and our deepest sorrows. The pleasure and the pain go together; indeed, they emanate from the same region in our hearts. We cannot live without the yearning, and yet the yearning sets us up for disappointment—sometimes deep and devastating disappointment. One storm claimed the lives of eight of Krakauer's companions in the Everest disaster of 1996. Should they not have tried? Many have said they were foolish even to begin. Do we reach for nothing in life because our reaching opens us up to tragedy? Because of its vulnerable nature, desire begins to feel like our worst enemy.

FRIEND OR FOE?

"I'm beginning to despise the hope." We were talking about life, a friend and I, and how hard it was to keep pressing on. David had been through a series of setbacks in his career, going from earning a six-figure income at a top Wall Street firm to driving a courier van, making deliveries. It's the hardest fall a man takes. He didn't want to be there; he wanted to climb out of the slump he was in. Occasionally, an opportunity would present itself. He'd get a call or a contact through a friend. Putting on a coat and tie, David would head out into the arena. The desire for something better would resurface, only to be thwarted. The interview seemed to go well at the time, but then he'd sit by the phone and the call would never come. Each time he reached for a rung up the ladder, the rung broke, and he found himself back at the bottom. After several years of the cycle, he found himself despising hope. "It just sets me up for another fall. Why bother?"

I think of another friend, Carol, whose life has been marked over the years by one disappointing relationship after another. Just when she is ready to call it quits on loving altogether, hope appears on the horizon. She ventures out cautiously. And several months later, her heart is broken again. Over lunch yesterday she used nearly the same words: "I hate hope." Hope rouses the desire from its slumber and makes us even more vulnerable to disappointment.

As Carol and I spoke about life and love, I thought of Fantine, one of the tragic characters in Victor Hugo's novel *Les Misérables*. Fantine is a young single mother who works in a factory to support her daughter, whom she had to send away to live with an innkeeper. Fired for refusing the sexual advances of the foreman, she finds herself on the streets without a job, a place to stay, or a means of caring for her child. Those of you who have seen the musical will recall the hauntingly beautiful song she sings, entitled "I Dreamed a Dream."

> I had a dream in time gone by
> When hope was high

And life worth living
I dreamed that love would never die
I dreamed that God would be forgiving.

She remembers being young and unafraid, that time in our lives when dreams are "made and used and wasted." She tells of a love that came to her, filling her days with endless wonder. He became the father of her child and then, one day, disappeared. She dreams he will return, but knows he never will. I know too many women who have lived through this nightmare. Their lives are filled with weariness, loneliness, and resignation. Fantine ends by singing,

I had a dream my life would be
So different from this hell I'm living
So different now from what it seemed
Now life has killed the dream I dreamed.

WHEN DREAMS DIE

I understand. I know the dilemma of desire. Brent was killed on the doorstep of our dreams. You see, as our friendship deepened over the years, we discovered within us a similar hope. Long before I met him, I had begun to dream of having a ranch where people could come to recover their hearts, a place of beauty and adventure where one could learn about life's journey. I was shy to even mention it; heaven knows I had hidden it from everyone for years. How stunned with delight I was to find that he held the same desire. C. S. Lewis knew:

Are not all lifelong friendships born at the moment when at last you meet another human being who has some inkling . . .

of that something which you were born desiring, and which, beneath the flux of other desires and in all the momentary silences between the louder passions, night and day, year by year, from childhood to old age, you are looking for, watching for, listening for? (*The Problem of Pain*)

God seemed to be affirming that dream as we partnered together, speaking at conferences, writing, counseling. Still, it felt like courage even to allow ourselves to dream. We had both known enough disappointment in our lives to be wary of hope; maybe we'd both grown more than a little resigned. Both of us had been failed deeply by key men in our lives. Dare we trust?

Yet something deeper in us urged us to move forward. Alexander Pope knew that "hope springs eternal in the human breast." We planned to begin this great ascent of our desire last May, inviting a small group of men to join us on a ranch for a long weekend of conversation and adventure. It would be the inaugural voyage, the test flight for our dream. On the afternoon of the second day, Brent was killed. The rocks on which he was standing eighty feet above the ground crumbled beneath him.

"Despair," wrote James Houston, "is the fate of the desiring soul." Or as Scripture says, "Hope deferred makes the heart sick" (Prov. 13:12 NLT). How agonizing it can be to awaken desire! Over the past year I have wrestled deeply with what it means to go on. God has come to me again and again, insisting that I not give up the dream. I have ranted and railed, fought him and dismissed him. It feels crazy to desire anymore. What does it mean to live the rest of my life without my closest friend? I think of Lewis and Clark, those inseparable wilderness explorers, how we cannot think of one without the other. Lewis said of his companion, "I could neither hope, wish, nor expect from a union with any man on earth, more perfect support or further aid in the discharge of my mission, than that, which I am confident I shall derive from being associated with yourself." I know I shall never find another like him.

But I am not alone in this. Most of you will by this time have lost a parent, a spouse, even a child. Your hopes for your career have not panned out. Your health has given way. Relationships have turned sour. We all know the dilemma of desire, how awful it feels to open our hearts to joy, only to have grief come in. They go together. We know that. What we don't know is what to do with it, how to live in this world with desire so deep in us and disappointment lurking behind every corner. After we've taken a few arrows, dare we even desire?

I have come to the point that I am able to start looking at ranches again, but I can barely open myself to friendship. Still, something in me knows that to kill desire is to kill my heart altogether. Langston Hughes wrote,

> Hold fast to dreams
> For if dreams die
> Life is a broken-winged bird
> That cannot fly.
> Hold fast to dreams
> For when dreams go
> Life is a barren field
> Frozen with snow. ("Dreams")

Do we form no friendships because our friends might be taken from us? Do we refuse to love because we may be hurt? Do we forsake our dreams because hope has been deferred? To desire is to open our hearts to the possibility of pain; to shut down our hearts is to die altogether. The full proverb reads this way:

"Hope deferred makes the heart sick, *but when dreams come true, there is life and joy.*"

The road to life and joy lies through, not around, the heart-sickness of hope deferred. A good friend came to this realization recently. As we sat talking over breakfast, he put words to our dilemma: "I stand at the crossroads, and I am afraid of the desire. For forty-one years I've tried to control my life by killing the desire, but I can't. Now I know it. But to allow it to be, to let it out is frightening because I know I'll have to give up the control of my life. Is there another option?"

The option most of us have chosen is to reduce our desire to a more manageable size. We allow it out only in small doses—just what we can arrange for. Dinner out, a new sofa, a vacation to look forward to, a little too much to drink. It's not working. The tremors of the earthquake inside are beginning to break out.

THE BATTLE BETWEEN US

I haven't been the friendliest driver lately. Oh, I'm fine—until I'm provoked. When people cut me off, I'm furious. Just the other day, a car began to get on the highway as I was passing by. The fellow ignored all the rules of merging and cut in front of me as I was doing full speed. I hit my brakes to avoid him and honked my horn. He looked back, snarled, and yelled something unprintable. That did it. Only the fear of higher insurance premiums kept me from running him off the road. But oh, how I wanted to. Of course, this never happens to you. You are kind and benevolent when someone cuts you off. Why, you're practically happy when he steals your parking place, darts in right ahead of you. You smile and offer a blessing.

What is causing the quarrels and fights among you? Isn't it the whole army of evil desires at war within you? You want what you don't have, so you scheme and kill to get it. You are jealous for what others have, and you can't possess it, so you fight and quarrel to take it away from them. (James 4:1–2 NLT)

What do you make of all the road rage that's been surfacing? You don't think it's really about traffic etiquette, do you? People are shooting at each other on the freeway. This is not about bad manners or a need for driver's ed. There is something deeper, something pent up inside us. The fellow who cut me off didn't really endanger my life; but the violation felt like a symbol of a deeper, ongoing reality. Dan Allender points out,

> In every person there is a passionate, driving desire for more . . . The dilemma is that our longings for material joy are almost always partially blocked; our desires for better health and deeper relationships are never entirely possible; and the illusion of world peace seems no more attainable than the gold at the end of the rainbow. Our passion is more than usually stymied. The world simply does not bend to the desires that roar or whimper inside us. Our desires—from picking the quickest line at the bank to the overwhelming hope that our children will walk righteously with the Lord—are rarely satisfied in a way that relieves the ache of incompleteness . . . Our heart seems to rage against the ache. Our typical response to the heartbreak and sorrow of disappointment is murderous rage . . . We want someone to pay. (*Bold Love*)

The life we have is so far from the life we truly want, and it doesn't take us long to find someone to blame. In order for our longings to be filled, we need the cooperation of others. I long for a loving embrace and a kind word when I get home. I long for my boys to listen attentively when I talk about important life lessons. I want my work to be appreciated. I want my friends to be there for me in hard times. "No man is an island," wrote John Donne, and he could have been speaking of desire. We need others—it's part of our design. Very few of our desires are self-fulfilling; *all* our deepest longings require others to come through for us. Inevitably, someone stands in the way.

At its best, the world is indifferent to my desires. The air traffic controllers aren't the least affected when I've been traveling for a week and the plane they've chosen to cancel is my last chance to get home to my family. So long as it doesn't affect them, they couldn't care less. We suffer the violation of indifference on a daily basis, from friends, from family, from complete strangers. We think we've grown to accept it as part of life, but the effect is building inside us. We weren't made to be ignored. And though we try to pretend it doesn't really matter, the collective effect of living in a world apathetic to our existence is doing damage to our souls. Events such as bad traffic or delayed flights are merely the *occasions* for our true desperation to come out. As our desires come into direct conflict with the desires of another person, things get downright hostile.

We fought the Gulf War because Saddam Hussein wanted the rich oil fields of Kuwait. Phil and Diane fought the bedroom war over pork chops. They had invited another couple for dinner, and as Diane went out for the afternoon, she asked Phil to get the pork chops out of the freezer to thaw. He was working on the lawn mower and forgot. Dinnertime arrived, and Diane asked Phil to put the chops on the grill. He suddenly remembered that they were still hard as rocks in the freezer. You know the phrase "if looks could kill"? Diane couldn't say what she wanted to say. Their guests were sitting right there, and she had an image to maintain. She let Phil have it with a look and later that night finished the job off when they were alone.

Søren Kierkegaard said that resentment is the "constituent principle" of the modern era, this simmering anger at our blocked desires. We shove them beneath the surface for as long as possible, only to have them erupt on the freeway, in the classroom, or at home in a burst of physical or verbal retaliation. Our anger is rarely proportionate to the event. I yelled at my five-year-old son, Luke, at dinner tonight because he was being disrespectful to his mom. But is that all that was behind my stern rebuke? Aren't events like that the triggers, opening the doors to a reservoir of disappointment we pretend for the most part we have risen above? We try to get beyond the pain of desire by burying it, but it does not go away. It surfaces in other ways.

And so, Scripture says, we find ourselves in a civil war of desire. The horrors of this war go well beyond spoiled dinners and a little marital tension. We will sacrifice anything on the altar of our anger, the rage that is slowly building from a lifetime of thwarted desire—our marriages, our child's self-esteem, someone's very life. At the same moment that Krakauer's companions were battling for their lives on Everest's southeast ridge, three Indian climbers were stranded by the storm on the other side of the mountain as they attempted the summit from the northeast. Unable to work their way down, they spent the night on the face of the mountain without shelter in a howling blizzard. The following morning, two Japanese climbers ascending by the same route came across the climbers, now near death. They offered no assistance; no food or water, no bottled oxygen. They didn't even speak to them, but stepped aside and took their rest a few hundred feet beyond. The Japanese climbers made the summit; then they left the Indians to die as they passed them again on their way back down.

There is a reason Jesus chose lust and murder as examples of what happens when desire goes mad within us. He knew what our desperate hearts naturally do when our desires come into conflict. He knew to what lengths we would go to seek satisfaction of our soul's hunger. For the battle of desire rages not only between us, but *within* us.

THE BEAST WITHIN

Jeremy called and asked to see me to talk about "a little financial problem" he was having. I told him, sure, I could spare an hour of my Saturday. I thought he might need a small loan or some help with his checkbook. But when I saw the look on his face, I knew an hour wasn't going to be enough. Jeremy's little problem was that he had taken every credit card he owned to the limit, accumulating thousands of dollars in debt. Knowing he was unemployed at the time, with no prospect at all of paying off such a load, he was panic-stricken. "Good grief," I asked, "how did it happen?" The story proved more outrageous than the debt. He had booked himself a week at a five-star resort. Posing as a wealthy physician, Jeremy entertained a variety of women—"gold diggers"—purchasing their affections with lavish gifts and gourmet dinners. By the end of his self-created fantasy island trip he had lost his integrity and about ten thousand dollars.

I would never have believed it unless he himself had told me, through tears of shame and regret. He is a quiet and unassuming man, the complete opposite of some jet-setting gigolo. No one would have dreamed he was capable of such a thing. But then again, we wonder: *What am I capable of? Dare I even begin to feel my desire?* We may not go so far, but we know that there is a ravenous beast within us. Years of living in an indifferent and often hostile world create a deep sense of unsettledness within us. A friend asked the other day: "How important are feelings of desire? I ask because I have a seeming overabundance of desire, but it sometimes goes astray in a crazed and hopeless pursuit of brownies or something of the sort."

> Something has gone wrong deep within me and gets the better of me every time. It happens so regularly that it's predictable. The moment I decide to do good, sin is there to trip me up. I truly delight in God's commands, but it's pretty obvious that not all of me joins in that delight. Parts of me covertly rebel, and just when I least expect it, they take charge. (Rom. 7:20–23 *The Message*)

> For the sinful nature desires what is contrary to the Spirit, and the Spirit what is contrary to the sinful nature. They are in conflict with each other, so that you do not do what you want. (Gal. 5:17 NIV)

There is a nagging awareness inside us, warning that we'd better not feel our hunger too deeply or it will undo us. We might do something crazed, desperate. We are caught on the horns of a dilemma; our unmet desires are a source of trouble, and it feels as if it will get worse if we allow ourselves to feel how much we do desire. Not only that, we often don't even know what we desire. Dan, a passionate young friend now finishing college, just sent this e-mail:

> Chris McCandless wrote, "All hail the Phantom Bear, the beast within us all." Well the "Bear" so to speak has really been growling loud as of late. I seem to be daily wanting more out of my life than what I have been living. Leo Tolstoy wrote, "I felt in myself a superabundance of energy which found no outlet in my quiet life." And that really describes me well. I want more . . .

more of God in my life . . . more intimacy with my friends . . . and I feel bad for wanting it. Everyone seems so content here and simple . . . and also I feel like I'm longing for nothing I'm certain of.

We try food, tennis, television, or sex, going from one thing to another, never quite finding satisfaction. The reason we don't know what we want is that we're so *unacquainted* with our desire. We try to keep a safe distance between our daily lives and our heart's desire because it causes us so much trouble. We're surprised by our anger and threatened by what feels like a ravenous bear within us. Do we really want to open Pandora's box? If you remember the Greek myth, Pandora was the wife of Epimetheus, given to him by Zeus. The gods provided many gifts to her, including a mysterious box, which she was warned never to open. Eventually, her curiosity got the better of her, and she lifted the lid. Immediately, a host of evils flew out, plagues against the mind and body of mankind. She tried to close the box, but to no avail; the troubles had been loosed.

Dare we awaken our hearts to their true desires? Dare we come alive? Is it better, as the saying goes, to have loved and lost than never to have loved at all? We're not so sure. After his divorce, a friend's father decided to remain single the rest of his life. He told his son, "It's easier to stay out than to get out." Our dilemma is this: we can't seem to live with desire, and we can't live without it. In the face of this quandary most people decide to bury the whole question and put as much distance as they can between themselves and their desires. It is a logical and tragic act. The tragedy is increased tenfold when this suicide of soul is committed under the conviction that this is precisely what Christianity recommends. We have never been more mistaken.

⸺ HAD YOU JOURNEYED in those days through the barren lands, you might have seen the sea lion for yourself. Quite often in the evening, he would go and sit upon his favorite rock, a very large boulder, which lifted him off the burning sand and allowed him a view of the entire country.

There he would remain for hours into the night, silhouetted against the sky. And on the best nights, when the wind shifted to the east, a faint smell of salt air would come to him on the breeze. Then he would close his eyes and imagine himself once more at the sea. When he lay himself down to sleep, he would dream of a vast, deep ocean. Twisting and turning, diving and twirling, he would swim and swim and swim. When he woke, he thought he heard the sound of breakers.

The sea was calling to him.

CHAPTER THREE

DARE WE DESIRE?

But for real proof you must look at your own longings and aspirations; you must listen to the deep themes of your own life story.

—GERALD MAY

Longing is the heart's treasury.

—AUGUSTINE

What do you want?

—JESUS OF NAZARETH

The shriveled figure lay in the sun like a pile of rags dumped there by accident. It hardly appeared to be human. But those who used the gate to go in and out of Jerusalem recognized him. It was his spot and had been for as long as anyone could remember. He was disabled, dropped off there every morning by someone in his family, and picked up again at the end of the day. Over the years, a sort of gallery of human brokenness gathered by the pool of Bethesda—the lame, the blind, the deaf, lepers, you name it. A rumor was going around that sometimes (no one really knew when) an angel would stir the waters, and the first one in would be healed. Sort of a lottery, if you will. And as with every lottery, the desperate gathered round, hoping for a miracle. So—technically speaking—the man was never alone. But it had been so long since anyone had actually *spoken* to him, he thought the question was meant for someone else. Squinting upward into the sun, he didn't recognize the figure standing above him. The misshapen man asked the fellow to repeat himself; perhaps he had misheard. Although the voice was kind, the question felt harsh, even cruel.

"Do you want to get well?"

He sat speechless, blinking into the sun. Slowly, the words seeped into his consciousness, like a voice calling him out of a dream. *Do I want to get well?* Slowly, like a wheel long rusted, his mind began to turn over. *What kind of question is that? Why else would I be lying here? Why else would I have spent every day for the past thirty-eight seasons lying here? He is mocking me.* The man was familiar with mockery and had endured his share of ridicule. But now that his vision had adjusted to the glare, he could see the inquisitor's face, his eyes. There was no hint of mockery. The face was as kind as the voice he heard. Apparently, the man meant what he said, and he was waiting for an answer. "Do you want to get well? What is it that you want?"

"Hey, there, you without the legs—what are you lying here for? Wouldn't you love to get up, stretch yourself a bit, have a walk around?" Who dared ask something so callous? It was Jesus who posed the question, so there must be something we're missing here. He is love incarnate. Why did he ask the paraplegic such an embarrassing question? Of course the fellow wanted to get well. You don't have to be God to see the obvious. Or was it? As with most of the questions he posed, Jesus was probing for something we do not see. He knew the answer, of course—but did the man? Do we? Think of the fellow on the ground for a moment; put yourself, literally, in his shoes. His entire life has been shaped by his brokenness. All his days he has wanted one thing. Forget riches. Forget fame. Life for this man was captured in one simple, unreachable desire. When the other children ran and played, he sat and watched. When his family stood at the temple to pray, he lay on the ground. Every time he needed to have a drink or to go to the bathroom, someone had to pick him up and take him there.

So he had gone there for the past thirty-eight years, hoping to hit the jackpot. Sure, it was a long shot, but it was all he had. At what point did he begin to lose hope? First a year, then two went by. Nothing, at least for him. Maybe someone else got a miracle; that would buy him some time. What about after five years with no results? Ten? How long can we sustain desire against continual disappointment? Some hold out longer than others, but eventually, we all move to a place of resignation or cynicism or bitterness. As the years rolled on, this man, like all of us, began to lose any vital heart-connection to what he wanted. He was present, but not accounted for. The calluses had formed—not in the heart of Jesus, but over the man's heart. He had abandoned desire. Jesus took him back into the secret of his own heart. By asking him what he wanted, Jesus took the man *back into* his desire. Why?

It is where we must go if we are to meet God.

AN INVITATION TO DESIRE

This may come as a surprise to you: Christianity is not an invitation to become a moral person. It is not a program for getting us in line or for reforming society. It has a powerful effect upon our lives, but when transformation comes, it is always the *aftereffect* of something else, something at the level of our hearts. At its core, Christianity begins with an invitation to *desire*. Look again at the way Jesus relates to people. As he did with the fellow at the Sheep Gate, he is continually taking them into their hearts, to their deepest desires.

The story of the two blind men on the road to Jericho repeats the theme. Jesus is passing by the spot where these two men have sat looking for a handout for who knows how long. They learn that Jesus is going by, and they cry out for him. Though the crowd tries to shut them up, they succeed in shouting over the ruckus and capturing the Master's attention. The parade stops. Jesus steps to the side of the road, and standing there before him are two men, nothing clearer than the fact that they are blind. "What do you want me to do for you?" Again the question. Again the obvious that must not be so obvious after all.

Then there is the Samaritan woman whom Jesus meets at the well. She has come alone in the heat of the day to draw water, and they both know why. By coming when the sun is high, she is less likely to run into anyone. You see, her sexual lifestyle has earned her a "reputation." Back in those days, having one partner after another wasn't looked so highly upon. She's on her sixth lover, and so she'd rather bear the scorching rays of the sun than face the searing words of the "decent" women of the town who come at evening to draw water. She succeeds in avoiding the women, but runs into God instead. What does he choose to talk to her about—her immorality? No, he speaks to her about her *thirst*: "If you knew the generosity of God and who I am, you would be asking *me* for a drink, and I would give you fresh, living water" (John 4:10 *The Message*). Remarkable. He doesn't give a little sermon about purity; he doesn't even mention it, except to say that he knows what her life has been like: "You've had five husbands, and the man you're living with now isn't even your husband" (John 4:18 *The Message*). In other words, now that we both know it, let's talk about your heart's real thirst, since the life you've chosen obviously isn't working. "The water I give will be an artesian spring within, gushing fountains of endless life" (John 4:14 *The Message*).

Later in the gospel of John, Jesus extends the offer to anyone who realizes that his life just isn't touching his deep desire: "If you are thirsty, come to me! If you believe in me, come and drink! For the Scriptures declare that rivers of living water will flow out from within" (John 7:37–38 NLT). His message wasn't something new, but it confounded the religious leaders of the day. Surely, those scripturally learned Jews must have recalled God's long-standing invitation to them, spoken seven hundred years earlier through the prophet Isaiah:

> Come, all you who are thirsty,
>   come to the waters;
> and you who have no money,
>   come, buy and eat!
> Come, buy wine and milk
>   without money and without cost.
> Why spend money on what is not bread,
>   and your labor on what does not satisfy?
> Listen, listen to me, and eat what is good,
>   and your soul will delight in the richest of fare.
>   (Isa. 55:1–2 NIV)

Somehow, the message had gotten lost by the time Jesus showed up on the scene. The Jews of his day were practicing a very soul-killing spirituality, a lifeless religion of duty and obligation. They had abandoned desire and replaced it with knowledge and performance as the key to life. The synagogue was the place to go to learn how to get with the program. Desire was out of the question; duty was the path that people must walk. No wonder they feared Jesus. He came along and started *appealing* to desire.

To the weary, Jesus speaks of rest. To the lost, he speaks of finding your way. Again and again and again, Jesus takes people back to their desires: "Ask and it will be given to you; seek and you will find; knock and the door will be opened to you" (Matt. 7:7 NIV). These are outrageous words, provocative words. *Ask, seek, knock*—these words invite and *arouse* desire. What is it that you *want*? They fall on deaf ears if there is nothing you want, nothing you're looking for, nothing you're hungry enough to bang on a door over.

Jesus provokes desire; he awakens it; he heightens it. The religious watchdogs accuse him of heresy. He says, "Not at all. This *is* the invitation God has been sending all along." He continues,

> You have your heads in your Bibles constantly because you think you'll find eternal life there. But you miss the forest for the trees. These Scriptures are all about *me!* And here I am, standing right before you, and you aren't willing to receive from me the life you say you want. (John 5:39–40 *The Message*)

LIFE IN ALL ITS FULLNESS

Eternal life—we tend to think of it in terms of existence that never comes to an end. And the existence it seems to imply—a sort of religious experience in the sky—leaves us wondering if we *would* want it to go on forever. But Jesus is quite clear that when he speaks of eternal life, what he means is life that is absolutely wonderful and can never be diminished or stolen from you. He says, "I have come that they may have life, and have it to the full" (John 10:10 NIV). Not, "I have come to threaten you into line," or "I have come to exhaust you with a long list of demands." Not even, "I have come primarily to forgive you." But simply, *My purpose is to bring you life in all its fullness.* Dallas Willard writes in *The Divine Conspiracy,*

Jesus offers himself as God's doorway into the life that is truly life. Confidence in him leads us today, as in other times, to become his apprentices in eternal living. "Those who come through me will be safe," he said. "They will go in and out and find all they need. I have come into their world that they may have life, and life to the limit."

In other words, eternal life is not primarily *duration* but *quality* of life, "life to the limit." It cannot be stolen from us, and so it does go on. But the focus is on the life itself. "In him was life," the apostle John said of Jesus, "and that life was the light of men" (John 1:4 NIV). Notice that the people who aren't so good at keeping up with the program but who are very aware of their souls' deep thirst are captured by Jesus' message. Common folk tear the roofs off houses to get to him. They literally trample each other in an effort to get closer to this man. I've never seen anyone acting like this in order to get a chance to serve on some church committee or to hear a sermon on why dancing is "of the devil." People act like this when it's a matter of life and death. Crowds trample each other to get out of a burning building; they press into the mob to reach a food line. When life is at stake and the answer is within reach, that's when you see human desire unmasked in all its desperation.

The Pharisees miss the boat entirely. Their hearts are hardened by the very law they claimed would bring them life. They put their hope in rules and regulations, in knowing and doing things perfectly. Having killed their souls' thirst with duty, they went on to kill their souls' only Hope, thinking they were doing their duty.

GOOD NEWS THAT'S NOT REALLY

Things appear to have come full circle. The promise of life and the invitation to desire have again been lost beneath a pile of religious teachings that put the focus on knowledge and performance.

> History has brought us to the point where the Christian message is thought to be essentially concerned only with how to deal with sin: with wrongdoing or wrong-being and its effects. Life, our actual existence, is not included in what is now presented as the heart of the Christian message, or it is included only marginally. (*The Divine Conspiracy*)

Thus Willard describes the Gospels we have today as "gospels of sin management." Sin is the bottom line, and we have the cure. Typically, it is a system of knowledge or performance, or a mixture of both. Those in the knowledge camp put the emphasis on getting our doctrine in line. Right belief is seen as the means to life. Desire is irrelevant; *content* is what matters. But notice this—the Pharisees knew more about the Bible than most of us ever will, and it *hardened* their hearts. Knowledge just isn't all it's cracked up to be. If you are familiar with the biblical narrative, you will remember that there were two special trees in Eden—the Tree of Knowledge of Good and Evil and the Tree of Life. We got the wrong tree. We got knowledge, and it hasn't done us much good. T. S. Eliot lamented,

> Endless invention, endless experiment,
> Brings knowledge of motion, but not of stillness;
> Knowledge of speech, but not of silence;
> Knowledge of words, and ignorance of the Word.
> Where is the Life we have lost in living?
> Where is the wisdom we have lost in knowledge?
> ("Choruses from the Rock")

Christianity is often presented as essentially the transfer of a body of knowledge. We learn about where the Philistines were from, and how much a drachma would be worth today, and all sorts of things about the original Greek. The information presented could not seem more irrelevant to our deepest desires.

Then there are the systems aimed at getting our behavior in line, one way or another. Regardless of where you go to church, there is nearly always an unspoken list of what you shouldn't do (tailored to your denomination and culture, but typically rather long) and a list of what you may do (usually much shorter—mostly religious activity that seems totally unrelated to our deepest desires and leaves us only exhausted).

And this, we are told, is the good news. Know the right thing; do the right thing. This is life? When it doesn't strike us as something to get excited about, we feel we must not be spiritual enough. Perhaps once we have kept the list long enough, we will understand.

We don't need more facts, and we certainly don't need more things to do. We need *Life*, and we've been looking for it ever since we lost Paradise. Jesus appeals to our desire because he came to speak to it. When we abandon desire, we no longer hear or understand what he is saying. But we have returned to the message of the synagogue; we are preaching the law. And desire is the enemy. After all, desire is the single major hindrance to the goal—getting us in line. We are told to kill desire and call it sanctification. Or as Jesus put it to the Pharisees, "You load people down with rules and regulations, nearly breaking their backs, but never lift even a finger to help" (Luke 11:46 *The Message*). As a result, Willard says, "The souls of human beings are left to shrivel and die on the plains of life because they are not introduced into the environment for which they were made."

"I began to seriously question my faith," wrote a friend, "when

I was suffering my second year of depression. People in church saw my depressed face, and they complimented me on how I was such a good Christian." I am not making this up. This poor fellow was actually cheered for doing well spiritually when it became apparent his soul was dying. "I thought the best way for a person to live is to keep his desires to a minimum so that he will be prepared to serve God." Isn't that the message? It may not be explicit (what we truly believe rarely is), but it's clear enough. Get rid of desire, and get with the program.

Compare the shriveled life held up as a model of Christian maturity with the life revealed in the book of Psalms:

> You have made known to me the path of life;
> > you will fill me with joy in your presence,
> > with eternal pleasures at your right hand.
> > > (16:11 NIV)

> As the deer pants for streams of water,
> > so my soul pants for you, O God.
> My soul thirsts for God, for the living God.
> > When can I go and meet with God?
> > > (42:1–2 NIV)

> O God, you are my God,
> > earnestly I seek you;
> My soul thirsts for you,
> > my body longs for you,
> in a dry and weary land,
> > where there is no water.
> > > (63:1 NIV)

Ask yourself, Could this person be promoted to a position of leadership in my church? Heavens, no. He is far too unstable, too passionate, too desirous. It's all about pleasure and desire and thirst. And David, who wrote most of the psalms, was called by God a "man after his own heart" (1 Sam. 13:14 NIV).

Christianity has nothing to say to the person who is completely happy with the way things are. Its message is for those who hunger and thirst—for those who desire life as it was meant to be. Why does Jesus appeal to desire? Because it is essential to his goal: bringing us life. He heals the fellow at the pool of Bethesda, by the way. The two blind men get their sight, and the woman at the well finds the love she has been seeking. Reflecting on these events, the apostle John looked at what Jesus offered and what he delivered and said, "He who has the Son has life" (1 John 5:12 NIV).

THE STORY OF DESIRE

We misunderstand the good news Jesus announced when we hear it outside the story God is telling. Good news, a report that brings us relief and joy at the same time, is news that speaks to our dilemma. Hearing from your doctor that the lump is benign is good news. Receiving a notice from the IRS that you will not be audited after all is good news. Getting a call from the police to say that they've found your daughter is good news. Being offered tips and techniques for living a more dutiful life isn't even in the field of good news. We know in our hearts that our dilemma cannot be, "I sure wish I could be a more decent chap. What I really need is a program to improve my morals." Now, Jesus seemed to think that what he was offering really and truly spoke to our dilemma. Those who grasped what he was saying agreed. So what is our dilemma? What do we need most desperately to hear? Where are we in the story?

Let us ask the storytellers. In many ways, Hollywood has mastered the art of speaking to the human predicament. Consider the success of James Cameron's 1997 film *Titanic*. Not only did it sweep the Oscars, but the movie has become the all-time leading box office hit, passing even *Gone with the Wind*. Ticket sales have reached nearly $2 billion. I know people who have seen it not once or twice, but multiple times. It is a phenomenon whose appeal surpassed generational and cultural boundaries. Why? Christian critiques of the film missed the mark entirely, focusing almost exclusively on moral issues (sin management brought to film review). I cannot help thinking that if those reviewers were at the well when the Samaritan woman came by, they would have given her an earful.

But much more is going on here. Obviously, the film touched a nerve; it tapped into the reservoir of human longing for life. What is its story line? The film begins with romance, a story of passionate love, set within an exciting journey. Those who saw *Titanic* will recall the scene early in the film where the two lovers are standing on the prow of the great ship as it slices through a golden sea into a luscious sunset. Romance, beauty, adventure. Eden. The life we've all been searching for because it's the life we all were made for. Have we forgotten—or never been told? Once upon a time, in the beginning of humanity's sojourn on earth, we lived in a garden that was exotic and lush, inviting and full of adventure. It was "the environment for which we were made," as the sea lion was made for the sea. Now, those of you who learned about Eden in Sunday school maybe missed something here. Using flannel graphs to depict Paradise somehow doesn't do it. Picture Maui at sunset with your dearest love. A world of intimacy and beauty and adventure.

But then tragedy strikes. I'm sure I won't ruin the story for anyone if I tell you the ship goes down. How awful, how haunting are those scenes of the slow but irreversible plunge of the great ocean liner, leaving behind a sea of humanity to freeze to death in the Arctic waters. Everything is gone—the beauty, the romance, the adventure. Paradise is lost. And we know it. More than ever before, we know it. There was a time earlier in this century when we believed in the future, in something called progress. Not anymore, especially not the younger generations. I have yet to meet a young person who believes that his life will be better in a few years. As Chesterton said, we all somehow know that we are the "survivors of a wreck, the crew of a golden ship that had gone down before the beginning of the world." The ship has gone down. We are all adrift in the water, hoping to find some wreckage to crawl upon to save ourselves.

But that is not all. The secret of the film's success is found in the final scene. As the camera takes us once more to the bottom of the sea and we are given a last look at the rotting hulk of the once great ship, something happens. The *Titanic* begins to transform before our eyes. Light floods in through the windows. The rust and decay melt away as the pristine beauty of the ship is restored. The doors fly open, and there are all the great hearts of the story, not dead at all, but quite alive and rejoicing. A party is under way; a wedding party. The heroine, dressed in a beautiful white gown, ascends the staircase into the embrace of her lover. Everything is restored. Tragedy does not have the final word. Somehow, beyond all hope, Paradise has been regained.

Isn't this our dilemma? Isn't this the news we have been longing for? A return of the life we prize? Look again at what Jesus offers. There is bread enough for everyone. There is healing for every brokenness. The lost are found. The weary are given rest. There is life available—life to the limit.

I am the Gate. Anyone who goes through me will be cared for—will freely go in and out, and find pasture. A thief is only there to steal and kill and destroy. I came so they can have real and eternal life, more and better life than they ever dreamed of. (John 10:9–10 *The Message*)

DESIRE AND GOODNESS

But doesn't Christianity condemn desire—the Puritans and all that? Not at all. Quite the contrary. Christianity takes desire seriously, far more seriously than the Stoic or the mere hedonist. Christianity refuses to budge from the fact that man was made for pleasure, that his beginning and his end is a paradise, and that the goal of living is to find Life. Jesus knows the dilemma of desire, and he speaks to it in nearly everything he says.

When it comes to the moral question, it is not simply whether we say yes or no to desire, but always what we *do* with desire. Christianity recognizes that we have desire gone mad within us. But it does not seek to rectify the problem by killing desire; rather, it seeks the healing of desire, just as it seeks the healing of every other part of our human being.

"Two things contribute to our sanctification," wrote Pascal. "Pains and pleasures." And while we know that our journey is strewn with danger and difficulty, "the difficulties they meet with are not without pleasure, *and cannot be overcome without pleasure.*" Where do you find Jesus saying, "The problem with you people is, you want too much. If you'd just learn to be happy with less, we'd all get along just fine"? Not anywhere. Quite the contrary. "My commands are for your good," he says, "always."

Something has gone wrong in us, very wrong indeed. So wrong that we have to be told that joy is found not in having another man's wife, but in having our own. But the point is not the law; the point is the joy. Need I say more than this: modern Christianity has brought an entire group of people to the point where they have to be told that sex is, in the words of one book, "intended for pleasure."

God is realistic. He knows that ecstasy is not an option; we are made for bliss, and we must have it, one way or another. He also knows that happiness is fragile and rests upon a foundation greater than happiness. All the Christian disciplines were formulated at one time or another in an attempt to heal desire's waywardness and so, by means of obedience, bring us home to bliss. Walter Brueggemann suggests that faith on its way to maturity moves from "duty to delight." If it is not moving, then it has become stagnant. If it has changed the goal from delight to duty, it has gone backward; it is *regressing*. This is the great lost truth of the Christian faith, that correction of Judaism made by Jesus and passed on to us: the goal of morality is not morality—it is ecstasy. *You* are intended for pleasure!

WHO, THEN, CAN BE SAVED?

Look again at the story Jesus told about the prodigal son. It might be called the story of desire. Consider what each character does with his desire. You have the younger son, whose desires get him into a world of trouble. Then there is the father, whose desire for the lost boy is so deep that he sees him coming from a long way off—he has been watching, waiting. Forgiveness is assumed; it's a given. He's grateful just to have the boy home again. And then there is the older brother. He's the party pooper, if you recall. His younger brother is "back from the dead," as the father says, and the older brother won't even come in for the celebration. He stands outside, sulking. Let's pick up the story there:

> The older brother was angry and wouldn't go in. His father came
> out and begged him, but he replied, "All these years I've worked

hard for you and never once refused to do a single thing you told me to. And in all that time you never gave me even one young goat for a feast with my friends. Yet when this son of yours comes back after squandering your money on prostitutes, you celebrate by killing the finest calf we have." His father said to him, "Look, dear son, you and I are very close, and everything I have is yours. We had to celebrate this happy day. For your brother was dead and has come back to life! He was lost, but now he is found!" (Luke 15:28–32 NLT)

The older brother is the picture of the man who has lived his entire life from duty and obligation. When the wayward son returns from his shipwreck of desire, his brother is furious because he gets a party and not a trip behind the barn with the broadside of a paddle. He tells his father that he has been had; that all these years he hasn't gotten a thing in return for his life of service. The father's reply cuts to the chase: "All that is mine has always been yours." In other words, "You never asked." Rembrandt captures all this powerfully in his now-famous painting *The Return of the Prodigal Son*. In the painting, the elder brother stands a step *above* the reunion of father and son. He will not step down, enter in. He is above it all. But who receives redemption? The scandalous message of the story is this: those who kill desire—the legalists, the dutiful—are not the ones who experience the father's embrace. The question is not, Dare we desire, but dare we *not* desire?

THE SEA LION loved his rock, and he even loved waiting night after night for the sea breezes that might come. Especially he loved the dreams those memories would stir. But as you well know, even the best of dreams cannot go on, and in the morning when the sea lion woke, he was still in the barren lands. Sometimes he would close his eyes and try to fall back asleep. It never seemed to work, for the sun was always very bright.

Eventually, it became too much for him to bear. He began to visit his rock only on occasion. "I have too much to do," he told himself. "I cannot waste my time just idling about." He really did not have so much to do. The truth of it was, waking so far from home was such a disappointment, he did not want to have those wonderful dreams anymore. The day finally came when he stopped going to his rock altogether, and he no longer lifted his nose to the wind when the sea breezes blew.

CHAPTER FOUR

DISOWNED DESIRE

The danger is that the soul should persuade itself that it is not hungry. It can only persuade itself of this by lying.

—SIMONE WEIL

Everybody's got a hungry heart.

—BRUCE SPRINGSTEEN

I n his essay "Screwtape Proposes a Toast," C. S. Lewis portrays the old devil delivering the annual commencement speech for the Tempter's Training College for Young Devils. Screwtape begins his address by lamenting that "the human souls on whose anguish we have been feasting tonight were of a pretty poor quality." He laments that there are so few truly great sinners available at present; they could capture only passive milksops.

Here were vermin so muddled in mind, so passively responsive to environment, that it was very hard to raise them to that level of clarity and deliberateness at which mortal sin becomes possible. To raise them just enough; but not that fatal millimeter of "too much." For then of course all might possibly have been lost. They might have seen; they might have repented.

Screwtape decides that perhaps this is all for the best because there are real dangers when a soul is capable of deep desire. He knows what we have forgotten: "The great (and toothsome) sinners are made out of the very same material as those horrible phenomena, the great Saints."

Dare we forget King David? Yes, his passions got him in a heap of trouble—and gave us our book of *worship*, the Psalms. Sure, Peter was a hotheaded disciple always quick with a reply. Remember in the Garden of Gethsemane—he's the one who lopped off the ear of the high priest's servant. But he was also the first to acknowledge that Jesus was the Messiah, and despite his Good Friday betrayals, he became a key apostle, contributed important pieces to the Scripture, and followed Jesus all the way to his own crucifixion, asking to be nailed to the cross upside down because he was not worthy to die in the manner of his Lord. Surely, we remember that Paul was once Saul, the fiery young Pharisee "advancing in Judaism beyond many Jews of my own age and . . . extremely zealous for the traditions of my fathers" (Gal. 1:14 NIV). His zeal made him the foremost persecutor of the church. When Christ knocked him off his donkey on the Damascus road, Paul was hunting down the church, "uttering threats with every breath" (Acts 9:1 NLT). Christ captured his zeal, and after Damascus it led him to work "harder than all the other apostles" (1 Cor. 15:10 NLT).

Augustine was also a passionate young man, sexually licentious, enamored with the pleasures of Rome, "scratching the sore of lust," as he would call it after Christ got hold of him. He went on to become one of the great pillars of the church, laying the foundation for the rise of Christendom after the fall of Rome. "Tempered in the fires of his own sensuality, toughened by his arduous explorations of the heresies of the age," he became, in Malcolm Muggeridge's words, "a latter-day Noah . . . constrained to construct an ark, in his case Orthodoxy, wherein the Church could survive through the dark days that lay ahead" (*A Third Testament*).

The great saints come from the same material as the "tooth-some sinners." Desire, a burning passion for more, is at the heart of both. Those who would kill the passion altogether would murder the very essence that makes heroes of the faith. They remind me of those misguided physicians of a hundred years ago, who would attempt to cure a fever by "bleeding" their patients, cutting a vein and draining them of bowls of blood, depriving them of the very life force they needed to get better. It's a wonder so many survived. Augustine would later write,

> Give me a man in love; he knows what I mean. Give me one who yearns; give me one who is hungry; give me one far away in this desert, who is thirsty and sighs for the spring of the Eternal Country. Give me that sort of man; he knows what I mean. But if I speak to a cold man, he just doesn't know what I am talking about. (Quoted by Muggeridge in *A Third Testament*)

BLESSED ARE THE NICE?

And so Screwtape reveals the enemy's ploy—first make humans flabby, with small passions and desires, then offer a sop to those diminished passions so that their experience is one of contentment. They know nothing of great joy or great sorrow. They are merely *nice*. One young woman wrote to me,

> My parents always told me to be a "nice little girl." I simply assumed that being nice meant not getting upset or being angry with anyone . . . I was nice because I wanted to be liked, and I figured that people would like someone who was always nice. My senior year of high school I was voted "Nicest Senior" for the senior awards, and it was true. I was nice and I was proud of it. I thought there was no higher virtue than niceness.

Christianity has come to the point where we believe that there is no higher aspiration for the human soul than to be nice. We are producing a generation of men and women whose greatest virtue is that they don't offend anyone. Then we wonder why there is not more passion for Christ. How can we hunger and thirst after righteousness if we have ceased hungering and thirsting altogether? As C. S. Lewis said, "We castrate the gelding and bid him be fruitful."

The greatest enemy of holiness is not passion; it is apathy. Look at Jesus. He was no milksop. His life was charged with passion. After he drove the crooks from the temple, "his disciples remembered that it is written: 'Zeal for your house will consume me'" (John 2:17 NIV). This isn't quite the pictures we have in Sunday school, Jesus with a lamb and a child or two, looking for all the world like Mr. Rogers with a beard. The world's nicest guy. He was something far more powerful. He was holy. G. K. Chesterton wrote,

> Instead of looking at books and pictures about the New Testament I looked at the New Testament. There I found an account, not in the least of a person with His hair parted in the middle or His hands clasped in appeal, but of an extraordinary being with lips of thunder and acts of lurid decision, flinging down tables, casting out devils, passing with the wild scenery of the wind from mountain isolation to a sort of dreadful demagogy; a being who acted like an angry god—and always like a god . . . The diction used about Christ has been . . . sweet and submissive. But the diction used by Christ is quite gigantesque; it is full of camels leaping through needles and mountains hurled into the sea. (*Orthodoxy*)

If the way to avoid the murderous rage and deceptive allures of desire is to kill it, if deadness is next to godliness, then Jesus had to be the deadest person ever. But he is called the *living* God. "It is a dreadful thing," the writer of Hebrews says, "to fall into the hands of the living God . . . For our 'God is a consuming fire'" (Heb. 10:31; 12:29 NIV). And what is this consuming fire? His jealous love (Deut. 4:24). God is a deeply, profoundly passionate person. Zeal consumes him. It is the secret of his life, the writer of Hebrews says. The "joy set before him" enabled Jesus to endure the agony of the Cross (Heb. 12:2 NIV). In other words, his profound desire for something greater sustained him at the moment of his deepest trial. We cannot hope to live like him without a similar depth of passion. Many people find that the dilemma of desire is too much to live with, and so they abandon, they disown their desire. This is certainly true of a majority of Christians at present. Somehow we believe that we can get on without it. We are mistaken.

THE MAN WHO WANTED NOTHING

Initially, Gary and Jill had come to me because their marriage had become merely functional. No major issues—no one was throwing dishes; neither was having an affair. As I realized later, that would have been better, at least a sign of life. Their marriage had all the passion of yesterday's oatmeal. Jill was the one who called because she was afraid that she was losing Gary, that they were "drifting apart." It didn't take long to see why. Gary had checked out. He was still going to work, paying the bills, and cutting the grass, but that was it. There was no emotion, no investment, no reaction to anything. The more vital parts of him were shut down. I asked if he and I might spend some time just talking about his life. As the weeks rolled by, I learned that he had been a faithful church attender, never missing a Sunday. He served on a committee and offered help to those in need. But obviously, something was missing.

I was surprised, frankly, when he showed up each week. Going to counseling can feel like the emotional equivalent of attempting Everest, but I found in him nothing near the desire to make the ascent. After months of getting nowhere, I asked the obvious: "Gary, why are you a Christian?" He sat in silence for what must have been five minutes. "I don't know. I guess because it's the right thing to do." "Is there anything you're hoping to enjoy as a result of your faith?" "No . . . not really." "So what is it that you *want*, Gary?" An even longer silence. I waited patiently. "I don't desire anything." Our sessions ended shortly thereafter, and I felt bad that I was unable to help him. You cannot help someone who doesn't want a thing. All his life Gary had been a good boy. A gelding. And geldings, though they are nicer and much more well behaved than stallions, do not bring life. They are sterile.

I thought of the last story we have from the life of the prophet Elisha. Jehoash was king of Israel at the time, and he went to visit Elisha on his sickbed. He knew that without the help of the great prophet, the future of Israel was looking dim. Enemies were closing in on every side, waiting for the kill. Elisha told the king to take in hand some arrows.

> And the king took them. Elisha told him, "Strike the ground."
> He struck it three times and stopped. The man of God was
> angry with him and said, "You should have struck the ground
> five or six times; then you would have defeated [your enemies]
> completely . . . But now you will defeat [them] only three
> times." Elisha died and was buried. (2 Kings 13:18–20 NIV)

That's it? What a strange story! Why was the old prophet so angry? Because the king was nonchalant; he was passionless, indifferent. He gave the ground a whack or two. His heart wasn't in it. God says, in effect, "If that is how little you care about the future of your people, that is all the help you will get." In other words, if your heart's not in it, well then, neither is mine. You can't lead a country, let alone flourish in a marriage, with an attitude like that. To abandon desire is to say, "I don't really need you; I don't really want you. But I will live with you because, well, I'm supposed to." It is a grotesque corruption of what was meant to be a beautiful dance between desire and devotion.

Your heart longs, and you go to seek the one you desire. She responds to your seeking because it touches her heart's desire to be longed for. Yes, commitment plays a vital role—but only as the *expression* of desire. Duty reduces the dance to a drill. It's as if you showed up with a bouquet of flowers for your anniversary. Your wife is delighted, but then you say, "Think nothing of it, my dear. It's my obligation." John Piper opens his book *Desiring God* with this illustration, showing the deadly effect of duty on a relationship: "Dutiful roses are a contradiction in terms." A woman doesn't want to be an object of duty; she wants to be *desired*. So does God. Thus A. W. Tozer asserted, "God waits to be wanted."

At one point I had asked Gary about his prayer life. "I never ask God for anything," he replied. I wasn't surprised. You see, the real dilemma of desire is that it *humbles* us. It takes us way beyond our own resources where we need to ask for help.

FAITH AS DESIRE

You may recall the story Jesus told of the man who entrusted three of his servants with thousands of dollars (literally, "talents"), urging them to handle his affairs well while he was away. When he returned, he listened eagerly to their reports. The first two fellows went out into the marketplace and doubled their investment. As a result, they were handsomely rewarded.

The third servant was not so fortunate. His gold was taken from him, and he was thrown into "outer darkness, where there will be weeping and gnashing of teeth." My goodness. Why? All he did was bury the money under the porch until his master's return. Most of us would probably agree with the path he chose—at least the money was safe there. But listen to his reasoning. Speaking to his master, he said, "I know you are a hard man, harvesting crops you didn't plant and gathering crops you didn't cultivate. I was afraid I would lose your money, so I hid it." (See Matt. 25:14–30 NLT.) He was afraid of the master, whom he saw as a hard man. He didn't trust his master's heart.

The issue isn't capital gains—it's what we think of God. When we bury our desires, we are saying the same thing: "God, I don't dare desire because I fear you; I think you are hard-hearted."

Just yesterday evening I was taking a walk in our neighborhood, talking to the Lord about going forward and establishing the ranch I have mentioned. I had been moving toward the creation of this place of ministry in what felt like sheer obedience, dragging my heart along behind me. God had been confirming the direction with many signs and affirmations. And yet I sensed that something was wrong. I was asking him what he wanted the ranch to be. He said, *What do you want it to be? What's in your heart?* I was embarrassed by the honesty of my reply: "What do you care about my desires?" There is this hurt and angry place inside, a very old wound, that harbors some rather strong doubts about how much God really cares for me.

We all have this place. Life has not turned out the way we want, and we know God could have handled things differently. Even though we may profess at one level a genuine faith in him, at another level we are like the third servant. Our obedience is not so much out of love as it is out of carefulness. "Just tell me what to do, God, and I'll do it." Killing desire may look like sanctification, but it's really godlessness. Literally, our way of handling life without God.

"But when the Son of Man comes, will he find faith on the earth?" Jesus had been talking about prayer by telling the story of a persistent widow who wasn't getting the justice she deserved from a belligerent judge. The woman won her case because she refused to let up. Jesus used her as a picture of unrelenting desire; he urged us not only to ask, but also to keep on asking. And then he ended the parable by wondering out loud, "When I return, will I find anyone who really lives by faith?" (see Luke 18:1–8 NIV).

We know in our hearts the connection he is making, though we haven't admitted it to ourselves. To live with desire is to choose vulnerability over self-protection; to admit our desire and seek help beyond ourselves is even more vulnerable. It is an act of trust. In other words, those who know their desire and refuse to kill it, or refuse to act as though they don't need help, they are the ones who live by faith. Those who do not ask do not trust God enough to desire. *They have no faith.* The deepest moral issue is always what we, in the heart of hearts, believe about God. And nothing reveals this belief as clearly as what we do with our desire.

PRAYER AS THE LANGUAGE OF DESIRE

The book of Hebrews describes the prayer life of Jesus in the following way: "While Jesus was here on earth, he offered prayers and pleadings, with a loud cry and tears, to the one who could deliver him" (5:7 NLT). That doesn't sound like the way that prayers are offered up in most churches on a typical Sunday morning. "Dear Lord, we thank you for this day, and we ask you to be with us in all we say and do. Amen." No pleading here, no loud cries and tears. Our prayers are cordial, modest, even reverent. Eugene Peterson calls them "cut-flower prayers." They are not like Jesus' prayers or, for that matter, like the psalms. The ranting and raving, the passion and ecstasy, the fury and desolation found in the psalms are so far from our religious expression that it seems hard to believe they were given to us as our *guide* to prayer. They seem so, well, *desperate*. Yet E. M. Bounds reminds us,

> Desire gives fervor to prayer. The soul cannot be listless when some great desire fixes and inflames it . . . Strong desires make strong prayers . . . The neglect of prayer is the fearful token of dead spiritual desires . . . There can be no true praying without desire. (*E. M. Bounds: Man of Prayer*)

A young woman came to see me, as most seeking counseling do, because she was at the end of her rope. What had begun a year earlier as mild depression had sunk deeper and deeper until she found herself contemplating suicide. We met for many weeks, and I came to know a delightful woman with a poet's heart, whose soul was buried beneath years not so much of tragedy but of neglect. This one particular afternoon, we had spoken for more than an hour of how deeply she longed for love, how almost completely ignored and misunderstood she felt her entire life. It was a tender, honest, and deeply moving session. As our time drew to a close, I asked her if she would pray with me. I could hardly believe what came next. She assumed a rather bland, religious tone to her voice and said something to the effect of "God, thank you for being here. Show me what I ought to do." I found myself speechless. *You've got to be kidding me*, I thought. *That's not how you feel at all. I know your heart's true cry. You are far more desperate than that.*

I wish she'd prayed like my son Luke. He is our youngest son and very wise for all of his five years. He knows what he wants and what it means to lose it. "My life is over." Luke laid his head down on the table and sighed, a picture of lament. I had just told him he couldn't have chocolate-covered sugar bombs for breakfast, and he was devastated. There was no longer any reason to go on. Life as he knew it was over. I enjoy Luke because he has more undisguised and unadulterated desire than anyone I know. He is "out there" with his desire and his disappointments. When we go over to someone's house for dinner, the first thing he'll ask will always be, "Is there dessert?" Part of me has tried to train this out of him; part of me admires the fact that he isn't embarrassed by his desire, like the rest of us. He is unashamed. We hide our true desire and call it maturity. Jesus is not impressed. He points to the less sophisticated attitude of a child as a better way to live.

Why are we so embarrassed by our desire? Why do we pretend that we're doing fine, thank you, that we don't need a thing? The persistent widow wasn't too proud to seek help. Neither was the psalmist. Their humility allowed them to express their desire. How little we come to God with what really matters to us. How rare it is that we even admit it to ourselves. "Is there dessert?" We don't pray like Jesus because we don't allow ourselves to be nearly so *alive*. We don't allow ourselves to feel how desperate our situation truly is. We sense that our desire will undo us if we let it rise up in all its fullness. Wouldn't it be better to bury the disappointment and the yearning and just get on with life? As Larry Crabb has pointed out, pretending seems a much more reliable road to Christian maturity. The only price we pay is a loss of soul, of communion with God, a loss of direction, and a loss of hope.

DRIFTING WITHOUT DESIRE

As a teacher, counselor, and author, I love what I do for a living. But it hasn't always been so. I spent a lifetime in Washington, DC, several years ago. They were two of the most miserable years of my life. I don't like government, and I abhor politics. Harry Truman was right: "If you want a friend in Washington, buy a dog." What in the world was I doing there? I didn't really want to go; my employer talked me into accepting a transfer. But I can't put the blame on them. The truth is, I had come to a point where I didn't really know what I wanted in life. My real passion had been the theater, and for a number of years I pursued that dream with great joy. I had my own theater company and loved it. Through a series of events and what felt like betrayals, I had gotten deeply hurt. I left the theater and just went off to find a job. The Washington offer came up, and even though my heart wasn't in it, I let the opinions of people I admired dictate my course. Without a deep and burning desire of our own, we will be ruled by the desires of others.

Ann didn't know whether she should marry the man she was dating. They'd been dating for the last three years of college, and in many ways they enjoyed being together. But now that the possibility of engagement was becoming a reality, she found herself lost as to what she should do. "Do you want to marry him?" I asked. "I don't know. I guess so. I'm not sure." Ann is a very bright and energetic young woman. A youth pastor, she is rarely at a loss for ideas and energy. People regularly turn to her for counsel and encouragement. Ann always knows the "right" thing to do. But she was stumped. There was no "right" course to take. Her boyfriend was a committed Christian and a good man who loved her. She loved him too.

The problem was simply this: Ann had lived her entire life

based on what was right and had never once made a decision based on her desire. The oldest daughter in a family with some very high needs, Ann had been required to grow up much sooner than the others. She was highly responsible, and found her security in meeting the expectations and demands placed upon her. When the moment came for her to live out of her desire, she was out of practice. There was no one to tell her what to do.

I have met many Christians in the same position. I think of Charles, an attorney in his fifties who still doesn't know what he wants to be when he grows up. His wife left him last year. There is Paul, a young man in his twenties who doesn't know what to do with himself now that college is over. He focused on grades and left his heart behind. Jamie isn't sure if she should get married or stay single. Barbara hates her job but hasn't the slightest idea what she'd do if she left. They have all tried to bury their heart under the porch and seek a safer life. The poet David Whyte states,

> The hope is to stay in the background away from the fire, and wait for someone or something to come along and grant us immunity from these difficulties and sacrifices, someone to offer reassurance, saying perhaps, "Take the safe way, not the way of passion and creativity, as the path to your destiny, the life you desire. Follow it and you will never be touched . . ." [But] we cannot neglect our inner fire without damaging ourselves in the process. (*The Heart Aroused*)

The damage, of course, is a life lost unto itself. Millions of souls drifting through life, without an inner compass to give them direction. They take their cues from others and live out scripts from someone else's life. It's a high price to pay. Too high.

HOPELESS WITHOUT DESIRE

A curious warning is given to us in Peter's first epistle. There he tells us to be ready to give the reason for the hope that lies within us to everyone who asks (3:15). Now, what's strange about that passage is this: no one ever asks. When was the last time someone stopped you to inquire about the reason for the hope that lies within you? You're at the market, say, in the frozen food section. A friend you haven't seen for some time comes up to you, grasps you by both shoulders, and pleads, "Please, you've got to tell me. Be honest now. How can you live with such hope? Where does it come from? I must know the reason." In talking with hundreds of Christians, I've met only one or two who have experienced something like this.

Yet God tells us to be ready, so what's wrong? To be blunt, nothing about our lives is worth asking about. There's nothing intriguing about our hopes, nothing to make anyone curious. Not that we don't have hopes; we do. We hope we'll have enough after taxes this year to take a summer vacation. We hope our kids don't wreck the car. We hope our favorite team goes to the World Series. We hope our health doesn't give out, and so on. Nothing wrong with any of those hopes; nothing unusual, either. Everyone has hopes like that, so why bother asking us? It's life as usual. Sanctified resignation has become the new abiding place of contemporary Christians. No wonder nobody asks. Do *you* want the life of any Christian you know?

Having abandoned desire, we have lost hope. C. S. Lewis summed it up: "We can only hope for what we desire." No desire, no hope. Now, desire doesn't always translate into hope. There are many things I desire that I have little hope for. I desire to have lots more money than I do, but I see little reason to think it will come. But there isn't one thing I hope for that I don't *also* desire. This is Lewis's point. Bland assurances of the sweet by-and-by don't inflame the soul. Our hopes are deeply tied to our real desires, and so killing desire has meant a hopeless life for too many. It's as if we've already entered Dante's *Inferno*, where the sign over hell reads, "Abandon hope, all ye who enter here."

The effect has been disastrous, not only for individual Christians, but also for the message of the gospel as a whole. People aren't exactly ripping the roofs off churches to get inside. We see the enemy's ploy: drain all the life and beauty and adventure away from the gospel, bury Christians in duty, and nobody will want to take a closer look. It's so very unappealing.

THE DANGER OF DISOWNED DESIRE

Jenny fell in love in Ecuador. She wasn't looking for love, mind you. She had gone to South America on a missions trip. Her heart has long been devoted to bringing the gospel to Third World peoples, and frankly, she can be pretty intense about it. With her focus on the mission at hand, love was the last thing on her mind. It came as a great surprise. Perhaps it was the romance of being in a foreign country. The beauty of the mountains and the jungles, the exotic flowers and birds, and the intrigues of a Latin culture certainly provided a lush setting for romance to blossom. And then there was the fact that the man she was with was charming and intelligent and just a little bit dashing. Moreover, he was interested in her. His sincere questions, their shared laughter, a mutual sense of purpose added to the powerful potion. There was only one small problem: he was married.

It was with a deep sense of shame that Jenny told me her story. Nothing happened between them, but she let her heart go farther than it should. She was embarrassed, humiliated. I wasn't in the least surprised, not because Jenny is a flirt—far from it. But I've known her for a while now, and I know the story of her heart. Jenny is afraid of intimacy, and she has tried hard to live beyond her longing for love. She has known the betrayal of love and carries the wounds to prove it. Of course, she enjoyed his attention. We were made for that, remember? Like all of us, Jenny is designed for intimacy and adventure. What made me mad was that she was about to draw the wrong conclusion, a conclusion the church has long jumped to: desire gets me into trouble; I must avoid it at all costs. Jenny's story is not about the dangers of desire, but about the dangers of *disowned* desire. Just because she pretends she doesn't really want romance doesn't make the desire go away. It goes underground, to surface somewhere else at some other time.

David Whyte calls this the "devouring animal of our disowned desire." It is the reason behind most affairs in the church. The pastor lives out of duty, trying to deny his thirst for many years. One day, the young secretary smiles at him and it's over. Because he has so long been out of touch with his desire, it becomes overwhelming when it does show up. The danger of disowning desire is that it sets us up for a fall. We are unable to distinguish real life from a tempting imitation. We are fooled by the impostors. Eventually, we find some means of procuring a taste of the life we were meant for.

———— THE SEA LION was not entirely alone in those parts. For it was there he met the tortoise. Now this tortoise was an ancient creature, so weathered by his life in the barren lands that at first, the sea lion mistook him for a rock. He told the tortoise of his plight, hoping that this wise one might be able to help him. "Perhaps," the tortoise mused, "this is the sea." His eyes appeared to be shut against the bright sun, but he was watching the sea lion very closely. The sea lion swept his flippers once against his side, gliding to the end of the water hole and back. "I don't know," he said. "It isn't very deep." "Isn't it?" "Somehow, I thought the sea would be broader, deeper. At least, I hoped so."

"You must learn to be happy here," the tortoise told him one day. "For it is unlikely you shall ever find this sea of yours." Deep in his old and shriveled heart, the tortoise envied the sea lion and his sea. "But I belong to the sea. We are made for each other." "Perhaps. But you have been gone so long now, the sea has probably forgotten you." This thought had never occurred to the sea lion. But it was true, he had been gone for a long, long time. "If this is not my home, how can I ever feel at home here?" the sea lion asked. "You will, in time." The tortoise appeared to be squinting, his eyes a thin slit. "I have seen the sea, and it is no better than what you have found here." "You have seen the sea!" "Yes. Come closer," whispered the tortoise, "and I will tell you a secret. I am not a tortoise. I am a sea turtle. But I left the sea of my own accord, many years ago, in search of better things. If you stay with me, I will tell you stories of my adventures."

The stories of the ancient tortoise were enchanting and soon cast their spell upon the sea lion. As weeks passed into months, his memory of the sea faded. "The desert," whispered the tortoise, "is all that is, or was, or ever will be." When the sun grew fierce and burned his skin, the sea lion would hide in the shade of the tree, listening to the tales woven by the tortoise. When the dry winds cracked his flippers and filled his eyes with dust, the sea lion would retreat to the water hole. And so the sea lion remained, living his days between water hole and tree. The sea no longer filled his dreams.

CHAPTER FIVE

MOCKING OUR DESIRE— THE IMPOSTORS

*We have sailed too close to shore; having fallen in love with life, we
have lost our thirst for the waters of Life.*

—SIR FRANCIS DRAKE

*And my desires, like fell and cruel hounds,
E'er since pursue me.*

—SHAKESPEARE

The problem with desire is, you want everything.

—PAUL SIMON

In fourteen hundred and ninety-two, as we all remember,
Columbus sailed the ocean blue. Instead of opening a trade
route to Asia, he unleashed something in the European
imagination when he reported discovering a New World. What
followed is simply amazing. First, it was the Fountain of Youth.
Ponce de León (who sailed with Columbus on his second voyage
to the Caribbean) learned from the natives of a mythical island
called Bimini. A spring was reported to flow there, whose waters
bestowed eternal youth. He actually obtained the backing of
King Ferdinand to lead a party in search of that coveted fount.

Failing to discover Bimini, Ponce de León stumbled upon Florida, which many aging Americans apparently have found to be nearly as good. Unfortunately, Ponce de León's own life was cut short by the discovery. Apparently, the natives didn't take to his attempt at conquest (and the future prospect of mobile home parks), so they killed him.

Then came El Dorado, the Lost City of Gold. As conquistadores penetrated the mainland of Central and South America, they were enchanted by a legend telling of a kingdom of unfathomable riches located somewhere in the Americas. The finder of this hidden treasure would become wealthy beyond his wildest dreams. In 1535, Sebastian de Belalcazar led a three-year search for the fabled city through the jungles of Colombia. He failed, lost control of Peru, and died of fever. You'd think his fate would have cast a chill on the whole enterprise. Not at all.

Two years later, Francisco de Orellana led an expedition down the Amazon, which also ended in disaster. About the same time, Coronado and his soldiers were marching into northern Mexico, searching for the Seven Cities of Cibola (reputed to be flowing with gold). They returned empty-handed. After a number of additional Spanish failures, Sir Walter Raleigh decided he'd give it a go. Not once, but twice he came in search of El Dorado. On his second expedition in 1616, he violated the express orders of King James I of England and attacked a Spanish settlement in Guyana. His son was killed, and Raleigh was beheaded upon his return to England.

THE SEARCH CONTINUES

What *was* it with those guys? If only Raleigh had given up on his first disappointment. But something in us will not be daunted once we've smelled the promised land. I was supposed to be writing last night, but instead sat on the couch thumbing through a Williams-Sonoma catalog. It calls itself "a catalog for cooks," but really, it's a catalog of the life we wish we had. Everything is beautiful, delicious, elegant. The kitchens portrayed are immaculate—there are no messes. Cooking there would be a joy. The tables are sumptuous with their beautiful china place settings, wine glasses brimming with nectar, gourmet foods deliciously prepared, invitingly presented. Fresh flowers abound. The homes are lovely and spacious; the view out the windows is always a mountain lake, a beach, or perhaps an English garden. Everything is as it ought to be. Glancing through its pages, you get a sense of rest. Life is good. *You see,* the images whisper, *it can be done. Life is within your grasp.* And so the quest continues. But of course. Our address used to be Paradise, remember?

And oh, how we yearn for another shot at it. Flip with me for a moment through the photo album of your heart, and collect a few of your most treasured memories. Recall a time in your life when you felt really special, a time when you *knew* you were loved. The day you got engaged perhaps. Or a childhood Christmas. Maybe a time with your grandparents. I remember one birthday in particular. My wife planned a surprise party and kept it a perfect secret. All day long, I thought everyone had forgotten me; I was thoroughly depressed. I have a hard time with birthdays anyway—the longings they rouse. I had pretty much killed my desire for something special by evening when we went to dinner at one of our favorite restaurants. There were all my friends. I was stunned, humbled, delighted all at once. It was a wonderful evening of laughter and conversation—for me, to celebrate me. A simple event, but I recall the feelings I had even still.

Hold your memory while you gather another, a time of real adventure, such as when you first learned to ride a bike, or galloped on a horse, or perhaps did something exciting on a vacation.

Stasi and I spent our tenth anniversary snorkeling in Kauai, off the Na Pali Coast. We tried to catch up to the sea turtles and grab their flippers, hoping for a ride. It was exotic and more than a little funny. I remember falling asleep that night to the sound of the waves. Now, we were meant to live in a world like that—every day. Just as our lungs are made to breathe oxygen, our souls are designed to flourish in an atmosphere rich in love and meaning, security and significance, *intimacy* and *adventure*. But we don't live in that world anymore. Far from it. Though we try to resolve the dilemma by disowning our desire, it doesn't work. It is the soul's equivalent of holding our breath. Eventually, we find ourselves gasping for air. As Allender said, "Can any human being live with a loss of soul—a loss of his or her very essence?" Of course not. Something will come along and touch those essential places in us, offering a taste of intimacy or adventure.

LOOKING FOR THE GOLDEN PERSON

"Love can touch us one time and last for a lifetime." You had to have been hibernating to have missed Celine Dion singing the theme song of *Titanic* at least once in 1998. It played constantly, in grocery stores, over the radio, and on more than nine million copies of the best-selling CD. A hauntingly beautiful song to be sure, with its Celtic strains, and made all the more powerful by the central myth of our day. Though I believe the film's success was due to its remarkable parallels to the gospel—to our longing for heroic intimacy—that is not why millions were *consciously* drawn to it. *Titanic* roused our desire for Eden, then reaffirmed the leading alternative. It offered romantic love as the answer to the heart's deepest yearnings. The idea is that someone is out there for you, and if you can find him, his love will carry you for a lifetime. How many women in particular were fueled by this film in their search for the Golden Person, their own Jack? As C. S. Lewis warned, "Another personality can become to us 'our America, our New-found-land.'"

You don't think you've been immune to all this, do you? Culture has been chanting that mantra for a long time. Of all the films, songs, television shows, musicals, dramas, poetry, and novels you've partaken of in your life, can you name more than five in which human love is *not* held up as the pinnacle of our quest? It's done so often, we don't give it a second thought when Paradise is relocated in the ideal lover. *Romeo and Juliet; Casablanca; Phantom of the Opera; The Sound of Music; Cinderella; Out of Africa; Forrest Gump.* How many couples came to the altar (or dream of coming) with this expectation? "And they all lived happily ever after." We've been fed this from childhood. Please understand me—of course, we long to be loved by another person. "It is not good for man to be alone." Most people live incredibly lonely lives. Our worst pain comes from our ever-present isolation. We are surrounded by people, but truly known by so few—if any. How we long for a soul-to-soul connection. But something else is going on here, something at the level of *worship*.

Not long ago I received a letter from a woman whose husband had left her. Having been married for ten years, she was understandably devastated. My heart broke as she poured out the pain of her divorce. But as I read on, I became more and more concerned. She said she was weeping constantly and shaking uncontrollably. She wanted to die and was seriously considering taking her own life. It was not initial shock; the letter was penned many months after their breakup. Grief is an expected and appropriate response to the loss of love. But she was reacting as though she had lost her *life*. Which is, of course, what happens when you make someone else your life.

Shortly after that, a young man whom I hadn't spoken with for a number of years called. Through his sobs, I gathered that his wife had left him and the children. He explained that she'd "met someone" on the Internet, and their relationship became her obsession. "It's my turn for love," she declared, "and I'm taking it."

If we could get some distance from it, we'd see it's no less crazy than the search for El Dorado or the Fountain of Youth. Cyber relationships have launched the search for the golden man or woman to a new level because the mystique can be maintained much longer. Internet love doesn't ever have bad breath, you don't get an STD from a terminal, and no one ever has to know. Most people don't take their search to adultery. Instead, they find other, "safer" ways to taste idyllic intimacy. It may be as subtle as that second glance or maybe never quite giving up those letters from a high school sweetheart. When that's not enough, pornography becomes the next level for men. Most women go to fantasy, fed by romance novels, soap operas, or films such as *Titanic*. How else are we to explain our revolving-door marriage policy? *It's out there*, we are told, and like those earlier explorers, we'll destroy families, homes, and careers to get it.

The potion becomes intoxicating the more openly sexual it gets. Sarah McLachlan sings in "Elsewhere,"

> I am drunk in my desire,
> I love the way your hands reach out and hold me near,
> I believe, I believe this is heaven.

You might have seen *City of Angels*, another film released in the late '90s. It tells the story of how one celestial being chooses to fall from grace into the arms of a mortal woman, who happens to be Meg Ryan. While going about his angelic duties, the angel, played by Nicolas Cage, encounters Ryan. He discovers that paradise is not where you'd expect an angel to find it (in paradise) but in her embrace. Renouncing eternity, he becomes a mortal, and they share one exquisite night together. The next morning, Ryan is killed by a bus. Even still, Cage decides it was worth it. He'd do it all again, forfeit heaven "for one smell of her perfume, one touch of her hair." It's a beautiful, powerful story, and we leave the theater with the sound track still playing in our minds, a song called "Iris" by the Goo Goo Dolls.

> And I'd give up forever to touch you,
> 'Cause I know that you feel me somehow,
> You're the closest to heaven that I'll ever be.

Sexual ecstasy has long been the leading rival to the Sacred Romance, but never has it been worshiped so blatantly. Allow me one more example.

> One dark night,
> fired with love's urgent longings
> —ah, the sheer grace!—
> I went out unseen
> my house being now stilled.
> On that glad night
> in secret, for no one saw me,
> nor did I look at anything
> with no other light or guide
> than the one that burned in my heart.
> This guided me
> more surely than the light of noon
> to where he was waiting for me
> —him I knew so well—

there in a place where no one appeared.
O guiding night!
O night more lovely than the dawn!
O night that has united
the Lover with his beloved,
transforming the beloved in her Lover.
Upon my flowering breast,
which I kept wholly for him alone.

No, this is not a recent pop hit. Nor is it the theme to yet another film celebrating human love. It is taken from *The Dark Night*, penned by St. John of the Cross in the 1500s. The Lover in the poem is God, and St. John the beloved. The passion and ecstasy expressed here by this Christian mystic come from a long tradition that finds its roots in Scripture. The psalmists sang, "My soul thirsts for you, my body longs for you. Your love is better than life, my soul clings to you. Whom have I in heaven but you? And earth has nothing I desire besides you." How far we have come. Loreena McKennitt released a CD containing a song of St. John's *Dark Night*—rewritten to adore an earthly lover. She admits that St. John wrote it to "his god" (notice the small *g*), but like all of us, she chooses another god. "How skilled you are at pursuing love!" God laments. "You have lived as a prostitute with many lovers" (Jer. 2:33; 3:1 NIV).

REACHING FOR THE GOLDEN MOMENT

We do the same thing with our hunger for adventure. I imagine there must have been great excitement at the outset for those early explorers—that is, before the mosquitoes and hostile natives became realities. Most of us are not so daring; we prefer our adventure on a more modest scale. Shopping, if you can believe it, has become for most people their experience of a sort of conquest. What do you make of the credit card debt in the U.S.? More than 1.5 billion cards in circulation, with an average balance of $5,000 on each card. (How do you explain *your* current balance?)

We say we worship money, but it's not that simple. Money is merely the means to get what we really want—clothes that give us an image of attractiveness, equipment to provide excitement. Sport-utility vehicles were the top-selling line in the past ten years, but the irony is that less than 5 percent of them are ever actually taken off road. We want the illusion of adventure without really having to risk it. There is big money in outdoor gear right now; the "look" of the expedition is in. Thirty years ago you wouldn't have found a gym in every strip mall. There, in our air-conditioned sanctuaries, we tone our bodies while watching television. We'll take our adventure *vicariously*, preferring for the most part to be voyeurs of the extreme sport rage or our favorite sports teams.

I was surprised when Steven asked to see me about a problem he was having with football. He was engaged to a wonderful young woman, and things were moving along well in their relationship. "So what's wrong?" I asked. "Well . . . her dad, you see . . . he roots for the state rival of my college football team. It's kinda becoming a big deal." I had never encountered this before. This young man had a full-blown addiction to college football. He spent Monday through Friday anticipating the games, Saturday watching the games, and Sunday talking about the outcome. He knew nearly every player's name and his stats by heart. During final exams week, he tried to get away from it by securing himself in a friend's apartment with no TV. It lasted about an hour before he dialed up the Internet and picked up live coverage of his team.

As we talked about what it all meant to him, he described the thrill of going with his dad to see their team win the national play-offs. "I have a picture at home, with all of us in it—my brothers, my dad. I've never seen him so happy, so alive." Notice how important it is that it's the *home* team. We need to feel as though we are a part of the excitement.

I had an affair of my own this past summer—with an internal frame backpack. It was outrageously expensive and totally unnecessary (I have a backpack already). But still, I became obsessed. I dreamed about it during the day. At night, I pored over the catalog, comparing it with others, deepening my conviction that this was all I needed for life to be good. As Dick Keyes has pointed out, most of our idols come in pairs. There is the "nearby idol," the thing close at hand, which gives us a sense of control over our world. And then there is the "faraway idol," which provides the taste of transcendence. In my case, the backpack was the thing within reach, which promised adventure down the road. In sexuality, we work hard on our appearance (what we can control), which in turn draws others to us, bringing, we hope, a sense of being loved. The bottom line is, we don't want to wait for the promise of God to be fulfilled.

We're not the first generation to give it a go; the spirit of it goes back at least as far as the Tower of Babel. But certainly, mankind's *options* have never been greater. The technology, the finances, and the cleverness at our disposal are unsurpassed in the history of the world. The angel may be barring our way back into Eden, but we're bound and determined to get something going on our own. Wal-Mart is open twenty-four hours a day now, with a dozen restaurants nearby. Next door, a multiplex theater with thirty screens. Or stay home—we have more than a hundred channels on the TV. Then there are computer games and the Internet. We've discovered gourmet coffee (tell your grandfather you're paying five dollars for a cup), gourmet jelly beans, gourmet popcorn—you name it. We've nearly perfected our little pleasures. When the going gets tough, the tough go shopping or fishing or out to dinner. They're all impostors—every one. But we're so taken by the dizzying array of choices, we never have to stop and take a good look at what we're doing.

THE NARCOTIC OF PLEASURE

G. K. Chesterton thought that everybody ought to get drunk once a year because if that didn't do you good, the repentance in the morning would. There's nothing like waking up to what you've done, whether it's having too much to drink or eat, or letting your anger fly. The remorse after a flagrant sin often brings a sense of clarity and resolution. (How many New Year's resolutions are made the morning after?) But if we don't quite overdo it, if we keep our indulgence at a more moderate level, such clarity never comes. We never see it in black and white, for we're always under the influence. No one stops to think about it. Pleasure isn't nearly so much about true enjoyment as it is about anesthetizing ourselves. Think about the relief your idols provide: Is your desire truly and deeply satisfied, or does the relief come more through the temporary *absence* of desire?

I've had a nagging sense I was more pleasure-oriented than might be good, but I didn't see the function of pleasure in my life until I had to face intense grief and loss. I tried every drug I could, and nothing worked. Not food. Not sleep. Not work. Not reading. Not even sex. I could not get away from the pain. And then it occurred to me: If I am trying to use pleasure as a drug in this case, how many of my so-called enjoyments are merely the same thing on a lesser scale? Reading Pascal, I found he'd already hit upon the same thing. Unable to get out of the dilemma of desire, we've found a powerful drug—distraction.

> The way to render a man happy, is to engage him with an object that will make him forget his private troubles. What can be the reason that this man, who not long ago lost his only son, and this very morning was engaged almost to distraction in a law suit, now does not give his troubles a thought? You need not be astonished; he is taken up with watching a stag, which his hounds have been in full chase after, for six hours. However great his distress may have been, in this he finds ample consolation. In short, prevail upon a man to join in any amusement whatever, and as long as that lasts he will be happy; but it will be a false and imaginary happiness, arising not from the possession of real and solid good, but from a levity of spirit that obliterates the recollection of his real miseries, and fixes his thoughts upon mean and ridiculous objects, unworthy of his attention, and still less deserving of his love. (*Pensées*)

Don't be fooled by the apparent innocence of the object you've chosen. What is its *function*? Most of our idols also have a perfectly legitimate place in our lives. That's their cover. That's how we get away with our infidelity. The prophet Isaiah gives an example when he marvels at a man who cuts down a tree in the forest and then puts it to two very different uses:

> Half of the wood he burns in the fire;
> over it he prepares his meal,
> he roasts his meat and eats his fill.

Nothing wrong here. That's the perfectly appropriate use of wood. But it doesn't end here (it rarely does):

From the rest he makes a god, his idol;
>   he bows down to it and worships.
He prays to it and says,
>   "Save me; you are my god."

The prophet is incredulous. *Doesn't he see what he's doing?* he wonders.

No one stops to think,
>   no one has the knowledge or understanding to say,
>   "Half of it I used for fuel;
>   I even baked bread over its coals,
>   I roasted meat and I ate.
Shall I make a detestable thing from what is left?
>   Shall I bow down to a block of wood?"
He feeds on ashes, a deluded heart misleads him;
>   he cannot save himself or say,
>   "Is not this thing in my right hand a lie?"
>   (Isa. 44:16–17, 19–20 NIV)

So there you have it: no one stops to think. We don't want to take a good, hard look at what we are really doing, for then we might see the lie. We would expose the impostors. We would see the water hole for the muddy puddle it is. Our idols become the *means* by which we forget who we truly are and where we truly come from. They numb us. Like Hansel and Gretel, we're following a sugared path to our destruction. Or perhaps it's the Pied Piper who's got us skipping along. (There's a reason we used to tell those fairy tales. They contained wisdom we desperately need.) How else can we explain our apparent happiness when we are so far from home? Pascal observed,

Mankind, unable to escape death, trouble and ignorance, in order to make themselves happy, have hit upon the plan of never thinking about these things; the utmost efforts of their ingenuity can suggest no better consolation for such prodigious evils. But it is most miserable consolation, since it does not cure the evil, but merely to conceal it a little while; and by concealing it, prevents men from attempting to obtain a thorough cure. (*Pensées*)

THE ASSAULT ON OUR DESIRE

The battle of desire is not something that just takes place within us or even between us. It is also taking place *against* us, all the time. Our desire is under nearly constant attack. "We come into the world longing," says Gil Bailie, "for we know not what. We *are* desire. And desire is good, for it's what takes us to God. But our desire is not hard-wired to God."

We look to others to teach us what to desire. We are intensely imitative creatures, as Aristotle pointed out. It is how we learn language; it is how we master just about anything in life. It is also how we come to seize upon the objects of our desire. We all know this, though we don't like to admit it.

One example should suffice. I was at a garage sale, looking for some tools. There was a table saw at a wonderful price. Another fellow was sort of browsing around, standing in front of the saw but not seeming particularly interested. I opened my mouth and made the fatal error: "Wow, that's a great price on that saw." You know what happened next. Immediately, his nonchalance became intense interest, and since he was there before me, he drove off with a table saw that five minutes earlier he couldn't have given two hoots about.

Madison Avenue plays on this with a cynical brilliance. Look at fashion, for example. It lives on this dynamic. We don't wear what we want to wear; we wear what everyone else is wearing this year. The new line of cars that rolls out each year survives on this as well. Do we really imagine there's a significant difference in the actual car itself? Or notice what happens every Christmas. Quite often one toy emerges as the "must have" toy. A few years ago it was a little doll called Tickle Me Elmo, after the Sesame Street character. There was a rush on the doll. Suppliers ran out. People went mad, paying hundreds and thousands of dollars to get their hands on a little red character that retails for $29.99. Incidentally, you can go to the store tomorrow and get as many as you'd like. The mimetic fever is over—or has changed focus.

Advertisers play on this constantly, urging us to desire this and that by creating the image that "everyone who is anyone" has the object for sale, and we are surely a loser if we don't join the frenzy. Sadly, the ploy works. Bailie perceives that

> we live in a world inundated by these mimetic passions. What we call "modernity" is a world of feverishly mimetic desires and fascinations. With powers of telecommunication of which the Aztecs could not have dreamed, we are given models to emulate incessantly. We are inspired to envy, desire, compete, resent, aspire and be ambitious. (*Violence Unveiled*)

The constant effort to arouse our desire and capture it can be described only as an assault. From the time we get up to the time we go to bed, we are inundated with one underlying message: *it can be done.* The life you are longing for *can* be achieved. Only buy this product, see this movie, drive this car, take this vacation, join this gym, what have you. The only disagreement is over the means, but everyone agrees on the end: we can find life now.

I suppose the architects of Madison Avenue are for the most part motivated merely by success. It's their job to sell. But behind the whole mimetic madness is an even more brilliant schemer. The evil one has basically two ploys. If he cannot get us to kill our hearts and bury our desire, then he is delighted to seduce our desire into a trap. Once we give over our desire for life to any object other than God, we become ensnared. Think of the phrase, "She's a slave to fashion." We become slaves to any number of things, which at the outset we thought would serve us. In this light, repression of desire is a much less dangerous stage in the process. Addiction is far worse, for as May explains,

> Our addictions are our own worst enemies. They enslave us with chains that are of our own making and yet that, paradoxically, are virtually beyond our control. Addiction also makes idolaters of us all, because it forces us to worship these objects of attachment, thereby preventing us from truly, freely loving God and one another. (*Addiction and Grace*)

Like the rich young ruler, we find we cannot give up our treasured possessions, whatever they may be, even though God himself is standing before us with a better offer. If you think his sad story is not also your own, you are out of touch with yourself. I remember standing in the East River several summers ago. It was a gorgeous summer evening, and I was about to enjoy some great fly-fishing. I had just begun to cast when God spoke to me. *Put down the rod*, he said. *I'd like to spend some time with you.* I was irritated. *Now?* I replied. *You want to talk to me now? Why not later on the drive home? There's plenty of time in the car.* Good grief. What an addict I am! Thus the father of lies turns our most precious treasure—our longing for God and for his kingdom—into our worst enemy. It is truly diabolical. We wind up serving our desire slavishly or resenting it, or a little of both.

OUR TIMING IS OFF

"And envy."

It was three days after Brent's fall, and I was talking to a mutual friend of ours on the phone, telling him what I had been feeling— anger, rage, grief, numbness, exhaustion. Dan said, "And envy." He went on to describe his own feelings of a sort of jealousy, that Brent was home, that he had moved "from the battle to the banquet." I didn't reply. I didn't know what to say. I wasn't feeling envy; it hadn't even crossed my mind. Certainly, part of that can be written off to what I was going through. But not all of it.

Dan's comment exposed my basic commitment to find life here and now. It is a commitment nearly all of us share, at a far deeper level than we'd like to admit. There's something just a little hurt and angry in all of us as we find that life is not coming through. A song by Don Henley called "The End of the Innocence" captures the relation between our heartache and our use of pleasure in a very sad sort of way. The opening lines go like this:

> Remember when the days were long
> And rolled beneath a deep blue sky
> Didn't have a care in the world
> With mommy and daddy standin' by
> But "happily ever after" fails
> And we've been poisoned by these fairy tales
> The lawyers clean up all details
> Since daddy had to fly

The man in the song lost the love he was meant to know as a boy when his parents divorced. It was the end of the innocence for him, his personal encounter with life after the Fall. Hurt and angry, he searches for something now to give at least a taste of what was meant to be. Like so many men, he chooses sexual intimacy as his impostor.

> But I know a place where we can go
> Still untouched by man . . .
> So lay your head back on the ground
> Let your hair fall all round
> Offer up your best defense
> But this is the end of the innocence

Have we really been poisoned by fairy tales? No, we've merely gotten the timing wrong. Although our desire has taken us to a thousand "other lovers," we must not make a fatal error and try one more time to get rid of it. We cannot revert to killing our hearts. Instead, we must accept the first lesson in the journey of desire: ecstasy is *not* an option. We must have life. The only problem is in our refusal to wait. That is why God must rescue us from the very things we thought would save us.

—— IT WAS IN *May that the winds began to blow. The sea lion had grown used to wind, and at first he did not pay much heed at all. Years of desert life had taught him to turn his back in the direction from which the wind came and cover his eyes with his flippers, so that the dust would not get in. Eventually, the winds would always pass.*

But not this time. Day and night it came, howling across the barren lands. There was nothing to stop its fury, nothing to even slow it down. For forty days and forty nights the wind blew. And then, just as suddenly as it had begun, it stopped. The sea lion lifted himself to have a look around. He could hardly believe his eyes.

Every single leaf had been stripped from his tree. The branches that remained, with only a twig or two upon them, looked like an old scarecrow. And I do not need to tell you that there was no longer any shade in which to hide. But worse than this, much worse indeed, was what the sea lion saw next. The water hole was completely dry.

CHAPTER SIX

THE DIVINE THWARTER

Someone has altered the script.
My lines have been changed . . .
I thought I was writing this play.

—MADELEINE L'ENGLE

I can't get no satisfaction.

—THE ROLLING STONES

Devise your plan. It will be thwarted.

—GOD

It started five years ago with my annual fishing trip. Those of you unfamiliar with *fly*-fishing must rid your minds of the images of that other kind—guys in their lawn chairs down at the city pond, chugging cheap beer while they attempt to fool fish with fluorescent pink, garlic-flavored cheese balls beneath an enormous bobber. You wonder if they haven't met their match. To compare that with a day on a high mountain stream pursuing wild trout through the elegance and serenity of fly-fishing is like comparing the mini mart at your gas station to Nordstrom's, or professional wrestling to gymnastics, or the Simpsons to Shakespeare. Enough said.

This yearly pilgrimage has always been for me a time of consummate pleasure, a banquet of beauty with deep friendship and adventure. Then it all began to unravel. I had scheduled a few days on the Frying Pan River in Colorado in late May. The fishing there is legendary, and recent reports had been phenomenal. But as a friend and I drove up to the river, it began to rain. *Not to worry,* I thought. *Late spring often brings rain. It'll blow over in an hour or two.* As we climbed into the mountains, the rain turned into a snowstorm that lasted the entire trip.

I began to play chess with God. The following year, I planned our trip for July to eliminate all possibility of snow. I booked several days at a private ranch that caters to fly fishermen, with a guide to take us out on the upper Rio Grande. The night before we were to leave, I received a call telling me that no, it had not snowed, but thunderstorms had created mudslides and the fishing was impossible. They offered to refund my money.

I sensed that God had made a countermove, and that my king was in danger. Grabbing my phone book, I found the number of another guide on a different river and called him. Yes, the fishing was fabulous. Yes, he could take us out tomorrow. I hung up the phone with a smile. Your move, God. When we arrived early the next morning, the fellow told us sadly, "It's the strangest thing, but they opened the dam last night and the river's flooded. Sorry 'bout that."

The next year it was a drought; the year after that we still don't know what happened. High in the meadows of the Eastern Sierra, the fish had seemed to simply vanish from the San Joaquin. I was losing the game, as you can tell. But I hadn't been cornered; not yet.

Last year I was invited to speak at a conference near Bend, Oregon. It is a place very dear to me, full of memories from my childhood. The Deschutes River flows through there, and I was looking forward (can you believe my tenacity?) to some great time on the water with my new fly rod. (Country musicians use a *fiddle*, but to play Mozart, you use a *violin*. Bait fishermen use *poles*, while fly fishermen use *rods*.) I made what I felt would be my winning move. A friend arranged access for me to a private stretch of the Deschutes, a ranch visited each year by only a handful of people. The caretaker was an old master fly fisherman. When the owner of the shop in town learned where I was headed, he looked around furtively, leaned across the counter, and whispered, "Mister, that may be the best one hundred yards of fishing in the United States." Something smiled in my heart and said, *Check*.

Old Bill was a marvelous fisherman, and as we walked down to the water, he realized, "I'm thinkin' . . . let's see . . . you're the first guy to fish this since last October." *Six months ago*, I thought. *This is going to be incredible.* You know what's coming next. Nothing. We caught nothing. Bill had a funny look on his face. "John," he said, "people come from all over the world to fish this ranch. I've never had a day like this . . . ever." Feeling for all the world like Jonah, I said, "Bill, this is not about you. The fishing will be great tomorrow after I've gone." Checkmate.

CRUEL OR KIND?

This is the point at which God most feels like our enemy. It seems at times that he will go to any length to thwart the very thing we most deeply want. We can't get a job. Our attempt to find a spouse never pans out. The doctors aren't able to help us with our infertility. Isn't this precisely the reason we fear to desire in the first place? Life is hard enough as it is, but to think that God himself is working against us is more than disheartening. Job cried out, "What do you gain by oppressing me? . . . You hunt me like a lion and display your awesome power against me" (10:3, 16 NLT).

I want to state very clearly that not every trial in life is specially arranged for us by God. Much of the heartache we know comes from living in a broken world filled with broken people. And we have an enemy in the evil one who hates us deeply. But there are times when God himself seems to be set *against* us. Unless we understand our desperate hearts and our incredible tenacity to arrange for the life we want, these events will just seem cruel.

When we lived in Eden, there was virtually no restriction on the pleasure around us. We could eat *freely* from any tree in the Garden. Our desire was innocent and fully satisfied. I cannot even imagine what five minutes in total bliss would be like. We had it all, but we threw it away. By mistrusting God's heart, by reaching to take control of what we wanted, Adam and Eve set in motion a process in our hearts, a desperate grasping that can be described only as *addiction*. Desire goes mad within us. May observes, "Once they gave in to that temptation, their freedom was invaded by attachment. They experienced the need for more. God knew that they would not—*could not*—stop with just the one tree."

Our first parents are banished from Paradise as an act of mercy. The thought of the human race gaining immortality—eating from the Tree of Life—in a fallen state is too horrible to imagine. We would be evil forever. And though we are sent from the Garden, "the story of Eden is not over." Every day we reenact the Fall as we turn in our desire to the very things that will destroy us. As May reminds us,

> Addiction exists wherever persons are internally compelled to give energy to things that are not their true desires. To define it directly, addiction is a state of compulsion, obsession, or preoccupation that enslaves a person's will and desire. Addiction side-

tracks and eclipses the energy of our deepest, truest desire for love and goodness. We succumb because the energy of our desire becomes attached, nailed, to specific behaviors, objects or people. (*Addiction and Grace*)

Addiction may seem too strong a term to some of you. The woman who is serving so faithfully at church—surely, there's nothing wrong with that. And who can blame the man who stays long at the office to provide for his family? Sure, you may look forward to the next meal more than most people do, and your hobbies can be a nuisance sometimes, but to call any of this an addiction seems to stretch the word a bit too far.

I have one simple response: give it up. If you don't think you're a chess player, too, then prove it by letting go of the things that provide you with a sense of security, or comfort, or excitement, or relief. You will soon discover the tentacles of attachment deep in your soul. There will be an anxiousness; you'll begin to think about work or food or golf even more. Withdrawal will set in. If you can make it a week or two out of sheer willpower, you will find a sadness growing in your soul, a deep sense of loss. Lethargy and a lack of motivation follow.

Remember, we will make an idol of anything, especially a good thing. So distant now from Eden, we are *desperate* for life, and we come to believe that we must arrange for it as best we can, or no one will. God must thwart us to save us.

FUTILITY AND FAILURE

Adam and Eve stand before God with nothing but fig leaves to hide their shame. Knowing what has happened in our hearts, what desire can and will do divorced from its true source of happiness, God moves to intervene. With deep wisdom and kindness, he curses our lives. To Adam—and all his sons after him—God says,

> Because you listened to your wife and ate the fruit I told you not to eat, I have placed a curse on the ground. All your life you will struggle to scratch a living from it. It will grow thorns and this-tles for you, though you will eat of its grains. All your life you will sweat to produce food, until your dying day. (Gen. 3:17–19 NLT)

God thwarts men where it hurts most—in the field. He strikes a blow in the arena of our labor, our strength. This is our most vulnerable spot. We draw our sense of worth from it. I am not minimizing the importance of intimacy to a man; not at all. But when men get together, they don't talk about how everyone's relationship is doing. "Did you hear about Sally and Bill? I won-der if everything's okay. Maybe we should give them a call." No, they talk about their *achievements* (typically with a little embel-lishment). "I bagged the Zonax account today. Yep. Won't be long now before I'm running Sales." A man's impostors are most often born out of this place in his heart. Either they offer a false sense of strength, or they relieve a man from having to be strong. Pornography, for example, does both. The woman says, "I will make you feel like a man by giving myself to you, and you don't have to do anything at all. You can have the pleasure of a woman without having to *live* with her." A man's deepest desires always relate to his strength, one way or another, and so the curse for a man strikes him at the core.

As Dan Allender has pointed out, this is obviously about more than literal thorns and thistles, or every man who is not a farmer gets to escape the curse. Those who live in an apartment and work on Wall Street would get off scot-free. If only it were that easy. If only our worst enemy were dandelions and crabgrass. But every man knows the reality of the curse because every man must face the ongoing frustration of *futility* and *failure*. No matter how much a man achieves, it is never enough. He has to go out tomorrow and do it all again. If you hit a home run in last week's game, there is such a short time of joy. Next time you're at the plate, everyone expects you to do it again. And again. Futility. And even if you do seem to beat the odds and secure yourself financially, the curse is waiting for you somewhere else in your life—in your marriage or with your children. That is why a man's worst fear is not measuring up. A woman isn't affected by defeat the way a man is. It may hurt, but typically, she bounces back from failure. Not so for a man; in some cases, failure can be debilitating for life.

LONELINESS AND HEARTACHE

When God turns to the issues of a woman's wayward heart, he brings a very different curse. To Eve and all her daughters, he says, "You will bear children with intense pain and suffering. And though your desire will be for your husband, he will be your master" (Gen. 3:16 NLT).

This is obviously about more than babies and marriage, or every single woman without children gets to escape the curse. Some of our dearest friends are in that situation, and I can tell you that they do not live in Paradise. Every woman knows the reality of the curse because every woman lives with *relational heartache* and *loneliness*. With the skill of a surgeon going after a cancer, God thwarts a woman where it matters most—in her relationships. Are not her deepest tears shed over issues of failed intimacy? When women get together, they don't talk about work, unless it's to talk about their work *relationships*. This observation is not condescending in the least. A woman's glory is her heart for others, her keen sense of interpersonal dynamics, her commitment to maintaining relational connections. A woman who knows she is deeply loved typically survives a career setback that would send a man into a tailspin.

A woman's impostors are nearly always an attempt to somehow fill that ache for love or pretend she doesn't need love. The feminist movement has tried hard to assert that women can be as tough as men; they, too, can compete, can achieve, can conquer. It's tired and overdone. Like Lady Macbeth, it was an attempt by certain women to deal with the dilemma of their desire by "unsexing" themselves. Such contempt for tenderness and vulnerability reveals only how much they fear both, how deeply they have been hurt in that place. In a backhanded way, it confirms their design.

The worst fear for a woman is *abandonment*. Like a man who refuses to play the man for fear of failing, a woman who shuns intimacy only reveals her fear of rejection by refusing to face it honestly, openly. As for the love substitutes, men aren't buying Danielle Steel romances. They have to be dragged to the next "love finally finds her" movie. Women often create colorful fantasy worlds, a kind of pornography that guarantees rich intimacy in spite of the emptiness of daily life. The writers of soaps know this tendency only too well.

THE HARDEST LESSON TO LEARN

God *promises* every man futility and failure; he *guarantees* every woman relational heartache and loneliness. We spend most of our waking hours attempting to end-run the curse. We will fight this truth with all we've got. Sure, other people suffer defeat. Other people face loneliness. But not me. I can beat the odds. We see the neighbor's kids go off the deep end, and we make a mental note: *they didn't pray for their kids every day*. And we make praying for our kids every day part of our plan. It doesn't have to happen to us. We watch a colleague suffer a financial setback, and we make another note: *he was always a little lax with his money*. We set up a rigid budget and stick to it.

Isn't there something defensive that rises up in you at the idea that you cannot make life work out? Isn't there something just a little bit stubborn, an inner voice that says, *I can do it?* Thus Pascal writes,

> All men seek happiness. This is without exception. Whatever different means they employ, they all tend to this end . . . This is the motive of every action of every man. *But example teaches us little*. No resemblance is ever so perfect that there is not some slight difference, and hence we expect that *our* hope will not be deceived on this occasion as before. And thus, while the present never satisfies us, experience dupes us and from misfortune to misfortune leads us to death. (*Pensées*)

It can't be done. No matter how hard we try, no matter how clever our plan, we cannot arrange for the life we desire. Set the book down for a moment and ask yourself this question: Will life ever be what I so deeply want it to be, in a way that cannot be lost? This is the second lesson we must learn, and in many ways the hardest to accept. We must have life; we cannot arrange for it.

People will avoid this lesson all their days, changing their plans, their jobs, even their mates, rather than facing the truth.

> You were wearied by all your ways,
>> but you would not say, "It is hopeless."
> You found renewal of your strength,
>> and so you did not faint. (Isa. 57:10 NIV)

These are the majority of folks out there, Christian and pagan, who are still giving it a go. Yes, a smaller number have collided against failure and heartache in such a devastating way that they have come to see it can't be done, but they have faded into resignation, or bitterness, or despair. They have taken their revenge on the God who has thwarted them by killing their desire.

How do we accept that *it can't be done* with an open heart? How do we sustain desire in the face of ongoing failure and loneliness? It all depends on what we do with hope.

MISPLACED HOPE

"In this world you will have trouble." No kidding. Jesus, the master of understatement, captures in one sentence the story of our lives. He adds, "But take heart! I have overcome the world" (John 16:33 NIV). Why aren't we more encouraged? (Sometimes we'll try to *feel* encouraged when we hear a "religious" passage like this, but it never really lasts.) The reason is that we are still committed to arranging for life now. Be honest. Isn't there a disappointment when you realize that I'm not going to offer you the seven secrets of a really great life today? If I wanted to make millions, that's the book I would write. The only thing is, I would have to lie. It can't be done. Not *yet*. And that *yet* makes all the difference in the world because desire cannot live without hope. But hope in what? *For* what?

"Set your hope *fully* on the grace to be given you when Jesus Christ is revealed" (1 Peter 1:13 NIV, emphasis added). I read a passage like this, and I don't know whether to laugh or to cry. Fully? We don't even set our hope *partially* on the life to come. Not really, not in the desires of our hearts. Heaven may be coming. Great. But it's a long way off and who really knows, so I'm getting what I can now. Our search is limited only by our finances, our options, and our morals. Those with fewer misgivings and greater financial discretion go farther with it. For most Christians, heaven is a backup plan. Our primary work is finding a life we can at least get a little pleasure from here. Heaven is an investment we've made, like Treasury bonds or a retirement account, which we're hoping will take care of us in the future sometime, but which we do not give much thought to at present. It's tucked away in a drawer at the back of our minds, while we throw our immediate energies into playing the stock market. God comes in like a corporate raider, ruining our plans as we watch our "stocks" go into a tailspin.

"Remember how the LORD your God led you all the way in the desert these forty years, to humble you and to test you in order to know what was in your heart . . . He humbled you, causing you to hunger" (Deut. 8:2–3 NIV). When the Israelites left Egypt, they headed across the Red Sea to Mount Sinai. From there it was only about a two-week journey into the promised land. Fourteen days turned into *forty years*. A blind camel would have found its way sooner than that. God designed a supernaturally long trail in order to deal with what was in their hearts. During my five-year chess match with God, I often wrestled with his reasons for thwarting me. *I am serving you faithfully, God. Why won't you let me have this little pleasure?* Trip after trip was supernaturally foiled. It felt to me so unfair, even cruel. I mean, we're talking about fishing, for heaven's sake. It's not as if I were trying to have an affair. Or was I?

The day after my miraculous not-even-one-little-strike disaster on the Deschutes, I was driving around the back roads of that gorgeous country in central Oregon, looking at ranches and daydreaming. For years I've had a desire for a place of my own, several hundred acres with some riverfront, maybe here in Oregon. My longing for a ranch preceded by years any thought of using it for "ministry." No, ever since I was a child, the ranch has meant to me something else, my little heaven on earth. I rolled down the windows of my four-wheel drive and drank in the beauty and the solitude, the warmth of the sun, the sight of horses grazing in the fields, and the smell of the hay meadows. As I allowed myself to feel that quiet and long-buried desire, a sentence popped up out of my heart: *I really could be happy here without God*. It was completely unlooked for and remarkably honest. The thwarting had worked; now I could see what God was after in my heart. It all fell into place, and I simply said, *Oh . . . now I understand*.

God must take away the heaven we create, or it will become our hell. You may not think your efforts to arrange for a little of what you desire are anything like heaven on earth. I certainly didn't; not, at least, in the more conscious regions of my heart. But some deep and tender part of us gets trapped there in those times and places where we have had a taste of the life we long for. There in the ranch lands of central Oregon, I realized that the real issue is this: I haven't wanted to be an eternal person. I've wanted to find life here somehow. And not somehow, but through golden days on western streams, with men I love. For it was there I felt most alive, most loved, most hopeful.

As I sat there in my Jeep, surrounded by the visions and aromas—horses in a field, the pine and sage—I was transported to a time long ago in my youth, with all the promise in the air of the day ahead. And I thought, *I would give anything to return to that time in my life*. It's as if the golden center of my heart is back there in those golden days, and God wants to free it from there, to bring it into the present for the future.

I returned home a different man. Not entirely healed, not fully delivered, but still, something deep in me had shifted. The arranging had begun to stop. My heart was beginning to lift its eyes beyond the horizon toward those eternal pastures. Two weeks later Brent was killed. I began to see the hand of God in all of it, preparing me for what was coming. I think at any time during those years of thwarting, had you asked me if I truly longed for eternity, I would have said yes. My answer would not have been dishonest, but it would not have been entirely true, either. George MacDonald explained the thwarting,

> Thy hand unloved its pleasure must restrain,
> Nor spoil both gift and child by lavishing too soon.
>
> (*Diary of an Old Soul*)

THE ULTIMATE BLOW

The phone just rang. A friend's father has died of a heart attack. One minute he is going about his business like all the other drivers on the road—like us—and the next minute is his last. He was sitting at a stoplight, waiting to make a turn, and suddenly, he was gone. It was just a few months ago that I received another call, from a different friend, telling me that her little brother had died of some complications that developed from a congenital defect. He was three years old. The day before he had been out in the yard, playing on the swings and laughing.

How can we possibly continue to bet on our arranging in the face of such an overwhelming enemy as death? It is beyond me. It certainly is a testimony to our unlimited capacity for denial. As Pascal observed, it is as if we are all under a spell.

> Nothing is so important to man as his own state, nothing is so formidable to him as eternity; and thus it is not natural that there should be men indifferent to the loss of their existence, and to the perils of everlasting suffering. They are quite different with

regard to all other things. They are afraid of mere trifles; they foresee them; they feel them. And this same man who spends so many days and nights in rage and despair at the loss of an office, or for some imaginary insult to his honor, is the very one who knows without anxiety and without emotion that he will lose all by death. It is a monstrous thing to see in the same heart and at the same time this sensibility to trifles and this strange insensibility to the greatest objects. It is an incomprehensible enchantment. (*Pensées*)

In the years that followed the Fall and our exile from Eden, mankind got worse and worse. Cain killed Abel; Lamech threatened to kill everybody else. The wickedness of the human heart seemed out of control and unstoppable, even by the curses. People were living for seven, eight, even nine *hundred* years. Can you imagine the arranging that one person could accomplish with that sort of time on his hands? Stubbornness seems to come with old age. Haven't you heard your grandmother sigh and say of your grandfather, "He's set in his ways"? Multiply that by a factor of eight or nine and you get the picture. So God dealt the ultimate blow. Then the Lord said, "My Spirit will not contend with man forever, for he is mortal; his days will be a hundred and twenty years" (Gen. 6:3 NIV). He cut our life short; nobody gets to pass 120. However clever we might be in our ability to conjure Paradise, we can never get around death. It is the final thwarting.

You must follow me very carefully now. We can never fully explain the reasons surrounding someone's death. We've come to accept it for the aged, and we try to console ourselves with thoughts like, *He's had a full life*. But death is *never* natural; it was not meant to be. That is why those left behind experience such excruciating pain. The agony is only worsened when the death is what we call premature, when it takes a life in full bloom, or just as the bud begins to open. Each death can begin to be understood only within the larger story God is telling. Much of that story remains for the moment a mystery.

Many people were shattered by Brent's death. I know I was. Not even on my worst enemies would I wish such pain. But I also know this: the shattering was good. Living apart from God comes naturally; all the striving and arranging is so second nature to me that to have it stopped in its tracks was a great good. I would wake in the morning in those early days of grief, and instead of my desires "rushing at me like a pack of wild animals" as Lewis said, I knew *it can't be done*. I knew it more deeply and more personally than I had ever known it before. We must learn this lesson, at whatever cost, or the spell will not be broken and we will never discover true hope.

WHAT THEN?

"There's nothing now but heaven." It was one of those truly honest moments, when my heart speaks what I most deeply believe. Stasi and I had just finished watching *A River Runs Through It*, and the warm tears rolled quietly down my face as I sat looking out the back window of our home into the night. In a subtle and unlooked-for way, the film had brought the reality of all my losses flooding back to me. The only time and place I ever really connected with my father was when we were fishing the rivers and streams of the West. But even that could not hold us together. As time passed our trips came to an end, and we drifted apart.

Years later, as a grown man, I came home distraught from a day alone on the river. I was agitated, and though I did not know why, I knew it was not because I had not caught anything. As

Stasi and I spoke about my frustration and disappointment, the words of truth slipped from my mouth: "I'll never find him out there." I hadn't known until that moment what I had been looking for in all those years of fly-fishing.

A River Runs Through It beautifully captures the author's time of boyhood innocence, and fly-fishing trips in Montana with his father, and losing it all. The story ends with the author, now an old man, standing alone in a river, fishing. "Now, all those I loved and did not understand in my youth are gone . . . But I still reach out to them." The words were true for me; they are true for all of us. It can't be done; yet the desire remains. This is the most crucial moment for our hearts. Once we come to accept that we can never find or hang on to the life we have been seeking, what then? As Dallas Willard writes, it matters for all the world to know that life is ahead of us.

> I meet many faithful Christians who, in spite of their faith, are deeply disappointed in how their lives have turned out. Sometimes it is simply a matter of how they experience aging, which they take to mean they no longer have a future. But often, due to circumstances or wrongful decisions and actions by others, what they had hoped to accomplish in life they did not . . . Much of the distress of these good people comes from a failure to realize that their life lies before them . . . the life that lies endlessly before us in the kingdom of God. (*The Divine Conspiracy*)

Pascal also observed, "We are never living, but hoping to live; and whilst we are always preparing to be happy, it is certain, we never shall be so, if we aspire to no other happiness than what can be enjoyed in this life."

Desire cannot live without hope. Yet we can only hope for

what we desire. There simply must be something more, something out there on the road ahead of us, that offers the life we prize. To sustain the life of the heart, the life of deep desire, we desperately need to possess a clearer picture of the life that lies before us.

CHAPTER SEVEN

THE GREAT RESTORATION

We shall not cease from exploration
And the end of all our exploring
Will be to arrive where we started
And know the place for the first time.

—T. S. ELIOT

Look, I am making all things new!

—JESUS OF NAZARETH

See! The winter is past;
    the rains are over and gone.
Flowers appear on the earth;
    the season of singing has come.

—SONG OF SONGS 2:11–12 NIV

I was walking in the woods and fields behind our house one evening, four months after Brent's death. My heart was so aware of the loss—not only of Brent, but in some ways, of everything that mattered. I knew that one by one, I would lose everyone I cared about and the life I am still seeking. In the east, a full moon was rising, bright and beautiful and enormous as it seems when it is just above the horizon. Toward the west, the clouds were turning peach and pink against a topaz sky. Telling myself to long for eternity feels like telling myself to let go of all I love—forever. It feels like accepting the teaching of Eastern religions, a *denial* of life and all God created. We lose it all too soon, before we can begin to live and love. But what if? What if nature is speaking to us? What if sunrise and sunset tell the tale every day, remembering Eden's glory, prophesying Eden's return? What if it shall all be restored?

THE SECRET OF SPRING

Winter tarries long at six thousand feet. Here in the Rocky Mountains, spring comes late and fitfully. We had snow again last week—the second week in May. Our boys are about to get out of school for summer vacation, and it's snowing. I've come to accept that spring here is really a wrestling match between winter and summer, as if winter doesn't want to let go its grip until it absolutely has to. It makes for a long time of waiting. You see, the flowers are pretty much gone in September. The first of October, the aspens start turning gold and drop their leaves in a week or two. Come November all is gray. Initially, I don't mind. The coming of winter has its joys, and there are Thanksgiving and Christmastime to look forward to.

But after the new year, things begin to drag on. Through February and then March, the earth remains lifeless. The whole world lies shadowed in brown and gray tones, like an old photograph. Winter's novelty is long past, and by April we are longing for some sign of life—some color, some hope. Instead, we get dumped on. It's our biggest snow month. While the azaleas are coming out in full glory in Atlanta, and the dogwoods are blooming pink and white in Portland, we are shoveling several feet of snow. It's too long.

And then, just this afternoon, I rounded the corner into our neighborhood, and suddenly, the world was green again. The bluffs behind our house were transformed. What had been rock and twig and dead mulch was a rich oriental carpet of green. I was shocked, stunned. How did it happen? As if in disbelief, I got out of my car and began to walk through the woods, touching every leaf. Just yesterday the scrub oaks had the twisted, gnarled look of the hands of an old witch. Now they are beautiful, tender, supple like a maiden. The birds are back as well, waking us in the morning with their glad songs. All the chirps and cheeps and whistles and twitters, a raucous melody of simple joy. It happened suddenly. In the twinkling of an eye.

My surprise is telling. It seems natural to long for spring; it is another thing to be completely stunned by its return. I am truly and genuinely surprised, as if my reaction were, *Really? What are you doing here?* And then I realized, *I never thought I'd see you again*. I think in some deep place inside, I had accepted the fact that winter is what is really true. As I lived through the first year of my grief, I had unconsciously settled into resignation. Empty and still, the world outside seemed a confirmation, the only fitting backdrop to the world within. I am shocked by the return of spring. And I wonder, *Can the same thing happen for my soul?*

> Grief melts away
> Like snow in May
> As if there were no such cold thing.
> Who would have thought my shrivl'd heart
> Could have recover'd greennesse? It was gone
> Quite underground
>
> And now in age I bud again,
> After so many deaths I live and write;
> I once more smell the dew and rain,

> And relish versing: O my only light
> It cannot be
> That I am he
> On whom thy tempests fell all night.
> ("The Flower" George Herbert)

Can it really happen? Can things in our lives be green again? No matter what our creeds may tell us, our hearts have settled into another belief. We have accepted the winter of this world as the final word and tried to get on without the hope of spring. *It will never come*, we have assumed, *and so I must find whatever life here I can*. We have been so committed to arranging for our happiness that we have missed the signs of spring. We haven't given any serious thought to what might be around the corner. Were eternity to appear tomorrow, we would be as shocked as I have been with the return of spring this week, only more so. Our practical agnosticism would be revealed. Pascal declared, "Our imagination so powerfully magnifies time, by continual reflections upon it, and so diminishes eternity . . . for want of reflection, that we make a nothing of eternity and an eternity of nothing."

MORE THAN CHURCH FOREVER

But of course we aspire to happiness we can enjoy now. Our hearts have no place else to go. We have made a nothing of eternity. If I told you that your income would triple next year, and that European vacation you've wanted is just around the corner, you'd be excited, hopeful. The future would look promising. It seems possible, *desirable*. But our ideas of heaven, while possible, aren't all that desirable. Whatever it is we think is coming in the next season of our existence, we don't think it is worth getting all that excited about. We make a nothing of eternity by enlarging the significance of this life and by diminishing the reality of what the next life is all about. Nearly every Christian I have spoken with has some idea that eternity is an unending church service. After all, the Bible says that the saints "worship God in heaven," and without giving it much more thought we have settled on an image of the never-ending sing-along in the sky, one great hymn after another, forever and ever, amen.

And our heart sinks. *Forever and ever? That's it? That's the good news?* And then we sigh and feel guilty that we are not more "spiritual." We lose heart, and we turn once more to the present to find what life we can. Eternity ends up having no bearing on our search for life whatsoever. It feels like the end of the search. And since we're not all that sure about what comes after, we search hard now. Remember, *we can only hope for what we desire.* How can the church service that never ends be more desirable than the richest experiences of life here? It would be no small difference if you knew in your heart that the life you prize is just around the corner, that your deepest desires have been whispering to you all along about what's coming. You see, Scripture tells us that God has "set eternity" in our hearts (Eccl. 3:11 NIV). Where in our hearts? In our *desires.*

The return of spring brings such relief and joy and anticipation. Life has returned, and with it sunshine, warmth, color, and the long summer days of adventure together. We break out the lawn chairs and the barbecue grill. We tend the garden and drink in all the beauty. We head off for vacations. Isn't this what we most deeply long for? To leave the winter of the world behind, what Shakespeare called "the winter of our discontent," and find ourselves suddenly in the open meadows of summer?

I am standing in my hotel room, which looks like every other hotel room I've been in over the past ten years. When you travel for a living, the excitement of hotel stays wears off pretty quickly.

There is a picture on the wall, a painting of a small harbor town. It appears to be somewhere in the Mediterranean, with its azure seas and whitewashed walls. I think of the Greek islands, perhaps Santorini. Sunlight fills the place, and small boats drift lazily in the bay. There are cafes, I am sure, filled with laughter. Along the plaza, lovers stroll hand in hand. The seas are warm and inviting. It evokes a longing, but not for vacation. Vacations end. The longing evoked by the painting is for a life that never ends.

Now . . . what if spring and summer are nature's way of expressing what Jesus was in fact trying to tell us? After all, nature is God's word to us also (Rom. 1:20). If we paid close attention, we would discover something of great joy and wonder: the restoration of the world played out before us each spring and summer is *precisely* what God is promising us about our lives. Jesus preached far more than the gospel of sin management. The good news he brought was much, much greater than forgiveness. Jesus came to announce the coming of "the kingdom of God."

> Jesus went throughout Galilee, teaching in their synagogues, preaching the good news of the kingdom. (Matt. 4:23 NIV)

> The time has come . . . The kingdom of God is near. Repent and believe the good news! (Mark 1:15 NIV)

> After this, Jesus traveled about from one town and village to another, proclaiming the good news of the kingdom of God. (Luke 8:1 NIV)

> After his suffering, he showed himself to these men and gave many convincing proofs that he was alive. He appeared to them over a period of forty days and spoke about the kingdom of God. (Acts 1:3 NIV)

And what exactly is this "kingdom of God"? What does it mean for our lives? A kingdom is a realm, quite simply, where the king's word has full sway. What the king desires is what happens. God's kingdom come means that his will is done "on *earth* as it is in heaven." Now in heaven, things are not stained or broken; everything is as it was meant to be. Think for a moment of the wonder of this. Isn't every one of our sorrows on earth the result of things *not* being as they were meant to be? And so when the kingdom of God comes to earth, wonderful things begin to unfold. Look at the evidence; watch what happens to people as they are touched by the kingdom of God through Jesus. As he went about "preaching the good news of the kingdom," Jesus was also "healing every disease and sickness among the people" (Matt. 4:23 NIV). When he "spoke to them about the kingdom of God," he "healed those who needed healing" (Luke 9:11 NIV). A direct connection is being made here. The actions of Jesus are the illustrations for the sermon.

What happens when we find ourselves in the kingdom of God? The disabled jump to their feet and start doing a jig. The deaf go out and buy themselves stereo equipment. The blind are headed to the movies. The dead are not at all dead anymore, but very much alive. They show up for dinner. In other words, human brokenness in all its forms is healed. The kingdom of God brings *restoration*. Life is restored to what it was meant to be. "In the beginning," back in Eden, all of creation was pronounced good because all of creation was exactly as God meant for it to be. For it to be good again is not for it to be destroyed, but healed, renewed, brought back to its goodness.

Those glimpses we see in the miracles of Jesus were the first-fruits. When he announces the full coming of the kingdom, Jesus says, "Look, I am making *all things* new!" (Rev. 21:5 NLT, emphasis added). He does not say, "I am making all new things." He means that the things that have been so badly broken will be restored and then some. "You mean I'll get a new pair of glasses?" my son Sam asked. "Or do you mean I'll get a new pair of eyes, so I won't need glasses?" What do you think? Jesus didn't hand out crutches to help the disabled.

THE JOY OF RESTORATION

Those of you who have been miraculously healed from a serious illness or injury will be ahead of me on this. You know firsthand the wonder and joy of restoration. But most of us have not experienced something quite so dramatic (not yet). So let me use a more common illustration, something most of you will remember—the flu. Several years ago, at Christmastime, my whole family was hit with a really vicious bug. It knocked us on our backs—literally. We brought blankets and pillows downstairs into the family room because no one had it in him to make it to his bedroom. For five days all we could do was lie on the floor, moaning. We ate nothing and drank nothing. Our house looked like an infirmary. You'll remember how awful it feels—the fever, the aches, the boredom.

One by one, we began to recover. Our first drink was simply water. It tasted like a living spring. I would have sworn it was from a different tap than we'd been using all those years. We moved up to fruit juice. It was exotic, as if we had never tasted anything like it in our lives. Each "new" food was an adventure. While I was lying in misery, I was dreaming of the day we'd go down to our favorite Mexican restaurant. It was off the charts, a sensory paradise. All things were new and absolutely delightful. It was a joy just to be alive. Our bodies had been "restored."

And going outside, after being closed in for a week, was like being released from prison. I wanted to run around, do everything all at once. I can only imagine what it would be like to walk for the very first time ever. Or to have been blind all my life and then have my sight restored. Such joy, such wonder. In *Pilgrim at Tinker Creek,* Annie Dillard recounts the stories that were reported of blind men and women who received some of the first cataract operations:

> A little girl visits a garden. "She is greatly astonished, and can scarcely be persuaded to answer, stands speechless in front of the tree, which she only names on taking hold of it, and then as 'the tree with the lights in it.'" . . . One girl was eager to tell her blind friend that "men do not really look like trees at all," and astounded to discover that her every visitor had an utterly different face. Finally, a twenty-two-year-old girl was dazzled by the world's brightness and kept her eyes shut for two weeks. When at the end of that time she opened her eyes again, she did not recognize any objects, but, "the more she now directed her gaze upon everything about her, the more it could be seen how an expression of gratification and astonishment over-spread her features; she repeatedly exclaimed: 'Oh God! How beautiful!'"

How beautiful indeed. Can you imagine seeing wildflowers for the first time? Gerard Manley Hopkins was right: "The world is charged with the grandeur of God." Perhaps the reason there is reported a silence for half an hour of eternity is that we are all quite speechless (Rev. 8:1). And perhaps the gratification and astonishment that swell up afterward are the chorus of worship we are told about. "Look at this! Look there at that! Oh God! How beautiful!" Even for those of us who have always enjoyed our sight, it will be as if we are seeing for the first time. T. S. Eliot wrote in "Little Gidding,"

> The end of all our exploring
> Will be to arrive where we started
> And know the place for the first time.

OUR RESTORATION

Yes, dear friends, we are already God's children, and we can't even imagine what we will be like when Christ returns. But we do know that when he comes we will be like him, for we will see him as he really is. (1 John 3:2 NLT)

We have an expression that we use to describe someone who's out of sorts, who's not acting like the person we know her to be: "She's just not herself today." It's a marvelous, gracious phrase, for in a very real way, no one is quite himself today. There is more to us than we have seen. I know my wife is a goddess. I know she is more beautiful than she imagines. I have seen it slip out, seen moments of her glory. Suddenly, her beauty shines through, as though a veil has been lifted. It happened one night last fall.

We had slipped away from life for a long weekend in Mexico, a time to heal and rest and just be together again. We chose a hotel away from the crowds and the *turistas*. So we were almost entirely alone one evening as we ate dinner on a veranda overlooking the Sea of Cortez. Night had fallen, and the sky was so deeply black, the stars were shining right down to the horizon of the water. We sat gazing out to sea, listening to the mariachis and the breakers and our own hearts. I turned to steal a glimpse at my wife. She was beautiful, there in the moonlight, tanned from the sun, rested, serene. She was simply beautiful in a way that life often prevents her from being, but in a way she was destined to be.

All of us have moments like this, glimpses of our true creation. They come unexpectedly and then fade again. Life for the most part keeps our glory hidden, cloaked by sin, or sorrow, or merely weariness. When I see an older woman, doubled over with arthritis, the hard years etched into her face, I want to cry, *Eve, what happened?* How truly wonderful it will be to see her in her youth again, the full flower of her beauty restored.

When the disciples saw Jesus on the Mount of Transfiguration, they got a peek at his glory. He was radiant, beautiful, magnificent. He was Jesus, the Jesus they knew and loved—only *more so.* And we shall be glorious as well. Jesus called himself the Son of man to state clearly that he is what mankind was meant to be. What we see in Jesus is our personal destiny. Is this not the secret of every fairy tale? As Frederick Buechner reminds us,

> Maybe above all they are tales of transformation where all creatures are revealed in the end as what they truly are—the ugly duckling becomes a great white swan, the frog is revealed to be a prince, and the beautiful but wicked queen is unmasked in all her ugliness. They are tales of transformation where the ones who live happily ever after, as by no means everybody does in fairy tales, are transformed into what they have it in them at their best to be. (*Telling the Truth*)

I've spoken with many people who believe that we become "spirits" when we die; that we lose our bodies and float around. Some even believe we become angels. But I don't want to lose my body; I very much want it to be renewed. When we conceive of our future existence as something ghostly, mysterious, completely "other" than anything we've ever known, we place it beyond all hoping for. (You can only hope for what you desire.) The "otherness" of it takes away its power. But look at the first

example—Jesus. What happens to him after he dies? He is res-
urrected, of course. As someone or something else? No, as himself, only healed and very much alive. Then what—float around?
No, he has breakfast.

> Early in the morning, Jesus stood on the shore, but the disci-
> ples did not realize that it was Jesus. He called out to them,
> "Friends, haven't you any fish?" "No," they answered. He said,
> "Throw your net on the right side of the boat and you will find
> some." When they did, they were unable to haul the net in
> because of the large number of fish. Then the disciple whom
> Jesus loved said to Peter, "It is the Lord!" . . . When they
> landed, they saw a fire of burning coals there with fish on it,
> and some bread . . . Jesus said to them, "Come and have break-
> fast." (John 21:4–12 NIV)

Now think about this for a minute. You're the Son of God.
You've just accomplished the greatest work of your life, the stunning rescue of mankind. You rose from the dead. What would
you do next? Have a cookout with a few friends? It seems so
unspiritual, so *ordinary*. Do you see that eternal life does not
become something totally "other," but rather that life goes on—
only as it should be?

Jesus did not vanish into a mystical spirituality, becoming one
with the cosmic vibration. Jesus has a body, and it's *his* body. His
wounds have been healed, but the scars remain—not gruesome,
but lovely, a remembrance of all he did for us. His friends recognize him. They share a bite to eat. This is our future as well—
our lives will be healed and we shall go on, never to taste death
again. And so MacDonald writes in a letter to his wife,

> We may however say to ourselves—one day these souls of ours
> will blossom into the full sunshine—when all that is desirable in

the commonness of daily love, and all we long for of wonder and mystery and the look of Christmas time will be joined in one, and we shall walk as in a wondrous dream yet with more sense of reality than our most waking joy now gives us. (*The Heart of George MacDonald*)

The creation, we are told, groans for this day, the day when we—the sons and daughters of God—are revealed for who we truly are.

THE EARTH IS RESTORED

The creation waits in eager expectation for the sons of God to be revealed. For the creation was subjected to frustration, not by its own choice, but by the will of the one who subjected it, in hope that the creation itself will be liberated from its bondage to decay and brought into the glorious freedom of the children of God. (Rom. 8:19–21 NIV)

The created world itself can hardly wait for what's coming next. Everything in creation is being more or less held back. God reins it in until both creation and all the creatures are ready and can be released at the same moment into the glorious times ahead. Meanwhile, the joyful anticipation deepens. (Rom. 8:19–21 *The Message*)

How wondrous this will be! Creation can be so breathtaking *now*. What shall it be like when it is released to its full glory? Reading the journals of Lewis and Clark's journey across the West, I am filled with longing to see what they saw. The Great Plains were filled with wildlife; the buffalo dwelled in herds of hundreds of thousands. One of the first white men to see this paradise, Meriwether Lewis wrote in his journal,

I ascended to the top of the cut bluff this morning, from whence I had a most delightful view of the country—immense herds of buffalo, elk, deer and antelopes feeding in one common and boundless pasture. The buffalo, elk and antelope are so gentle that we pass near them while feeding, without appearing to excite any alarm among them, and when we attract their attention, they frequently approach us more nearly to discover what we are . . . The country is beautiful in the extreme.

It was the world "with dew still on it," to use MacLean's delightful phrase. And it will be our Paradise again. We seem to have forgotten—or perhaps we've never been told—that we get the earth back as well. Too many of us have placed eternity somewhere "out there," in a wispy and ethereal "heaven" that we cannot imagine; in the clouds perhaps. "I love the earth," wrote a friend, "and it makes me sad to think it will all be destroyed one day." We have all probably shared in this sadness. But we needn't. "Behold," says the Lord, "I will create new heavens and a new earth" (Isa. 65:17; Rev. 21:1 NIV). When he says he is making all things new, he includes the earth.

But won't the earth be destroyed, and won't we all go "up" to heaven? Peter wrote some pretty ominous words about the end of this age: "That day will bring about the destruction of the heavens by fire, and the elements will melt in the heat" (2 Peter 3:12 NIV). It looks like the whole cosmos is going down in a ball of flames. But wait—by way of comparison, Peter pointed to the Flood of Noah's day as an allegory for the "day of the Lord." He said about the Flood, "By these waters also the world of that time was deluged and destroyed" (v. 6 NIV). Now, we know that the earth was *not* destroyed by the Flood. The earth remained; the ark didn't land on Mars. What was destroyed was all the wickedness and corruption of mankind (Gen. 6–7). The Flood *cleansed* the earth, renewed it. Noah stepped out with his family onto a restored earth to begin again.

Fire is also used for cleansing throughout the Scriptures. Paul declared that our life's work will be tested in the fire, like gold. Only the dross is burned away (1 Cor. 3:13–15). This is the fire Peter refers to when he says, "But the day of the Lord will come like a thief. The heavens will disappear with a roar; the elements will be destroyed by fire, and the earth and everything in it will be *laid bare*" (2 Peter 3:10 NIV, emphasis added). The meaning of the word used here is not *destroyed,* but much closer translated as *revealed.* In other words, the world will be "exposed to judgment," and the earth will be cleansed of all unrighteousness. And a good scrubbing it needs. After declaring that the earth is full of the grandeur of God, Hopkins goes on to ask why we no longer see the glory of God in it.

Generations have trod, have trod, have trod;
    And all is seared with trade; bleared, smeared with toil;
    And wears man's smudge and shares man's smell: the soil
Is bare now, nor can foot feel, being shod.

All the strip mines and strip malls, all the incredibly ugly things we've done to the earth. No wonder the fire of God's jealous love will burn; he intends to cleanse the earth, once more, once and for all. Thus John (the writer of Revelation) sees the New Jerusalem not floating in the clouds, but descending from heaven *to the earth,* and he hears "a loud voice from the throne saying, 'Now the dwelling of God is with men, and he will live with them. They will be his people, and God himself will be with them and be their God'" (21:2–3 NIV). So Dallas Willard assures us, *"The life we now have as the persons we now are will continue in the universe in which we now exist."* The earth has been our home and will be our home in eternity. This is a great consolation. When we place eternity "out there somewhere," in a place we cannot conceive of, we are left longing for home. To lose the only world we have ever known—a world so full of memories, so rich and beautiful, with so much left to explore—is to lose something deep and priceless to our hearts.

ALL SHALL BE WELL

At the end of *The Chronicles of Narnia*, Aslan seems to have brought that delightful kingdom to an end, and the children are left to mourn its loss.

> "So," said Peter, "night falls on Narnia. What, Lucy! You're not *crying*? With Aslan ahead, and all of us here?" "Don't try to stop me, Peter," said Lucy, "I am sure Aslan would not. I am sure it is not wrong to mourn for Narnia. Think of all that lies dead and frozen behind that door." "Yes, and I *did* hope," said Jill, "that it might go on forever. I knew *our* world couldn't. I did think Narnia might." "Sirs," said Tirian. "The ladies do well to weep. See, I do so myself. I have seen my mother's death. What world but Narnia have I ever known? It were no virtue, but great discourtesy, if we did not mourn."

But as the children venture farther into Aslan's country, they begin to recognize every rock and stream and tree. They have been there before. And then they discover, to their wonder and joy, that Narnia exists forever in Aslan's country, that the world they loved has been preserved, though more rich and more real than ever.

It was the Unicorn who summed up what everyone was feeling. He stamped his right fore-hoof on the ground and neighed, and then cried: "I have come home at last! This is my real country! I belong here. This is the land I have been looking for all my life, though I never knew it till now. The reason why we loved the old Narnia is that it sometimes looked a little like this."

Our search for the Golden Moment is not a search in vain; not at all. We've only had the timing wrong. We do not know exactly how God will do it, but we do know this: the kingdom of God brings restoration. The only things destroyed are the things outside God's realm—sin, disease, death. But we who are God's children, the heavens and the earth he has made, will go on. "The wolf will live with the lamb, the leopard will lie down with the goat, the calf and the lion and the yearling together" (Isa. 11:6 NIV). "And Jerusalem will be known as the Desirable Place," the place of the fulfillment of all our desires (Isa. 62:12 NLT). This is significant because it touches upon the question, What will we *do* in eternity? If all we've got are halos and harps, our options are pretty limited. But to have the whole cosmos before us—wow. Thus MacDonald writes to his daughter, whom he will soon lose to tuberculosis,

> I do live expecting great things in the life that is ripening for me and all mine—when we shall have all the universe for our own, and be good merry helpful children in the great house of our father. Then, darling, you and I and all will have the grand liberty wherewith Christ makes free—opening his hand to send us out like white doves to range the universe. (*The Heart of George MacDonald*)

CHAPTER EIGHT

THE GRAND AFFAIR

Thy fishes breathe but where thy waters roll;
Thy birds fly but within thy airy sea;
My soul breathes only in thy infinite soul;
I breathe, I think, I love, I live but thee.
Oh, breathe, oh, sink—O Love, live into me.

—GEORGE MACDONALD

Happiness can be found neither in ourselves nor in external
things, but in God and in ourselves as united to him.

—PASCAL

And the people came together and the people came to dance and
they danced like a wave upon the sea.

—WILLIAM BUTLER YEATS

Several years ago I gave a series of lectures on eternity to a group of career-age singles on the East Coast. Over lunch one afternoon, several of the women asked if they might have a word with me. I sensed they wanted to ask a question that they didn't feel comfortable raising during our group discussion time. After a bit of nervous hemming and hawing, they got down to the point. Though quite successful professionally, they were feeling the ache and disappointment of singleness. And as the years seemed to be racing by, they weren't feeling so young anymore. A lifetime of singleness was becoming more and more a reality for each one, though by no means her heart's desire. What I had been saying about heaven was certainly attractive, but still, they could not shake a fear that they will forever miss one of the deepest joys of human experience. "Will there be sex in heaven?" I smiled at their courage; it's a question many haven't let themselves wonder, even though they do wonder.

THE UNION THAT WE CRAVE

To understand the importance of the question, you've got to recognize the ache that seems to be met only through sexual union. When God created Eve, as you will recall, he took her straight from Adam's side. None of us have fully recovered from the surgery. There is an aloneness, an *incompleteness* that we experience every day of our lives. How often do you feel deeply and truly known? Is there another soul to whom a simple glance is all that is necessary to communicate depth of understanding? Do you have someone with whom you can commune in love? This is our inconsolable longing—to know and to be known. It is our deepest ache, which we feel to be healed only in our union with another. Even physically, there is an incompleteness until our bodies are joined together.

But let's take a closer look. What are we looking for in the opposite sex? The Beloved in Song of Songs captures something of what the heart of a woman is seeking:

> Listen! My lover!
> Look! Here he comes,
> leaping across the mountains,
> bounding over the hills.

My lover is like a gazelle or a young stag.
(2:8–9 NIV)

Picture the opening sequences of the film *Last of the Mohicans*. It is 1757. England is at war with France for possession of the American colonies. "Three men, the last of a vanishing people, are on the frontier west of the Hudson River." Before us is a vast panorama of untamed wilderness. Mountain and forest as far as the eye can see. The camera takes us down into those woods, and we discover the men, running at full speed through the deep forest. Leaping across ravines, bounding with grace and speed through the heavy undergrowth, they are clearly on a great mission.

This is our first glimpse of Nathaniel, the hero of the story. Raised by the Mohawk, he is rugged, wild, *alive*. Out here on the edge of the frontier, there is something dangerous about these men. But it does not make us afraid; rather, we are all the more drawn to them. No words are spoken in this scene; no words need to be spoken. It is an image of masculinity in motion. This is what has stirred the woman's heart in Songs—to see her man's strength. And she invites that strength to come to her in the night:

> Until the day breaks
>   and the shadows flee,
> turn, my lover,
>   and be like a gazelle
> or like a young stag
>   on the rugged hills.
> (2:17 NIV)

There is an emptiness in the woman that only her man can fill. Is it not physically true? But it is more than just physically true. Our bodies are an outward sign of an inward reality. So, too, the woman completes her man in a uniquely beautiful way. Come to me, she says, and let your strength be fully expressed in the garden of my beauty. Is this not the invitation that stirs a man's heart? For these are the qualities of the Beloved that captivate her Lover in the Song. He says,

> How beautiful you are, my darling!
>> Oh, how beautiful!
>> Your eyes behind your veil are doves . . .
> Your lips are like a scarlet ribbon;
>> your mouth is lovely . . .
> Your two breasts are like two fawns,
>> like twin fawns of a gazelle
>> that browse among the lilies.
>>>> (4:1, 3, 5 NIV)

Shortly after the opening sequence of the *Mohicans* in the forest, we are given our first glimpse of Cora, the heroine of the film. And such a contrast to the warriors she is. Cora is British; she wears a lovely white dress, fringed with lace and flowing to the ground. Beauty and grace have come to the frontier. She wears a summer hat with a wide brim, which for a moment veils her dark eyes, rich and deep as pools of water, soft as doves. She is mysterious, but her mystery is not one that forbids. Rather, she is captivating. Her lips are red, like the Beloved in Songs, and her fitted bodice, in no way immodest, is alluring. Though an entire war party of Hurons is not enough to trap Nathaniel, he is captured by Cora's femininity, "held captive" by her long black hair, just as the Lover is in the Song.

> My lover has gone down to his garden,
>> to the beds of spices,

> to browse in the gardens
> and to gather lilies.
> I am my lover's and my lover is mine;
> he browses among the lilies.
> (6:2–3 NIV)

There is no union on earth like the consummation of the love between a man and a woman. No other connection reaches as deeply as this oneness was meant to; no other passion is nearly so intense. People don't jump off bridges because they lost a grandparent. If their friend makes another friend, they don't shoot them both. No one has ruined home and career for a rendezvous at the library. Troy didn't go down in flames because somebody lost a pet. The passion that spousal love evokes is instinctive, irrational, intense, and dare I say, immortal. As the Song says,

> Love is as strong as death,
> its jealousy unyielding as the grave.
> It burns like a blazing fire,
> like a mighty flame.
> Many waters cannot quench love;
> rivers cannot wash it away.
> (8:6–7 NIV)

Small wonder that many people experience sexual passion as their highest transcendence on this earth. This love surpasses all others as the source of the world's most beautiful poetry, art, and music. Lovers reach for the stars to find words fitting enough to express what the beloved means to them and still feel those words fall short. Granted, much of it is hyperbole, expressing more the dream than the reality. But that is precisely my point. It is not merely hormones and sex drives projected outward. It is a clue to a deeper reality, a reach for something that does exist. For this exotic intimacy was given to us as a picture of something else, something truly out of this world.

OUR LOVE AFFAIR WITH GOD

After creating this stunning portrait of a total union, the man and woman becoming one, God turns the universe on its head when he tells us that this is what *he* is seeking with *us*. In fact, Paul says it is *why* God created gender and sexuality and marriage—to serve as a living metaphor. He quotes Genesis, then takes it to the nth degree: "'For this reason a man will leave his father and mother and be united to his wife, and the two will become one flesh.' This is a profound mystery—but I am talking about Christ and the church" (Eph. 5:31–32 NIV).

A profound mystery indeed. All the breathtaking things in life are. The Cross is a great mystery, but we are helped in understanding it by looking back into the Old Testament and finding there the pattern of the sacrificial lamb. Those early believers did not understand the full meaning of what they were doing, but once Christ came, the whole period of ritual sacrifice was seen in a new light, and in turn gave a richer depth to our understanding of the Cross.

We must do the same with this stunning passage; we must look back and see the Bible for what it is—the greatest romance ever written. God creates mankind for intimacy with himself, as his beloved. We see it right at the start, when he gives us the highest freedom of all—the freedom to reject him. The reason is obvious: love is possible only when it is freely chosen. True love is never constrained; our hearts cannot be taken by force. So God sets out to woo his beloved and make her his queen:

I remember the devotion of your youth,
　　how as a bride you loved me
and followed me through the desert,
　　through a land not sown.
Israel was holy to the LORD,
　　the firstfruits of his harvest;
all who devoured her were held guilty,
　　and disaster overtook them.

(Jer. 2:2–3 NIV)

I gave you my solemn oath and entered into a covenant with you, declares the Sovereign LORD, and you became mine . . . I dressed you in fine linen and covered you with costly garments. I adorned you with jewelry . . . You became very beautiful and rose to be a queen. And your fame spread among the nations on account of your beauty, because the splendor I had given you made your beauty perfect. (Ezek. 16:8, 10–11, 13–14 NIV)

If you're writing a romance, love is the goal; you must allow for the possibility of betrayal. That is precisely what God calls our turning away from him. The Hebrews thought that he would be satisfied with some religious rituals and rule keeping. God calls them an "adulterous" wife, of all things:

Long ago you broke off your yoke
　　and tore off your bonds;
　　you said, "I will not serve you!"
Indeed, on every high hill
　　and under every spreading tree
　　you lay down as a prostitute.

(Jer. 2:20 NIV)

But you trusted in your beauty and used your fame to become a prostitute. You lavished your favors on anyone who passed by and your beauty became his. (Ezek. 16:15 NIV)

The hero's heart has been broken. He rails with a jealous fury that flows only from a Lover who has been rejected:

> Because you have forgotten me
>   and trusted in false gods.
> I will pull up your skirts over your face
>   that your shame may be seen—
> your adulteries and lustful neighings,
>   your shameless prostitution!
>   (Jer. 13:25–27 NIV)

I will sentence you to the punishment of women who commit adultery and who shed blood; I will bring upon you the blood vengeance of my wrath and jealous anger. (Ezek. 16:38 NIV)

But the story does not finish with their divorce. True love never fails; it always perseveres. God will fight for his beloved. So the Old Testament ends with a promise of reconciliation:

> Therefore I will block her path with thornbushes;
>   I will wall her in so that she cannot find her way.
> She will chase after her lovers but not catch them;
>   she will look for them but not find them.
> Then she will say,
>   "I will go back to my husband as at first . . ."
> Therefore I am now going to allure her;
>   I will lead her into the desert
>   and speak tenderly to her . . .

"In that day," declares the LORD,
  "you will call me 'my husband';
you will no longer call me 'my master.'"
                    (Hos. 2:6–7, 14, 16 NIV)

"That day" comes when Jesus appears on the scene and announces himself as the Bridegroom (Matt. 9:15). And when he says to us, "I am going there to prepare a place for you. And if I go and prepare a place for you, I will come back and take you to be with me that you also may be where I am," he is making his proposal (John 14:2–3 NIV). In the culture of the day, these are the very words a young man would say to his fiancée. Once the suitor secured the hand of his bride, he would return to his father's house and build the additional room that would be their bridal suite. (Couples moved into the home of the groom's parents.) It was "preparing a place for her." When all was ready, he would come for her and take her to be with him, so that where he is, she would also be.

We, the beloved, have become betrothed to the Bridegroom. John the Baptist said, "The bride belongs to the bridegroom. The friend who attends the bridegroom waits and listens for him, and is full of joy when he hears the bridegroom's voice" (John 3:29 NIV). We are in the time of waiting for the Bridegroom to return. By the end of the love story in Revelation 22 (vv. 17, 20 NIV), the church is practically panting for the return of Christ:

> The Spirit and the bride say, "Come!" And let him who hears say, "Come!" Whoever is thirsty, let him come; and whoever wishes, let him take the free gift of the water of life . . . He who testifies to these things says, "Yes, I am coming soon." Amen. Come, Lord Jesus.

Notice that it is the *bride* who is panting. How does a bride pant? As if for a lover who has long been away. She pants like the Beloved in Song of Songs: "Come, my lover, let us go to the countryside . . . There I will give you my love" (7:11–12 NIV). We are waiting for our Love to come. Augustine declared, "The whole life of the good Christian is a holy longing. What you desire ardently, as yet you do not see . . . By withholding of the vision, God extends the longing; through longing he extends the soul, by extending he makes room in it." So, said Augustine, "let us long because we are to be filled . . . that is our life, to be exercised by longing." And when the Bridegroom of our souls comes, what then? This engagement is headed toward a consummation.

THE CONSUMMATION OF THE AFFAIR
(What Is Worship, After All?)

The older Christian wedding vows contained these amazing words: "With my body, I thee worship." Maybe our forefathers weren't so prudish after all; maybe they understood sex far better than we do. To give yourself over to another, passionately and nakedly, to adore that person body, soul, and spirit—we know there is something special, even sacramental about sex. It requires trust and abandonment, guided by a wholehearted devotion. What else can this be but worship? After all, God employs explicitly sexual language to describe faithfulness (and unfaithfulness) to him. For us creatures of the flesh, sexual intimacy is the closest parallel we have to real worship. Even the world knows this. Why else would sexual ecstasy become the number one rival to communion with God? The best impostors succeed because they are nearly indistinguishable from what they are trying to imitate. We worship sex because we don't know how to worship God. But we will. Peter Kreeft writes,

This spiritual intercourse with God is the ecstasy hinted at in all earthly intercourse, physical or spiritual. It is the ultimate reason why sexual passion is so strong, so different from other passions, so heavy with suggestions of profound meanings that just elude our grasp. (*Everything You Wanted to Know About Heaven*)

Don't let your disappointing experiences cloud your understanding of this. We have grown cynical, as a society, about whether intimacy is really possible. To the degree that we have abandoned soul-oneness, we have sought out merely sex, physical sex, to ease the pain. But the full union is no longer there; the orgasm comes incomplete; its heart has been taken away. Many have been deeply hurt. Sometimes, we must learn from what we have not known, let it teach us what *ought* to be.

God's design was that the two shall become one flesh. The physical oneness was meant to be the expression of a total interweaving of being. Is it any wonder that we crave this? Our alienation is removed, if only for a moment, and in the paradox of love, we are at the same time known and taken beyond ourselves. In *The Mystery of Marriage* Mike Mason asserts,

> For many people, certainly, sex is the most powerful and moving experience that life has to offer, and more overwhelmingly holy than anything that happens in church. For great masses of people, sex is the one force which can actually tip men and women completely off their accustomed centers of gravity and lift them, however briefly, right out of themselves.

As Allender says, our hearts live for "an experience of worship that fills our beings with a joy that is so deeply in awe of the other that we are barely aware of ourselves." Many people have a hard time conceiving of this kind of intimacy with God. For their entire lives they have related to him in a distant, though reverent way. Our worship services don't get anywhere near something like our wedding nights. Men in particular have a hard time relating to the bridal imagery used in Scripture. Do we take on femininity to relate to God? What does it mean to *know* God as our Lover?

THE BEAUTY AND STRENGTH OF GOD

It is a mystery almost too great to mention, but God is the expression of the very thing we seek in each other. For do we not bear God's image? Are we not a living portrait of God? Indeed we are, and in a most surprising place—in our *gender*. "So God created man in his own image, in the image of God he created him; male and female he created them" (Gen. 1:27 NIV). Follow me closely now. Gender—masculinity and femininity—is how we bear the image of God. "I thought that there was only one kind of soul," said a shocked friend. "And God sort of poured those souls into male or female bodies." Many people believe something like that. But it contradicts the Word of God. We bear his image as men and women, and God does not have a body. So it must be at the level of the soul—the eternal part of us—that we reflect God. The text is clear; it is *as a man* or *as a woman* that the image is bestowed.

God wanted to show the world something of his strength. Is he not a great warrior? Has he not performed the daring rescue of his beloved? And this is why he gave us the sculpture that is man. Men bear the image of God in their dangerous, yet inviting strength. Women, too, bear the image of God, but in a much different way. Is not God a being of great mystery and beauty? Is there not something tender and alluring about the essence of the Divine? And this is why he gave us the sculpture that is woman.

You men will know what Mason means, though perhaps you've never made the connection:

> My wife's body is brighter and more fascinating than a flower, shier than any animal, and more breathtaking than a thousand sunsets. To me her body is the most awesome thing in creation. Trying to look at her, just trying to take in her wild, glorious beauty . . . I catch a glimpse of what it means that men and women have been made in the image of God. If even the image is this dazzling, what must the Original be like? (*The Mystery of Marriage*)

What, indeed. God is the source of all masculine power; God is also the fountain of all feminine allure. Come to think of it, he is the wellspring of everything that has ever romanced your heart. The thundering strength of a waterfall, the delicacy of a flower, the stirring capacity of music, the richness of wine. The masculine and the feminine that fill all creation come from the same heart. What we have sought, what we have tasted in part with our earthly lovers, we will come face-to-face with in our True Love. For the incompleteness that we seek to relieve in the deep embrace of our earthly love is never fully healed. The union does not last, whatever the poets and pop artists may say. Morning comes and we've got to get out of bed and off to our day, incomplete once more. But oh, to have it healed forever; to drink deeply from that fount of which we've had only a sip; to dive into that sea in which we have only waded.

And so a man like Charles Wesley can pen these words: "Jesus, Lover of my soul, let me to thy bosom fly," while Catherine of Siena can pray, "O fire surpassing every fire because you alone are the fire that burns without consuming! . . . Yet your consuming does not distress the soul but fattens her with insatiable love."

The French mystic Madame Guyon can write, "I slept not all night, because Thy love, O my God, flowed in me like delicious oil, and burned as a fire . . . I love God far more than the most affectionate lover among men loves his earthly attachment." And at the same time a monk, St. John of the Cross, can say,

> I abandoned and forgot myself,
> laying my face on my Beloved;
> all things ceased; I went out from myself
> leaving my cares
> forgotten among the lilies.

Where else are we told about oil and lilies? In Song of Songs. Is there sex in heaven? It would be better to ask, Is there worship in heaven?

THE SHARED AFFAIR

"O, rejoice beyond a common joy, and set it down with gold on lasting pillars!" This is the cry sent up at the end of Shakespeare's play *The Tempest*. What is the reason for such uncommon rejoicing? That though treason, and foul play, and a shipwreck had for so long separated families, lovers, even kingdoms, they have all been reunited. In hope against hope, they have been restored to one another.

> In one voyage
> Did Claribel her husband find at Tunis,
> And Ferdinand, her brother, found a wife
> Where he himself was lost, Prospero his dukedom
> In a poor isle, and all of us ourselves
> When no man was his own.

It is a manifestation of the humility of God that he creates a kingdom so rich in love that he should not be our all, but that others should be precious to us as well. Even in Eden, before the Fall, while Adam walked in Paradise with his God, even then God said, "It is not good for the man to be alone" (Gen. 2:18 NIV). He gives to us the joy of community, of family and friends to share in the Sacred Romance.

Is it not the nature of true love—to be generous in love? This is something of the reason that married couples long to have children; they want others to share in their happiness. The embrace of lovers does not stay confined to the lovers; rather, it builds a home, it fills a household. And so our longing for intimacy reaches beyond our "one and only." We come to discover that others mean so very much to us. There is no joy like the joy of reunion because there is no sorrow like the sorrow of separation. To lose those we love and wonder if we shall ever see them again—this is our deepest grief.

In 1991, Eric Clapton lost his only son, five-year-old Connor. The little boy fell from a window of their Manhattan apartment, plunging forty-nine stories to his death. Clapton channeled his grief into writing the heart-wrenching song "Tears in Heaven." In it he puts words to one of our deepest questions,

> Would you know my name
> If I saw you in heaven?
> Would it be the same
> If I saw you in heaven?

Oh, how much hangs on the word *if*. Jesus wept at the funeral of his dear friend Lazarus. I'm not sure we understand his tears because we do not share his strange carelessness about death. He has told us again and again not to fear it. (At the approach of his own death, he tells his closest friends to be *glad*, for heaven's sake.) On reaching Lazarus's grieving sister Martha, Jesus makes the astounding statement that those who are his will simply "never die" (John 11:26 NIV). He then comes to the grave site and weeps. Certainly, the tears are not for Lazarus, for according to Jesus, Lazarus is quite well. Jesus weeps for Martha and Mary, and for all of us who suffer loss. I think he weeps not only for our loss, but also for our inability to see beyond it. Dare I say, sometimes our refusal to see beyond it?

I have tasted grief, drunk deeply from its bitter cup. It is the most awful experience in this life. Death truly is the enemy (1 Cor. 15:26). But much of our grief comes because we have not dislodged that *if* from our hearts. As Willard explains,

> Once we have grasped our situation in God's full world, the startling disregard Jesus and the New Testament writers had for "physical death" suddenly makes sense. Paul bluntly states . . . that Jesus abolished death—simply did away with it.

> To one group of his day, who believed that "physical death" was the cessation of the individual's existence, Jesus said, "God is not the God of the dead, but of the living" (Luke 20:38). His meaning was that those who love and are loved by God are not allowed to cease to exist, because they are God's treasures. He delights in them and intends to hold onto them. He has even prepared for them an individualized eternal work in his vast universe. (*The Divine Conspiracy*)

I'll say more about that work in the next chapter. What is vital for us to grasp now, Willard says, is simply this: *"The life we now have as the persons we now are will continue in the universe in which we now exist."* By all means we shall know each other's name—not *if*—but *when* we see each other in God's great kingdom. We'll hold each other's hands, and far better than that. The naked intimacy, the real knowing that we enjoy with God, we shall enjoy with each other. George MacDonald wrote, "I think we shall be able to pass into and through each other's very souls as we please, knowing each other's thought and being, along with our own, and so being *like* God."

Brent used to call it multiple intimacy without promiscuity. It is what the ancients meant by the communion of saints. All of the joy that awaits us in the sea of God's love will be multiplied over and over as we share with each other in the Grand Affair. John Donne captures this beautifully:

> All mankind is of one author, and is one volume; when one man dies, one chapter is not torn out of the book, but translated into a better language; and every chapter must be so translated; God employs several translators: some pieces are translated by age, some by sickness, some by war, some by justice; but God's hand is in every translation; *and his hand shall bind up all our scattered leaves again*, for that library where every book shall lie open to one another.

Imagine the stories that we'll hear. And all the questions that shall finally have answers. "What were you thinking when you drove the old Ford out on the ice?" "Did you hear that Betty and Dan got back together? But of course you did—you were probably involved in that, weren't you?" "How come you never told us about your time in the war?" "Did you ever know how much I loved you?" And the answers won't be one-word answers, but story after story, a feast of wonder and laughter and glad tears.

The setting for this will be a great party, the wedding feast of the Lamb. Now, you've got to get images of Baptist receptions entirely out of your mind—folks milling around in the church gym, holding Styrofoam cups of punch, wondering what to do with themselves. You've got to picture an Italian wedding or, better, a Jewish wedding. They roll up the rugs and push back the furniture. There is *dancing*: "Then maidens will dance and be glad, young men and old as well" (Jer. 31:13 NIV). There is *feasting*: "On this mountain the LORD Almighty will prepare a feast of rich food for all peoples" (Isa. 25:6 NIV). (Can you imagine what kind of cook God must be?) And there is *drinking*—the feast God says he is preparing includes "a banquet of aged wine—the best of meats and the finest of wines." In fact, at his Last Supper our Bridegroom said he will not drink of "the fruit of the vine until the kingdom of God comes" (Luke 22:18 NIV). Then he'll pop a cork.

> And the people came together
> and the people came to dance
> and they danced like a wave upon the sea.

It was one of Brent's favorite lines from the poet Yeats. Stasi reminded me the other night of the last time Brent was in our home. For several years he and Ginny shared their lives with us and two other couples, all dear friends, in a covenant group. We'd meet twice a month or so, to talk about life. It was a place to know and be known, to come in out of the winds of the world and mend your sails. On this night, I'd asked everyone to bring a piece of art that he loved—a song, or a poem, or perhaps a film clip. Art is a glimpse into our hearts, and you can learn so much about someone when he shares with you something that has stirred his soul. Our conversation flowed from laughter to tears as we talked about each person's "window of the soul." The evening was winding to a close when Leigh offered to play the song she had brought. "It makes me think of heaven," she said, a little embarrassed. Heaven hadn't been part of the discussion 'til that moment. It was a joyful, upbeat, you've-got-to-get-up-and-dance kind of song, and soon we all were; swinging and jitter-bugging and just sort of hopping around the living room, none of us great dancers, but everyone celebrating the banquet to come. It was the last time we would all be together.

Until the Party begins.

CHAPTER NINE

THE ADVENTURE BEGINS

And in the perfect time, O perfect God,
When we are in our home, our natal home,
When joy shall carry every sacred load,
And from its life and peace no heart shall roam,
What if thou make us able to make like thee—
To light with moons, to clothe with greenery,
To hang gold sunsets o'er a rose and purple sea!

—GEORGE MACDONALD

Enter into the joy of your master.

—JESUS OF NAZARETH

We must explore one more aspect of our future if we are to recover heart for the journey of our lives. For though it will be unspeakable joy to live forever in a fully restored universe with the company of the truly intimate, it is not enough. There is something core to our being and set within our deepest desires that remains untouched. For as the nineteenth-century preacher Thomas Chalmers wrote, one of the "Grand Essentials" of human happiness is having something to *do*. I think the fear of being bored is an unspoken fear of many people about the life that is coming. After all, the never-ending sing-along in the sky isn't exactly breathtaking. Spending a weekend at the beach beats that hands down. Our lives in the coming kingdom will be surrounded with great beauty and our hearts filled with love, but what will we *do* with ourselves forever and ever? I have yet to meet a Christian who has more than the faintest notion of what his life will entail beyond the eternal church service. "I guess it will be good," sighed one friend. But guesses are not good enough in the journey of desire. We must *know*.

We've somehow overlooked a line in the parable of the talents, a single sentence that speaks volumes about the connection between our present and future life. As you'll recall, the landowner in the story has been away on a journey. In the parallel version told in Luke, the parable of the minas, he is a man of "noble birth" who has gone to "a distant country to have himself appointed king" (19:11–27 NIV). Upon his return, he rewards those faithful members of his staff in a way that at first seems, well, like no reward at all: "You have been faithful with a few things; I will put you in charge of many things." Luke's version has it this way: "Because you have been trustworthy in a very small manner, take charge of ten cities." This is their bonus— more to do? Wouldn't a vacation make a better reward? My boys clean their rooms so they can go out and play, not so they can clean the rest of the house. Yet Jesus thinks that he is sharing something delightful with us. The landowner then says, "Come and share your master's happiness." Or, as the King James has it, "Enter thou into the joy of thy lord" (Matt. 25:23). To understand what he means, we must have a closer look at God's joyful activity and our inherent design.

THE JOY OF THE MASTER

How marvelous it is to watch a master artist at work. We enjoyed a wonderful performance of Chausson's *Poeme for Violin and Orchestra* last night. The young woman who played the lead violin was simply beautiful in her long white gown, her graceful arms working the bow and strings with finesse. It was a joy just to watch her play. And the *Poeme* itself is an enchanting piece of music, almost ethereal. It fit her and the mood of the summer evening perfectly. And so it was with one accord that the audience rose in applause at the close of the performance.

Something similar happened at the opening of Genesis. As creation was unfolding from the hands of the Master, like wet clay on a potter's wheel, a great ovation erupted: "The morning stars sang together and all the angels shouted for joy" (Job 38:7 NIV). But of course. He has just finished sculpting the islands of Greece so that their white sandy beaches perfectly rim those azure seas. Then he watered the jungles of Malaysia to sustain an exotic array of orchids, after which he painted sunsets over the Sahara and hurled the Himalayas upward, treacherous peaks scraping the roof of the world.

And he doesn't stop there. Into this breathtaking setting of a thousand different habitats God places "the fish of the sea and the birds of the air and . . . every living creature that moves on the ground" (Gen. 1:28 NIV). Chameleons and caribou, porcupines and porpoises. How do we begin to describe this God whose image we bear? *Artistic* is the only word that even comes close. *Powerful, awesome, majestic*—yet *intricate, delicate, whimsical. Creative,* without a doubt. And that was just the beginning. Although God rested on the seventh day, he hasn't been lying around ever since.

Jesus said, "My Father is always at his work to this very day, and I, too, am working" (John 5:17 NIV). For many people this is a new thought—that God is still quite active. Life has led them to believe that he may have gotten things off to a great start, but then he left on vacation or perhaps went to attend to more important matters. But the creative overture recorded in Genesis was only the first movement of a great symphony that has been swelling ever since. The opening notes were not *staccato*, but *sostenuto*, ongoing, unfolding. He's not just sitting around on a throne somewhere. The psalmist proclaimed of God's work today,

> He wraps himself in light as with a garment;
>> he stretches out the heavens like a tent
>> and lays the beams of his upper chambers on their waters.
> He makes the clouds his chariot
>> and rides on the wings of the wind . . .
> He makes springs pour water into the ravines;
>> it flows between the mountains.
> They give water to all the beasts of the field;
>> the wild donkeys quench their thirst.
> The birds of the air nest by the waters;
>> they sing among the branches.
> He waters the mountains from his upper chambers;
>> the earth is satisfied by the fruit of his work.
> He makes grass grow for the cattle,
>> and plants for man to cultivate—
>> bringing forth food from the earth:
> wine that gladdens the heart of man,
>> oil to make his face shine,
>> and bread that sustains his heart.
>>> (Ps. 104:2–3, 10–15 NIV)

The only way to describe his ongoing creative activity is *extravagant*. Thunderclouds gather over the prairies, and afterward he scatters wildflowers as far as the eye can see. He fills the oceans with orcas and urchins and who knows what. A single maple leaf is woven with greater intricacy than the finest French lace—even though it will fall with the winds of autumn. New stars are born every day; a new sunset painted and swept away each night. Such magnificent generosity. No composer ever gave so many free concerts. MacDonald had it right: "Gloriously wasteful, O my Lord, art thou!"

You don't suppose he experiences his part in running the universe as drudgery, do you? Did Margot Fonteyn and Rudolf Nureyev love to dance? Does Michael Jordan love to play basketball? So God loves his work. He isn't ashamed to call it all "very good." Like a Master Craftsman offering a glimpse into his workshop, he asks Job,

> Have you ever given orders to the morning,
>> or shown the dawn its place? . . .
> Have you journeyed to the springs of the sea
>> or walked in the recesses of the deep? . . .
> Have you entered the storehouses of the snow
>> or seen the storehouses of the hail? . . .
> Can you bind the beautiful Pleiades?
>> Can you loose the cords of Orion?
> Can you bring forth the constellations in their seasons
>> or lead out the Bear with its cubs? . . .
> Do you send the lightning bolts on their way?
>> Do they report to you, "Here we are"? . . .
> Do you hunt the prey for the lioness
>> and satisfy the hunger of the lions? . . .
> Do you give the horse his strength
>> or clothe his neck with a flowing mane?
>>>> (Job 38:12–40; 39:19 NIV)

On and on he goes with a pride that befits his grandeur. You see, Job has come to the point where he wonders, rather loudly, whether God is "on the job" anymore. This is God's answer, and it goes on for two more chapters. The frost each morning? That's mine. The ostrich and hippo—mine too. I'm watching over the young doe when she gives birth; the eagle soars at my command. A jealous indignation characterizes these words, the sort of emotion that is aroused when someone criticizes our most cherished work. You see, it is God's *delight* to do all these things. Dallas Willard notes,

> We should, to begin with, think that God leads a very interesting life, and that he is full of joy. Undoubtedly he is the most joyous being in the universe. The abundance of his love and generosity is inseparable from his infinite joy. All of the good and beautiful things from which we occasionally drink tiny droplets of soul-exhilarating joy, God continuously experiences in all their breadth and depth . . . We are enraptured by a well-done movie sequence or by a few bars from an opera or lines from a poem. We treasure our great experiences for a lifetime, and we may have very few of them. But he is simply one great inexhaustible and eternal experience of all that is good and true and beautiful and right. This is what we must think of when we hear theologians and philosophers speak of him as a perfect being. *This is his life.* (*The Divine Conspiracy*)

And it is *this* life, with all its joyful creativity and power and unending happiness, that he says he is going to share with us. This is "the joy of your master" that we are to be welcomed into. It rather beats harps and halos, wouldn't you say? For we long to find our place in the world, caring for and developing creation in all its diverse potential. It is this for which we were made.

LITTLE GODS

"So God created man in his own image, in the image of God he created him; male and female he created them." Thus is humanity trumpeted onto the scene in verse 27 of the first chapter of Genesis (NIV). It is a passage familiar to most of us. Too familiar perhaps, for we rarely wonder about what it means. Right here, at the beginning of our existence, is the single phrase our Creator uses to characterize us, and most of us haven't the foggiest idea what it implies. If we were reading the Scripture for the story it is (and not like an encyclopedia, as many do), we would have in mind all that has transpired up to this moment. We have been watching the God whose image we bear. What do we know about him at this point? What has he been up to? Creating the heavens and the earth. Islands and caribou and wildflowers. This is what he has been doing. *This is all we know of God* when we reach the point at which we are compared to him.

If you were meeting a young man for the first time, and he was introduced to you as the "son of Einstein," you'd probably expect him to be rather bright. If you met a young woman as the "daughter of Nadia Comancci," the Russian gymnast, you might assume she could turn a decent cartwheel. We expect greatness from the offspring of the great. To be introduced as the image bearers of God is full of anticipation. It would be as though we were introduced as the sons of a renowned artist, perhaps a Monet, or as the daughters of a graceful dancer, such as Martha Graham. It leads us to what to expect next. Jesus said, "Is it not written in your Law, 'I have said you are gods'?" (John 10:34 NIV). Why is it, then, that creativity rarely comes to mind when we think of how we reflect God? More often than not we think of godliness in moral terms. When we hear that so-and-so is a "godly person," we assume that he is devout, or perhaps self-sacrificing, and certainly more virtuous than most. But when Genesis declares we are God's image, it is describing not certain qualities of our character but *capacities of our nature*. This is why, when the essence of our likeness to God is announced, it is in the context of our *position* upon the earth, our place in creation:

> Then God said, "Let us make man in our image, in our likeness, *and let them rule* over the fish of the sea and the birds of the air, over the livestock, over all the earth, and over all the creatures that move along the ground." (Gen. 1:26 NIV, emphasis added)

In other words, we are *made* like God in our creative powers because we are to *be* like God in ruling the earth. The image implies a capacity, and the capacity assumes the creative legacy we shall carry on. "Those two phrases—'Let us make man in our Image,' and 'Let them rule'—must be taken together," says Ben Patterson. "Each modifies the other. To be like God is to rule the earth as he does. To rule the earth as he does is to be like God." Our original design was for a life of creative rule, to share in the overall care and development of God's creation. The poet writes because she is made in God's image; the builder loves to build for the same reason. Entrepreneurs risk capital ventures, baseball players go to the batting cages, and cooks experiment with spices all for the same reason. It is what we *are*.

ON MOZART AND MARTHA STEWART

"Somehow," notes Os Guinness, "we human beings are never happier than when we are expressing the deepest gifts that are truly us." Now, some children are gifted toward science, and others are born athletes. But whatever their specialty, *all* children are inherently creative. Give them a barrel of Legos and a free afternoon and my boys will produce an endless variety of spaceships and fortresses and who knows what. It comes naturally to children; it's in their *nature*, their design as little image bearers. Set a group of kindergartners down with sheets of paper and tubs of finger paint, and you don't have to provide directions. They know what to do. In fact, paint and paper aren't even necessary; chocolate pudding and a nearby wall will do nicely. A pack of boys let loose in a wood soon becomes a major Civil War reenactment. A chorus of girls, upon discovering a trunk of skirts and dresses, will burst into the *Nutcracker Suite*. The right opportunity reveals the creative nature.

This is precisely what happens when God shares with mankind his own artistic capacity and then sets us down in a paradise of unlimited potential. It is an act of creative *invitation*, like providing Monet with a studio for the summer, stocked full of brushes and oils and empty canvases. Or like giving Mozart full use of an orchestra and a concert hall for an autumn of composing. Or like setting Martha Stewart loose in a gourmet kitchen on a snowy winter weekend, just before the holidays. You needn't provide instructions or motivation; all you have to do is release them to be who they are, and remarkable things will result. As the poet Hopkins wrote, "What I do is me: for that I came."

Oh, how we long for this—for a great endeavor that draws upon our every faculty, a great "life's work" that we could throw ourselves into. "I was made for this," said one friend who after years of hesitation finally pursued his dream of becoming a high school teacher. "It energizes me." "After years in a wasteland," moaned another, "all I want is to be released to be who I am." His career had not panned out, and as he saw his most productive days slipping by, he longed to find his place. "God has created us and our gifts for a place of his choosing," says Guinness, "and we will only be ourselves when we are finally there." Our creative nature is essential to who we are as human beings—as image bearers—and it brings us great joy to live it out with freedom and skill. Even if it's a simple act such as working on your photo albums or puttering in the garden—these, too, are how we have a taste of what was meant to rule over a small part of God's great kingdom. Willard points out:

> Here is a truth that reaches into the deepest part of what it means to be a person . . . that we are made to "have dominion" within an appropriate domain of reality. This is the core of the likeness or image of God in us and is the basis of the destiny for which we were formed. We are, all of us, never-ceasing spiritual beings with a unique eternal calling to count for good in God's great universe . . . In creating human beings God made them to rule, to reign, to have dominion in a limited sphere. Only so can they be persons. (*The Divine Conspiracy*)

THE MISERIES OF A DETHRONED MONARCH

During a long layover at O'Hare, I studied the man who sells popcorn from a little stand in one of the terminal hallways. He sat silently on a stool as thousands of people rushed by. Occasionally, every fifteen minutes or so, someone would stop and buy a bag. He would scoop the popcorn from the bin, take the money, and make change—all without a word being spoken between them. When the brief encounter was over, he would resume his place on the stool, staring blankly, his shoulders hunched over. I wondered at his age; he seemed well past fifty. How long had that been his profession? Could he possibly make a living at it? His face wore a weary expression of resignation tinged with shame. *Adam,* I thought, *what happened?* Did he know how far his situation was from his true design? Somehow he knew, even if he didn't know the Story. His sadness was testimony to it. I thought of Pascal, that all our miseries prove our greatness: "They are the miseries of a dethroned monarch."

Some people love what they do. They are the fortunate souls, who have found a way to link what they are truly gifted at (and therefore what brings them joy) with a means of paying the bills. But most of the world merely toils to survive, and no one gets to use his gifts all the time. On top of that, there is the curse of thorns and thistles, the futility that tinges all human efforts at the moment. As a result, we've come to think of work as a result of the Fall. You can see our cynicism in the fact that we've chosen the cartoon character Dilbert as the icon of our working days. His is a hopeless life of futility and anonymity in the bowels of a large corporation. We don't even know what he does—only that it's meaningless. We identify with him, feeling at some deep level the apparent futility of our lives. Even if we are loved, it is not enough. We yearn to be *fruitful,* to do something of meaning and value that flows naturally out of the gifts and capacities of our souls. But of course—we were meant to be the kings and queens of the earth.

Dorothy Sayers once wrote, "Work is not, primarily, a thing one does to live, but the thing one lives to do." If only it were so; if only we could land our "dream job," where we'd be paid to do what we love. Some actually go out and do it. A friend took off several years ago to be a hunting and fishing guide in Alaska. He's having a ball. Another friend had a chance to work on Broadway; his wife said to me afterward, "John was made for this. All the experiences of his life had led up to this very thing." The rest of us look on from the sidelines with longing, held back from our dreams by fear or heartache or the demands of the life we do have. No wonder we hear the rewards in the parable with such disappointed ears—it sounds as though we'll lose even those few hours of private joy we manage to squeeze in on the weekend and take on some sort of eternal task. But what if it were the opposite? What if the master's invitation was to do, like Hopkins, what is *you*? What if you were given the *freedom* (the permission) and the *power* (all the resources necessary) to do exactly what you were always meant to do?

THE MONARCHY RESTORED

Let's come back for a moment to the restoration of the earth. In Romans 8 (NIV), Paul says something outrageous. He says that all our sufferings are "not worth comparing" with the glory that will be revealed in us. It seems hard to believe, given the way life can break your heart. The human race has seen an unspeakable amount of suffering. What can possibly make that seem like nothing? "The glory that will be revealed in us" (8:18). The Great Restoration. Paul then goes on to say, "The creation waits in eager expectation for the sons of God to be revealed" (8:19). The release of a fully restored creation is being more or less held back, waiting upon *our* restoration. Why? Because only then can we handle it. Only when we ourselves have been restored can we take our place again as the kings and queens of creation. Or did you not know? The day is coming when Christ will appoint you as one of his regents over his great and beautiful universe. This has been his plan all along.

When the Son of Man comes in his glory, and all the angels with him, he will sit on his throne in heavenly glory. All the nations will be gathered before him, and he will separate the people one from another as a shepherd separates the sheep from the goats. He will put the sheep on his right and the goats on his left. Then the King will say to those on his right, "Come, you who are blessed by my Father; take your inheritance, *the kingdom prepared for you since the creation of the world.*" (Matt. 25:31–34 NIV, emphasis added)

Who then is the faithful and wise servant, whom the master has put in charge of the servants in his household to give them their food at the proper time? It will be good for that servant whose master finds him doing so when he returns. I tell you the truth, *he will put him in charge of all his possessions.* (Matt. 24:45–47 NIV, emphasis added)

And they will *reign* for ever and ever. (Rev. 22:5 NIV, emphasis added)

Think for a moment. The One who created you and set all those loves and gifts in your heart, the One who has shaped all your life experiences (including the ones that seem to make no sense), this God has prepared a place for you that is a more than perfect fit for all your gifts and quirks and personality traits— even those you don't know you have. Christ is not joking when he says that we shall inherit the kingdom prepared for us and shall reign with him forever. We will take the position for which we have been uniquely made and will rule *as he does*—meaning with creativity and power.

I think back upon God's questions to Job: "Have you ever given orders to the morning? Do you hunt the prey for the lioness?" And like a young apprentice in the presence of a master, something in my heart says cautiously (yet eagerly), "No . . . but I'd like to!" And so Willard writes,

We will not sit around looking at one another or at God for eternity but will join the eternal Logos, "reign with him," in the endlessly ongoing creative work of God. It is for this that we were each individually intended, as both kings and priests (Exod. 19:6; Rev. 5:10) . . . A place in God's creative order has been reserved for each one of us from before the beginnings of cosmic existence. His plan is for us to develop, as apprentices to Jesus, to the point where we can take our place in the ongoing creativity of the universe. (*The Divine Conspiracy*)

Much of the activity of God in our lives is bringing us to the place where he can entrust us with this kind of influence. God takes our training so seriously because he fully intends to promote us. Will it be joy? Does Stephen Hawking enjoy physics? Does Mark McGwire enjoy hitting it out of the park? There are so many ways this "reigning" will be expressed—as unique and varied as there are human souls. God has quite a few "possessions," and it's going to take a lot of looking after by men and women uniquely fitted for the task.

I am not a scientist; but I am told by those who are of the great adventure in exploring the beauty revealed in the structures of physics or molecular biology. I don't go in for organizational structures and master planning, but I have friends who can talk about them for hours. To each his own—literally. Each person will live out the passion of his heart, set there by the Creator from before the beginning of time. I should like one day to paint with the grace of Monet, or plumb the wonders of physics with Einstein. Perhaps I shall. There is work enough to be done.

THE GLORIOUS FREEDOM

"Life," as a popular saying goes, "is not a dress rehearsal. Live it to the fullest." What a setup for a loss of heart. No one gets all he desires; no one even comes close. If this is it, we are lost. But what if life *is* a dress rehearsal? What if the real production is about to begin? That is precisely what Jesus says; he tells us that we are being shaped, prepared, groomed for a part in the grand drama that is coming. In *The Call*, Guinness writes about a delightful story told by Artie Shaw, a famous clarinetist during the big band era:

> Maybe twice in my life I reached what I wanted to. Once we were playing "These Foolish Things" and at the end the band stops and I play a little cadenza. That cadenza—no one can do it better. Let's say it's five bars. That's a very good thing to have done in a lifetime. An artist should be judged by his best, just as an athlete. Pick out my one or two best things and say, "That's what we did: all the rest was rehearsal."

All the rest was rehearsal—not for just a few shining moments, but for an eternity of joy. Realizing this is immensely freeing. How many of your plans take an unending future into account? "Let's see, I'm going to be alive forevermore, so . . . if I don't get this done now, I'll get to it later." This is so important, for no human life reaches its potential here.

I was talking with a playwright several years ago. His career was not panning out the way he deeply wanted it to, and he was becoming rather depressed. It wasn't a matter of being unqualified; he was, and is, a very gifted writer. But few playwrights achieve anything like success. Life wasn't inviting him to be who he was—yet. He had never once considered that he would be a great writer in the coming kingdom, and that he was merely in training now. His day was yet to come. Understanding that put his life in an entirely new light.

In Revelation 21, John describes the New Jerusalem, the city of God come to earth. It is a place of exquisite beauty and grandeur. And then he adds an odd statement: "The kings of the earth will bring *their* splendor into it" (v. 24 NIV, emphasis added). It seems hard to believe that we could add anything to the splendor God creates, but that is exactly what we are designed for and what our future involves. How amazing it will be to have our souls released into their true destiny, in a world no longer stained by sin or under the curse. To throw ourselves into some wonderful enterprise, unhindered by our own weaknesses or the frustrations typical of a broken world. Gardeners dream of a spot of ground with rich soil and not a weed or sow bug to be found. They shall have it. Architects dream of the day they shall build their own designs and not merely carry out the plans of another. They shall. Like children eager to show off our precious creations, we shall bring them to our Father in Jerusalem, for glory and praise.

The Grand Affair heals the curse of isolation. The Great Adventure heals the curse of futility. The "glorious freedom" of the children of God is the freedom of being all we were meant to be. We won't be held back by anything anymore; no, we will finally hit our stride. We all know the frustration of failure, of missing the mark—getting the equation wrong, hitting the ball into the rough, misdiagnosing the patient. And most of us at one time or another have tasted the joy of getting it right. Not only will we find our place, but we will be empowered to do the very things we aim to do, with and for God. As C. S. Lewis wrote,

> The miracles that have already happened are, of course, as the Scripture often says, the first fruits of that cosmic summer which is presently coming on. Christ has risen, and so we shall rise. St. Peter for a few seconds walked on the water; and the day will come when there will be a remade universe, infinitely obedient to the will of glorified and obedient men, when we can do all things, when we shall be those gods that we are described as being in Scripture. (*The Grand Miracle*)

—— THREE WEEKS AFTER *the wind ceased to blow, the sea lion had a dream. Now, as I told you before, there were other nights in which he had dreamed of the sea. But those were long ago and nearly forgotten. Even still, the ocean that filled his dreams this night was so beautiful and clear, so vast and deep, it was as if he were seeing it for the very first time. The sunlight glittered on its surface, and as he dived, the waters all around him shone like an emerald. If he swam quite deep, it turned to jade, cool and dark and mysterious. But he was never frightened; not at all. For I must tell you that in all his dreams of the sea, he had never before found himself in the company of other sea lions. This night there were many, round about him, diving and turning, spinning and twirling. They were playing.*

Oh, how he hated to wake from that wonderful dream. The tears running down his face were the first wet thing he had felt in three weeks. But he did not pause even to wipe them away; he did not pause, in fact, for anything at all. He set his face to the east, and he began to walk as best a sea lion can.

"Where are you going?" asked the tortoise.

"I am going to find the sea."

CHAPTER TEN

ENTERING MORE DEEPLY INTO DESIRE

Blessed are those who hunger and thirst.

—JESUS OF NAZARETH

And in me wake hope, fear, boundless desire.

—GEORGE MACDONALD

The devil sleepeth not; neither is the flesh as yet dead; therefore cease not to prepare thyself for the battle; for on thy right hand and on thy left are enemies who never rest.

—THOMAS À KEMPIS

I hope by now you see why I have spent three chapters trying to bring eternity out of the clouds and into our conscious lives. The dilemma of desire is the deepest dilemma we will ever face. Its dangers are deep and potentially fatal. How, then, shall we not lose heart? If we manage to somehow hang on to our desire, how do we keep from being consumed by it? The secret is known to all of us, though we may have forgotten that we know it. Who wants to fill up with snacks on Thanksgiving Day? Who goes out to buy presents for himself on Christmas Eve? Is there anyone in his right mind who looked for someone to date at his wedding rehearsal? When we are convinced that something delicious is about to be ours, we are free to live in expectation, and it draws us on in anticipation. There are three things that we must come to terms with in our deep heart. First, we must have life. Second, we cannot arrange for it. Third, it is coming. Now we are ready to proceed on our way.

BATTLE AND JOURNEY

Life is now a battle and a journey. As Eugene Peterson reminds us, "We must fight the forces that oppose our becoming whole; we must find our way through difficult and unfamiliar territory to our true home." It's not that there aren't joy and beauty, love and adventure now—there are. The invasion of the kingdom has begun. But life in its fullness has yet to come. So we must take seriously the care of our hearts. We must watch over our desire with a fierce love and vigilance, as if we were protecting our most precious possession. We must do battle with the enemies of our hearts—those sirens that would seduce and shipwreck our desire and those arrows that aim to kill it outright. And we must journey forward, toward God, toward the Great Restoration and the Adventures to come. How awful to reach the end of life's road and find we haven't brought our hearts along with us.

So let me say it again: life is now a battle and a journey. This is the truest explanation for what is going on, the only way to rightly understand our experience. Life is not a game of striving and indulgence. It is not a long march of duty and obligation. It is not, as Henry Ford once said, "one damn thing after another." Life is a desperate quest through dangerous country to a destination that is, beyond all our wildest hopes, indescribably good. Only by conceiving of our days in this manner can we find our way safely through. You see, different roads lead different places. To find the Land of Desire, you must take the journey of desire.

You can't get there by any other means. If we are to take up the trail and get on with our quest, we've got to get our hearts back, which means getting our desire back.

RECOVERING DESIRE

I continue to be stunned by the level of deadness that most people consider normal and seem to be contented to live with. It had been more than a year since Diane and Ted first came to see me for counseling. As with most marriages, the real issues lay buried under years of just getting by, hidden beneath the way we've learned to live with each other so as not to rock the boat. Sadly, this way involves killing large regions of our hearts. And so their struggle toward intimacy required a lot of pain and hard work. But they stuck with it until they began to taste the true life of a real marriage. At this point Diane asked Ted about his deepest desires: "If I could be more of what you wanted in a woman, what do you secretly wish I would offer you?" It's a question that most men are dying to be asked. His response? Clean socks. That's all he could come up with. Life would be better, his marriage would be richer, if Diane would keep his drawer filled with clean socks. I wanted to throw him out the window.

I wasn't angry with Ted because his answer was unbelievably shallow or because it mocked all that his wife was seeking to offer him. I was angry because *it's just not true.* We are made in the image of God; we carry within us the desire for our true life of intimacy and adventure. To say we want less than that is to lie. Ted may believe that clean socks would satisfy him, but he is deceived. His satisfaction comes at the price of his soul.

When I brought up this very issue with a colleague, he sort of dismissed it all with the comment, "Not everyone longs like you do." I had to admit that much. But we were *meant* to. I thought of

The Weight of Glory, where Lewis says that "when we consider the unblushing promises of reward and the staggering nature of the rewards promised in the Gospels, it would seem that our Lord finds our desires not too strong, but too weak." My point precisely. Lewis is right:

> We are half-hearted creatures, fooling about with drink and sex and ambition, when infinite joy is offered us, like an ignorant child who wants to go on making mud pies in a slum because he cannot imagine what is meant by the offer of a holiday at the sea. We are far too easily pleased.

If only it were as strong as drink and sex and ambition. We've been bought off by clean socks and television. We'll sell our birthright for a little bit of pleasure and some peace and quiet. I understand. It hasn't taken us long to realize that life is not going to offer what we truly want, and so we've learned to reduce our desires to a more manageable size. But let's be honest about what we've done, and call it what it is: sin. The first step in the journey of desire is to stop pretending that we'd be happy with our equivalent of clean socks. Simone Weil said, "The danger is that the soul should persuade itself that it is not hungry." Recovering our true heart's desire may involve facing some very deep disappointment. Undoubtedly, it will require painful self-examination. But we do not need to fear what we will find, for our heart is our ally in this journey.

OUR DEEPEST HEART

Many committed Christians are wary about getting in touch with their desires, not because they want to settle for less, but because they fear that they will discover some dark hunger lurking in their hearts. As I've said, the father of lies takes many people out of the battle and ends their journey by keeping them in the shallows of their desire, tossing them a bone of pleasure, and thus convincing them that they are satisfied. However, once we begin to move from that place, his strategy changes. He threatens us from going into the deep waters by telling us that our core desires are evil. You might recall the scene in *Pilgrim's Progress* that takes place as Christian is making his way along the dark and dangerous trail through the Valley of the Shadow of Death:

> One thing I would not let slip; I took notice that now poor Christian was so confounded that he did not know his own voice; and thus I perceived it. One of the wicked ones got behind him, and stepped up softly to him, and whisperingly suggested many grievous blasphemies to him, which he verily thought had proceeded from his own mind. This put Christian more to it than anything that he met with before, even to think that he should now blaspheme him that he loved so much before; yet if he could have helped it, he would not have done it; but he had not the discretion either to stop his ears, or to know from whence these [thoughts] came.

The crisis for Christian is that he did not know his own voice, his true voice. He was convinced that the whispers of the enemy were his own desires. Far too many Christians today make the same dangerous assumption—that every thought and desire they experience is their own. "I could just lose myself at work." David was angry and resentful as he said this. He is struggling deeply in his marriage just now. "And no one would know the difference. I would still look married." "You are not a coward," I said. "I know you . . . that is not your heart. That is not the man you really want to be."

Listen to the promise of God to us in the new covenant: "I will

give you a new heart and put a new spirit in you; I will remove
from you your heart of stone and give you a heart of flesh" (Ezek.
36:26 NIV). For those who have been born of the Spirit and
become new creatures in Christ, sin is no longer the truest thing
about us. Since the coming of Christ, everything has changed.
The joy of the new covenant is the transformation of our deepest being. As Christians, we have a new heart, and that means
nothing less than this: our core desires are good. "I will put my
law in their minds and write it on their hearts" (Jer. 31:33 NIV).
We don't need to fear recovering our desire because our desire is
from God and for God. That is what is most true about us. After
several silent moments David said, "You're right. This is not what
I most deeply want."

Yes, we still struggle with sin, with our tendency to kill desire
or give our hearts over to false desires. But that is not who and
what we truly are. If we really believe the new covenant, we'll be
able to embrace our desire. So, let's come back to the simple
question Jesus asks of us all: What do you want? Don't minimize
it; don't try to make sure it sounds spiritual; don't worry about
whether or not you can obtain it. Just stay with the question until
you begin to get an answer. This is the way we keep current with
our hearts.

WHAT DO YOU WANT?

"It's hard to be holy and passionate." Cindy sighed as she said
this. A bright young woman and a sincerely committed follower of
Christ, she's also a bit more vulnerable to men than she'd like to
be. It seems that the only way Cindy can keep from chasing after
physical intimacy with a man is to bury herself in grad school. But
as I've said earlier, the "run from desire" approach never works, and
she soon finds herself leaving the books for another compromis-

ing situation. "Why can't I get beyond this?" she asked. "I'm praying and reading my Bible every day. But still I fall." "What are you looking for?" I asked in return. We sat in silence for a few minutes. "I really don't know." "That's your problem . . . you don't know. And so your unexamined desires rule you." After a few moments she asked, "Is it pleasure? Excitement?" She was clueless. As intelligent as Cindy is, I wasn't surprised that she had no clue about why she couldn't break her addiction to men. As a rule, most of us live far from our hearts. We need to be much more acquainted with them. We need to know what we want.

The path to a clearer knowledge of our desire depends on how we've been handling it. Those who have buried desire beneath years of duty and obligation may need to give all that a rest so that their hearts can come to the surface. Abandon all but the most essential duties for a while. You still have to pay the bills, but everything you can jettison, you should. Do nothing unless it reflects your true desire. Remember the Pharisees—their religious activities deadened them to the point that they couldn't even recognize God when he stood before them. When our deepest treasure becomes our most dutiful burden, it really kills our hearts. You might even need to give up going to church for a while or reading your Bible. I stopped going to church for a year; it was one of the most refreshing years of my life. I hadn't abandoned God, and I very much sought out the company of my spiritual companions. What I gave up was the performance of having to show up every Sunday morning with my happy face on. I suggested something similar to a young woman who had really lost the joy of her faith. A few weeks later she wrote to me, "I actually had a desire to read the Bible and pray without its being a set time or a guilt trip! That's never happened before!"

Those who have been living to indulge desire will need to give that a rest too. What does your heart feel when I suggest you give up your obsession? Listen to the panic—there's something beneath it, something you need to know. Now, I understand that going cold turkey may seem overwhelming, unattainable. You may have tried that before and failed. Let me offer a more gentle approach. Simply stay in your desire for fifteen minutes longer than you usually do. When you're feeling a pull to the refrigerator or the gym or the bedroom, stop and let the desire just be; let it become more acute. Don't do anything with it. Let yourself feel it, and as you do, let your heart put some honest words to what you're feeling. You might be surprised what you find there.

I was walking down the hall at work one day, lost in my thoughts. Walking ahead of me, the same direction I was going, was a beautiful woman. I looked up and my heart said, *Wow!* Fearing that the beast of lust was rearing its ugly head, I tried to kill my reaction. It never works, and I knew it, so I decided instead to find out what was going on beneath what seemed to be an inappropriate response. Still walking along, with this beauty still in view, I asked my heart, *What do you mean by "wow"?* The next sentence literally popped out, unscripted, from someplace deep inside me: *The grand prize if you are truly a man.* I was stunned. I have lived that lie for a long time. How many young boys in our culture, just as they are entering adolescence, are introduced to sexuality as masculinity? Look at every ad designed for men. Whether it's for cars or sporting gear, clothes or beer, a beautiful siren is almost always posing seductively alongside. The message is beaten into us: if you're a man, you'll win the woman. I saw how long I had been haunted by that idea, and I also saw that what I was desiring was not an affair, but a truer sense of my masculinity.

This is something more than cognitive therapy, more than telling yourself the truth. It involves the hidden places of your heart, which are almost always revealed in your desire. But few of us take the time to look at the desire *beneath* the desire. A friend just spent thousands of dollars to undo a previous operation that tied her fallopian tubes. She wants to have another baby; no, she *needs* to have another baby. It has nothing to do with a baby. This is where she experiences being needed and wanted and loved. How many women derive their sense of self from their children? On and on it goes. Do we purchase a new home merely for more space, or does it mean security to us? We seek a better job. Might we be seeking a sense of identity, of being a successful person? It's not that the longing roused by any of these things is wrong. It's that we must learn what is actually *being* roused. The more attuned we are to our true desire, the less prone we'll be to impostors.

TEMPTATION

Then Jesus was led by the Spirit into the desert to be tempted by the devil. After fasting forty days and forty nights, he was hungry. The tempter came to him and said, "If you are the Son of God, tell these stones to become bread." Jesus answered, "It is written: 'Man does not live on bread alone, but on every word that comes from the mouth of God.'" (Matt. 4:1–4 NIV)

We can learn many things about the journey of desire in the story of Jesus' wilderness trial. First, "he was hungry." I am so grateful for that phrase. It helps me to believe in the humanity of Jesus. He didn't just glide along through life, untouched by the dilemma of desire. Because his hunger is real, we can learn something about ours. May says, "If we think of Jesus as truly human, as a real man who was truly vulnerable to attachment, then the way he responded to Satan's temptation reveals some things that are critically important." The first thing we learn is that we're going to hunger. It's normal; expect it. Jesus' hunger validates my own. I needn't be embarrassed by it, try to hide it, or diminish it in some way. Sometimes we feel guilty about the depth of our desire, and we end up repenting of the wrong thing.

The devil sees his opportune moment. He comes to Jesus as he comes to us—in our hunger. And what he says is simply this: "You don't have to stay hungry, you know. There are options." He's not lying at this point; there usually are options. There is often something we can do about our hunger, and the options increase the more we are willing to turn away from trusting God. The lie is that the options will bring us what we most deeply want and need. They won't. Every idol is an impostor. Jesus responds, "Those options are not true life." This is the first crucial moment—facing what the options really amount to and realizing "that's not really life." A deep, robust thirst—like we feel after a long, hot hike—can be quenched only by water. To be offered a hot fudge sundae wouldn't tempt us at all. And so we see the importance of entering into desire, of knowing full well what we're craving.

I look at what my friends eat—not one-tenth of it is real food. It is all impostors—canned this, microwaved that. Bread without any nutritional value; fruit juice that boasts "10 percent real juice." Thus they slowly starve themselves while feeling full. When we are out of shape, when we are in the habit of eating poorly, truly nourishing foods don't appeal to us. Better something rich, high in fat. Those mock our need while they appease our taste. But when we are fit, when we've been working out or just working hard in the field, we know what we want. Who would trade a hearty farmhouse dinner for a plate of marshmallows? The truly healthy desire knows what it wants. Had we desired more deeply, more clearly, we would have seen the offer for what it was. Knowing full well what our heart's real thirst was, we would have looked the impostor in the face and laughed. As Jesus did.

Then the devil took him to the holy city and had him stand on the highest point of the temple. "If you are the Son of God," he said, "throw yourself down. For it is written: 'He will command his angels concerning you, and they will lift you up in their hands, so that you will not strike your foot against a stone.'" Jesus answered him, "It is also written: 'Do not put the Lord your God to the test.'" (Matt. 4:5–7 NIV)

The second trial comes after we determine not to take matters into our own hands. By refusing to turn stones to bread, Jesus chooses to trust God. That is what we are saying when we refuse our options as well. Satan's reply is, "Oh, so you're going to trust your God. Fine. Prove he cares for you." He comes with an attack on God's heart toward us. This is almost inevitable for the thirsty soul. After we have chosen to remain in our thirst for a while, the doubts begin to creep in. *God, I know you love me. But I didn't expect I'd have to wait so long for what I desire.* We begin to wonder, *Do you care for me, God?* Satan jumps all over this, throwing fuel on the fire of our doubts. Jesus' response is our only hope: "I don't need to prove that God cares for me. He cares for me *now*." There is no other place to stand. As Allender says,

If God's goodness is looked for primarily in turns of fortune . . . then the verdict on his heart towards us will always be pending on a new set of facts. We will, then, become either a judge ("How can God be good, if he let my son die?!") or a bargainer ("God, I'll know you are good if you bring my husband back to me"). God does not seem to show his goodness to those who peer through the lens of a skeptical examiner or a demanding negotiator. The Evil One uses the pain and confusion of a fallen world to shadow doubt over God's goodness. (*Bold Love*)

Jesus came to answer once and for all our question, "Do you care for me, God?" That is why the ground before the cross is the only place we can take a firm stand against the doubts that come in the journey of desire. We don't need for God to prove his love for us; he has, at the cross.

> Again, the devil took him to a very high mountain and showed him all the kingdoms of the world and their splendor. "All this I will give you," he said, "if you will bow down and worship me." Jesus said to him, "Away from me, Satan! For it is written: 'Worship the Lord your God, and serve him only.'" Then the devil left him, and angels came and attended him. (Matt. 4:8–11 NIV)

The cat's out of the bag. Satan has revealed his true aim. "You don't have to take the route of suffering," he says. "There are shortcuts. Just give your heart away." It all comes down to worship. What will we give our hearts away to, in return for the promise of life? May says this is "the ultimate invitation to idolatry." Jesus shuts Satan down: "There are no shortcuts, and my heart belongs to God alone."

Once we realize what a precious thing this is, the heart's desire, we must see that to guard it is worth our all. To neglect it is foolishness. To kill it is suicide. To allow it to wander aimlessly, to be trapped by the seductions of the evil one, is disaster. We must be *serious* about our happiness. And so Thomas à Kempis urges,

> The greatest, and indeed the whole impediment, is that we are not disentangled from our passions and lusts, neither do we endeavor to enter into that path of perfection which the saints have walked before us; and when any small adversity befalleth us, we are too quickly dejected, and turn ourselves to human comforts. If we would endeavor, like men of courage, to stand in

the battle, surely we would feel the favorable assistance of God from heaven. For he who giveth us occasion to fight, to the end that we may get the victory, is ready to succor those that fight manfully, and do trust in his grace. *(The Imitation of Christ)*

TUNING THE INSTRUMENT

So I tell you this, and insist on it in the Lord, that you must no longer live as the Gentiles do, in the futility of their thinking. They are darkened in their understanding and separated from the life of God because of the ignorance that is in them due to the hardening of their hearts. Having lost all sensitivity, they have given themselves over to sensuality so as to indulge in every kind of impurity, with a continual lust for more. (Eph. 4:17–19 NIV)

The loss of sensitivity that Paul is referring to here is the dullness that most people accept as normal. It actually leads us into sin, to sensuality and lust. The deadened soul requires a greater and greater level of stimulation to arouse it. This is, of course, the downward spiral of any addiction. What began as an attraction to *Playboy* ends up for the porn addict in some really horrific stuff. Just look at the progression of television drama over the past thirty years. What we have now would have been considered shocking, even repulsive, to an earlier audience. Networks have to keep adding more sex, more violence, to keep our attention. We have become so sensual. This is why holiness is not numbness; it is sensitivity. It is being *more* attuned to our desires, to what we were truly made for and therefore what we truly want. Our problem is that we've grown quite used to seeking life in all kinds of things other than God.

For example, God wants to be our perfect lover, but instead we seek perfection in human relationships and are disappointed when our lovers cannot love us perfectly. God wants to provide our ultimate security, but we seek our safety in power and possessions and then we find we must continually worry about them. We seek satisfaction of our spiritual longing in a host of ways that may have very little to do with God. (*Addiction and Grace*)

And so May comments, "The more we become accustomed to seeking spiritual satisfaction through things other than God, the more abnormal and stressful it becomes to look for God directly." Our instrument is out of tune from years of misuse. This is where the Law is our help. Everything in you may be saying, "But you don't understand. I *want* to eat that whole box of chocolates (or sleep with my boyfriend, or let my anger really fly). That's what really seems like life to me right now." God says, "I know you do, but it'll kill you in the end. What you think is life is not. That's not the comfort (or the love, or the significance) you are seeking. You'll wind up destroying yourself." The commands of God become our tutor in the healing of our desire. We need the Law because our instrument is out of tune; we're not clear all the time on what it is we *really* desire.

And so the first command comes first. God tells us to love him with all our hearts and all our souls, with all our minds and all our strength. It's not a burden but a rescue, a trail out of the jungles of desire. When we don't look for God as our true life, our desire for him spills over into our other desires, giving them an ultimacy and urgency they were never intended to bear. We become desperate, grasping and arranging and worrying over all kinds of things, and once we get them, they end up ruling us. It's the difference between wants and needs. All we truly need is God. Prone to wander from him, we find we need all sorts of other things. Our desire becomes insatiable because we've taken our longing for the Infinite and placed it upon finite things. God saves us from the whole mimetic mess by turning our hearts back to him.

You may have heard an orchestra tuning up before a concert. It sounds like total chaos—oboes, cello, French horns, dozens of instruments all sounding off, everyone doing his own thing. Trills, groans, whistles, thumps—an absolute cacophony. This is how our desires seem most of the time. But then the first violin plays a long high C, and slowly, all the other instruments join in. They become focused, centered, ready to perform. Such is what happens with the chaos of our desires when we turn our souls to God in worship. All the other desires find their place as we give God his place. That is why the psalmist urges us, "Delight yourself in the LORD and he will give you the desires of your heart" (Ps. 37:4 NIV). Only as we truly delight in God is it safe to give us our desires, for then they are not likely to become idols. And by our delighting in God, he heals our false desires as our souls come true in the light of their Maker. *Worship* becomes the means by which we most deeply heal our desire.

WORSHIP—THE HEART'S HEALER

Henri Nouwen once asked Mother Teresa for spiritual direction. Spend one hour each day in adoration of your Lord, she said, and never do anything you know is wrong. Follow this, and you'll be fine. Such simple, yet profound advice. Worship is the act of the abandoned heart adoring its God. It is the union that we crave. Few of us experience anything like this on a regular basis, let alone for an hour each day. But it is what we need. Desperately. Simply showing up on Sunday is not even close to worship. Neither does singing songs with religious content pass for worship. What counts is *the posture of the soul* involved, the open heart pouring forth its love toward God and communing with him. It is a question of desire.

Worship occurs when we say to God, from the bottom of our

hearts, "You are the One whom I desire." As Thomas à Kempis prayed, "There is nothing created that can fully satisfy my desires. Make me one with You in a sure bond of heavenly love, for You alone are sufficient to Your lover, and without You all things are vain and of no substance."

I spent a year in the Psalms at the same time I was resting from the duty of Sunday morning. I wasn't studying them with my head; I was praying them from my heart. It gave me a voice for the cry of my soul—the anguish, the weariness, the joy, the sorrow. It's all there. What is remarkable is that no matter where the poet begins, he almost always ends in worship. This is no coincidence. It is where our journey must lead us. In the most often quoted phrase from Augustine, he says, "Our hearts are restless until they find their rest in Thee." He is referring to desire. Our only hope for rest from the incessant craving of our desire is in God, and us united to him. And so à Kempis prayed, "O faithful soul, make ready thy heart for this Bridegroom." He continued,

> Grant me, O most sweet and loving Jesus, to rest in thee above all creatures, above all health and beauty, above all glory and honor, above all power and dignity, above all knowledge and subtlety, above all riches and arts, above all joy and gladness, above all fame and praise, above all sweetness and comfort, above all hope and promise, above all desert and desire . . .

> Thou alone art most beautiful and loving, thou alone most noble and glorious above all things, in whom all good things together both perfectly are, and ever have been, and shall be.

The full union, of course, is coming. We rehearse for the wedding now through worship.

·

CHAPTER ELEVEN

LETTING GO

Grasp not at much for fear thou losest all.
— GEORGE HERBERT

For Jesus I have gladly suffered the loss of all things.
— THE APOSTLE PAUL

I f you're coming up from the south, the only way to get into the Lamar Valley in northeast Yellowstone is over Dunraven Pass. It's a narrow, winding road over the flanks of Mount Washburn and in recent years badly in need of repair. Still, I had come so far for this. It was three months after Brent's death, and I had made a sort of pilgrimage to Yellowstone. The last great adventure we shared together was here, fly-fishing among the wolves and bears in the Lamar Valley.

I had returned under the auspices of taking my family on vacation, but I sensed there was a deeper reason. Unbeknownst to them, I was on a pilgrimage, drawn here for a purpose only partially known to me. Down the desolate highways of Wyoming, across the Absarokas, up the Snake River from Jackson Hole, I had followed some inner call. There was much to see along the way, and many side trails explored with my family. But finally, we came to my real goal—the road over Dunraven Pass. It was closed.

The orange-and-white barriers stood there like a prophetic

beast out of a nightmare. ROAD CLOSED. *None shall pass.* It seems the Park Service crews had decided—that morning, with no prior warning—to close the road for repairs for the rest of the season. My journey would end here. I sat at the intersection staring dumbly at the barriers, the engine idling, cars piling up behind me. God began to speak to my sinking heart: *Your journey lies along another path. You've got to let all that go now.* I knew there was no arguing. I didn't even try to put up a fight. I've been known to plow through his barriers in the past, but not now. Remember checkmate? My grip has loosened in recent years, and I knew this was a call to loosen it even more. David Wilcox sings about this moment in "Slipping Through My Fist":

> I have drifted down a ways along the shoreline,
> I just watched these ropes give way
> where they were tied.
> I could have reached out quick when the ropes first
> slipped, if I had tried,
> but I was wondering where the wind was trying to take me
> overnight, if I never did resist, and
> what strange breezes make a sailor want to
> let it come to this,
> with lines untied, slipping through my fist.
> It is downhill all the way to the ocean,
> So of course the river wants to flow.
> The river's been here longer,
> It's older and stronger and knows where to go.

One thing I have come to embrace is this: we have to let it go. The more comfortable we are with mystery in our journey, the more rest we will know along the way. The Christian life is full of paradox (as if you hadn't noticed). Listen to how Paul describes his experience of the quest: "Sorrowful, yet always rejoicing; poor, yet making many rich; having nothing, and yet possessing everything" (2 Cor. 6:10 NIV). How true this is. If we will remain open to sorrow, we can know joy. Somehow being empty allows us to make others rich. And if we are willing to let go, we'll discover something most surprising—that all is ours. That is why reaching to possess is one danger of which the heart alive must be wary. Those who have given up caring aren't tempted by this. But once we *know* what we want, we must learn the grace of release.

WILLING TO THIRST

There is a widespread belief in the church that to be a Christian somehow satisfies our every desire. As one camp song has it, "I'm inright, outright, upright, downright happy all day long." What complete nonsense! Augustine emphasized, "The whole life of the good Christian is a holy longing. What you desire ardently, as yet you do not see." So, "let us long because we are to be filled . . . That is our life, to be exercised by longing." There's the mystery again. Longing leads to fullness somewhere down the road. Meanwhile, being content is not the same thing as being full.

Paul said he had "learned the secret of being content" (Phil. 4:12 NIV), and many Christians assume he no longer experienced the thirst of his soul. But earlier in the same epistle, the old saint said that he had *not* obtained his soul's desire, or "already been made perfect." Quite the contrary. He described himself as pressing on, "straining toward what is ahead" (Phil. 3:12–14 NIV). These are not the words of a man who no longer experienced longing because he had arrived. They are the account of a man propelled on his life quest by his desire.

Contentment is not freedom *from* desire, but freedom *of* desire. Being content is not pretending that everything is the way you wish it would be; it is not acting as though you have no wishes. Rather, it is no longer being *ruled* by your desires.

The fact is, at this point in our journey, we have only three options: (1) to be alive and thirsty, (2) to be dead, or (3) to be addicted. There are no other choices. Most of the world lives in addiction; most of the church has chosen deadness. The Christian is called to the life of holy longing. But we don't like to stay there. A. W. Tozer perceived that "there is within the human heart a tough, fibrous root of fallen life whose nature is to possess, always to possess." And why do we seek to possess? So that we do not have to live in thirst, trusting our hearts each day to the goodness of God. To live in thirst is to live with an ache. Every addiction comes from the attempt to get rid of the ache. How is it possible to satisfy an insatiable desire? Merely trying sets us on an unending chase that leads us farther and farther from home.

And thus life passes away. Men combat with a thousand difficulties for the sake of repose, and as soon as they have overcome them all, repose becomes intolerable. For their thoughts are turned either on existing evils, or on such as are impending. And when secure on all sides from danger, their inherent disquietude, destitute of objects it might just fix upon, still continues to shoot from the heart, its native soil, and overspreads the soul with its venom.

What can this incessant craving, and this impotence of attainment mean, unless there was once a happiness belonging to man, of which only the faintest traces remain, in that void which he attempts to fill with everything within his reach? But it is in vain he seeks from absent objects the relief things present cannot give, and which neither of them can give; because, in a soul that will live forever, there is an infinite void that nothing can fill, but an infinite unchangeable being. (*Pensées*)

You can be satisfied, says Pascal; you just can't be sated. There is great joy in a glass of cabernet; the whole bottle is another story. Intimate conversation satisfies a different thirst, but how awful to try to arrange for it again the next night and the night after that. The Israelites tried to hoard the manna—and it crawled with maggots. Our soul's insatiable desire becomes the venom Pascal warns of when it demands its fill here and now, through the otherwise beautiful and good gifts of our lives.

God grants us so much of our heart's desire as we delight in him: "You open your hand and satisfy the desires of every living thing" (Ps. 145:16 NIV). Not always, not on demand, but certainly more than we deserve. God delights to give good gifts to his beloved. But that old root would have us shift once more from giver to gift, and seek our rest through being full. This is the turn we must be vigilant to see, watching over our hearts with loving care. In his lovely poem "The Size," George Herbert prays,

> Content thee, greedie heart.
> Modest and moderate joys to those, that have
> Title to more hereafter when they part,
> Are passing brave.
>
> If thou hast wherewithall to spice a draught,
> When griefs prevail;
> And for the future time art heir
> To th' Isle of spices, is't not fair?
> To be in both worlds full
> Is more than God was, who was hungrie here.

Remember, pleasure is often more about drugging ourselves than it is about enjoying ourselves. And the things we do to avoid the ache are always worse in the end than the ache itself. I think of Jamie, a bright and energetic young woman who has tried so hard to know the right thing to do in every situation. She has tied herself in knots trying to figure out the will of God, solve all the theological quandaries, never miss a beat. She wrote to me recently, "I am caught in a tangle of trying to *do*, trying to live *right*. I don't know how to not think or worry or control. I don't know how to let go." It's driving her absolutely crazy. (Didn't Chesterton warn us, "Poets do not go mad; but chess-players do"?) Why can't she let go? "I want to predict what the Lord is going to do, so that it doesn't hurt so bad when it happens." Jamie grasped onto perfectionism to avoid pain and disappointment. It only made matters worse. As Carl Jung asserted, "Neurosis is always a substitute for legitimate suffering." So what do we do? How do we live with desire we cannot take care of and heartache we cannot prevent? We groan and wait.

WHAT HOPE FEELS LIKE

We know that the whole creation has been groaning as in the pains of childbirth right up to the present time. Not only so, but we ourselves, who have the firstfruits of the Spirit, groan inwardly as we wait eagerly for our adoption as sons, the redemption of our bodies. For in this hope we were saved. But hope that is seen is no hope at all. Who hopes for what he already has? But if we hope for what we do not yet have, we wait for it patiently. (Rom. 8:22–25 NIV)

Amazing. Paul is passing along to us the secret of the sojourning heart. We live in hope, and he says hoping is waiting. And groaning. When was the last time you heard that in a sermon or the title for a new book? *You, Too, Can Groan Inwardly While You Wait Eagerly!* Everything I've seen lately offers a sure-fire way to "get what you want." How to be a success at work. How to be a success at love. How to succeed in work *and* love at the same time.

Here are questions to ask yourself to see if you are a pilgrim or an arranger: What am I waiting for? Is there anything I ardently desire that I am doing nothing to secure? The first time I asked myself, I couldn't name a thing. There were many things I was working on, or fretting over, or had given up wanting. I am thankful that was some time ago. Things are different now. Now I wonder, What am I still arranging for? I should like to let it go too.

WAITING

To wait is to learn the spiritual grace of *detachment*, the freedom of desire. Not the absence of desire, but desire at rest. St. John of the Cross lamented that "the desires weary and fatigue the soul; for they are like restless and discontented children, who are ever demanding this or that from their mother, and are never contented." Detachment is coming to the place where those demanding children are at peace. As King David said,

> I have stilled and quieted my soul;
>> like a weaned child with its mother,
>> like a weaned child is my soul within me.
>
> (Ps 131:2 NIV)

Such a beautiful picture, a young one leaning against her mother's breast. There is no fussing, no insistent tears. She has learned to wait.

The word *detachment* might evoke wrong impressions. It is not a cold and indifferent attitude; not at all. May writes, "An authentic spiritual understanding of detachment devalues neither desire nor the objects of desire." Instead, it "aims at correcting one's own anxious grasping in order to free oneself for committed relationship to God."

Bethann told me this beautiful story after we both attended a conference in Denver: "After nine days of being with twelve hundred people, I wanted to breathe, to be alone, and to be free." So she went antique shopping downtown. The first shop she stepped into was very upscale. "It felt more like a museum or even cathedral than a shop. I felt out of place. Obviously, I couldn't buy anything here. I clutched my purse closely to make sure that I didn't knock anything over." Enormous English armoires, French marble fireplaces, an $18,000 Roman bathtub. Reaching the back of the store, Bethann turned into a narrow passage between pieces and was captivated by a stained glass window. "It must have come from a chalet in France. It was propped up against a window and the light that came through it seemed somehow purified; the shades of soft yellow and blue and rose flowing from an urn of profuse flowers with ribbons elegantly fluttering away. I don't know how long I stood there with my mouth open. It made my heart swell and fill and ache at the same time." Her mind began to race: How could she possess it for her own? But at $8,000, the window was beyond hoping for. "Resignation, hopelessness, and anger followed. Then out of nowhere, I rebounded. I *will* have it in my home—in heaven. Some guy making six figures may be able to have it for a few years, but I'll have it forever." It was the first time, she told me, that she saw her desires filled in the coming kingdom. *I've got the better end of the deal,* she said to herself and walked out.

As Thomas à Kempis declared, "Wait a little while, O my

soul, wait for the divine promise, and thou shalt have abundance of all good things in heaven." In this posture we discover that, indeed, we are expanded by longing. Something grows in us, a capacity if you will, for life and love and God. I think of Romans 8:24–25: "That is why waiting does not diminish us, any more than waiting diminishes a pregnant mother. We are enlarged in the waiting. We, of course, don't see what is enlarging us. But the longer we wait, the larger we become, and the more joyful our expectancy" (*The Message*). There is actually a sweet pain in longing if we will let it draw our hearts homeward.

AND GROANING

When I turned away from those barriers to the Lamar Valley, I accepted that I could not recover what had been lost. Not yet. My journey now lies along another path. And so we retreated from the road over Dunraven Pass, left Yellowstone through the south gate, and descended into the Tetons, staying there for several nights.

One morning I woke early and could not get back to sleep. My soul was agitated, restless. After what seemed like an hour of tossing and turning, I rose and slipped out of the cabin to take a walk. Waves of grief began to sweep over my soul. But it was not all about Brent or even primarily about him. His death was the lance that pierced the wound of all the ungrieved grief of my life. Sorrows from my marriage, from college days, from wounds I received as a child—all of them poured forth through this place of release. Why had I waited so many years to shed these tears? As I wept, I realized that Paul was absolutely right. How can we live without groaning? If we do not give our ache a voice, it doesn't go away. It becomes the undercurrent of our addictions. Pleasure becomes necessary in larger and larger doses, like morphine.

The paradox of grief is that it is healing; it somehow restores our souls, when all the while we thought it would leave us in despair. Control is the enemy; grief is our friend. Jamie came to realize this when her boyfriend decided he did not know if he could love her and broke off their relationship. She wrote,

> The problem is that I was already choosing to love him. How hard it was for me to let down the walls and care—risk. And it isn't that I did anything wrong in dating, so there is nothing that I can say I should have done or should not have done, besides love him. Oh, I don't know if this is making any sense, but through the breakup I have been real. I have not done my usual "cover up and pretend that I never cared in the first place." Instead I have hurt, I have embraced the pain and the reality that there is nothing that I can do besides wait for the healing. Embracing the pain has brought me to a place of more complete healing than I feel I could have known otherwise.

As she let go of her controlling, something better took its place—mourning. When the ministry of the Messiah is described in Isaiah 61, comfort for those who mourn and healing for the brokenhearted are placed at the center of his mission. None of this makes sense until we admit our brokenheartedness and give our sorrow a voice in mourning. Only then will we know his comfort. Until then, they are nice, religious-sounding words.

Solomon said that it is better to go to a house of mourning than it is to a house of feasting. I never understood this; I wrote it off as the pessimism of a depressed man. Now I think I know what he meant. Grief is good. It is cleansing. It undoes my world—and that is the best part of it. I need to be undone; simply undone. No regrouping. We need to mourn; it is the only way our hearts can remain both free and alive in this world. Why? Because it, like nothing else, puts a stop to the constant striving. Grief is the anti-dote to the incessant possessive demand within.

Another friend, Deborah, wrote,

How do I live in the world I have with my woundedness? How do I live as an alive woman in the world I have? I am so grateful every time God speaks deeply to my heart. I started to acknowledge my deep, deep loneliness, and when I did, everything has been happening in a rush, like a river freed, fast and tumultuous. I've been crying and it just keeps going—the kind of tears and feelings of grief that I've cried when family members have died . . . but it's oh so good, because it is also a feeling of being alive to who God made me to be and it's acknowledging the truth of how I see life and experience life.

Those who sow in tears
will reap with songs of joy.
He who goes out weeping,
carrying seed to sow,
will return with songs of joy,
carrying sheaves with him.
(Ps. 126:5-6 NIV)

I believe we must add two spiritual disciplines to everyday life. The first is worship. We must adore God deliberately, regularly. The other is grief. We must allow a time for sorrow to do our own personal sowing. I see no other way to care for our hearts.

Now making time to grieve might seem strange to you. "But I don't feel grief or sorrow at all." Just because we do not feel it doesn't mean it is not there. Our pleasant experience may be the result of the thousand distractions that fill our waking moments. Kierkegaard said that despair has become so rare not because the human race is doing suddenly better, but because we so effectively push it away. This is the "sickness unto death," to despair without ever despairing, to mourn without ever mourning.

I've found, therefore, that quite often grief has to sneak up on us, surprise us during our day. It may come through a song you hear or a movie you see. It may come as you choose to allow your soul twenty minutes of quiet during your lunch hour. Sometimes a small disappointment can be the door into a room of grief you never knew was there. However unexpectedly grief shows up, let us accept it as a welcome visitor.

This is the last journal entry I made *before* going to the mountains with Brent, the weekend he was killed: *Life is loss and I must grieve regularly, so as to give up trying to possess. I will not arrive in the golden place until I am home with God.* The last thing Jesus said to me before that weekend was, *Don't run from the suffering. Embrace it.* I had no idea what was coming. I had no idea how prophetic those words would be. I knew only the truth of them from the journey thus far. They are truer now.

LET BEAUTY HAVE ITS SAY

What can I possibly say to her? How can I begin to restore hope to her life? This is what was going through my mind as I listened to Kathleen. It was partly about being raped, and partly about the tensions in her marriage remaining years after, that she had come to see me. I wondered, *What can I offer this woman? What can I say to one who has known such terrible evil?* We sat in my office on a cold winter afternoon; outside all was gray. Perhaps that's the reason I first noticed the little flowers embroidered on the collar of her denim shirt. As she told me her tragic story, my eye kept coming back to those graceful little bouquets. Maybe I was surprised by them, but somehow I felt they were the clue to her restoration.

Kathleen finished her story, and we sat in silence. After a few moments, I couldn't help mentioning the flowers. "Oh," she said. "Ever since the rape, beauty has meant the world to me. No one seemed to understand why. Sometimes I would spend hours just gazing at my garden and the woods behind my house. Only beauty helps."

I understand completely. As the shock of Brent's death began to wear off, the searing pain of intense grief took its place. It was too difficult to read my Bible. Conversation required more than I was able to give. Frankly, I didn't want to talk to anyone, not even God. The only thing that helped was my wife's flower garden. The solace I found there was like nothing else on earth. I wrote in my journal, *Sitting outside this evening, the Shasta daisies swaying in the gentle breeze on their long stems, the aspens shimmering without light, the full moon rising over the pine-crested bluff . . . only beauty speaks what I need to hear. Only beauty helps.*

Simone Weil was absolutely right—beauty and affliction are the only two things that can pierce our hearts. Because this is so true, we must have a measure of beauty in our lives proportionate to our affliction. No, more. Much more. Is this not God's prescription for us? Just take a look around. The sights and sounds, the aromas and sensations—the world is overflowing with beauty. God seems to be rather enamored with it. Gloriously wasteful. Apparently, he feels that there ought to be plenty of it in our lives.

I am at a loss to say what I want to say regarding beauty. Somehow, that is as it ought to be. Our experience of beauty transcends our ability to speak about it, for its magic lies beyond the power of words. Wordsworth penned these lines:

> Thanks to the human heart by which we live,
> Thanks to its tenderness, its joys, and fears,

> To me the meanest flower that blows can give
> Thoughts that do often lie too deep for tears.

I want to speak of beauty's healing power, of how it comforts and soothes, yet also how it stirs us, how it moves and inspires. All that sounds ridiculous. You know your own experiences of beauty. Let me call upon them then. Think of your favorite music, or tapestry, or landscape. "We have had a couple of inspiring sunsets this week." A dear friend sent this in an e-mail: "It was as if the seams of our atmosphere split for a bit of heaven to plunge into the sea. I stood and applauded . . . simultaneously I wanted to kneel and weep." Yes—that's it. All I want to do is validate those irreplaceable moments, lift any obstacle you may have to filling your life with greater and greater amounts of beauty.

We need not fear indulging here. The experience of beauty is unique to all the other pleasures in this: there is no possessive quality to it. Just because you love the landscape doesn't mean you have to acquire the real estate. Simply to behold the flower is enough; there is nothing in me that wants to consume it. Beauty is the closest thing we have to fullness without possessing on this side of eternity. It heralds the Great Restoration. Perhaps that is why it is so healing—beauty is pure gift. It helps us in our letting go.

SURRENDER

The time has come for us to quit playing chess with God over our lives. We cannot win, but we can delay the victory, dragging on the pain of grasping and the poison of possessing. You see, there are two kinds of losses in life. The first is shared by all mankind—the losses that come to us. Call them what you will—accidents, fate, acts of God. The point is that we have no control over them. We do not determine when, where, what, or even how. There is no predicting these losses; they happen *to* us. We choose only how we respond. The second kind is known only to the pilgrim. They are losses that we *choose*. A chosen loss is different from repentance, when we give up something that was never ours to have. With a chosen loss, we place on the altar something very dear to us, something innocent, whose only danger is in its goodness, that we might come to love it too much. It is the act of *consecration*, where little by little or all at once, we give over our lives to the only One who can truly keep them.

Spiritual surrender is not resignation. It is not choosing to care no longer. Nor is it Eastern mysticism, an attempt to get beyond the suffering of this life by going completely numb. As my dear friend Jan describes, "It is surrender *with* desire, or *in* desire." Desire is still present, felt, welcomed even. But the will to secure is made subject to the divine will in an act of abandoned trust. Think of Jesus in the Garden of Gethsemane. Frederick Buechner has suggested that we contrast him with a picture we have of Buddha, so that we might see the difference of true surrender:

Buddha sits enthroned beneath the Bo-tree in the lotus position. His lips are faintly parted in the smile of one who has passed beyond every power in earth or heaven to touch him. "He who loves fifty has fifty woes, he who loves ten has ten woes, he who loves none has no woes," he has said. His eyes are closed.

Christ, on the other hand, stands in the garden of Gethsemane, angular, beleaguered. His face is lost in the shadows so that you can't even see his lips, and before all the powers on earth or heaven he is powerless. "This is my commandment, that you love one another as I have loved you," he has said. (*Now and Then*)

Christ is weeping freely; his prayers are marked by loud cries and tears. He makes it very, very clear what he desires. Not once, but three times he begs his Father to remove this awful cup from him: "Yet not my will, but thine be done." He surrenders with desire, in desire. Making himself poor, he opens up to us the treasures of heaven. Buddha abandons his desire; Christ surrenders his will. It is no small difference.

True surrender is not an easy out, calling it quits early in the game. This kind of surrender comes only *after* the night of wrestling. It comes only after we open our hearts to care deeply. Then we choose to surrender, or give over, our deepest desires to God. And with them we give over our hearts, our deepest selves. The freedom and beauty and rest that follow are among the greatest of all surprises.

After he lost his son, Wolterstorff did not remain passive: he wept; he railed; he lamented. I suppose it was his own Gethsemane. That trail of tears brought him to a place of true surrender. This is how he describes it:

> Let me try again. All these things I still recognize. I remember delighting in them—trees, art, house, music, pink morning sky, work well done, flowers, books. I still delight in them. I'm still grateful. But the zest is gone. The passion is cooled, the striving is quieted, the longing stilled. My attachment is loosened. No longer do I set my heart on them. I can do without them. They don't matter. Instead of rowing, I float. The joy that comes my way I savor. But the seeking, the clutching, the aiming is gone. (*Lament for a Son*)

I tasted this wonderful freedom a few months ago, canoeing on a high mountain lake. My boys had already gone in for the day, and so I was alone in the canoe, paddling across this beautiful lake at dusk. That was when the trout began to rise. The surface of the water was serene in the little cove I had found, and the dimples made by feeding rainbows were too numerous to count. It is the moment fly fishermen dream about. I set down the paddle and picked up my rod to begin casting. As the line unfurled, my fly alighted gently on the water in the middle of a dozen rise-rings. First one, then two trout took my offering. I knew that if the fish continued to rise, I would have my fill before it became too dark to fish anymore. But then, a gentle breeze began to blow down the valley. It was cool and fragrant and refreshing, and though it was soft, I noticed it was strong enough to carry my canoe along. A tremor of anxiety passed through me, for I knew I could not fish and paddle at the same time. To stay in this little cove, among the rising trout, I would have to put down the rod and pick up the paddle.

I smiled and sct down the rod. But I didn't take up the paddle. I let my hands rest along the gunwales and let the gentle breeze take me away, out across the surface of the lake. And as I drifted, I drank in the beauty of the mountain peaks around me, and the golden quality of the fading light, and the joy of the freedom of my desire. A little voice reminded me that fish were rising back in the cove.

> But I was wondering where the wind was trying to take me
> overnight, if I never did resist, and
> what strange breezes make a sailor want to
> let it come to this,
> with lines untied, slipping through my fist.

CHAPTER TWELVE

KEEPING HEART— TO THE END

Remember thee!
Yea, from the table of my memory
I'll wipe away all trivial fond records . . .
And thy commandment all alone shall live
Within the book and volume of my brain
Unmix'd with baser matter.

—HAMLET

Sometimes I wake, and, lo, I have forgot.
—GEORGE MACDONALD

But every now and anon a trumpet sounds from the hid battle-
ments of eternity.
—FRANCIS THOMPSON

Gabriel García Marquez's novel *One Hundred Years of Solitude* chronicles the life of the little Mexican town of Macondo and the families who call it home. At one point in their domestic journey, a plague of insomnia strikes the little village. The residents go weeks, then months without sleep. They begin to lose vital faculties. First to go is the memory—no small aspect for living. Even the simplest and most common household goods appear foreign, unfamiliar, forgotten. Aureliano, the silversmith, is working in his shop one day when he realizes he cannot remember the name for the little anvil he uses. His father, Jose, tells him the name.

Aureliano wrote the name on a piece of paper that he pasted to the base of the small anvil: *stake*. In that way he was sure of not forgetting it in the future. It did not occur to him that this was the first manifestation of a loss of memory, because the object had a difficult name to remember. But a few days later he discovered that he had trouble remembering almost every object in the laboratory. Then he marked them with their respective names so that all he had to do was read the inscription in order to identify them . . . [Jose] put it into practice all through the house and later on imposed it on the whole village. With an inked brush he marked everything with its name: *table, chair, clock, door, wall, bed, pan*. He went to the corral and marked the animals and plants: *cow, goat, pig, hen, cassava, caladium, banana*. Little by little, studying the infinite possibilities of a loss of memory, he realized that the day might come when things would be recognized by their inscriptions but that no one would remember their use. Then he was more explicit. The sign that he hung on the neck of the cow was an exemplary proof of the way in which the inhabitants of Macondo were prepared to fight against loss of memory: *This is the cow. She must be milked every morning so that she will produce milk, and the milk must be boiled in order to be mixed with coffee to make coffee and milk.*

. . . At the beginning of the road into the swamp they put up a sign that said *Macondo* and another larger one on the main street that said *God exists*.

OUR WORST ENEMY

The first time I read this story I simply laughed. But it haunted me, and on a second reading I began to realize that it's my story too. I said to myself, *It's not a bad plan. Right above my bed I think I shall hang a sign that says,* GOD EXISTS. You see, I wake most mornings an unbeliever. It seems that during the night, I slip into forgetfulness, and by the time the new day comes, I am lost. The deep and precious truths that God has brought to me over the years and even just yesterday seem a thousand miles away. It doesn't happen every morning, but enough to make it an ongoing reality. And I know I am not alone in this. As MacDonald confessed in *Diary of an Old Soul,*

> Sometimes I wake, and lo, I have forgot,
> And drifted out upon an ebbing sea!
> My soul that was at rest now resteth not,
> For I am with myself and not with thee;
> Truth seems a blind moon in a glaring morn,
> Where nothing is but sick-heart vanity.

Virtually every person I've ever counseled follows a similar pattern. Over the course of our time together, some wonderful things begin to happen. Not necessarily at first, and never on command, but God shows up. The lights turn on for these people; their heart is lifted; grateful tears flow. Suddenly, faith, hope, and love seem the only way to live. And I nearly dread the next session. When they return the following week, it is as though it never happened. The marvelous day is a distant memory. Life is hard, God is distant, and love is foolish. All is forgotten; all is sick-heart vanity. I want to grab them and shake them into sense, shouting, "Don't you *remember?* Why did you let it slip away?" Wisdom has kept me restrained so far.

Forgetting is no small problem. Of all the enemies our hearts must face, this may be the worst because it is insidious. Forgetfulness does not come against us like an enemy in full battle formation, banners waving. Nor does it come temptingly, seductively, the lady in red. It works slowly, commonly, unnoticed. My wife had a beautiful climbing rose vine that began to fill an arbor in her garden. We enjoyed the red blossoms it produced every summer. But last year, something happened. The vine suddenly turned brown, dropped its flowers, and died within the course of a week. After all that loving care we couldn't figure out what went wrong. A call to the nursery revealed that a worm had gotten into the stalk of the vine and eaten away at the life from the inside. Such is the work of forgetfulness. It cuts us off from our Life so slowly, we barely notice, until one day the blooms of our faith are suddenly gone.

BE FOREWARNED

We're certainly warned about forgetfulness in Scripture, both in word and by example. In the Old Testament, the pattern is so predictable, we come to expect it. God delivers his people from the cruel whips of Egypt by a stunning display of his power and his care—the plagues, the Passover, the Red Sea. The Israelites celebrate with singing and dancing. Three days later, they are complaining about the water supply. God provides sweet water from the bitter desert springs of Marah. They complain about the food. God drops breakfast out of the sky, every morning. Then it's the water again. God provides it from a rock. Enemies attack; God delivers. On and on it goes, for forty years. As they stand on the brink of the promised land, God issues a final warning: "Only be careful, and watch yourselves closely so that you do not forget the things your eyes have seen or *let them slip from your heart* as long as you live" (Deut. 4:9 NIV, emphasis added).

They do, of course, let it slip from their hearts. All of it. This becomes the pattern for the entire history of Israel. God shows up; he does amazing things; the people rejoice. Then they forget and go whoring after other gods. They fall under calamity and cry out for deliverance. God shows up; he does amazing things; the people rejoice—you get the picture. Round and round and round we go; where she stops, nobody knows.

And like that of the people of Macondo, their story is our story. Things aren't changed much in the New Testament, but the contrast is greater, and the stakes are even higher. God shows up *in person*, and before he leaves, he gives us the sacraments along with this plea: *Do this to remember me.*

They don't—remember him, that is. Paul is "shocked" by the Galatians: they are "turning away so soon from God, who in his love and mercy called you to share the eternal life he gives through Christ" (1:6 NLT). He has to send Timothy to the Corinthians, to "remind you of what I teach about Christ Jesus in all the churches wherever I go" (1 Cor 4:17 NLT). Peter, who knew firsthand the grief that comes from forgetting, writes his letters to combat this cancer of the soul: "So keep a firm grip on the faith. The suffering won't last forever. It won't be long before this generous God who has great plans for us in Christ—eternal and glorious plans they are!—will have you put together and on your feet for good" (1 Peter 5:10 *The Message*).

It happens to the best of us. Brent and I were having coffee with a pastor from Denver, whose wife was greatly helped by the things we wrote about in *The Sacred Romance.* He told us of her long exile in the desert of her soul, which was deepened by a bout with depression. Our words about life and God and the journey of the heart had been the means by which God had brought life to her parched heart. Her husband was truly grateful for the book, and he thanked us again and again for writing it. You would think both of us would have been quite moved. Authors live to hear such things. But Brent's comment betrayed a deeper reality: "Really? You mean, it's *true*?"

WHAT WILL WE CLING TO?

Life is a journey of the heart that requires the mind—not the other way around. The church sometimes gets this backward and makes knowing the right things the center of life. It's not; the heart is the center of life. Desire is always where the action is. However, staying alive to our desire is not enough; we know that only too well. We must bring the *truth* into our hearts to guard and to guide our desire; this is the other half of our mission. With a recovery of heart and soul taking place in many quarters, my fear now is that we will abandon the pursuit of truth and try to base our journey on our feelings and intuition. "Follow your heart" is becoming a popular message in our culture. Or as Sting sings, "Trust your soul." It will not work. Our spiritual fathers and mothers knew this only too well. In *The Imitation of Christ*, Thomas à Kempis warned, "Our own opinion and our own sense do often deceive us, and they discern but little." We must cling to the truth for dear life. And so our spiritual forbears urged us to bring *both* heart and mind together. As James Houston says in *The Heart's Desire*,

In medieval Christian thought, the idea of learning by heart was something that went far deeper than mathematical tables. It meant the re-orientation of one's life, by what Benedict called *haga*, bringing the thoughts of the mind into the heart, so that one's whole person stood in the presence of God. A Russian monk of the nineteenth century, Theophan the Recluse, gives weight to a similar idea: "The principal thing is to stand before God with the intellect in the heart, and to go on standing before him unceasingly day and night, until the end of life."

Now, not all truths help us descend with the mind into the heart. There is a way of talking about the truth that can actually deaden our hearts. Most of us were raised in the modern era, the age of reason and science. We came to believe that truth is best discovered in the scientific method—dissection. And if you will remember high school biology, we discovered quite a bit about the cat on the table before us—its respiratory system, its muscles and sinews, and all that. Only when the experiment is finished, you have nothing like a cat left at all. You have facts about a cat, but you are far from the real thing anymore. The coy, playful, aloof creature who stands waiting to be let out and walks back into the room once you've risen to open the door—the *living cat*—is gone.

Let me give another example: what is the truth of a kiss? Technically, in a modernistic sense, it is two sets of mandibles pressing together for a certain duration of time. Those of you who have experienced the wonders of a kiss will know that while true, this description is so untrue. It takes away everything beautiful and mysterious and passionate and intimate and leaves you with an icy cold fact. Those who know kissing feel robbed; those who don't are apt to say, "If that's what kissing is all about, I think I'd rather not."

We've done the same thing to theology. We have dissected God, and man, and the gospel, and we have thousands, if not millions, of facts—all of it quite dead. It's not that these insights aren't true; it's that they no longer speak. I could tell you a few facts about God, for example. He is omniscient, omnipotent, and immutable. There—don't you feel closer to him? All our statements about God forget that he is a person, and as Tozer says, "In the deep of His mighty nature He thinks, wills, enjoys, feels, loves, desires and suffers as any other person may." How do we get to know a person? Through stories. All the wild and sad and courageous tales that we tell—they are what reveal us to others. We must return to the Scriptures for the story that it is and stop approaching it as if it is an encyclopedia, looking for "tips and techniques."

Reminders of the story are everywhere—in films and novels, in children's fairy tales, in the natural world around us, and in the stories of our own lives. In fact, every story or movie or song or poem that has ever stirred your soul is telling you something you need to know about the Sacred Romance. Even nature is crying out to us of God's great heart and the drama that is unfolding. Sunrise and sunset tell the tale every day, remembering Eden's glory, prophesying Eden's return. These are the trumpet calls from the "hid battlements of eternity." We must capture them like precious treasure, and hold them close to our hearts.

HOW TO CLING

People tie strings around their fingers to offset forgetfulness. God told the Jews to bind what he told them to their foreheads. Some of them took him literally and strapped a little box to the brow in which they carried sections of Scripture. I used to read this with a sense of the ridiculous; now I read it with empathy. I need it strapped right there in front of me, every single day. *God exists.*

Blaise Pascal took it a step farther. On the night of his conversion to Christ, November 23, 1654, he penned these words to capture his encounter with the living God:

Fire. The God of Abraham, the God of Isaac, the God of Jacob . . . Certainty, Certainty, emotion, joy, peace, God of Jesus Christ. *Deum meum et Deum vestrum*, Thy God shall be my God. Oblivion of the world and of everything except God. Joy, Joy, Joy, tears of Joy!

When he died, they found this memorial sewn into his jacket, next to his heart. He had kept it there from the day of his conversion until his last breath.

We must do something similar if we are to keep our hearts with us to the end. For we lose the story every day. It is continually being stolen from us by the evil one—the ultimate deconstructionist. He twists and spins and pulls apart the truth until the fragments we have left are unrecognizable. Or we lose it ourselves in the marketplace of Vanity Fair. Bombarded by thousands of messages each day, every one of them marked urgent, we leave behind the truly important things, the only refuge for our hearts.

I remember a story from my childhood about a little pack rat named Put-it, Pick-it. He ventures out each morning with an important task to do, but then something catches his eye. It is a piece of blue glass. He drops what he is carrying and picks up the glass, determined to bring it home to show his mother. How proud she will be! Along the path, a silver sheen reflects the desert sun. He stops for a closer look. The glass is left behind, for now he has something even better—a bottle cap. On and on it goes. By the time he gets home, the true treasure is long gone.

We must be more intentional about holding on to the truth. The spiritual pilgrims who aligned themselves with St. Benedict took this task seriously—far more seriously than we do, I'm afraid. A typical day in the lives of Benedictine monks began in the middle of the night, when they arose for the Night Office. No less than twelve psalms would be said, together with three

Scripture readings, several hymns, and prayers. Sunrise brought the Morning Office, followed by six other breaks during the labors of the day for remembering: Prime, Terce, Sext, None, Vespers, and Compline in the evening. Seven times a day set aside for prayer and the recitation of psalms. Together with their night vigil, more than twenty-nine psalms would be said, not to mention numerous lessons, verses, prayers, and hymns.

Now, I'm not suggesting that we all adopt the Rule of Benedict. But think about this: these men left the distractions of the world to focus entirely on God. They lived in an environment *designed* to keep them standing before God, and what did they discover? They needed reminders every hour of the day and night! Do we, who live in the hostile chaos of the world, think we can do with an occasional visit? "Hey, Lord, I know it's been a while, but . . . um . . . thanks for being here and please help me get through this day." We are kidding ourselves if we think we can keep heart without a constant turning to the truth. So let me suggest a bit of monastic wisdom for contemporary pilgrims.

First, you must reduce the constant noise of your life. Turn off the television; it is an enemy of your heart. Having one is like inviting Vanity Fair to set up shop in your home. The whole operation runs on mimetic passion, a continual assault on your desire. Even the news is a problem because of its artificial importance. Have you noticed? Every night there's an urgency to the stories; that's what they have to do to sell the news. But if everything is urgent, then nothing is. I believe Thoreau said, "Don't read the Times; read the eternities." Given the pace of our lives, I doubt we have room for both. Simply unplug from all the clamor, and make room for eternity in your life. In *The Wisdom of the Desert*, Thomas Merton reminds us of the early Christians who fled to the deserts south of Palestine in order to draw near to God. They saw society "as a shipwreck from which every single man had to swim for his life." They believed that to "let oneself drift along, passively accepting the tenets and values of what they knew as society, was purely and simply a disaster."

TREASURES FOR OUR HEARTS

After the shepherds learn about the birth of Christ from the angels, they seek and find the Babe, lying in a manger. The whole village is astounded by their report, but Mary, we are told, "treasured up all these things and pondered them in her heart" (Luke 2:19 NIV). Later, when the boy Jesus is found in the temple holding forth with the religious leaders, we are told again that everyone is quite amazed. "But his mother treasured all these things in her heart" (Luke 2:51 NIV). It is more than a touching story of a mother's love; Mary is going to need those treasures when the tide turns against her son. At her darkest hour, when a sword pierces her soul, she does not lose heart. I believe this is why.

So if you do not have a way of seizing what God is speaking to you, begin journaling. Each year I take up a new journal in which to capture my heart's journey. *Journals* chronicle *journeys;* this is far different from simply recording the day's events in a diary, or worse still, the weekly goal sheets of the popular schedulers. A journal is about the interior life. At the back there is a section I have entitled "This New Day." There I am writing the central truths I must return to each morning (at least) to guide my desire home. My journal will be filled with all the twists and turns a year can bring, but here is the place I can go for the *interpretation* of the events and emotions and experiences. Like the Benedictines, we must keep before us the deepest truths—morning, noon, and night.

As my friend Craig and I sat in the warm sun, eating lunch

beside Four Mile Canyon, he picked up Pascal and read these words out loud: "It is awful to feel that everything we possess is hastening away, and to persist in our attachment, without being anxious, to examine if there is no object attainable that will be permanent." It was Thursday afternoon; that evening, our men's retreat was to begin. We had come up early to fish and to scout the area we would use for our rock-climbing sessions. Brent and the other guys would meet us later at the ranch.

The canyon is a beautiful place, with a lovely creek meandering through a meadow, framed on both sides by the high rock walls. It seemed strange to be talking about life slipping away when so much promise was in the air. A wonderful weekend lay ahead with some great men, doing the things I love best. I did not know why Craig had opened the *Pensées*, nor did I know the real story that was about to unfold. I would later realize that these were prophetic words, spoken to us by God at the opening of a very different scene.

God is speaking to us more often than we imagine. These are the treasures we must hide in our own hearts—sew them into our jackets if need be—for the dark hours that may come. As Buechner points out, "His word to us is both recoverable and precious beyond telling." And so I share a few of my notes, only in the hope that they will stir you to capture and hang on to the words and images that bring the romance back to you each new day:

- *The story continues*. This simple statement reminds me that life is unfolding, that we are headed somewhere, that the story is moving toward its happy ending. "What's past is prologue," as Shakespeare said. No event is the final word. Several weeks after Brent died, as I was walking from my car to my office, I said to myself, *The story has taken a tragic turn*. Somehow it mattered immensely to say it this way because it reminded me of all the tragic stories I have known and how they made me feel, how the heroes of those stories faced their tragedies, and so it gave weight to what I was living through. But it also kept me from despair because I found the moment in its context, not a random event but as Brent would often say, "A love affair in the midst of a life-and-death struggle." I was able to allow my heart to know it is not the end—the story continues. Dan Allender notes, "Faith increases to the degree we are aware of, caught up in, enthralled by, and participating in His and our story."

- *It can't be done.* By this I remember that I can't arrange for the life I prize. I am not fully healed yet of my addictions and my tendency—which seems so second nature—to arrange for my own little Eden now. To say again and again, "It can't be done," does not discourage me; quite the contrary, it frees my heart from the grasping and plotting and fretting over my life, which always accompany arranging. It reminds me to let it go. It breaks the power of the spell the evil one is trying to weave around us.

- *It is coming.* Oh, how I forget this most of all. How easy it is to slip back into thinking that it's now or never; that if it's not here, it's not at all. The life I prize is coming. The very thing that I am aching for now, missing now, seeking now in other things is exactly what's coming to me. This is how I interpret the promises that seem to be coming through the good and beautiful gifts we have now. As you raise your glass of wine, toast to the banquet to come; as you see anything beautiful you'd like to have (Bethann's window), say to yourself, *In a little while it shall be mine forever;* as you make love, remember it is rehearsal for the Grand Affair. That way your heart will not be trapped there. I recall the end of MacDonald's novel *Phantastes:* "A great good is coming—is coming—is coming to thee."

- *Battle and journey.* We are at war, and the bloody battle is over our

433

hearts. I am astounded how few Christians see this, how little they protect their hearts. We act as though we live in a sleepy little town during peacetime. We don't. We live in the spiritual equivalent of Bosnia or Beirut. Act like it. Watch over your heart. Don't let just anything in; don't let it go just anywhere. *What's this going to do to my heart?* is a question that I ask in every situation.

And thinking of life as a journey reminds me to stop trying to set up camp and call it home. It allows me to see life as process, with completion somewhere down the road. Thus I am freed from feeling like a failure when things are not finished, and hopeful that they will be as my journey comes to its end. I want adventure, and this reminds me I am living in it. Life is not a problem to be solved; it is an adventure to be lived.

I've written down many other thoughts and images over the years, but they couldn't possibly make sense to you. I will spare you the equivalent of looking at my home movies; I fear I have indulged myself already. But let me share one last image, captured in two words: *the meadowlark.*

- *The meadowlark.* The meadowlark has long been my favorite songbird. I suppose to many people it's a simple bird, not really all that colorful, none too spectacular in flight. But I love its song because it evokes so many summer days out in the fields and streams of the West. Because of my story, there is much romance for me in the meadowlark. Its song *means* summer, hay meadows, long lazy days, fly-fishing. More than anything else, it has become for me a symbol of hope. The meadowlark returns to Colorado in the early spring, and as I've mentioned, that typically means it arrives about the same time our major snowstorms hit. What courage; I'm sure if it were me, I'd wait until June when the weather warms up. But they come in spite of the snow, and take their place on fence posts and the tops of small trees, and begin singing. Hearing a midsummer song almost seems out of place when the flurries are whipping about your face. But that is exactly when we need it.

I heard two meadowlarks again this spring, calling and responding to each other on a cold and windy day. God began to speak through them. I heard him urging me to keep my own summer song, even though life's winter tries to throw into my spring cold wind and snow. *Do not throw away your confidence,* he said. *Do not budge from your perch, but sing your song, summer confident, sure of my great goodness toward you. You did not bring this spring, dear child; you do not have to arrange for the summer to follow. They come from thy Father's will, and they will come.* I thought of C. S. Lewis's essay, "The Grand Miracle," where he says,

> To be sure, it feels wintry enough still: but often in the very early spring it feels like that . . . the spring comes down slowly down this way; but the great thing is that the corner has been turned. There is, of course, this difference, that in the natural spring the crocus cannot choose whether it will respond or not. We can. We have the power either of withstanding the spring, and sinking back into the cosmic winter, or of going on into these "high mid-summer pomps" in which our leader, the Son of Man, already dwells, and to which he is calling us. It remains with us to follow or not, to die in this winter, or to go on into that spring and that summer.

Brent was buried on a Thursday afternoon. As we gathered by the graveside, his family and friends, Craig read these words: "I am the resurrection and the life. He who believes in me will live, even though he dies; and whoever lives and believes in me will never die" (John 11:25–26 NIV). He closed his Bible, and we all stood in silence, not really knowing what to say or do; no one wanted to leave; no one really wanted to stay. It seemed so final. At that moment, a meadowlark sang.

This is my song in return.

ABOUT THE AUTHOR

JOHN ELDREDGE is the author of numerous books including *Fathered by God*, *Walking with God*, *Epic*, *Waking the Dead*, *Wild at Heart* and coauthor of *Captivating* and *The Sacred Romance*. John, his wife, Stasi, and their three sons live in Colorado where they pursue adventure in the mountains, the woods, and on the rivers. He is also founder of Ransomed Heart, a ministry helping men and women discover the heart of God.

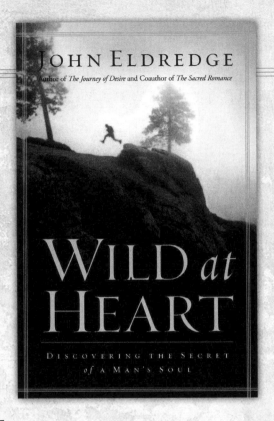

JOHN ELDREDGE
Author of *The Journey of Desire* and Coauthor of *The Sacred Romance*

WILD *at* HEART

DISCOVERING THE SECRET
of A MAN'S SOUL

Every man was once a boy. And every little boy has dreams, big dreams. But what happens to those dreams when they grow up? In *Wild at Heart*, John Eldredge invites men to recover their masculine heart, defined in the image of a passionate God. And he invites women to discover the secret of a man's soul and to delight in the strength and wildness men were created to offer.

THOMAS NELSON
Since 1798

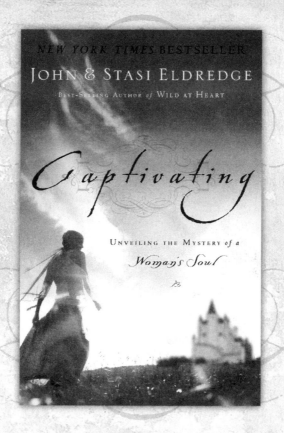

*B*y revealing the core desires every woman shares—to be romanced, to play an irreplaceable role in a grand adventure, and to unveil beauty—John and Stasi Eldredge invite women to recover their feminine hearts, created in the image of an intimate and passionate God. Further, they encourage men to discover the secret of a woman's soul and to delight in the beauty and strength women were created to offer.

 THOMAS NELSON
Since 1798